Enlightened Nationalism prov[...] synthesis in English of Prus[...] culture from the Napoleonic era to the Revolution of 1848. Matthew Levinger challenges the conventional notion that Prussia lagged behind Western Europe in its political development, demonstrating that Prussian leaders embraced a distinctive program of political modernization in response to their country's defeat by Napoleon in 1806-1807. Building on the eighteenth-century tradition of enlightened absolutism, Prussian leaders attempted to unite a rationalized monarchy with a politically active "nation," thus mobilizing the populace to resist the French oppressors. The new culture of "enlightened nationalism" influenced the political theory and program of both liberals and conservatives in nineteenth-century Prussia.

The book has important implications for understanding both subsequent German history and the history of nationalism in general. The author shows that the so-called authoritarian tendencies in Prussia's political culture resulted from its distinctive response to the challenges of the French Revolution and Napoleonic era, rather than from the persistence of premodern cultural or socioeconomic patterns. Likewise, by showing how nationalist activists drew on the cultural legacy of the Enlightenment, Levinger demonstrates that German nationalism cannot be understood as a uniquely pathological political phenomenon.

ENLIGHTENED NATIONALISM

ENLIGHTENED NATIONALISM
The Transformation of Prussian Political Culture
1806–1848

Matthew Levinger

OXFORD
UNIVERSITY PRESS

2000

OXFORD
UNIVERSITY PRESS

Oxford   New York
Athens   Auckland   Bangkok   Bogotá   Buenos Aires   Calcutta
Cape Town   Chennai   Dar es Salaam   Delhi   Florence   Hong Kong   Istanbul
Karachi   Kuala Lumpur   Madrid   Melbourne   Mexico City   Mumbai
Nairobi   Paris   São Paulo   Singapore   Taipei   Tokyo   Toronto   Warsaw

and associated companies in
Berlin   Ibadan

Copyright © 2000 by Oxford University Press

Published by Oxford University Press, Inc.
198 Madison Avenue, New York, New York 10016

Oxford is a registered trademark of Oxford University Press.

Library of Congress Cataloging-in-Publication Data
Levinger, Matthew Bernard, 1960–
Enlightened nationalism : the transformation of Prussian
political culture, 1806–1848 / Matthew Levinger.
p.   cm.
Includes bibliographical references and index.
ISBN 0-19-513185-1
1. Political culture—Germany—Prussia—History—19th century.
2. Nationalism—Germany—Prussia—History—19th century.
3. Enlightenment—Germany—Prussia.   4. Prussia
(Germany)—Historiography.   I. Title.
DD347 .L45   2000
943'.7—dc21   99-32583

Parts of chapter 2 appeared originally in "Kant and the Origins of Prussian Constitutionalism," *History of Political Thought*, vol. 19, no. 2 (Summer 1998). Parts of chapter 6 appeared originally in "Hardenberg, Wittgenstein, and the Constitutional Question in Prussia, 1815–22," *German History*, vol. 8, no. 3 (October 1990). Parts of chapters 3 and 8 appeared in "The Prussian Reform Movement and the Rise of Enlightened Nationalism," in *Re-thinking Prussian History*, ed. Philip Dwyer (London: Longman, 2000). The author gratefully acknowledges the permission to reproduce each of these passages.

1 3 5 7 9 8 6 4 2

Printed in the United States of America
on acid-free paper

For my parents
and in memory of Oma

PREFACE

Like many works of German history composed over the past half century, this book has its roots in the experience of exile. At the age of eight, in 1935, my father fled his birthplace, Berlin, with his family. My father's mother never set foot in Germany again, but she loved the literature of the German romantics and played Beethoven almost daily on the piano in her Manhattan apartment. My interest in history was sparked by the urge to understand Germany's disastrous turn to National Socialism between 1933 and 1945.

Perhaps because I have witnessed the effects of exile only at a distance, I approach this problem more obliquely than many historians. My analysis centers on Prussia, the largest northern German state, during the first half of the nineteenth century—an era in which Germany is often said to have embarked on a *Sonderweg,* or "separate path" of historical development from Western Europe. Some scholars have attributed this historical distinctiveness to Germans' rejection of modern Western cultural values of equality and individual freedom. Others have contended that the German states' belated industrialization, vis-à-vis their Western counterparts, allowed for the entrenchment of the authority of premodern political elites. Thus, whether for cultural or socioeconomic reasons, Prussia and the other German states are portrayed as having failed to modernize their political institutions at a critical historical moment.

Through an analysis of discourse involving the concept "nation," this book demonstrates that nineteenth-century Prussian political culture cannot be understood as fundamentally premodern. Rather than rejecting Western values, many influential Prussians, from the Napoleonic era onward, embraced the ideals of individual liberty and popular participation

in government. Proponents of political reform in Prussia expressed a
hybrid vision that combined the theories of eighteenth-century Enlightenment philosophers, such as Immanuel Kant and Adam Smith, with the
new nationalist ideas of the French Revolution. By forging a rational and
harmonious civil society, they hoped to overcome the contradiction between popular and monarchical sovereignty. The mobilization of the nation, they argued, would enhance rather than diminish the power of the
Prussian monarchy.

Although this "enlightened nationalism" was but one strand of nineteenth-century Prussian political culture, promoted primarily by reform-
minded civil servants and liberal activists, it profoundly influenced Prussia's political evolution. Ironically, by stressing the paramount importance of internal harmony, exponents of enlightened nationalism bol-
stered the legitimacy of the monarchical state and inhibited the
development of a pluralistic system of parliamentary rule. The very modernity of their political program, which aimed at the rationalization of
sovereign authority, contributed to the formation of a brittle regime that
was poorly suited to the productive management of social and political
conflict. In effect, the quest for an enlightened nation injected a powerful
utopian element into Prussian political culture, the counterpart of which
was an overexaggerated fear of the negative effects of domestic strife.
The inevitable disappointment of these utopian hopes for national harmony and unanimity may have been one factor that undermined the
stability of parliamentary institutions in Germany during the early twentieth century.

My work on this book came to fruition through the generous help of
many gifted colleagues and friends. I am deeply indebted to my won-
derful teachers at the University of Chicago: above all, Michael Geyer,
who supervised my dissertation project from its inception, Keith Baker,
John Boyer, Michael Silverstein, and François Furet. Reinhart Koselleck
provided indispensable guidance during the early stages of my research,
and I have also benefited from the wise counsel of James Sheehan, Gordon Craig, Reinhard Rürup, Hagen Schulze, Dieter Langewiesche, Andrea
Hofmeister-Hunger, Hans Erich Bödeker, Günther Höpfner, Eva Bliembach, and Jane Hunter. Three anonymous readers for Oxford University
Press, as well as Phil Stern, Eli Nathans, and Brendan Simms, offered
incisive critiques of the manuscript that allowed me to improve it greatly.
I am also grateful to Thomas LeBien and Susan Ferber of Oxford University Press for their faith in this project and for their inspired editing.

My research and writing was supported by fellowships from the University of Chicago and by a two-year grant from the Berlin Program for

Advanced German and European Studies of the Social Science Research Council and the Free University of Berlin (jointly funded by the Volkswagen Stiftung and the German Marshall Fund). While revising the manuscript, I received crucial support from Lewis and Clark College, including a junior faculty sabbatical and a summer research stipend, and a research grant from the German Academic Exchange Service. In Germany, I benefited from the expert assistance of archivists at the Geheimes Staatsarchiv Preußischer Kulturbesitz in Berlin-Dahlem, the Zentrales Staatsarchiv, Dienststelle Merseburg (since reincorporated into the Geheimes Staatsarchiv Preußischer Kulturbesitz), the Brandenburgisches Landeshauptarchiv, and the Bildarchiv Preußischer Kulturbesitz. The maps for the book were produced by Richard Wilkie, Sean FitzGerald, Donald Sluter, and David Ritchay of the University of Massachusetts Cartographic Laboratory.

A word of thanks to some others encountered along the way: John Warthen, Bill Hohenstein, John Spielman, Susan Fisher, Dario Biocca, Hartmut and Ulrike Püschel, and Heiner Legewie and Barbara Schervier-Legewie, all of whom have provided friendship and inspiration. I have been blessed by the love and companionship of my wife, Livia Nicolescu, who has helped me keep my sense of humor and who has made this work infinitely more rewarding. The company of our daughter, Alexandra, has made every enterprise more joyful. Above all, I thank my parents, George and Ann Levinger, for their love and unfailing support. I dedicate this book to them and to the memory of my grandmother Charlotte Levinger.

January 2000   M. L.
Portland, Oregon

CONTENTS

A NOTE ON TRANSLATION

In a study such as this, which explores subtle shifts in the meanings of words, consistency in translation is essential. Generally, when there is potential for ambiguity in an important phrase, I have indicated the original German words in parentheses. In translating certain critical terms, I have followed the rules indicated below (unless otherwise noted in the text):

Nation, Volk, völkisch, Volkstümlichkeit. The German term *Nation* is always translated here as "nation." For purposes of clarity, the term *Volk* is never translated as "nation." I have also avoided translating *völkisch* as "national," instead choosing the term "popular." The word *Volkstümlichkeit*, which might be translated as "national character" or "national essence," appears here as "tribalism." Translating the word *Volk* presents particular difficulties. Some of the authors whose writings are quoted here used this word in a relatively neutral sense, indicating the "populace" or "civil society." In these cases, I have chosen to translate *Volk* directly as "people." For other authors, the term was charged with connotations of ethnic or national community. When I have judged this to be the case, I have generally left the term *Volk* in the original German.

Stand, Stände, Landstände, Landschaft, Landtag, Rittergut, Ritterguts-besitzer. *Stand* and *Stände* may be translated literally as "estate" and "estates." The term *Stände*, however, may be employed in two very different senses, first, to refer to the various legally distinct strata of the population (e.g., the "noble estate" or the "estate of the peasantry"), and second, as a designation for the "assembly of the estates" in a diet. To make clear the distinction between these two usages, I have generally used the term "diet" when the term *Stände* is employed in the second

xiii

sense. I have also sometimes used the term "diet" to translate the words *Landschaft, Landstände,* and *Landtag.*

An additional wrinkle on this translation problem is posed by the word *Rittergut,* which (until 1807) denoted a landed estate that belonged to a member of the nobility. I have chosen to translate *Rittergut* as "noble property" or as "landed estate." The term *Rittergutsbesitzer* is translated here as "owner of noble property" or as "owner of a landed estate." A complication here stems from the peculiarity of the reform period legislation itself: after 1807, ownership of *Rittergüter* was opened to commoners. Thus, an "owner of noble property" was not necessarily a member of the nobility.

Verfassung, ständische Verfassung, landständische Verfassung, Konstitution. The words *Verfassung* and *Konstitution* are both translated here as "constitution." Of the two terms, *Verfassung* is by far the more common. The terms *ständische Verfassung* and *landständische Verfassung* referred to a constitution that would provide representation for each of the various estates—the nobility, the burghers, and the peasants—and perhaps also for corporate bodies such as the universities and the church. I have generally translated these terms as "constitution based on estates."

Bildung, Erziehung. The word *Bildung* carries rich connotations that are difficult to capture in English; it implies a process of organic maturation through which both intellect and character become fully formed. *Bildung* cannot be imposed entirely from above; instead, it involves spontaneous self-development, resulting in the capacity for ethical self-determination. To avoid overly cumbersome phrasing, I have translated *Bildung* simply as "education," but the reader should keep in mind that this term serves as a shorthand expression for a much richer idea. The word *Erziehung* may also be translated as "education," but I have instead employed the words "upbringing" or "schooling" to distinguish it from the more pregnant and heavily laden concept of *Bildung.*

All emphases within direct quotes are from the original works.

Because of space limitations, it has not been possible to include the original German quotations in the book along with the translations. (An exception has been made for three important, previously unpublished memoranda that explain the decision by King Frederick William III against the establishment of a constitution. These documents are reproduced in the notes to chapter 6.) The German-language quotations may be obtained by writing the author at the Department of History, Lewis and Clark College, 0615 S.W. Palatine Hill Road, Portland, OR 97219 (e-mail levinger@lclark.edu), or care of Oxford University Press.

ENLIGHTENED NATIONALISM

One

INTRODUCTION

The year 1806 marked a turning point in the history of Prussia and the other German states. With the establishment of the Confederation of the Rhine in July 1806, Napoleon consolidated France's control over much of German-speaking Europe. The following month, he forced the abolition of the Holy Roman Empire, which had been the supreme political entity in Central Europe for more than 800 years. Though the empire had long exercised only limited power, it had provided a legal and institutional framework that established a formal unity among the various German territories, which was now lost entirely. Finally, on 14 October 1806, Prussia's famed army collapsed in a single day, routed by the French in the battles of Auerstädt and Jena. Napoleon's military conquest left Prussia's government intact but stripped the country of nearly half its territory and imposed a humiliating punitive treaty, which was signed at Tilsit in July 1807. The war and the subsequent occupation ravaged all sectors of the population: food prices soared while land values plunged, and both the countryside and the cities were devastated by epidemics and famine.[1]

Prussia's experience under Napoleonic domination was a unique one: no other German state faced such humiliation while still preserving its governing institutions.[2] After the military devastation of 1806–1807, Prussia's leaders feared that their country had only two options: either to reinvigorate its social and political institutions by adopting the innovations of the enemy or to cease to exist as an independent state. Moreover, the abolition of the empire had created a constitutional vacuum in Central Europe, so that it was also necessary to redefine the political relationships between Prussia and the other territories of German-speaking Europe. Prussia's response to the Napoleonic challenge was led by a new cadre of officials, most of whom had held middle-level administrative posts before 1806, but who assumed positions of leadership after the old ruling elite was discredited by the military and diplomatic catastrophe. Most notable among the officials who spearheaded what came to be known as the Prussian reform movement were Freiherr Karl vom und zum Stein (1757–1831), Prussia's first minister in 1807–1808, and Karl August von Hardenberg (1750–1822), who served as state chancellor from 1810 until his death.

In analyzing Prussian history of the Stein-Hardenberg era, some historians have spoken of a "revolution from above" instigated by the civil service.[3] According to Reinhart Koselleck's classic analysis, the Prussian reformers attempted to establish a free market economy and liberal political institutions. The Prussian bourgeoisie, however, was still too undeveloped to sustain a viable system of parliamentary rule. Thus, these officials were forced to abandon their ambitions for political liberalization in order to achieve the implementation of their socioeconomic reforms.[4] Hans Rosenberg, while concurring with Koselleck about the immaturity of the Prussian bourgeoisie during this era, interprets the motives of Prussia's leading civil servants in a less altruistic light. The early nineteenth century, Rosenberg argues, witnessed a "revolution from within" that resulted in a "modified pattern" of aristocratic privilege and a political system based on "bureaucratic absolutism."[5]

More recent scholarship analyzes Prussia's political evolution in terms of a process of "partial" modernization or "defensive" modernization. Historians such as Herbert Obenaus, Barbara Vogel, and Hans-Ulrich Wehler stress the combination of challenges with which Prussia's leaders contended during the Napoleonic era, including the country's precarious international standing, its dire fiscal condition, its lack of internal integration, and the "legitimation deficit" that confronted the Prussian government. These challenges motivated concerted efforts at social and political reform by leading civil servants. While many important social and economic changes were successfully enacted, efforts at constitutional reform before 1848 proved largely abortive.[6]

The terms "revolution from above" and "partial modernization" both imply that while significant socioeconomic changes occurred in Prussia during the early nineteenth century, the authority of the monarchical state remained largely unchallenged. Prussia's political development, according to this view, was stunted by the absence of a more thoroughgoing "revolution from below," such as the one that had occurred in France. I demonstrate that this interpretation underestimates the political consequences of the events of the Napoleonic era, even though it may accurately describe the initial intentions of the Prussian reformers. These leaders were unable fully to control the consequences of their actions. Ultimately, what began as a narrowly circumscribed "revolution from above" escalated into a profound and irrevocable transformation of Prussian political culture.

Humiliated by Napoleon and facing the potential annihilation of their state, Prussian leaders sought to learn from their conqueror. Beginning with the outbreak of the revolutionary wars in 1792, France had enjoyed astonishing military success—in stark contrast with the many wars of the preceding century, in which it had achieved little territorial expansion despite fielding the largest army in Europe. Reformers such as Stein and Hardenberg believed that France's newfound military might stemmed largely from the mobilization of nationalist sentiments within the French populace. Yet the French example offered a far from perfect political model for the Prussian reformers. Apart from the problematic issue of whether Prussia itself constituted a nation, these leaders confronted a thorny strategic dilemma. As noblemen in the employ of the Prussian monarch, Stein, Hardenberg, and their compatriots were acutely sensitive to the danger of revolution. They sought a means of harnessing the power of the French Revolution while avoiding what they saw as the revolution's unfortunate side effects, such as the abolition of the aristocracy and the execution of the king.

My phrase "enlightened nationalism" is intended to highlight the hybrid nature of the Prussian reformers' political agenda. As was the case for the so-called enlightened absolutists of the eighteenth century, such as Frederick the Great, the reformers' paramount objective was to mobilize social resources on behalf of the state. Influenced by Enlightenment theorists such as Kant, Smith, and Turgot, they argued that the establishment of a rational social and political order would liberate the energies of the populace and foster harmony between the government and the citizenry. While this rationalizing impulse of the Prussian reform movement had its roots in eighteenth-century governing traditions, Stein and Hardenberg fused this prerevolutionary legacy with an effort to forge a politically active "nation." This aspect of their program was a specific response to the cataclysmic events of the revolutionary and Napoleonic eras.

The Prussian reformers' project contained powerful internal tensions: they insisted that the nation be politically mobilized but held equally fervently that the nation must express its will in harmony with the will of the king. Moreover, while calling for the establishment of a more egalitarian legal order, they also sought to preserve certain traditional social hierarchies. The rhetoric of enlightened nationalism aimed to resolve these incipient tensions within the reformers' legislative progam.

By educating the populace and by rationalizing Prussia's political and social institutions, they believed they could reconcile a politically active nation with a sovereign monarch.

This book traces the evolution of the concept "nation" in Prussia from the Napoleonic era up to the eve of the Revolution of 1848. Not surprisingly, the reformers' ideal of harmonious cooperation between the citizenry and the monarchical state proved unattainable. Nonetheless, their vision of national harmony and unanimity continued to shape Prussian political debate long after Napoleon's demise in 1815. Bourgeois liberal activists, like the bureaucratic reformers, came to believe that a constitutional order balancing monarchical and democratic elements could be forged through the education of the nation and the rationalization of the state. Other groups both on the right and the left of the political spectrum, from conservative aristocrats to radical republicans, also struggled to come to terms with the implications of enlightened nationalism. These groups were more skeptical than the liberals and the reform-minded civil servants about the feasibility of peacefully sharing sovereignty between the nation and the king. Nonetheless, they found it difficult to construct alternative political theories that would justify limiting or abolishing the authority of the monarchical state.

While my investigation is confined to Prussian history during the first half of the nineteenth century, it has broader implications both for the study of comparative political modernization and for the analysis of the role played by discourse in historical change. I present a new perspective on the question of whether, and in what sense, nineteenth-century Prussia may be said to have embarked on a distinctive path of political modernization. Moreover, by examining how competing political interest groups invoked the concept "nation" in order to articulate and enforce their claims, I seek to illuminate the interplay between the discursive strategies and the material interests that shaped the evolution of Prussian political culture during this era.

Revisiting the *Sonderweg*

The notion that modern Germany has followed a "special path" of historical development possesses a long pedigree. In the aftermath of World War II, scholars such as Hans Kohn maintained that Germans had long engaged in a "war against the West," rejecting Enlightenment ideals of freedom and individual autonomy in favor of a collectivist political creed.[7] According to Leonard Krieger, Germans occupied a position "half within and half without the western community." The "liberal spirit did affect German institutions," Krieger declared, but "the process was incomplete and unintegrated." The outcome of this partial transformation was a "peculiar 19th century version of political freedom which made the idea of liberty not the polar antithesis but the historical associate of princely authority."[8] Krieger's arguments paralleled those of sociologists such as Ralf Dahrendorf, who maintained that Germans showed evidence of an "authoritarian personality" that had predisposed them to the appeal of Nazism.[9]

In more recent decades, historians have expressed skepticism toward such global claims about Germans' cultural susceptibility to totalitarian politics. Instead, many scholars writing since the late 1950s have emphasized socioeconomic factors that rendered nineteenth-century Germany distinctive. In comparison to England and France, according to this view, most of the German states remained economically underdeveloped during the era of the French Revolution. The relative immaturity of the German bourgeoisie ensured the continuing political dominance of aristocrats and royal officials throughout the early nineteenth century. Even with Germany's rapid industrialization after 1850, the country experienced only uneven modernization: it developed an advanced capitalist economy, but the social and political elites remained "feudalized." Rather than demanding a transition to parliamentary rule, the new capitalist class in Germany imitated the ostentation of the aristocracy and acknowledged the political supremacy of the emperor.[10]

Yet this socioeconomic version of the *Sonderweg*, like the older cultural *Sonderweg* theory, has encountered strong criticism in recent years. The latest wave of revisionism has been motivated partly by new comparative research on French and German social history. Scholars have discovered that industrial capitalism in eighteenth-century France was less advanced than they had previously presumed; conversely, they have increasingly emphasized the dynamism and vibrancy of the nineteenth-century German bourgeoisie. Thus, it appears difficult to account for differences between the French and German political trajectories primarily on the basis of different paths of socioeconomic development.[11]

Apart from these doubts about the degree of nineteenth-century Germany's socioeconomic distinctiveness, many historians have expressed unease about several fallacies associated with the *Sonderweg* interpretation, which may be labeled the essentialist, the teleological, and the normative.

The essentialist fallacy is found in works that make vast, undifferentiated claims about the "German character"—for example, that Germans possess an essentially authoritarian disposition or that virtually all Germans are anti–Semitic.[12] This type of argument is deeply problematic for at least two reasons. First, it both caricatures and scapegoats the

German people, while whitewashing the sins of other national cultures. Germans, for example, may be lambasted as fervent anti–Semites, while the pervasive anti–Semitism in many other European countries is ignored. Second, this type of argument provides little insight into the historical mechanisms that contributed to the rise and fall of authoritarianism or anti–Semitism in Germany. By stating one's claims in such global terms, one forecloses the possibility for nuanced historical interpretation.

The teleological fallacy is closely related to the essentialist fallacy: it is the argument that all paths of German history lead to National Socialism. Certain scholars have gone so far as to trace a straight line from Luther to Hitler.[13] More commonly, historians begin their story in the eighteenth or the nineteenth century, identifying various pathological features of German society that allegedly contributed to the breakdown of democracy and the rise of Nazism in the 1930s. The problem with this approach is that it fosters a kind of historical tunnel vision. Not only does it make a single twelve-year period, 1933–1945, the logical culmination of all German history, but it leads scholars to overemphasize certain negative characteristics of German society and culture, while neglecting other tendencies that cannot be linked to the Nazi phenomenon.

Finally, the normative fallacy involves the premise that Germany's historical development was pathologically aberrant because it followed a different pattern than the so-called Western nations. As David Blackbourn and Geoff Eley observe, this normative vision reflects "an idealized picture of what the 'western' pattern actually was, a picture which historians of Britain, the USA, or France themselves would usually regard as quasi-mythical."[14] Indeed, American and British historians, like historians of Germany, frequently make claims about the exceptional character of their own country's historical trajectory. In a real sense, every nation's history is unique, so one must be careful not to read too much into the fact of Germany's distinctiveness.

For all of these qualifications, however, the notion that German history is somehow distinctive has proved difficult to banish from scholarly debate. Germany's pattern of constitutional development during the nineteenth and early twentieth centuries did indeed differ strikingly from that of many Western nations. In most of the industrializing states of Western Europe and the Americas during this era, monarchy was either abolished or rendered largely symbolic. Germany, by contrast, retained a strong monarchy until the end of World War I, with the Kaiser continuing to play a central role in vital affairs of state and with the civil service enjoying exceptionally strong prestige.[15] Even after the abolition of the German monarchy in 1918, the parliamentary institutions of the

Weimar Republic proved more vulnerable to challenge than those of most Western European states.

Broadly speaking, most explanations of these distinctive aspects of German political culture have gravitated toward one of two methodological poles: idealism or materialism. The idealists include old-school German scholars, such as Friedrich Meinecke,[16] as well as postwar historians, such as Krieger and Kohn. They emphasize cultural factors that made Germany unique. The materialists, who have been in the majority among German historians since the 1960s, focus primarily on the competition among interest groups. They maintain that, in large part, political outcomes may be derived from the interplay of socioeconomic forces.

This study seeks to forge a link between the idealist and materialist traditions of German historiography. Anthropologist Clifford Geertz depicts politics as symbolic action, as activity undertaken in reference to "authoritative concepts that render it meaningful."[17] My analysis focuses on precisely this reciprocal link between symbols and action: I explore the ways in which the language of nineteenth-century Prussian politics was shaped by socioeconomic interests and, conversely, how patterns of discourse defined the horizon of political possibilities.

Rather than explaining Prussia's political evolution on the basis of global social or cultural characteristics—such as the immaturity of the bourgeoisie or an alleged predisposition to authoritarianism—I stress the ways in which the conjunction of contingent, localized phenomena produced distinctive political results. Of signal importance for Prussia's political evolution was that the reform movement was motivated by an external threat. This fact led the bureaucratic reformers to place strong emphasis on the need for the internal unanimity of the "nation" to repel the Napoleonic challenge. Other interest groups, such as landed aristocrats concerned about the loss of their traditional privileges, and marginalized bourgeois intellectuals striving to enhance their own social status, seized on this ideal of a unanimous "national spirit" for reasons of their own. In effect, a new authoritative symbolic order of politics arose out of the struggle among competing factions that were striving to attain strategic advantage.

Method and Sources

A political culture consists, in part, of the "values, expectations, and implicit rules that express and shape collective intentions and actions."[18] It also comprises the habitual patterns of political activity within a given society—whether dictated by law or by custom. The culture of enlightened nationalism in Prussia manifested itself at both of these levels. In discourse, it appeared in discussions about the need to create a rational, educated, and harmonious national community. In practice, it displayed itself through the creation of new political institutions, such as municipal and provincial assemblies, as well as in popular activities, such as petition-writing campaigns and nationalist festivals.

The transformation of political culture in early nineteenth-century Prussia is best understood as the product of shifting strategies of persuasion. In seeking to articulate new political goals and to appeal to new audiences, the Prussian reformers were forced to recast the underlying symbolic order of the polity. Methodologically, my analysis is influenced by the discipline of historical semantics, developed by scholars such as Reinhart Koselleck, Rolf Reichardt, and Hans-Ulrich Gumbrecht.[19] These scholars seek to identify linguistic and cultural norms that "exercise compulsion over an individual's freedom of expression, narrowing the possibilities offered by the system within the frame of traditional realizations."[20] Language, according to this conception, does not simply serve to communicate ideas and interests; rather, it also shapes the ways in which speakers articulate and perceive their own interests. In Koselleck's formulation, concepts "contain the structural possibilities . . . which are not detectable in the historical flow of events."[21]

This work on historical semantics is part of a growing body of literature that has explored the role played by discourse in social and political change. As Kathleen Canning observes, many historians have come to see "language as constitutive, not merely reflective, of historical events and human consciousness."[22] This concern with language is reflected in a wide-ranging theoretical debate over the virtues of the "linguistic turn" in historical scholarship.[23] Historians have also written case studies that have sought to apply discourse analysis to various historical problems, for example, the origins of the French Revolution,[24] the formation of working-class and middle-class identities during the Industrial Revolution,[25] the transformation of gender roles and family structures in nineteenth-century Europe,[26] and the emergence and spread of nationalism.[27]

At the heart of all the debates over the linguistic turn lies one central methodological question: to what extent does language reflect social reality, and to what extent does it constitute it? Most historians are rightly uneasy about the suggestion that discourse alone determines the course of political and social events. Koselleck, for example, while asserting that words possess an autonomous force in politics, elaborates on this claim with greater nuance:

Without common concepts there is no society, and above all, no political field of action. Conversely, our concepts are founded in politicosocial systems that are far more complex than would be indicated by treating them simply as linguistic communities organized around specific key concepts. A "society" and its "concepts" exist in a relation of tension.[28]

Likewise, French revolutionary historians, such as Keith Michael Baker, as well as British social historians, such as Dror Wahrman, emphasize the dynamic tension between ideas and action. Baker observes that "meaning is a dimension of all social action"; he proposes a view of "politics as constituted within a field of discourse, and of political language as elaborated in the course of political action."[29] This analytical approach, in other words, strikes a middle ground between two methodological extremes. It rejects the neo–Marxist assumption that political ideas and events may be derived from allegedly more fundamental socioeconomic phenomena. Conversely, it also rejects the premises of linguistic determinism, which endows "language with the ultimate power to determine the outcome of historical developments."[30]

While numerous historians have proclaimed the need for an analytical method that combines social and linguistic history, fewer have provided practical models for such work. For example, while Koselleck argues that it is essential to explore the interactions between "society and its concepts," his magisterial seven-volume lexicon of "foundational historical concepts" (*Geschichtliche Grundbegriffe*) displays a more traditional approach than one might anticipate from his theoretical writings. The articles in this lexicon provide comprehensive descriptions of the shifting nuances of key social and political concepts but little systematic analysis of the relationship between social and linguistic change.[31] Similarly, Baker's essays on the ideological origins of the French Revolution offer elegant exegeses of various strands of political discourse at the end of the Old Regime but do not elucidate the specific social and political forces that served as catalysts for discursive change.[32]

Like the works cited above, this book is first and foremost a history of political ideas. I explore the evolution of a single concept, the "nation," in a single German state during the early nineteenth century. While this book contains little social history in a formal sense, it analyzes political rhetoric as a point of intersection between the realm of ideology and the realm of social action. My study presumes that participants in political debate seek to manipulate ideological claims in order to advance their own interests. Thus, at one level, political rhetoric reflects social interests. Yet, conversely, rhetorical conventions play an important role in defining how participants in political debate perceive their own interests, as well as in delineating the political possibilities in a given era. I seek to illuminate the reciprocal processes by which social interests shape discursive forms and by which discourses shape interests.

In order to highlight the relationship between ideas and their contexts, I focus less on the realm of high theory (for example, the works of political philosophers, such as Hegel and Fichte) than on the complex "middle ground . . . in which there is a consciousness of ideas at play in social life."[33] I concentrate primarily on documents whose authors and political intent are clearly identifiable: memoranda and letters exchanged among Prussia's leading officials, petitions to the king composed by the nobility and the urban elites, popular pamphlet literature, and so forth. Many of the documents analyzed in this study represent arguments either for or against the adoption of a constitution in Prussia. Throughout the forty years beginning with the Napoleonic conquest, the question of whether the king should grant his people a "national representation" was one of the most prominent and volatile issues in Prussian political debate. King Frederick William III publicly promised to create a central representative assembly several times between 1810 and 1820 before ultimately deciding against the idea. His son and successor, Frederick William IV, raised the issue again shortly after his accession to the throne in 1840 and ultimately granted a constitution under the compulsion of the revolutionary events of 1848. The ongoing debates between 1806 and 1848 over this issue, both within the Prussian government and in the broader public sphere, revealed a great deal about competing conceptions concerning the identity and social organization of the nation, the nature of political representation, and the relationships binding the nation with the king and the administrative authorities of the state.

Because I have chosen to rely primarily on written sources, my inquiry is necessarily restricted to the views of literate, politically active Prussians. To identify as broad as possible a range of literate public opinion, I examine sources that stem from a wide variety of social locations and that represent diverse political views. They include works composed by state officials, nobles, artisans, bourgeois journalists, and student activists, among others. Some of these figures were highly influential proponents or opponents of a constitution, others were relatively unknown minor figures. Interestingly, those who expressed fringe opinions—who were ridiculed, jailed, or denounced as insane—prove to be particularly significant in developing a clearer sense of the boundaries of legitimate discourse within a political culture. This analysis makes it possible to map the shifting conceptual universe of Prussian politics during the early nineteenth century—to observe which premises were widely shared across the political and social spectrum and which were contested.

My analysis is informed by Michel Foucault's concept of the "historical a priori," which he introduces in *The Archaeology of Knowledge*. Foucault argues that the history of thought may be visualized as a series of archaeological strata, each of which represents a particular "discursive formation," or set of rules that define how one thinks and speaks about the world. These strata are set off from each other by "ruptures," which mark sudden changes in the underlying assumptions of political and social discourse.[34] The historical a priori may be defined as a set of common premises shared by all participants in legitimate political discourse. Thus, for example, the principle that the king ruled by divine right constituted an a priori assumption of seventeenth- and eighteenth-century French political discourse, whereas the notion that legitimate government reflects the will of the people has become an a priori premise of political discourse during the nineteenth and twentieth centuries.[35]

To observe that the theory of divine-right monarchy was part of the seventeenth-century French historical a priori does not necessarily imply that everyone in seventeenth-century France truly believed that the monarch was ordained by God. It does imply, however, that even the most robust atheist of that day had to employ that premise in order to participate in legitimate political discourse. A petitioner for tax relief, for example, might rail at the short-sightedness and venality of the royal ministers, but to question the king's own wisdom and benevolence would be to expose oneself to the charge of heresy. Likewise, in the twentieth century, many observers doubt that most government decisions stem from the "people's will." To participate effectively in the democratic political process, however, one needs to claim that one's views reflect the voice of the people (rather than the voice of God). Concepts such as "divine right" and the "will of the people," in other words, are necessary fictions that serve as organizing principles for political debate.

Though Foucault's notion of the historical a priori provides a conceptual starting point for this study, the method of inquiry here differs substantially from the one he proposes. Unlike Foucault, whose archaeological metaphor suggests a rigid and radical break between the successive "strata" of political discourse, my analysis highlights the open-ended and ambiguous character of much rhetorical usage. Fundamental changes in political theory often occur not through a total rejection of past arguments but through subtle shifts of emphasis and terminology or through the articulation of old ideas in new contexts.[36] Thus, rather than employing the boldly categorical term "historical a priori," I have generally chosen to speak of "consensual features" of Prussian political discourse, a phrase intended to capture the fluid and shifting nature of rhetorical conventions. Alongside these elements of discursive consensus were certain "contested features" that attracted heated debate. Throughout the period analyzed in this study, the concept "nation" represented an amalgam of consensual and contested features, which are identified in the following chapters.

In discussing the periods of transition when one historical a priori gives way to another, Foucault refused to speculate either about the causes of these ruptures or about the mechanisms by which they occur. This is precisely the problem that this study will address. I conclude that the concept "nation" was shaped in Prussia both by cultural factors and by the specific political constellations of the Napoleonic era. Part I explores the origins of enlightened nationalism in Prussia. Chapter 2 focuses on the eighteenth-century intellectual antecedents of the Prussian reform movement, which included the writings of the German cameralists, the French physiocrats, and the authors of the Scottish Enlightenment, along with the political theories of the French revolutionaries and philosopher Immanuel Kant. Chapter 3 documents how, in the wake of the devastating defeat by Napoleon in 1806–1807, Prussian leaders drew on these varied traditions in seeking to forge a harmonious relationship between a sovereign king and a politically mobilized nation.

The Prussian reformers envisioned the nation as a body of loyal citizens who would gladly sacrifice their fortunes and their lives in the service of the monarchical state. Yet, by invoking the concept of the nation, they opened the gates of contention about the precise nature of this new political community. The resulting controversies over the concept "nation" are analyzed in part II of this book. Chapter 4 focuses on the rhetoric of Prussia's traditional social elites, who invoked this concept in order to oppose many of the tax increases and social reforms proposed by the Prussian ministry. These figures argued that the traditional legal privileges of the aristocracy, the urban guilds, and other corporate bodies must be preserved in the new nation. Chapter 5 analyzes the rhetoric of another set of political actors: the (largely bourgeois) intellectuals, journalists, and popular activists, many of whom called for the abolition of aristocratic privilege and the unification of all Germans into a single state. In their view, the nation was an organic union based on a common language, culture, and religion: they were critical of social and legal privileges that divided Germans from one another.

In the face of the volatile and unpredictable character of the new nationalist rhetoric, the Prussian king and his leading ministers struggled to come to terms with the shifting political landscape. Chapter 6 documents the crystallization of the concept "nation" during the decade after the Vienna Settlement of 1815, a period commonly known as the Restoration. According to an increasingly vocal faction within the Prussian administration and aristocracy, the nation represented a potential rival center of sovereignty, which (if nourished) would ultimately subvert the authority of the monarch. A politically active nation, this group argued, was inevitably a revolutionary nation. Thus, the only way to preserve the stability of the state was strenuously to oppose any movement toward a constitution and to deny the very existence of a national political community. Because many conservative leaders rejected the ideal of nationhood during this period, liberals and radicals prevailed in the struggle to define the nation as a pan–German community founded on the principle of civil equality.

While parts I and II of this study analyze how the concept "nation" took shape in the heat of Prussian political debate during the early nineteenth century, part III examines how the concept itself came to influence Prussia's subsequent political evolution. The idea of nationhood remained highly fluid during the first decades of the nineteenth century, and the new definitions, like the old, were subject to rearticulation and renegotiation. Nonetheless, my analysis demonstrates strong continuities in certain features of this concept, which proved significant in structuring political debate. In particular, the consensus over the ideally unitary and harmonious character of the nation had important consequences for the evolution of both conservative and liberal political theory in nineteenth-century Prussia. Chapter 7 examines more closely the rhetoric and program of the conservative faction that emerged in Prussia during the 1820s and 1830s. My account emphasizes the modern and experimental character of Prussian conservatism during this period. Conservative leaders sought to fuse older notions of a paternalistic social order with the new principles of a free market economy and universal legal equality. Some sought, with limited success, to deny the existence of the nation altogether. Others, by embracing new notions of public politics, undermined traditional claims about the unique political status and rights of the aristocracy. Once introduced during the Napoleonic era, the concept of the politically active nation thus proved impossible to eradicate from Prussian political discourse. Chapter 8 explores how Prussian liberals articulated the relationship between the nation and the monarchy during the period 1820–1848. Building on the Enlightenment legacy, liberals emphasized the importance of education, political participation, and harmony between the citizenry and the state. In effect, by defining conflict as illegitimate, liberals were inhibited from establishing an effective language of opposition to state authority. Indeed, most Prussian liberals remained staunch monarchists, rather than republicans, throughout the nineteenth century.

Ultimately, the legacy of enlightened nationalism in Prussia was a mixed one. The ideal of a unified and harmonious nation fostered a laudable commitment to public education and the rationalization of government institutions. But this ideal also resulted in exaggerated fears of political dissent, inhibiting the capacity of parliamentary institutions to provide a forum for competing views. This book investigates how, during the first half of the nineteenth century, new forms of intolerance were born out of eighteenth-century ambitions for enlightened political reform.

I

GENESIS

Two

THE POLITICS OF HARMONY IN
EIGHTEENTH-CENTURY PRUSSIA

"Kings are . . . but human, and all humans are equal."[1] This remark, from a treatise by the youthful Frederick the Great, illustrates a deep tension that existed within the theory of Prussian enlightened absolutism—a tension between egalitarian principles and authoritarian practice. From the mid–seventeenth century onward, the Hohenzollern kings had sought to consolidate their control over the realm and to diminish the political power of the Prussian nobility. Frederick's predecessors had established a centralized bureaucracy and a large standing army under their direct command. They had levied taxes without consulting the *Landstände*, the traditional representative assemblies of the Prussian provinces. Only in the local and county diets, many of which still convened on a regular basis, did the Prussian nobility continue to play an active governing role.[2]

By the era of Frederick the Great (who ruled from 1740 to 1786), Prussia's Hohenzollern dynasty had succeeded in forging a highly centralized and tightly regimented administrative apparatus, as well as in thwarting any serious internal challenges to royal authority. Yet even as Prussian absolutism triumphed, a new philosophical movement was emerging that undermined traditional arguments for the legitimacy of royal authority. In medieval Europe, inequality of social rank—not universal equality—was considered the natural human condition. Each person was said to hold a distinct position in the "chain of being," a grand ordering principle that established a hierarchy of all living things from plants to angels. Kings, who occupied the highest rank in the human world, were said to rule "by the grace of God."[3] Frederick the Great broke from this traditional logic. He rejected both the notion of the divine right of kingship and the principle of natural social hierarchy, justifying his right to rule simply by claiming to be the first—and best—"servant of the state."[4]

Reinhart Koselleck has termed the century between 1750 and 1850 a critical "bridge period" (*Sattelzeit*) between the early modern and the modern age.[5] Throughout Europe, this period was marked by the emergence of increasingly ambitious states that imposed ever-greater obligations on their subjects, as well as by growing popular demands for involvement in the processes of government. It was also characterized by the transition from the traditional hierarchical order, consisting of particular corporate bodies, each possessing its own specific legal rights and privileges, to a social order founded on universal egalitarian and individualistic principles. In French, this traditional form of social organization was termed the *société d'ordres;* in German, it was called the *Ständegesellschaft.* Both of these translate roughly as "society of orders" or "society of estates," though there is no precise English equivalent for these terms.[6]

This chapter explores the political and intellectual framework out of which the Prussian reform movement emerged. While Prussia must be understood as an integral part of Europe, rather than as following a deviant path of historical development, Prussian political and social thought of the late eighteenth and early nineteenth centuries was distinctive in certain critical respects. Put simply, this era was marked by two fundamental struggles: politically, the struggle between monarchy and democracy, and socially, the struggle between the principles of legal hierarchy and legal equality. In Prussia, partly because of the continuing vitality of traditional social institutions and partly because of particularities of the Prussian legal and philosophical heritage, intellectuals and political leaders strove mightily to reconcile old and new governing principles. Politically, they sought to create a government that combined monarchical and democratic elements. Socially, they sought to create a new order that would make room both for the preservation of traditional hierarchies *and* for the new principle of universal equality before the law. To achieve these unlikely goals, these leaders placed particular emphasis on the doctrine of the common good, as articulated by political philosophers from Aristotle to Kant. The Prussian reformers argued that rulers and their subjects could be reconciled if only they recognized the true unity of their interests. The creation of "public spirit," the reformers claimed, would forge an organic solidarity among all Prussians regardless of their social status. The "politics of harmony" thus evolved as a valiant effort to resolve the contradictions that lay at the heart of the project of enlightened monarchy.[7]

Prussia and the European Setting

Eighteenth-century Brandenburg-Prussia was the newest and most rapidly expanding European great power. Beginning in the reign of Frederick William, the Great Elector (who ruled from 1640 to 1688), the Hohenzollern monarchs had embarked on a series of ambitious conquests and annexations, and within a century they had transformed a small barren northern realm into the largest and most powerful German state after the Austrian Habsburg Empire. By the time of the French Revolution, Prussia's territory extended in a wide band across east central Europe south of the Baltic Sea, from Lithuania and parts of Poland in the east to the territories of Brandenburg, along the Elbe River, in the west. Through dynastic alliances, the Hohenzollern kings had also become the rulers of other territories to the south and west, including Ansbach-Bayreuth, sections of Westphalia and the Rhineland, and the Swiss canton of Neuchâtel.

At the beginning of the nineteenth century, Prussia remained sparsely populated compared to its western neighbors. The population density of France was about fifty people per square kilometer, in England it was fifty-eight; in Prussia's eastern provinces, the population density was only thirty-seven per square kilometer.[8] Prussia still lacked any cities as large as Paris or London. Berlin, which had been a town of only 12,000 residents in 1650, had grown rapidly over the subsequent century and a half. By 1800, it numbered 173,000 inhabitants. (Paris, in comparison, had 581,000 residents in 1800, while greater London had a population of more than 1.1 million.) Only two other Prussian cities had more than 50,000 inhabitants at the beginning of the nineteenth century: Königsberg in East Prussia and Breslau in Silesia. About three-quarters of the Prussian population still lived in communities with fewer than 2,000 inhabitants. Indeed, in all of German-speaking Europe, there were only sixty-four cities with a population of more than 10,000.[9]

From the mid–eighteenth century onward, however, Prussia participated in a massive European-wide population expansion, which some scholars have termed the demographic revolution. Between 1750 and 1800, the population of Prussia's old territories expanded almost 40 percent. Between 1816 and 1864, Prussia's total population grew by an additional 86 percent, from 10.4 to 19.3 million inhabitants. By 1850, the population of Berlin had more than doubled from fifty years earlier, to 419,000.[10]

These demographic characteristics of Prussia and the other German states had important consequences for the evolution of political culture in Central Europe. The absence of a metropolis like Paris meant that German cultural life remained highly decentralized and rooted within traditional local institutions. The German Enlightenment, notes one scholar, "lacked the extremes" of the Enlightenment in France. Rather than displaying the ardent anticlericalism of Voltaire or the radical republicanism of Rousseau, German intellectuals presented more modest critiques of existing institutions, advocating either "limited reform within the corporate structures of the Estates or legal emancipation within absolute monarchy."[11] The rapid population expansion in Central Europe after 1750, however, undermined the stability of the traditional order by creating a more mobile populace that could not be adequately absorbed into the old institutions of rural and village life.

Economically, the German states lagged somewhat behind their western neighbors in the development of urban industry, though not to the extent that has sometimes been depicted in historical accounts. England underwent the first wave of industrialization in the latter half of the eighteenth century; France and Belgium entered the industrial age during the first half of the nineteenth century. In the German states, the period of "industrial takeoff" began only in the 1830s and 1840s, accelerating rapidly after 1850.[12] Over the course of the eighteenth century, however, a gradual "protoindustrialization" had occurred in much of Central Europe, with the expansion of commerce and rural manufacturing. The new rural industries, generally employing traditional artisanal methods of production, emerged in part as a challenge to the urban guilds, which continued to exercise monopolies over economic life in the towns. Along with this expansion of rural manufacturing, Prussian agriculture was becoming increasingly driven by market forces. By the beginning of the nineteenth century, Prussia's East Elbian farms supplied 50 percent of British grain imports. The modernization of farming methods, which led to larger harvests, together with significant increases in grain prices after 1750, resulted in a wave of land speculation as the prices of landed estates skyrocketed at the end of the eighteenth century.[13]

Socially and economically, Prussia thus stood on the threshold between two worlds during the era of the French Revolution. In the towns, the guilds remained economically dominant, but they were beginning to be challenged by unregulated rural manufacturers. In the countryside, large landowners were increasingly transforming themselves into agrarian capitalists. At the same time, however, the landed nobles fiercely clung to their traditional legal privileges, ranging from special tax exemptions to hunting rights and monopolies over milling and brewing, to patrimonial police and justice powers over their serfs. In most of Western Europe, the legal condition of hereditary serfdom had largely disappeared by the eighteenth century. In Prussia, however, two types of serfdom remained in existence until the Napoleonic era: *Erbuntertän-igkeit*, or "hereditary subjection," and the even more onerous *Leibeigen-schaft*, whereby the lord was literally the "owner of the body" of the peasant.

If the eighteenth century marked a transformation of Prussian social and economic life, it also witnessed changes in the political relations of the Hohenzollern monarchs both with the Prussian nobility and with the Holy Roman Empire. Since the late thirteenth century, the nobles of various German territories had periodically convened in diets (*Land-stände*), which were intended both to apportion taxes and to represent the common interests of the land. In practice, the *Landstände* functioned more as a negative than as a positive political force, exerting their energies to uphold the rights and privileges of the nobility and to restrict the ambitions of the territorial princes. At the local level, rural territories were administered through county diets (*Kreistage*), which were dominated by the leading nobles of the area; and on the individual estates, lords enjoyed virtually unrestricted police and judicial powers over their peasants.[14]

With the rising power of the dynastic states in the seventeenth and eighteenth centuries, political rulers throughout Europe came to intervene more and more intensively in the lives of their subjects. The army of Louis XIV, comprising 400,000 soldiers, was several times as large as the grandest European military force of the previous century, the Spanish Host. Frederick the Great's Prussian army of the mid–eighteenth century, as a proportion of the overall population, was four to five times as large as the army of France.[15] To support these growing military machines, European states developed larger bureaucratic structures with the mission both of extracting resources from the population and of encouraging the growth of wealth through the regulation of commerce and industry.[16]

In Prussia, the Hohenzollern princes intervened with increasing vigor in the life of the municipalities from the mid–seventeenth century onward. In the countryside, however, they left the social and legal privileges of the nobility largely untouched. The strategy of Prussian absolutism was to achieve the "depoliticization and privatization of the estates" by eliminating, for example, the authority of the *Landstände* over taxation and by requiring the sons of nobles to attend royal military academies and subsequently to serve as officers in the army of the king. Once in the army, the lives of nobles were regimented to an extreme degree: officers were forbidden to marry without the king's consent (which was frequently withheld), and they were not allowed to travel abroad without permission. These policies were intended not to destroy the authority of the aristocracy but to neutralize its capacity to organize political dissent. Viewing a vigorous nobility as a key source of support for the throne, Prussia's monarchs supported the preservation of aristocrats' ruling powers on their own estates. Unlike the French absolute monarchs, who regularly sold offices and titles as a source of revenue for the crown, the Hohenzollern kings sought to preserve the integrity of the nobility by limiting the ennoblement of members of the bourgeoisie.[17]

The struggle for supremacy between monarchs and nobles was a common feature of political life throughout Europe in the early modern era. One feature of German politics that differentiated it from the rest of Europe, however, was the institution of the Holy Roman Empire of the German Nation, which remained intact until 1806. The empire was a federative structure of more than 1,800 semiautonomous political entities, including independently governed church lands, the imperial cities, and the lands of the so-called imperial (reichsunmittelbare) nobility, who owed allegiance to the emperor alone. All of these entities, along with the larger German states, were subordinated at least in theory to the emperor and the imperial diet (Reichstag). The rulers of these political territories, because they were subjected to the feudal legal and political order of the empire, did not exercise full sovereign authority either over their own subjects or in their dealings with other states. Nor could the emperor himself be considered to be sovereign, because he depended on the support of the imperial diet and the imperial princes, and he exercised little de facto military or diplomatic power.[18]

By the end of the eighteenth century, German political writers, expecting sovereign authority to be "united, compact, and uniform," were becoming increasingly exasperated by the empire's weakness and its lack of centralized authority. Already in the mid–seventeenth century, Samuel Pufendorf had called the empire "an irregular, monster-like hybrid" doomed to remain in a "situation of permanent conflict."[19] In 1801, the young Georg Wilhelm Friedrich Hegel began a treatise on "The Constitution of the German Empire" with the claim that "Germany is no longer a state. What can no longer be comprehended [begriffen] no longer exists."[20]

These criticisms of the old Reich, however, were not entirely just, for the empire was never intended to be a unified nation-state in the modern sense of the word. Rather, the empire was primarily a symbolic community, as well as a "community of justice" whose courts resolved disputes within its territories, often serving to protect independent towns and small principalities from the designs of their ambitious neighbors.[21] As one scholar observes, the constitution of the empire must be understood in terms of the premises of the older "universalist tradition in European public life" out of which it evolved:

> The Reich came from a historical world in which nationality had no political meaning and states did not command total sovereignty. Unlike nations and states, the Reich did not insist upon preeminent political authority and unquestioning allegiance. Its goal was not to clarify and dominate but rather to order and balance fragmented institutions and multiple loyalties.[22]

Though the institutions of the Holy Roman Empire were formally abolished in 1806, this mission of establishing order and harmony among the various constituent parts of the realm would continue to motivate political leaders in Prussia and other German states well into the nineteenth century. During the Napoleonic era, influenced by writers such as Edmund Burke, Justus Möser, and August Wilhelm Rehberg, many leading Prussian political figures expressed reverence for traditional institutions. Stein, for example, hoped to revitalize the nobility so that it would serve as the bulwark of the throne. Stein's Municipal Ordinance of 1808 sought to strengthen local traditions of self-government. Even the most rationalistic of the Prussian reformers, such as Hardenberg, called for the modification rather than the outright abolition of the traditional estates. Hardenberg wanted to establish a "rational order of ranks,"[23] in which individuals' status would correspond to the social and economic functions they performed, to replace what he viewed as an outmoded and baroque system of privileges. In attempting to create balance and unity within diversity, rather than to renovate the social order from the ground up, the Prussian reformers owed much to the governing spirit of the old Reich.

The Problem of Cohesion: Recasting Civil Society

This emphasis on the importance of attaining domestic harmony was a central feature of Prussian political and social discourse of the late eighteenth century. According to the dominant science of government of the age, cameralism (*Cameralwissenschaft*), one essential function of the ruler was to carry out the function of "police" (*Polizei*). The term "police" had a much broader meaning than its modern sense: Johann Justi (1705?– 1771), one of the most influential cameralist theorists, defined it as "that science whose aim it is to keep the well-being of the individual families constantly in precise harmonious relation with what is best for the whole."[24] For Justi, the common good depended upon "cohesion" (*Zu-*

sammenhang), which, in turn, made possible both prosperity and the "perfection of our moral condition." Lack of cohesion, on the other hand, caused stagnation and poverty. Thus, the good of the state was synonymous with the good of the people: harmony was to be maintained through judicious regulation, as well as through the creation of a limited degree of individual economic freedom.[25]

Justi's arguments about cohesion exhibited an internal tension that would become far more prominent in the writings of social and political theorists of subsequent decades. On the one hand, Justi maintained that government had both the right and the obligation to intervene so as to preserve the proper relations among the various elements of the social order. On the other hand, he held that the establishment of economic freedom and the recognition of certain universal natural rights might be the best ways to attain cohesion "among the productive estates of the whole country."[26] This tension between traditional prerogatives and universal principles was seen, for example, in the provisions of the Prussian General Code (*Allgemeines Landrecht*) of 1794, which was written under the direction of jurist Carl Gottlieb Svarez. Alexis de Tocqueville mocked this law code as a "monstrous . . . compromise between two creations."[27] The code's statement of principles, Tocqueville noted, resembled the Declaration of the Rights of Man in the French constitution of 1791; but rather than abolishing antiquated institutions, such as serfdom, the code preserved intact virtually the entire fabric of legal privileges undergirding the traditional social order.

Tocqueville's judgment, though a harsh one, effectively captures the spirit of many of the efforts at social and political reform in Prussia prior to 1806. During this period, Prussian statesmen and jurists sought not so much to revolutionize the traditional order as to reconcile it with modern political principles, such as universal freedom and the rule of law. According to the traditional notion of the *Ständegesellschaft*, the society of estates consisted of a hierarchy of legally defined orders that were kept in balance by the authority of the monarch.[28] The new civil society, on the other hand, was held to be a sphere separate and at least partially autonomous from the state, consisting of free and legally equal individuals. The General Code attempted to establish a middle ground: it redefined the traditional estates (the nobility, the bourgeoisie, the clerical orders, and the peasantry) as *Staatsstände*—literally, "estates of the state"—thus maintaining their particularistic character but only in subordination to a unified set of laws enacted by the central state.[29]

In seeking to balance the principles of state interventionism and individual freedom, Prussian scholars of the late eighteenth century drew on the economic theories of both the Scottish and the French Enlightenment. Adam Smith's *Wealth of Nations* (1776) represented one attempt to define principles by which social order and harmony could be preserved in an autonomous civil society: the "invisible hand" of the market served as a Newtonian "law of motion" by which society regulated itself. In France, the physiocratic school founded by François Quesnay, which favored free trade and investment in agriculture, was a continental analogue.[30]

Though Adam Smith's writings initially attracted little attention in the German states, by the 1790s they had gained prominent supporters among the faculties of the Universities of Göttingen and Königsberg, where many of the leading Prussian reformers studied. In Königsberg, the lectures of Smith's main exponent, Christian Jakob Kraus, were attended by many aristocrats and by military officers stationed in the city; and by 1806, these doctrines had been disseminated throughout Prussia's ruling elite.[31] One of Stein's collaborators, Friedrich Ludwig von Vincke, referred to the Scottish economist as "the divine Smith."[32] For Vincke, as for many other German statesmen and intellectuals, free market economics provided a model for understanding how harmony could be maintained within a free and autonomous civil society.

Smith's theories provided one source of inspiration for the new discipline of "national economy" (*Nationalökonomie*), which emerged during the first decade of the nineteenth century. One economist, writing in 1805, defined the purpose of *Nationalökonomie* to be "the highest perfection of the physical condition of sociable mankind." He continued:

> But the study of *Nazional-Oekonomie* cannot be in any respects empirical. It is a purely intellectual abstraction, resting upon unchanging, certain and considered principles, which identifies the general regulator in *human relationships and passions*, arranges the mechanism in accordance with this (just like the omnipotent genius which created the world), *but then* quietly allows it to proceed, watching over its calm but steady progress.[33]

Like the eighteenth-century deists, the national economists believed in a "watchmaker God," who ordered the universe according to rational laws. By discovering these true governing principles, it might become possible to create an entirely self-regulating social order. This ambition was shared by the physiocrats in France, as attested to by the following apocryphal conversation between François Quesnay and the heir to the French throne:

> "What," the Dauphin asked, "would you do if you were king?"
> Quesnay: "Nothing."
> The Dauphin: "Then who would govern?"
> Quesnay: "The law."[34]

Like the French physiocrats, the national economists held out hope that the law might become king, that a rational government might reconcile new notions of freedom and equality with the preservation of social harmony. For many Prussian intellectuals of this era, however, cultural reform was equally as important as rational administration. In 1791, for example, the youthful Wilhelm von Humboldt denounced the paternalistic state in a treatise entitled *The Limits of State Action*. Unlike John Stuart Mill and other subsequent liberal theorists (many of whom were influenced by this treatise), Humboldt grounded his political theory not on the principle of utility but on an ethical foundation. The "true end of Man," Humboldt declared, was "the highest and most harmonious development of his powers to a complete and consistent whole." But the paternalistic state, by treating its subjects as immature, denied them the freedom that was the "indispensable condition" for the full development of human capabilities. Rational governance, in other words, was an essential precondition for popular education (*Bildung*).[35]

These ideals of education and harmony permeated many new eighteenth-century associations, from elite groups such as the Berlin *Mittwochsgesellschaft*, whose members included writers Moses Mendelssohn and Christian Wilhelm Dohm, and the distinguished jurist Carl Gottlieb Svarez,[36] to the burgeoning numbers of local reading societies in German towns, a large proportion of which bore the names Harmony Society or Concordia.[37] Likewise, the late eighteenth century marked the beginning of what Suzanne Marchand terms a German "cultural obsession" with the world of the ancient Greeks, who were idealized for their aesthetic sensibility and their devotion to individual cultivation.[38]

In a more mystical and arcane sense, the ideal of harmony was central to the society of the Freemasons. Founded in its modern form in England in 1723, Freemasonry spread to numerous German cities, including Hamburg, Königsberg, Göttingen, and Berlin, by the mid–eighteenth century. Though the initial Freemasons were drawn from the ranks of the bourgeoisie, the lodges came to attract numerous aristocrats as members as well. At the end of the eighteenth century, the Freemasons counted as members some of the most eminent literary and philosophical figures in the German states, including Kant, Herder, Fichte, Lessing, and Goethe. In Prussia, Frederick the Great dabbled in Freemasonic ideas as a youth, and many of the figures who became leading lights of the reform party after 1806 were Masons, among them Hardenberg, Theodor von Schön, and Johann Gottfried Frey.[39]

The ideology of Freemasonry combined a mystical regard for the secrets of the ancients with a rationalistic and egalitarian social philosophy.

The society was organized according to a democratic form that recognized no differences among its members based upon their occupation or social rank. The lodges were intended, in part, as a model for a new social order based on universal freedom and equal rights for all citizens. During the late eighteenth century, German Masons founded a secret order known as the Illuminati, which was intended to advance a progressive political agenda by placing its adherents in high government posts. This plan met with at least partial success: Hardenberg, as well as the Bavarian reformer Maximilian von Montgelas, were both at one time members of the Illuminati.[40]

During the late eighteenth century, Prussian intellectuals faced the challenge of identifying new principles of cohesion within a social order that consisted of free and equal individuals, rather than of hierarchies of legally defined orders whose mutual relations were determined by royal decree. In their view, rational administration and the *Bildung* of the populace offered two potential, mutually reinforcing solutions to this challenge. Governing according to the true principles of natural law, the monarch would have no need to resort to arbitrary and divisive acts of will, rather, he could allow society to function according to its own innate logic. The formation of an educated citizenry would facilitate this transition to a self-regulating social order by enhancing the rationality of human behavior. Both of these recipes for social reform—rationalization from above and education from below—would be developed much more explicitly in the aftermath of Prussia's military catastrophe of 1806–1807.

The Problem of Sovereignty: Immanuel Kant and Other Revolutionaries

When Louis XVI ascended to the French throne in 1774, he chose as his controller general of finance an adherent of the physiocratic doctrines, Anne-Robert-Jacques Turgot (1727–1781). One of Turgot's abortive proposals for governmental reform illustrates particularly clearly the effort to reconcile monarchical rule with new rational and egalitarian principles of social organization. In 1775, Turgot prepared a proposal for a system of municipal and provincial representative assemblies in France. The memorandum declared:

> The cause of the evil, sire, goes back to the fact that your nation has no constitution. It is a society composed of different orders, badly united, and of a people in which there are but very few social ties among the

members. . . . You are forced to decree on everything, in most cases, by particular acts of will, whereas you could govern like God, by general laws, if the various parts composing your realm had a regular organization and a clear understanding of their relations.[41]

For Turgot, a "constitution" meant an orderly social and political structure. Rather than glorifying the traditional hierarchical order, in the manner of Montesquieu and other authors, Turgot saw the existence of legally mandated inequalities as a fatal defect that prevented the establishment of true unity among the people. Any viable constitution, Turgot argued, must begin from the principle of "the rights of men united in society, [which] are founded not on their history but on their nature." Thus, for example, all property owners must be taxed on an equal basis, and all individual subjects must be treated as equals under the law. To prepare the way for these reforms, Turgot called for the creation of two new types of institutions. First, he favored instituting a national educational system to encourage the formation of public spirit. Second, he proposed establishing a hierarchy of representative assemblies throughout France to determine taxes and to vote on public works projects. Initially, he wanted to create these assemblies at the local and provincial levels; ultimately, when the rational discourse in these assemblies had reached a sufficiently elevated level, he believed it would be possible to establish a national assembly as well. The combination of all of these reforms, Turgot argued, would have spectacular success in revitalizing the French nation. If these plans were adopted, he declared

that in ten years [His Majesty's] nation would no longer be recognizable; and that, by its knowledge, by its good customs, by its enlightened zeal for His service and for service to the fatherland, it would be infinitely above all other peoples.[42]

Turgot's proposals envisioned two complementary movements for national renewal, one occurring from the top down and the other from the bottom up. From above, he sought to rationalize France's governing institutions. He declared that, ideally, the king should rule not by particular and arbitrary "acts of will" but rather "like God, by general laws." The new representative assemblies would assist in this process of rationalization by providing an accurate portrayal of the condition and desires of the nation, which would help ensure informed decision making. For the reforms imposed from above to be successful, however, it was essential that the nation reconstitute itself from below, transforming itself from a "society composed of different orders, badly united" into an enlightened and patriotic community. The people of France must therefore be linked together more closely, both through the establishment of conditions of legal equality and through educational and political reforms. Turgot's entire enterprise rested on one basic assumption: that the interests of the nation were in harmony with those of the king. An educated and properly constituted nation, he declared, would zealously serve both king and fatherland, so that politics could be reduced to a purely rational process, free of the contest of will between competing factions.[43]

Turgot fared poorly in his two-year tenure as France's controller general. After seeking unsuccessfully to abolish the guild system, to liberalize the grain trade, and to reform the tax system, he was ultimately driven from office by the outraged protests of France's privileged elites. His memorandum on municipal government was apparently never even sent to the king and was made public only in 1787, six years after his death. The fall of Turgot has long provided inspiration for thought experiments by French historians, who have speculated whether the revolution and much of the turbulence of subsequent French history might have been averted if Turgot had prevailed over his opponents.[44]

As the present study will show, one can gain insight into this question about the French Revolution by studying the Prussian reform movement. In a real sense, Turgot *did* prevail in Prussia. In April 1806, six months before the military catastrophes at Auerstädt and Jena, Karl vom Stein sent a memorandum to King Frederick William III, arguing for administrative reform:

> The Prussian state has no state constitution: supreme power is not divided between the head [*Oberhaupt*] and delegates [*Stellvertretern*] of the nation. It is a very new aggregation of many individual provinces brought together through inheritance, purchase, and conquest.

The fractured nature of the Prussian state, argued Stein, was exacerbated by the "mistaken organization" of its uppermost administrative authorities. The Prussian king ruled "under the influence of his cabinet" (a council that existed independently from the rest of the Prussian administration), and he remained "in complete seclusion from his ministers." As a consequence, Stein claimed, Prussian administrators had "sunk quite low in public opinion"; and, in the absence of administrative reforms, "it is to be expected that the state will either disintegrate or lose its independence, and the love and respect of its subjects will completely disappear."[45] The leaders of the Prussian reform movement, both in their rhetoric and in their legislative proposals, articulated many of the same notions about enlightened monarchy that were central to Turgot's project. The nation, they argued, must be linked together by organic social ties based on civic equality, and the citizenry must be educated and permitted to participate in the political process. The rationalization of the state administration from above and the formation of national spirit from below would forge a harmonious and vibrant bond between the monarch and his people.[46]

If French theories of enlightened monarchy served as one source of inspiration for the Prussian reformers, there were also important indigenous influences. Foremost among these were the writings of Immanuel Kant (1724–1804), who was a professor at the University of Königsberg and the most eminent Prussian philosopher of his age. Kant exerted tremendous intellectual authority both over his contemporaries and over the generation of reformers that would lead Prussia after 1806.[47] For example, Theodor von Schön and Johann Gottlieb Fichte both studied with Kant, and Stein expressed deep admiration for Kant's writings. Other leading reformers, such as Friedrich Leopold von Schrötter and Johann Gottfried Frey, were friends of Kant in Königsberg, as well as fellow Freemasons in Kant's lodge. Humboldt spent many months immersed in an exegesis of Kant's *Critique of Pure Reason*.[48]

As a political philosopher, Kant has often been depicted as the archetypal "apolitical German," an apologist for Prussian absolutism, who insisted on the freedom of the "public use of one's reason" but denied the public any practical political power. "*Argue* as much as you like and about whatever you like, *but obey*,"[49] declared Kant in his famous essay of 1784, "What Is Enlightenment?" In the view of historians such as Leonard Krieger, Kant offered an emasculated vision of political liberty that "moralized the traditional organs of state power."[50]

Reconstructing Kant's political theory is a challenging enterprise. Unlike predecessors such as Locke, Montesquieu, and Rousseau, who devoted treatises to the subject, Kant scattered fragments of his political theory among a series of occasional essays he published between the ages of sixty and seventy-five.[51] To argue that Kant's political theory legitimated authoritarian government, however, is to underestimate the significance of his project. Consider another passage from Kant's political writings, this one from *The Contest of the Faculties* of 1798:

> [I]t is . . . the duty of monarchs, even if they rule *autocratically*, to govern *in a republican manner [republikanisch]* . . . —that is, to treat the people in a manner consistent with the spirit of the laws of freedom (as a people with fully developed reason would direct itself).[52]

To grasp the meaning of this perplexing passage, it is essential to explore the distinction Kant draws between the "form of sovereignty" (*forma imperii*) and the "form of government" (*forma regimnis*). Following Aristotle, Kant held that the forms of sovereignty in a state may be divided into "autocracy, aristocracy, and democracy—the power of a prince, the power of a nobility, and the power of the people." Yet an even more important classification was the form of government, which "relates to the way in which the state, setting out from its constitution, . . . makes use of its plenary power." The form of government may be either "republican" or "despotic":

> *Republicanism* is that political principle whereby the executive power (the government) is separated from the legislative power. *Despotism* prevails in a state if the laws are made and arbitrarily executed by one and the same power, and it reflects the will of the people only in so far as the ruler treats the will of the people as his own private will.[53]

At first blush, it might appear that Kant was offering a fairly conventional defense of the "mixed constitution," such as is found in the works of Aristotle or Montesquieu. As both of these earlier authors argued, a polity is more likely to remain stable if various elements of civil society check each other's power. The best way to distill an expression of the public good, according to this logic, is through continual compromises among competing factions: thus, the best government is one that allows the public good to emerge out of the competition among private interests.

Yet, for Kant, the matter was not so simple. Republicanism, he argued, lay less in the form of a state's constitution than in the principles that any rightful government must uphold:

1. The *freedom* of every member of society, as a *person*.
2. The *equality* of the same with everyone else, as a *subject*.
3. The *autonomy* of every member of a commonwealth, as a *citizen*.[54]

Thus, any government that always acts to uphold the freedom and equality of the citizenry is a republican one (at least in spirit); while any government in which the ruler "treats the will of the people as his own private will" is a despotic one.

By this measure, Kant argued, a direct democracy

> is necessarily a *despotism*, because it establishes an executive power through which all the citizens may make decisions about (and indeed against) the single individual without his consent . . . ; and this means that the general will is in contradiction with itself, and thus also with freedom.[55]

But a limited monarchy such as the one that existed in Britain could also be despotic. The British monarchy, according to Kant, possessed the form but not the spirit of a representative system: though the "illusion" of representation existed there, the representatives, "won over by bribery, secretly subject [the people] to an *absolute monarch*."[56]

Paradoxically, Kant maintained, the government that was the most republican in spirit might be the one that was the least republican in form. Under a democratic constitution, "everyone . . . wants to be a ruler"; but an absolute monarch, such as Frederick the Great, who considers himself "the highest servant of the state," may function as the protector of the rights of man and the truest representative of the people. In general, "the smaller the number of ruling persons in a state and the greater their powers of representation, the more the constitution will approximate to its republican potentiality, which it may hope to realize eventually by gradual reforms." Thus, while an aristocracy is more likely to function in a republican manner than a direct democracy, a monarchy is most likely of all to attain "this one and only perfectly lawful kind of constitution."[57]

Added to this paradox concerning the relationship between monarchy and republicanism was a further one. On the one hand, Kant was a devotee of Rousseau and such an enthusiast of the French Revolution that some of his contemporaries labeled him a "Jacobin."[58] On the other hand, he denied that the people possessed the right of physical resistance against their ruler. Kant declared:

> A revolution may bring about the end of a personal despotism or of av-
> aricious and tyrannical oppression, but never a true reform of modes of
> thought. New prejudices will serve, in place of the old, as guidelines for
> the unthinking multitude.[59]

In attempting to explain the deep internal tensions in Kant's political writings, a few historians have rightly pointed to Kant's delicate position in Prussia during the era of the French Revolution.[60] As a professor in Königsberg, Kant was both a Prussian civil servant and the country's most famous philosopher. Following Frederick the Great's death in 1786, press censorship had tightened considerably in Prussia, and Kant faced pressure to avoid inflammatory statements in order to preserve his right to publish freely.

Yet some critics have overstated the degree of internal contradiction in Kant's political writings. Kant derived his principles of republicanism from the "original contract" or "civil constitution," which he said provided the foundation for any government and which, he argued, could arise "solely from the general (united) will of the people." According to the terms of the civil constitution, he wrote, the people surrendered the right of political decision making to the "head of state" (*Staatsoberhaupt*). In the event of a dispute between the people and their ruler, he noted, neither party could arbitrate the matter without acting "as a judge in his own case." To adjudicate the issue properly, "there would need to be a supreme head [*Oberhaupt*] above the supreme head, who would decide between him and the people—and this is a contradiction." Given the impossibility of impartially mediating such a dispute, Kant concluded, subjects must always obey their ruler's commands.[61]

The fact of obedience, however, did not guarantee that a ruler's decrees were legitimate. Kant criticized as "appalling" Hobbes's tenet that "the head of state has no contractual obligations to the people, and cannot do an injustice to the citizen." Kant proposed a simple test of the legitimacy of any law: "Whatever a people cannot resolve concerning itself, neither can the lawgiver resolve concerning the people." Under the civil constitution, every legislator is obliged "to make his laws as if they *could* have arisen out of the united will of an entire people." Thus, for example, a law that granted "a certain class of *subjects* the hereditary preference of the *ruling estate*" would be unjust, because it would be "*impossible* that an entire people *could* give its agreement" to such a measure.[62] In other words, since one part of the people would never agree to subordinate itself hereditarily to another part of the people, such a law would violate the civil constitution.

As these passages illustrate, Kant cared less about who ruled a state than about how they ruled. Rather than being an apologist for absolutism, Kant was an advocate of the tutelary state: he believed that the government had a duty to educate its people for citizenship. He considered monarchy to be an imperfect form of government but one that would serve to represent the interests of the people until such time as the people had shed the shackles of irrationality and subservience.[63] In Kant's view, governments should nurture the process of enlightenment by allowing their subjects freely to develop their faculty of reason. The ultimate objective, he argued, should be a society of free, equal, and self-determining citizens.[64] Given Kant's conviction that human nature possessed elements of radical evil, even a fully cultivated citizenry might always need to be constrained by governing institutions—and his acute awareness of evil may have tempered his enthusiasm for revolution. Other figures influenced by Kant, however, who were more sanguine about the character of humanity, expressed more unambiguously optimistic conclusions about the potential of this educational process. In an essay written in 1794, Kant's one-time disciple Fichte expressed the logical conclusion of his teacher's political philosophy: "The state, like all human institutions that are mere instruments, seeks its own annihilation: the goal of all government is to make government superfluous."[65]

The political writings of Turgot and Kant present a remarkable study in parallels and contrasts. Both authors portrayed civic equality as the bedrock foundation of any just and viable social order. Both also held that a monarchical form of sovereignty, if combined with a rational governing spirit, could be optimal for attaining the public good. Indeed, Kant's paradoxical notion of a republican monarchy may have inspired Hardenberg's famous remark in the Riga Memorandum of 1807 that the Prussian state should establish "democratic principles in a monarchical government."[66] Finally, Kant and Turgot concurred that the citizenry must be educated to achieve political maturity before it would become capable of governing itself.

Along with these similarities, however, were important differences between the two theorists' claims. Turgot employed the rhetoric of efficiency. In his view, the primary objective of political and social rationalization was to maximize the productivity of the French populace, as well as the government's ability to extract resources from the population. Kant's writings, on the other hand, were steeped in more traditional Aristotelian categories. Kant viewed the republic as a vehicle for achieving the common good; he was less interested in mobilizing resources for the benefit of the government than in the moral improvement of individual citizens. The writings of the Prussian reformers exhibited concern with both of these goals: first, mobilizing social resources, and second, fostering the "maturity" of the Prussian citizenry.

Well before the Napoleonic conquest, the rhetoric of political rationalization had gained wide currency among Prussia's ruling elite. In 1791–1792, jurist Carl Gottlieb Svarez presented a series of lectures on political theory and public law to the Prussian crown prince, who would reign as King Frederick William III from 1797 until 1840. Like Frederick the Great, who had declared that "the ruler represents the state,"[67] Svarez argued that "unrestricted monarchy" was the best form of government in Prussia. Svarez declared in his lectures to the crown prince: "The regent can never, provided he has correct conceptions, possess an interest different from or hostile to the people."[68] Thus, in order to achieve a harmonious political order, it was simply necessary to ensure that both the ruler and the ruled properly understood their own true interests. For example, Svarez warned that unrestricted monarchy could degenerate into despotism as a result of the ruler's "lack of insight or weakness of character." To guard against this tendency, he wrote, Prussia's kings should periodically convene assemblies of the estates, which would bring "the voice of truth before the throne." The estates would thus cooperate with the monarch without limiting his sovereignty.[69] His pupil, the crown prince, adopted this notion of sovereignty in an essay composed shortly before he ascended to the throne in 1797. The future Frederick William III declared that princes must rule for the "good of their land" and the "true best of the state [besten des Staats]." Any monarch who failed to heed this principle, he warned, risked plunging his country into revolution as, he argued, the recent events in France had shown.[70]

Though Svarez considered the interest of the monarch to be compatible with that of the people, he argued that both parties required assistance in order correctly to *perceive* their own true interests. The monarch needed the guidance of the laws and of the estates; his subjects needed to be educated to exercise their faculty of reason, which alone would allow them to discover their proper interest. Given the imperfect rationality of the people, Svarez argued, "insights can be incorrect, and then a person desires something that he should not desire." In such cases, he declared, the state had the right to "compel [a subject] to act against his conviction, but it cannot compel him to want anything other than what he recognizes as good and reasonable."[71] The state, according to this view, needed to foster the moral and intellectual development of its people. Svarez hoped to stimulate this process by granting the subjects "moral freedom"; he favored, for example, establishing a general right of freedom of expression.[72]

The above-cited passages from Svarez's lectures foreshadow the idea of the *Erziehungsstaat*—the "tutelary state"—which came to full fruition in Fichte's *Addresses to the German Nation*. The state, according to this view, needed to foster the moral and intellectual development of its people. In subsequent chapters, we will witness the idea of the *Erziehungsstaat* in various guises. This tutelary ideal became central to Prussian political discourse largely because many intellectuals and political leaders believed that it was vitally necessary to harmonize the desires of the people with the will of the state. Fichte's own development exemplified this movement from an anti-statist to a state-centered approach. In 1794, Fichte pronounced that "the goal of all government is to make government superfluous." By 1808, he sanctioned the state's right "to coerce those who are not mature [die Unmündigen] . . . for their own welfare."[73] If fostering the maturity (Mündigkeit) of the subjects was one of the key goals of the Prussian reform movement, it also proved to be a highly elusive objective.

Conclusion: The Paradoxes of Enlightened Monarchy

According to seventeenth-century German chemist and economist Johann Joachim Becher (1635–1682), the proper goal of governance was

"beauty" (*Schönheit*). Sovereignty, in turn, was the art of "beautiful police," which aimed at preserving the proper symmetry and harmony
among the various estates that constituted the community.[74] Becher's
premises about the nature of governance were shared by many European
intellectuals and political leaders of the seventeenth and eighteenth centuries. German cameralists, following Aristotle, held that politics was the
science of the "communal life of human beings" and that the proper role
of political authority was to intervene in the community so as to enhance
the good of all (*Glückseligkeit*).[75] Likewise, the new discourses about the
"self-regulating society" in Europe at the end of the eighteenth century—Adam Smith's free market theory in Britain, the physiocratic
movement in France, *Nationalökonomie* in the German states—should be
seen not simply as harbingers of an emerging liberal social order but also
as attempts to rearticulate traditional concerns about justice and communal harmony in a new philosophical language.

A fundamental premise of all these discourses was that an identifiable
common good existed: that civilized humans did not subsist in a Hob-
besian war of each against all, but rather were bound together by some
unity of collective interests. In the premodern era, this collective unity
had been portrayed in terms of a divinely ordained, hierarchical chain
of being. The philosophers of the Enlightenment, proceeding from the
new assumption that all humans were ideally equal, sought to discover
secular and rational laws by which the common good might be defined
and attained.

The project of enlightened monarchy was rent with internal tensions,
both philosophical and practical in nature. Prussia's eighteenth-century
rulers sought to combine a traditional Aristotelian view of government,
emphasizing the preservation of justice and harmony, with new efforts
to mobilize social resources on behalf of the state. Rather than abandoning old institutions, they attempted to transform them to accord with
Enlightenment principles and absolutist objectives. Thus, for example,
the Prussian General Code of 1794 juxtaposed a declaration of universal
human rights with the preservation of serfdom and aristocratic privileges. Likewise, administrative theorists, such as Justi, tried to reconcile
a dynamic theory of individual economic freedom with older notions of
a static social order that could be preserved only by judicious government regulation. In the realm of political theory, Kant justified absolute
monarchy on the basis of republican political ideals.

In short, Prussian enlightened absolutism must be understood as an
unstable governing project that sought to unite fundamentally irrecon-
cilable political and philosophical principles. Ultimately it proved im-

possible to forge a society that reconciled corporate privilege with universal equality or a government that was both monarchical and republican in nature. The eighteenth-century political legacies discussed in this chapter, however, played a powerful role in shaping the agendas of the Prussian reformers of the Napoleonic era.

Three

INVOKING THE NATION

On 14 October 1806, Prussia's famed army collapsed in a single day, routed by the French at the battles of Auerstädt and Jena. Two weeks later, Napoleon entered Berlin, as the Prussian court fled eastward toward Memel, a small Lithuanian seaport near the Russian border. Throughout the following winter and spring, the Prussian military forces were besieged in the towns of Prussia's eastern marches. Major August Neithardt von Gneisenau, commander of the garrison at Kolberg, conveyed his desperation in a letter of May 1807, two months before the Prussian capitulation to Napoleon at Tilsit:

> What can we believe, what shall we hope, what must we do? These three Kantian questions apply directly to us. If only the German were more vigorous. But he is stupid: he believes the French pretenses, he bears like a beast of burden, instead of rising up with flails, pitchforks, and scythes, and exterminating the foreigner from our land.[1]

Gneisenau was not the only disciple of Kant in the upper ranks of the Prussian army. Generals Gerhard von Scharnhorst and Hermann von Boyen, who would collaborate with Gneisenau in the reorganization of the Prussian army after 1807, were both close students of Kant's writings—indeed, Boyen had attended Kant's lectures on anthropology as a student in Königsberg during the 1780s. In the new era of warfare, Boyen declared, "impetuous raw force" must be placed "under the guardianship of human reason," so that even in the "bustle of war the sense of humanity will progressively develop with every century."[2]

This curious blend of Kantian ethics with the most passionate nationalism reveals much about the impulses behind the Prussian reform movement. Leaders of the defeated and diminished Prussian state sought a means of combining strong monarchical authority with a politically active populace. Their constitutional proposals presumed that properly designed representative institutions would produce a unitary expression of the true national interest, rather than simply give voice to a cacophony of competing factions. By rationalizing the institutions of the Prussian administration and by educating the populace for political participation, they hoped ultimately to harmonize democratic and monarchical forms of government. Popular enlightenment, they hoped, would ultimately serve as a tool for national mobilization.

The Crises of 1806–1807

The military disasters of 1806–1807 were only the most spectacular of a series of profound crises that shook Prussia during those years. In July 1806, Napoleon established the Confederation of the Rhine, an association that initially comprised sixteen states in southern and western Germany that he recognized as sovereign, on the condition that they provide support for France's military efforts. This proved to be the final nail in the coffin for the nearly 900-year-old Holy Roman Empire, and on 6 August 1806 Francis II of Austria abdicated the office of Roman emperor and dissolved the Reich. The abolition of the Old Reich had little immediate practical effect on Prussia, but by annihilating the overarching constitutional structure within which the Prussian state had existed until that year, it drew the nature of sovereign authority into question.[3] All of the Prussian political reforms of the Napoleonic era, therefore, took place in the shadow of this event. Prussia's bureaucratic reformers were challenged not only to establish a new constitutional order to replace the old but also to define a new principle of political community in Central Europe. The community of the nation, in other words, functioned in part as a replacement for the old imperial order.

More urgent problems were created by the French military occupation and the punitive Treaty of Tilsit, signed by King Frederick William III in July 1807, which humiliated Prussia's ruling elite and imposed intense suffering on all sectors of the population. According to the terms of this treaty, Prussia lost half of its territory, home to more than half of its subjects, including its new Polish possessions and all of its lands west of the Elbe River. It also agreed to shoulder crippling war tributes to France as a condition for the withdrawal of the French troops occupying the entire region west of the Vistula River. For almost three years, the Prussian court remained exiled from Berlin in Memel, and until 1809 the government maintained full administrative control only over the province of East Prussia and the Silesian county of Glatz.

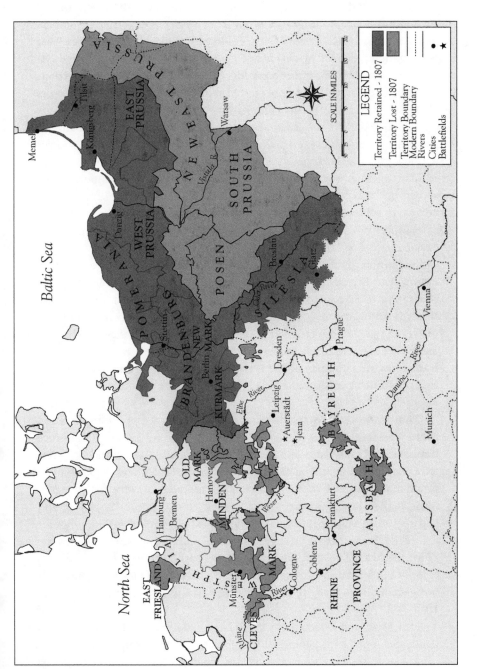

Prussia in 1806–1807

The war and the subsequent occupation ravaged all sectors of the population: food prices soared while land values plunged; the numbers of livestock in East Prussia fell to between 2 and 5 percent of prewar levels; and epidemics of dysentery, cholera, and typhoid devastated cities. Berlin's infant mortality rate in 1807–1808 approached 75 percent. The Napoleonic blockade bankrupted many grain and timber exporters along the Baltic Sea. French requisitions ruined landlords and peasants alike. Altogether, it is estimated that in the two years after the battle of Jena, the French extracted from the rump Prussian territories resources equivalent to approximately sixteen times the Prussian government's annual revenue from before 1806. In the words of contemporary observer Carl von Clausewitz, "The bankruptcies here are endless. . . . what was achieved in this sandy waste throughout centuries in the way of prosperity, culture, and trade, will now be destroyed in perhaps a decade."[4]

In addition to impoverishing large portions of the population, Prussia's defeat also discredited the traditional ruling elites and brought a new generation of leaders to the center of political power. In 1806, virtually the entire Prussian officer corps was of aristocratic extraction, and half of the 142 generals were over sixty years old. These officers, who had made their careers in the wars of Frederick the Great, were reluctant to learn from the triumphs of the French revolutionary armies. A coterie of royal favorites constituted the cabinet, serving as the king's closest advisers.[5]

Confronted by the disasters of war and the prospect of the annihilation of the Prussian state, Frederick William III was forced to seek assistance from an ambitious cadre of reform-minded officials. Two of these figures, Karl vom und zum Stein and Karl August von Hardenberg, had achieved prominent positions in the Prussian government already before 1806. Most of their key supporters were in their thirties and early forties, and had served in middle-level civil service posts before 1806. These figures included Hardenberg's protégé Karl von Stein zum Altenstein (1770–1840), Heinrich Theodor von Schön (1773–1856), Wilhelm von Humboldt (1767–1835), Johann August Sack (1764–1831), Friedrich August von Staegemann (1763–1840), and Friedrich Ludwig von Vincke (1774–1844).[6]

Both Stein and Hardenberg came from outside Prussia. Stein, whose family belonged to the imperial knights and owned estates in the Rhineland, attended the University of Göttingen and served in Westphalia before joining the Prussian administration in 1780. In 1804, Stein was named minister of economic affairs, though the king dismissed him for insubordination in January 1807. Hardenberg, who was born to a wealthy landowning family in Hanover, also studied at the University of Göttingen and served as an official in Hanover and Brunswick before accepting an appointment in the Prussian civil service, where he made his reputation as the administrator of Prussia's new territories in Ansbach-Bayreuth and as a member of the General Directory in Berlin after 1798. From 1804 to 1806, Hardenberg served as Prussian foreign minister. In this capacity, he played a pivotal role in formulating Prussia's foreign policy, initially supporting rapprochement with France and then advocating war. Hardenberg's effectiveness as foreign minister was limited by bitter infighting with his rival, Christian von Haugwitz, one of the king's cabinet councilors. Six months before the outbreak of hostilities with France, Frederick William III dismissed Hardenberg from office under pressure from French officials, who were upset by Hardenberg's support for an alliance with Britain. In January 1807, Hardenberg returned to office as the king's chief adviser, but Napoleon forced his dismissal in October of the same year.[7]

Though Stein and Hardenberg both wielded immense political power during the Napoleonic era, it is important to recognize that their status in the Prussian administration was doubly unstable. First, they were both geographical outsiders and were criticized as such by Prussian nobles incensed by their reform proposals. Second, before being named to head the Prussian ministry, both of them had already been fired at least once by the Prussian king. Stein served as first minister for only thirteen months, from October 1807 until November 1808, when he was dismissed on Napoleon's demand after a French spy intercepted a letter that linked Stein to a group advocating a rebellion against France. From November 1808 until June 1810, Altenstein and Count Alexander von Dohna (1771–1831) headed the so-called interim ministry, which ended with Hardenberg's appointment as state chancellor (*Staatskanzler*), a post that he held for twelve years without interruption until his death in 1822. One factor contributing to Hardenberg's longevity in office may have been that he took care to avoid directly confronting either the monarch or entrenched aristocratic interests. Hardenberg has often been criticized by historians as lacking firm principles and as excessively willing to compromise[8]; these attributes, however, may have stemmed in part from his earlier struggles to establish his authority within the Prussian administration.

Much recent scholarship on Prussian history of the Napoleonic era emphasizes the instrumental motives behind the reform movement. After 1807, the Prussian government confronted a critical fiscal crisis. In the Treaty of Tilsit, Napoleon had demanded a war tribute from Prussia of 154 million francs—later reduced to 120 million—as a condition of withdrawing his troops, which occupied all of Prussia west of the Vistula River. In December 1808, the French army vacated the country, reserving the right to return should Prussia default on its remaining payments. Thus, throughout the reform period, Prussia's political autonomy remained contingent on its fiscal solvency. These economic pressures were particularly acute when Hardenberg was appointed state chancellor in 1810. With Prussia having fallen in arrears in its war tribute installments, Napoleon was demanding either full payment or the cession of the province of Silesia to France. Thus, some historians have concluded that the fundamental objective behind all of Hardenberg's reforms was "the augmentation of national income."[9] Along with this fiscal crisis, scholars have pointed to other challenges that stemmed from the new "structural conditions" of early nineteenth-century politics, including "the growing need for social, for 'national' integration" and "the demand for an improved legitimation of state activity."[10] Certain scholars have gone so far as to claim that Hardenberg and his associates proposed establishing representative institutions primarily for "propagandistic effect."[11]

Though these challenges facing the Prussian state were essential preconditions for the reformers' initiatives, it is important to recognize that the specific form of their response to these challenges reflected the cultural legacy of the Enlightenment. Hardenberg set the tone for the reform movement in his Riga Memorandum of September 1807, calling for

> a revolution in a positive sense, one leading to the ennoblement of mankind, to be made not through violent impulses from below or outside, but through the wisdom of the government. . . . Democratic principles in a monarchical government—this seems to me to be the appropriate form for the spirit of our age.[12]

Stein concurred with Hardenberg about the need to elevate the level of popular participation in government, declaring in a letter of December 1807:

> It is essential that the nation become accustomed to managing its own affairs, so that it will emerge from this state of infancy in which an anxious and officious government attempts to keep the people.[13]

Both Stein and Hardenberg viewed the project of nation building as inextricably linked with the "ennoblement of mankind" through the establishment of individual freedom. Like Kant, they believed that the education of the Prussian populace would make it possible to overcome the opposition between rulers and subjects, which had caused such misery in revolutionary France.

Harmony as a Consensual Feature of the Concept
"Nation"

Anthropologist Claude Lévi-Strauss, in analyzing the construction of
myths and rites that serve as a culture's common "memory bank," draws
an analogy to the activities of the *bricoleur*, or jack-of-all-trades. Such
an individual completes projects by utilizing whatever tools and materials happen to be at hand: the ultimate product is a *bricolage*, patched
together from a variety of odds and ends lying around the workshop.
Cultural myths, he argues, arise through a similar (although less self-
conscious) process. "The characteristic feature of mythical thought,"
Lévi-Strauss writes, "is that it expresses itself by means of a heteroge-
neous repertoire which, even if extensive, is nevertheless limited. It has
to use this repertoire, however, whatever the task in hand because it has
nothing else at its disposal." Thus, mythical thought "builds ideological
castles out of the debris of what was once a social discourse"; it patches
together the remnants of old myths and theories in constructing something fundamentally new.[14]

The construction of the concept "nation" in nineteenth-century Prussia occurred through precisely such a process of "mythical" thinking.
This concept was a *bricolage* formed by combining older notions of political community in new ways. In part, the nation was modeled on the
Holy Roman Empire; in part, it reflected the Kantian ideal of the rational
republic, as well as cameralist theories of the well-ordered state and the
utopian social vision of the Freemasons. Nineteenth-century nationalists
in Prussia also drew their inspiration from the literature of romanticism,
from Herder's musings about the German *Kulturnation*, and from the political writings of the revolutionaries in France. Thus, the concept "nation" represented a synthesis of a wide range of disparate sources. While
some of these sources were quite old, this act of cultural synthesis itself
produced a novel result.

While Lévi-Strauss's notion of *bricolage* helps illustrate the synthetic
nature of the concept "nation," it tells us little about the specific form
of this cultural synthesis. A second analytical category, drawn from the
writings of Sigmund Freud, is useful in this regard, namely, the concept
of "overdetermination." Freud argues that the symptoms of psychological
illness generally flow from multiple causes, each one of which is capable
of producing the same consequence independently. Because these multiple causes are mutually reinforcing, they produce an intensification of
symptoms, exaggerating the tendency of the afflicted person to think
and act in a certain manner.[15]

The concept of overdetermination provides a useful tool for analyzing the specific type of *bricolage* involved in the construction of the concept nation in Prussia. One of the central claims of this book is that, in Prussia during the early nineteenth century, the "nation" became defined as an ideally harmonious political community possessing a unitary interest and a unitary will. These ideals of national unity and harmony, I conclude, played an important role in inhibiting the formation of a pluralistic system of parliamentary government. Freud's notion of overdetermination helps explain the intensity with which these premises about the nation came to be articulated in Prussia during this era.

As was demonstrated in chapter 2, a variety of intellectual traditions in eighteenth-century Europe pointed to the ideal of a harmonious political and social order, to be attained through rational governance. Toward the end of that century, another set of discourses emerged, both within the German states and elsewhere in Europe, depicting the nation as a primary cultural and political community. These discourses also emphasized the ideals of harmony and unity. The Weimar consistorial councilor Johann Gottfried Herder (1744–1803) defined the nation mainly as a cultural and linguistic community. He portrayed the *Volk* as "the invisible, hidden medium that links minds through ideas, hearts through inclinations and impulses, the senses through impressions and forms, civil society through laws and institutions, generations through examples, modes of living and education."[16] The development of national identity, Herder argued, would make possible the peaceful coexistence of humanity, both within individual nations and among the nations of the world. Herder was far from the only German of his age to portray nationhood in cultural terms. In 1776, Johann Christoph Adelung's dictionary had defined "nation" as

> the indigenous inhabitants of a country, in so far as they have a common origin, speak a common language and are, in a more specific sense, distinguished from other peoples by a characteristic mode of thought or action, or by their national spirit, whether they constitute a state of their own or are dispersed throughout a number of states.[17]

A more specifically political understanding of nationhood was derived from the rhetoric of the French revolutionaries. Inspired partly by Rousseau's *Social Contract*, leading revolutionaries in France insisted on the unanimous character of the "general will" of the nation. As François Furet has shown, in the French Revolution the nation came to be understood as

> ... the homogeneous and unanimous group of citizens who have recovered their rights. Society is thus conceived of in terms of the nation: the

multiplicity of individuals and of private interests is immediately cancelled out and reaggregated by the existence of a historical contract harking back to the nation's origins.[18]

The French revolutionaries' emphasis on the need for a unanimous and dedicated national will was reinforced during the revolutionary and the Napoleonic wars, when such patriotic appeals were used to mobilize the resources of France against its external enemies.

At the beginning of the nineteenth century, Prussian leaders, acting as *bricoleurs*, thus drew on a wide range of political and cultural traditions that made it plausible to define the nation as a unified and harmonious political community. In this sense, the ideals of national unity and harmony were overdetermined: they were the product of multiple, mutually reinforcing causes. The most important overdetermining factor of all, however, was the specific political crisis that confronted Prussian leaders after 1806. In response to the devastating defeat by Napoleon, this group of civil servants sought to mobilize the energies of the nation in defense of the monarchical state. Thus, they sought to forge a political community that would work in harmony with the monarchy, rather than one fraught with internal strife.

The overdetermined character of the ideals of national unity and harmony contributed to the intensity with which these ideals were expressed. Indeed, the emphasis on the need for harmony was a constant feature of the Prussian reformers' political proposals. Like earlier political writers, such as Turgot, Kant, and Svarez, leading Prussian civil servants of the Napoleonic era held that the monarch's interests coincided perfectly with those of his people. For the true common good to be recognized, however, the faculty of reason had to be cultivated on both sides. Both Stein and Hardenberg called for the rationalization of the state administration—for example, through the abolition of the royal cabinet, which was dominated by the king's cronies—and the establishment of a Council of State (*Staatsrat*) that would facilitate the more orderly exercise of sovereign authority. Stein, Hardenberg, and other leading reformers also considered the formation of a "national representation" to be critical for the establishment of a harmonious political order. Such a representative body, Stein argued, would contribute to the formation of a "public and common spirit."[19]

The ideal of a harmonious and unified national community appeared regularly both in the reformers' broad programmatic writings and in their specific proposals for constitutional reform. For example, in the Nassau Memorandum of June 1807, Stein claimed that representative institutions would result in

the awakening of a spirit of community and civic pride, the employment
of dormant or misapplied energies and of unused knowledge, harmony
between the views and desires of the nation and those of the administrative authorities of the state, the revival of patriotism and the desire for
national honor and independence.[20]

The document known as Stein's "Political Testament," which was drafted
by Theodor von Schön following Stein's dismissal from office in November 1808, portrayed the role of representative institutions in similar
terms. Stein's goal, the "Testament" declared, had been "to abolish the
disharmony that existed among the people; to eradicate the strife between estates that made us miserable." After listing the reforms that had
already been enacted, Schön proceeded to describe the work that still
lay ahead. The next important task, he wrote, was a "general national
representation" (allgemeine Nationalrepräsentation). Schön declared:

> The right [Recht] and the unlimited authority of our king was sacrosanct
> to me, and remains so to us! But in order for this right and this unlimited
> power to achieve the good that lies within it, it seemed to me necessary
> to give the highest power a means through which it can become ac-
> quainted with the wishes of the people and through which it can give life
> to their determinations.

Only through the "participation of the people in the operations of the
state," wrote Schön, could the "national spirit [Nationalgeist] be positively aroused and animated."[21]

While both Stein and Hardenberg believed that it was essential to
mobilize the nation politically, their plans for the adoption of a Prussian
national representation evolved only gradually during the Napoleonic
era. In April 1806, Stein wrote a memorandum calling for the abolition
of the king's cabinet. In its place, he proposed creating a council of five
ministers, made up of the heads of each of the Prussian administrative
departments, who would deliberate with the king concerning legislative
proposals. Any new decree, he wrote, would be valid only if signed both
by the king and by the members of the ministerial council. Laws would
thus obtain their legitimacy not from the person of the monarch but from
the duly constituted administrative authorities of the state.[22] Stein's proposal was fully consistent with Svarez's earlier project of rationalizing
the exercise of state power to ensure that the king would be guided by
the true interests of the state and of the people, rather than by arbitrary
whims.

Stein's memorandum on cabinet government also hinted at a more
radical agenda for constitutional reform. "Supreme power," Stein declared, should be "divided between the head [Oberhaupt] and delegates

[*Stellvertretern*] of the nation." The nature of this division of powers, however, was left completely undefined. Hardenberg, in his Riga Memorandum, called for a national representation, but he rejected the idea of establishing a national assembly on the French model. Instead, he proposed the "amalgamation of representatives into the administration," which he declared would be the most productive form of popular representation, as well as the one that would pose the least danger to monarchical sovereignty. This proposal was the narrowest possible plan for a national representation: no independent assembly at all but simply a group of three delegates, who would collaborate with the central administrative authorities, along with various deputies advising the provincial administrative departments.[23]

In the aftermath of the military defeat of 1806–1807, the Prussian ministry moved cautiously toward expanding the role of representative assemblies, initially establishing provincial diets and later, during Hardenberg's administration, creating experimental national representative bodies. The history of these institutions illustrates the convergence between immediate financial exigencies and the broader project of nation building. King Frederick William III and his ministers had two urgent financial motives for convening provincial diets after 1807. In order to pay the draconian war tribute installments imposed by Napoleon in the Treaty of Tilsit, the king's advisers proposed to adopt two measures, first, to mortgage (and eventually sell) lands from the royal domains, and second, to establish an income tax throughout the Prussian provinces. But, for several reasons, neither of these measures could be adopted without their acceptance by the provincial estates. To begin with the sale of the royal domains, a decree of 1713 by King Frederick William I had proclaimed these lands to be permanently "inalienable." In order to waive the terms of this proclamation, the king needed to secure the estates' approval. Their cooperation was especially important because the government wanted the nobles' provincial credit associations (*Landschaften*) to guarantee the new mortgage notes on the royal lands. The income tax required the estates' approval for another reason. Napoleon had demanded that Prussia's war tribute be paid not by the central government but by the individual provinces. He had identified the *Landschaften* as the appropriate institutions for making these payments. The income tax could be implemented, therefore, only with the assent of the *Landschaften*, so the government had to consult with these institutions to secure its adoption.[24]

That the provincial assemblies were modeled on the nobles' provincial credit institutes (*Landschaften*), rather than on the traditional provincial diets (*Landstände*), was in itself significant. Until the late seventeenth century, any new taxes in Prussia had required the approval of the *Land-stände*. With the rise of the centralizing monarchy, however, the diets had been convened only sporadically. The East Prussian diet, for example, had assembled only twice after 1740 (in the years 1786 and 1798) and on these occasions simply in order to pay homage to new kings upon their accession to the throne. The *Landschaften*, by contrast, were relatively new institutions that had been established in order to provide credit to the landholding nobility, either for improving their estates or for purchasing new land. Frederick the Great had founded the first *Land-schaft*, for Silesia, in 1770; the East Prussian *Landschaft* had been formed in 1788.[25]

In convening the East Prussian diet of 1808, Stein and his associates transformed both the organization and the function of the *Landschaft*. They wanted it to serve not only as a credit institute that would guarantee the mortgages on the royal domain lands but also as a model for a new general representative assembly. Thus they expanded the membership of the assembly to include non-noble large landowners (the *Köl-mer*) as well as aristocrats. (The towns, however, remained unrepresented in this first diet because they had no connection with the estate owners' mortgage fund.) Presiding over the assembly was a royal commissioner, Hans von Auerswald, rather than an official appointed by the provincial nobles, as had been customary. The government not only restructured the East Prussian *Landschaft* but also granted it a much broader sphere of activity than it had previously possessed. The delegates, declared a royal cabinet order, should deliberate "not only over matters concerning the credit system, but also over those concerning the country [*Land*] in general."[26] The government thus changed the *Landschaft* from a purely financial institution into one with the right to consult over legislation.

In a break from traditional practice, deputies to the East Prussian diet were explicitly forbidden to accept binding instructions from their constituents.[27] The king's cabinet order of January 1808, which dictated voting procedures, declared: "The deputies cannot be bound at all by instructions from the districts that elect them; otherwise all voting freedom and the usefulness of a general assembly would be vitiated." Rather, the order declared, each deputy must "candidly state and submit his opinion according to his insight and conviction."[28] Auerswald's opening speech to the assembly on 2 February 1808 expressed the logic behind these stipulations: the deputies, he declared, must strive to act for "the good of the whole, which is based on the voluntary sacrifice of every one-sided private perspective."[29] These changes in the composition and voting procedures of the *Landschaft* aimed at erasing its traditional corporate character, thereby allowing it to serve the common cause of the "national welfare."[30]

For Stein, the diet of 1808 represented only the first step in reforming the provincial estates and ultimately in moving toward the formation of a national representative body. He envisioned yearly provincial diets, organized according to new principles, which would contribute to the "preservation of common spirit, of national feeling, and of participation in the welfare of the whole."[31] Auerswald shared Stein's enthusiasm: "The general diet," he wrote in May 1808, "can possess no interest other than that of the nation." He recommended that the East Prussian diet meet annually in a purely advisory capacity, convening in a single chamber and publishing its proceedings in order to maintain close contact with "public opinion." Such a diet, he argued, would cause "no restriction of the legislative power of the ruler, but rather its reinforcement: by liberating it from personal interest and from the restricted views of officials, and by uniting the public voice and general trust with the legal provisions."[32]

For Hardenberg, as for Stein, Prussia's fiscal crisis provided the immediate motivation for developing plans for parliamentary institutions. In March 1809, fifteen months before being named Prussian chancellor, Hardenberg proposed gathering a group of bankers and estate owners from the various provinces to approve a plan for liquidating the state debt. As he was himself an estate owner in Brandenburg's Kurmark, Hardenberg could observe from close quarters the proceedings of the diet there. Remarking on the inadequacy of the provincial representation as then arranged, he argued that the "first and most urgent" priority should be "to organize a truly *functional* representation of the estates." He returned to this idea the following spring, when Altenstein and Dohna proved unable to cover the remaining war tribute payments. In April 1810, he wrote to Altenstein urging the adoption of "a forced loan, a national bank, the gathering of insightful and honest bankers and members of the estates."[33]

Hardenberg developed the idea further in several memoranda written during the next few months. In a memorandum of May 1810, calling for the establishment of a national bank, he also proposed a "gathering of insightful men from the whole monarchy," including high civil servants, estate owners, municipal officers, and bankers to deliberate on the proper organization of the national bank and on the government's plans for debt liquidation. Serving "as an organ of Your Royal Majesty," it was to "communicate the results of Your resolutions to the estates, representing those plans . . . as acceptable and as capable of fulfilling the goal; thus awakening patriotism and zeal for the salvation of the Fatherland."[34] This assembly, in other words, was not intended to represent the people to the king but rather to represent the king's policy to the people, thus facilitating its implementation.

In August 1810, even after shelving his plans for a national bank, Hardenberg argued that the creation of a "proper national representation" was essential:

> In any case, publicity with respect to the finances is thoroughly necessary, [and] helps to awaken trust . . . The king gives the state a constitution, a consultative representation, whose members he initially names, and annually submits to it the condition of the nation and of the finances.[35]

On Hardenberg's request, his adviser Friedrich von Raumer produced a plan for such a national representation. Raumer favored the creation of a small assembly that would meet in a single chamber. It should be strictly separated from the administrative authorities, he argued, "in order that the different viewpoint leads to the truth along a different path." Finally, he emphasized that the assembly should be granted a purely consultative and subordinate political role: "The new representation must emanate directly from the government alone; it must come down as a good gift from above."[36] It was an assembly of this nature that Hardenberg had in mind when he drafted Prussia's "first constitutional promise," which was contained in the Finance Edict of 27 October 1810. This promise gave no details and no timetable, it simply said that the king "reserved" to himself the role of "giving the nation an appropriately arranged representation, both in the provinces and for the whole, whose counsel we will gladly use."[37] Though the king would repeat this promise several times—in decrees published in 1811, 1815, and 1820—ultimately it would remain unfulfilled until the year 1847.

While the leading reformers within the Prussian civil service believed that a national representation should coexist harmoniously with the monarchical state, in practice they were reluctant to cede significant authority to parliamentary institutions. Hardenberg, in particular, sought to limit the independence of the new representative bodies, both by controlling the selection of delegates and by limiting them to a purely advisory political role. Despite this initial caution regarding the establishment of representative government, the bureaucratic reformers' rhetorical appeals to national unity and harmony proved highly influential. Other constituencies in Prussia soon would invoke these same premises about the nation in order to challenge the political monopoly of the monarchical state.

Equality and Its Limits: Contested Features of National Identity

In June 1807, four months before returning to head the Prussian ministry, Stein summarized his goals for social and political reform in his Nassau Memorandum:

> The nation, despite all of its flaws, possesses a noble pride, energy, valor, and willingness to sacrifice itself for fatherland and freedom . . . If the nation is to be ennobled, the oppressed part of it must be given freedom, independence, and property; and this oppressed part must be granted the protection of the laws.[38]

For the Prussian reformers, universal freedom and some degree of civil equality were fundamental prerequisites for the forging of a national community. As Altenstein put it succinctly, "the slave has no interest in the state."[39] The citizenry, the reformers argued, could be bound together by a common spirit only if they existed under common legal conditions and were released from arbitrary rule. Nonetheless, two strategic considerations dictated a cautious approach in attacking the privileges of Prussia's traditional elites. First, the reformers wanted to avoid destabilizing the social order through an excessively radical legislative program, and second, they were eager to secure the cooperation of the aristocracy in attempting to mobilize resources against the French threat.

For these reasons, the proposals of Stein and Hardenberg reflected an uneasy compromise between the older principles of the particularistic, hierarchical social order and the newer, egalitarian, and universalistic principles of the Enlightenment and the French Revolution. Though these leaders portrayed the nation as a community of equals, they also emphasized the importance of preserving elements of the traditional corporate order. Stein, in particular, was devoted to reinvigorating, rather than annihilating, what he saw as old organic institutions. These conflicting tendencies may be illustrated through an examination of several key reform measures: Stein's October Edict of 1807, which emancipated the serfs and abolished many of the traditional barriers between the bourgeoisie and the aristocracy, Stein's Municipal Ordinance (*Städteordnung*) of October 1808, and Hardenberg's free trade legislation and proposed fiscal reforms of 1810.

The October Edict. The first great reform measure adopted during Stein's ministry was the edict of 9 October 1807, which declared momentously, "After 11 November 1810, there will be only free people" throughout the Prussian realm.[40] In keeping with the language of Stein's memorandum, the provisions of this edict were directed toward two goals, first, to forge a liberal economic order that would allow each individual to achieve prosperity "according to the measure of his energies," and second, to create a legal system under which all inhabitants of Prussia would become "citizens of the state" (*Staatsbürger*), and all citizens would be considered equal before the law.[41]

The movement to abolish serfdom in Prussia had begun in the late eighteenth century. Between 1799 and 1806, Frederick William III had abolished the feudal obligations of the peasants who lived on the royal domains (about one-seventh of Prussia's agricultural population). In 1803, the king had also expressed support for a proposal that would have gradually eliminated hereditary servitude throughout the realm, but he withheld his final approval for this measure out of fear of provoking a conflict with the nobility.[42]

The October Edict not only abolished all hereditary servitude in Prussia but also eliminated certain traditional restrictions on the bourgeoisie and the nobility. Commoners obtained the right to purchase landed estates (*Rittergüter*), a privilege that had previously been reserved to the nobility. Conversely, nobles received the right to practice bourgeois professions without incurring any penalty to their status. Stein also favored other reforms, not included in the initial edict, that would have fundamentally transformed the relationship between lords and peasants. For example, he wanted to eliminate the nobility's traditional exemption from property taxes and, even more important, he sought to abolish the nobles' police and judicial powers over their estates, placing the entire realm directly under the legal authority of the state. These proposals foundered against bitter opposition from the landholding nobility. Ultimately, the Prussian nobles preserved their exemption from property taxes until 1861, and they kept their police powers until 1872.[43]

At one level, the theory behind Stein's plans was simple. He spoke of the need to secure the "original and inalienable rights of mankind" by establishing a social order based on the principles of freedom and the rule of law.[44] Yet the October Edict left many questions unresolved. For example, even though the serfs became officially free, the law did not abolish their compulsory labor obligations (*Frondienste*) to their former masters, nor did it grant them any ownership rights over the lands that they had farmed. Not until 1816 did the government finally settle the questions of how Prussian estate owners should be compensated for the loss of compulsory labor and how the lands should be distributed between them and the former peasants. This settlement worked largely to the advantage of the nobility, so that many of Prussia's peasants ended up living under worse material conditions than they had before 1807.[45]

A more fundamental ambiguity in Stein's political theory involved the status and function of the traditional estates. On the one hand, Stein wanted to abolish the nobility's hereditary exclusivity, as well as most of its privileges. Yet Stein also hoped to restore the nobility to the position of political preeminence that it had enjoyed prior to the eighteenth century. As a class consisting of Prussia's largest landowners, the nobility would play a leading role in the new representative assemblies that Stein planned to establish. Stein believed that a politically active nobility would support, rather than undermine, monarchical authority. In other words, rather than establishing full civil equality, Stein wanted to reinvigorate what he saw as Prussia's traditional hierarchical institutions. He favored increasing the degree of mobility between estates rather than abolishing outright the legal distinctions between different categories of the population.[46]

Stein's Municipal Ordinance. The provisions of the *Städteordnung*, enacted near the end of Stein's ministry in November 1808, revealed a similar ambivalence toward the traditional social institutions of Prussia's municipalities. Residents of the towns belonged to three main categories: "citizens" (*Bürger*), "protected residents" (*Schutzverwandten*), and "exempted" burghers (*Eximierten*). The status of citizenship was extended to only a small minority of the population; to qualify, one needed to be a self-sufficient practitioner of a "bourgeois trade." The protected residents, who were less prosperous urban dwellers, such as journeymen, day laborers, and domestic servants, lived under the authority of the towns' laws but possessed no political rights. Finally, certain residents, such as civil servants and members of the academic professions, were exempted from the towns' legal jurisdiction and, like the protected residents, they were excluded from voting or holding office in the town government.[47] Under this system, only the leading figures in the guilds and other corporate bodies were entitled to participate in the political life of the towns.

The Municipal Ordinance preserved all three of the traditional categories of residents, but it significantly expanded the class of *Bürger*, stipulating that any male resident of a town, as well as any unmarried female, could qualify for citizenship either by practicing a "municipal trade" (*städtische Gewerbe*) or by owning a house in the town. All male citizens who met certain property qualifications were permitted both to vote and to hold office in the town council, which was responsible for administering local institutions such as the police, schools, and poor relief. Not only did the Municipal Ordinance increase the number of citizens in the towns, it also established new local assemblies in many towns that had previously lacked representative institutions, and it broke the dominance of the guilds over existing municipal governments. The law stipulated that the town representatives be elected by geographical district, eliminating the traditional practice of selecting delegates to the municipal council from each of a town's leading corporate bodies. Moreover, it declared that delegates should be bound only by their own consciences in casting their votes, rather than by the traditional practice of a binding mandate from the electorate.[48]

Stein hoped that his Municipal Ordinance would produce a vigorous public spirit in Prussia's towns while still preserving their particularistic institutions. In the words of one historian, Stein's political theory stood "on the border between the old and the new constitutional thought." Though he wanted to maintain the traditional estates as discrete corporate entities, Stein perceived their character in an entirely new way. No longer did he view the estates as "beneficiaries of rights" that sought to defend their private privileges against encroachment by the monarchy. Rather, he saw the estates as institutions that derived their legitimacy from their performance of a public function and that were bound to serve the public good.[49]

Hardenberg's free trade legislation. Stein's reforms reflected a curious attempt to balance the hierarchical principles of the medieval social order with the new egalitarian ideals of the Enlightenment and the French Revolution. Hardenberg's reform plans, in contrast, attacked the very principle of a social order based on estates—though he stopped short of demanding the abolition of the nobility or other elements of the traditional corporate order. Proclaiming the precept of "equality before the law," he sought to abolish legal distinctions, such as the monopoly rights of the guilds, the nobility's tax exemptions and rural administrative powers, and the peasantry's compulsory labor obligations. Hardenberg rarely even used the word "estate," preferring the term "class," which at that time had a more neutral meaning.[50] His economic reforms, most of which were promulgated in a series of laws of October and November 1810, went a long way toward abolishing the remnants of aristocratic privilege in Prussia and liberalized the economies of the towns as well. Two of these measures were most significant: the Finance Edict of 27 October, which declared the state's intention to equalize tax burdens, reform the tariff and toll system, create freedom of enterprise, and secularize church lands, and the *Gewerbesteueredikt* of 2 November, which eliminated the guilds' monopolies over the practice of trades.

Hardenberg's economic reforms contributed to leveling the social status of the different estates both in rural and urban Prussia. The peasants, who had been formally freed by the edict of 9 October 1807, were now to be released from their economic obligations to the estate owners and to be granted ownership of part of the land they occupied. The nobility lost its exemptions from land taxes and consumption taxes, among other levies. In general, residents of the countryside were now to be taxed on the same basis as those of the towns. The nobles also lost their rights to administer various local and provincial funds, such as those providing mortgage credit and poor relief, as well as their monopoly rights over milling, brewing, and distilling in the countryside. In the towns, Hardenberg's program presented an equally forceful challenge to the position of the guilds. Though the guilds were permitted to remain in existence, they lost their exclusive rights to practice particular trades. Anyone, whether a resident of the countryside or the towns, could now begin practicing a trade simply by paying an annual "tax on enterprises" (Gewerbesteuer)—though one needed to obtain a certificate of competence from the government in order to work in certain specified occupations. In combination with the decree of October 1807, which had opened all professions to both nobles and bourgeois, the Gewerbesteueredikt constituted a significant step toward the creation of a fully free labor market in Prussia. It also enhanced the administrative powers of the central state by shifting the authority to regulate economic activity away from the guilds and towns.[51]

While some of Stein's reforms—notably his attacks on the aristocracy's tax exemptions, as well as on their police and judicial powers—met with opposition from Prussia's social elites, these groups accommodated themselves to much of the new legislation, often finding ways to turn it to their own economic advantage. Many nobles, for example, used the edict emancipating the serfs as a means of absorbing peasant lands into their estates.[52] Hardenberg's legislation, which represented a more radical assault on the traditional social order, provoked a storm of outrage that forced the government to retreat from many of its bolder plans.[53] For example, Hardenberg's tax reforms remained incomplete, and the Gendarmerie Edict of 30 July 1812, which sought to diminish the administrative powers of the nobility by creating a bureaucratic rural government in the French style, was ultimately revoked because of the vehement protests of the Prussian aristocracy.

Hardenberg's fiscal reforms. The leveling tendencies of Hardenberg's social vision were likewise evident in his proposals for tax reform and debt service, which were designed to overcome the dire fiscal crisis that Hardenberg inherited when he took control of the Prussian ministry in 1810. Confronted by a catastrophic shortfall in tax revenues, Altenstein and Dohna, who had headed the Prussian ministry since Stein's dismissal in November 1808, advised defaulting on Prussia's war tribute payments and ceding the province of Silesia to France. Appalled by these ministers' lack of courage and imagination, King Frederick William III and Queen Luise decided to appoint Hardenberg in their place.

Though Hardenberg's most pressing concern was to return the Prussian state to solvency, a second goal—which has been overlooked by most historians—was equally central to his legislative agenda, namely, he hoped that his new economic system would foster social cohesion and help build a politically unified nation. Hardenberg believed that the establishment of a free market for goods and labor would not simply maximize economic efficiency but also help forge a vibrant public spirit.[54] His plans reflected the premises of the new discipline of *Nationalökonomie* (national economy), whose doctrines were inspired both by Kantian philosophy and by the economic doctrines of the physiocrats and Adam Smith. Kant had argued that the king should attempt to free his subjects from "tutelage," so that they might become autonomous and self-determining beings. The national economists argued that the extension of human freedom to the sphere of economic life, by liberating the populace from the arbitrary power of the paternalistic state, would make possible "the highest perfection of the physical condition of sociable mankind."[55] Hardenberg attempted to establish precisely such a new sociability in Prussia. Through the establishment of a free market economy, Hardenberg hoped "that the individual classes of the state society [*Staatsgesellschaft*] mutually approach, support, and elevate each other; that perfect justice occur in the exchange of their products."[56]

Two fiscal reforms proposed in Prussia during the Napoleonic era illustrate this connection between finance and "national spirit": first, various ministers' early proposals for the establishment of an income tax, and second, Hardenberg's plan to consolidate debts incurred by the Prussian provinces into a single account managed by a Prussian national bank. To the modern observer, each of these proposals appears to be only tangentially related to the project of forging a unified and politically active nation. For Hardenberg and his compatriots, however, these economic reforms had profound political implications.

The initial plans for an income tax in Prussia were put forward during the Stein ministry of 1807–1808 as a means of covering the war tribute installments to France. Though Stein was able to obtain approval for this tax by the East Prussian diet in February 1808, this legislation encountered intense resistance when the Prussian ministry attempted to extend it to other Prussian provinces. Aristocrats in Brandenburg and other parts of the realm objected to this tax not simply because it involved an added financial burden but also because the imposition of an income tax represented a fundamental break from traditional Prussian administrative practice. Prussian "absolutism," as noted above in Chapter 2, had followed a different model than the French version, intruding to a much lesser extent on the management of local affairs. Through the end of the eighteenth century, the administrative authority of the central government essentially ceased at the county level; in the countryside, the nobles remained responsible for local administration, for exercising police and juridical powers over the peasantry, and for apportioning and collecting taxes.[57] An income tax would upset this traditional arrangement by giving the central government the authority to impose fiscal levies directly on individuals.

Indeed, it was precisely because the income tax promised to impose uniformity of fiscal administration throughout Prussia that leading reformers found it so attractive. Under this system, taxes would be assessed equitably on all Prussian residents as a proportion of their income, not on the basis of special legal privilege. This allocation of taxes would thus help break down particular corporate identities and forge a sense of common interest throughout the populace. Altenstein and Dohna, who were otherwise not especially energetic as political reformers, were both strong supporters of an income tax. Because it would be levied on the entire population of the country according to a common principle, Altenstein declared, such a tax would discipline the "egotism" of the estates, helping to break down particular corporate identities and to forge a sense of common interest throughout the populace. Ultimately, Altenstein argued, the income tax would prepare the way for a "representation of the nation and a constitution."[58] Fiscal reform, in other words, was an indispensable tool for the moral education of the Prussian populace and for fostering a sense of national unity.

Like Stein and Altenstein, Hardenberg supported the adoption of an income tax in Prussia, but he abandoned his attempt to extend this tax beyond East Prussia as a result of strenuous aristocratic opposition during 1810. Two proposals that were more central to Hardenberg's initial fiscal program were plans for the reorganization of Prussia's public debt and for the establishment of a national bank to manage this account. Hardenberg's plan, judged "dilettantish" by several historians,[59] called for the consolidation of all state debts and war tribute obligations (which had originally been imposed upon the individual Prussian provinces) into a single account managed by a national bank. The bank, which would be funded in part by land tax revenues, would be responsible for paying these debts and also for issuing paper money. By August 1810, in the face of opposition from Stein and others,[60] Hardenberg backed off from his demand for a national bank. But he insisted on the consolidation of war debts into a single central account. Such a policy was necessary, Hardenberg declared, "because we want not to perpetuate *provincialism*, but rather to establish *nationalism*."[61] This was among the earliest occurrences of the word "nationalism" in Hardenberg's writings—or indeed, in the writings of any of the Prussian reformers. It is no accident that the word first appeared in conjunction with a financial issue: the link between finance and national spirit surfaced constantly in Hardenberg's letters and memoranda.

Hardenberg and his allies viewed the rationalization of Prussia's economy and fiscal administration as intimately intertwined with the broader project of national renewal. Hardenberg sought not just to consolidate state power but, as Reinhart Koselleck notes, to "establish a common national interest, in which the financial engagement and political participation of all property owners would grow together."[62] By eliminating the social barriers that pitted the estates against each other and by founding a new order based on rational, egalitarian principles, he hoped to create a more productive and harmonious national community. His vision of the ideal society owed much to the eighteenth-century philosophical and economic theories discussed in the previous chapter. Hardenberg moved beyond the agendas of Smith and Kant, however, in linking the principles of *Nationalökonomie* to the project of forging "national spirit." By establishing economic freedom and by abolishing the legal barriers between the estates, he hoped to encourage a sense of unity and purpose among the Prussian population. His goal, in other words, was not simply to rationalize but also to mobilize civil society.

The legislative measures described above illustrate the tension between egalitarian and hierarchical tendencies in the reform measures promulgated in Prussia during the Napoleonic era. Though the reformers wanted to preserve Prussia's three traditional estates (nobles, burghers, and peasants) as formal categories, their legislation radically redefined the legal status and function of each estate, transforming hereditary legal statuses into predominantly functional distinctions: estate owner, urban worker, agricultural worker. The reformers hoped to establish a sufficient degree of legal equality to forge a unified civil society or, in Hardenberg's terminology, *Staatsgesellschaft* ("society of the state"). For Hardenberg and the other leading reformers, economic and fiscal reform was a critical prerequisite for national mobilization. A cohesive society, they believed, would inevitably become a patriotic one. Yet these figures disagreed over one fundamental problem: whether social cohesion would best be attained through the establishment of full civil equality or through the judicious preservation of certain traditional legal hierarchies.

A "Prussian" or a "German" Nation?
The Uses of Ambiguity

For all of the Prussian reformers' enthusiasm about the prospects for a national awakening, they studiously avoided one political question of critical importance: was the nation Prussia or Germany? The bureaucratic memoranda of the Napoleonic era were littered with the words national spirit, national interest, national consciousness, and so forth. But these memoranda rarely referred to the nation either as German or as Prussian. They identified the nation as possessing a unified political interest and will, but they steered clear of discussing the cultural, linguistic, or ethnic roots of national community.

The idea of the *Kulturnation* was certainly not unfamiliar to the Prussian reformers. Herder had insisted on the cultural foundations of national identity in the 1770s.[63] Likewise, Fichte's famous lectures of 1807–1808, the *Addresses to the German Nation*, advocated a program of national education that would forge a common culture and spirit of patriotism among all Germans. In 1808, Wilhelm von Humboldt, who would become the chief of the Section for Education and Religion in the Prussian Ministry of the Interior the following year, declared:

> I love Germany with my deepest soul, and there is mixed in my love even a materialism which often makes feelings less pure and noble but therefore only the more powerful. The misfortune of the age binds me still closer to it, and since I am firmly convinced that precisely this misfortune should be the motive for individuals to strive more courageously, to feel himself more for all, so I should like to see whether the same feeling rules others and to contribute to spreading it.[64]

For the most part, however, Prussia's leading ministers preferred to remain silent over whether the nation they had in mind was Prussia or Germany. There were good reasons behind this choice. As these officials were acutely aware, the Prussian state was an artificial construct, a patchwork quilt of territories whose inhabitants possessed little sense of common identity or common purpose. By appealing to "German" patriotism, they could tap into a more organic—and therefore potentially more compelling—identity. Such diffuse appeals might also serve to mobilize residents of other German states, as well as those of Prussia. To speak explicitly about mobilizing the German nation, however, was a highly problematic strategy for Prussian government officials during the Napoleonic era, for two reasons. First, they would thereby exclude Prussia's Polish and Lithuanian territories, fostering internal division in Prussia rather than unity of purpose. Second, such rhetoric might be viewed as a potential threat to the independence of other German states. Prussian leaders wanted to direct their energies toward fighting France not the rest of Germany.

This dilemma encouraged the articulation of implicit, rather than explicit, connections between Prussia and a greater German identity. On 17 March 1813, for example, King Frederick William III issued from Breslau a proclamation entitled "To My People." This decree, intended as a general call to arms against France, was addressed to the residents of the various Prussian provinces:

> Brandenburgers, Prussians, Silesians, Pomeranians, Lithuanians! You know what you have suffered for the past seven years; you know what your miserable fate will be, if we do not end the struggle that is now beginning with honor. Remember the time of antiquity, the great *Kurfürsten*, the great Frederick.

In the same decree, however, Frederick William embedded this Prussian identity within a broader German one, referring to the high sacrifices that would be demanded "if we don't want to stop being *Prussian* and *German*." This parallel between Prussian and German identity is drawn three times in the one-page proclamation.[65]

Another way to split the difference between Prussian and German patriotism was to use the word "fatherland" (*Vaterland*) alongside the word "nation." A royal decree of 1813 required all Prussian men to wear the black-and-white ribbon called the "national cockade" on their hats. The reasoning behind this measure was "that the inspirational general expression of true love of the fatherland [*Vaterlandsliebe*] demands an outward sign on the part of all citizens [*Staatsbürger*]."[66] The fatherland referred to here transcended the Prussian state but was not explicitly German. Likewise, within a week of Frederick William III's exhortation to his subjects in March 1813, Princess Marianne of Prussia called on the women of the realm to make donations of all kinds for the "rescue of the fatherland." Many women exchanged pieces of gold jewelry for replacements made of iron, which were inscribed with the motto "I gave gold for iron." In 1814, the royal ironworks in Berlin produced more than 40,000 pieces of iron jewelry as part of this campaign.[67] Strikingly,

Princess Marianne's proclamation points to the gendered character of this era's conception of national community. Women, though excluded from active citizenship, were called upon to lend their support for the patriotic effort. But women occupied a separate political sphere: it was apparently deemed appropriate that a princess confine her patriotic appeals to other women rather than addressing the populace at large. During the War of Liberation of 1813–1814, thousands of Prussian women joined patriotic associations with names such as the *Vaterländische Frauenverein*. These associations, however, confined themselves largely to tasks such as supporting the war effort and providing care for the poor and sick. Their members made few direct appeals to participate in political decision making. Thus, the question of female citizenship represented another fundamental silence in Prussian discourses about the nation.[68]

This absence of rhetoric about the cultural foundations of national community was mirrored in the reformers' political program. Apart from a few early memoranda alluding to the "Polish question," as well as the Jewish emancipation decree of 1812,[69] Prussia's leading civil servants of the Napoleonic era largely ignored the challenges of establishing ethnic and cultural solidarity within the nation. For example, these early reformers, unlike later generations of nationalists, did not emphasize the importance of establishing German as the sole language to be employed in government and in the schools. They rarely addressed the question of whether ethnic Poles could be citizens of the nation; likewise, they paid little heed to the problem of whether Catholics could be full members of the national community. (After 1815, with the integration of the predominantly Catholic territories of the Rhineland into Prussia, the status of the country's Catholic minority took on more immediate importance.) Not only did the bureaucratic reformers deemphasize the cultural foundations of national community, they also generally avoided specifying the territorial dimensions of the nation. Thus, for example, they rarely insisted that the nation's territories be contiguous, a standard demand of later nationalists both in Germany and elsewhere. Only at the conclusion of the War of Liberation did the leading reformers openly discuss the territorial extent of the nation: at that point, Stein, Hardenberg, and Humboldt all called for the creation of a closely bound German confederation under joint Austrian-Prussian leadership.[70] Thus, a strong correlation existed between the reformers' use of political concepts and their practical political priorities. Before 1815, the bureaucratic nationalists' main objective was to recover the autonomy of the Prussian state, not to establish internal cultural uniformity or to absorb other regions of German-speaking Europe.

Conclusion: Key Features of Bureaucratic Nationalism

This chapter has demonstrated how the interplay of cultural traditions and material interests shaped the concept "nation" in Prussian bureaucratic discourse during the Napoleonic era. My phrase "bureaucratic nationalism" must be understood as denoting an ideal type. In practice, a wide range of political views existed within the Prussian civil service. Nonetheless, this term is useful in calling attention to certain widespread discursive tendencies. The reformers' immediate strategic concern was to stabilize the Prussian state—and to secure their own political authority—by addressing the urgent fiscal crisis and legitimation crisis resulting from the catastrophic defeat of 1806–1807. In formulating their response to these challenges, Stein and Hardenberg drew on the logic articulated by earlier figures, such as Frederick the Great in Prussia and Turgot in France. The rationalization of the state and civil society, they argued, would enhance the productivity of the populace, as well as help forge a harmonious relationship between the monarch and his subjects.

While Stein and Hardenberg's social vision represented the logical conclusion of the enlightened absolutist tradition, their political reforms broke decisively from the eighteenth-century Prussian model. Unlike Frederick the Great, who had sought to monopolize political authority by eliminating the power of Prussia's traditional representative institutions, the Prussian reformers came to believe that their state could be saved only through the political mobilization of the nation. They hoped to achieve this task both through the establishment of parliamentary institutions and through the rationalization of civil society. In calling for the eradication of "strife between estates," Stein hoped to abolish the disparity of interests that encouraged the various elements of the Prussian population to focus on their private, corporate interests, rather than on the common good. When Hardenberg convened an Assembly of Notables in Berlin in February 1811, he asked the delegates to reject "prejudices and egotism" and to "subordinate the particular interest to that of the whole," by helping the government execute his economic reform decrees. The adoption of these principles, Hardenberg proclaimed, together with "cultivation" and "true religiosity," would lead to the formation of "*one* national spirit, *one* interest, and *one* sense [*Sinn*], on which our well-being and our security can be firmly grounded."[71] These premises of Prussian bureaucratic nationalism are schematized in table 3.1.

This table is intended as a rough heuristic device, which serves to highlight the fractured and ambivalent nature of the concept "nation." Prussia's leading civil servants shared several common premises about the nation, identified in the table as "consensual features." These di-

3.1 The Concept "Nation" in Prussian Bureaucratic Discourse, 1807–1815

Consensual features	Contested features
The nation is a harmonious community possessing one unified interest and will.	Can Jews be citizens?
The nation must possess a rational social order.	Must the old corporate bodies (e.g., the aristocracy) be abolished?
The nation must be politically educated.	Must all citizens be equal before the law?
The nation's interest is identical to the king's interest.	

mensions of the concept "nation" were *overdetermined*, in that they re-flected a variety of mutually reinforcing political and cultural influences, each one of which was an independent source of the same idea. The overdetermined character of the ideal of national unity and harmony meant that it was expressed with great intensity and frequency in Prussian bureaucratic discourse. Because this ideal had its origins in so many disparate cultural traditions and because it answered the political challenges of the age, it came to be a deeply rooted element of what Foucault terms the historical a priori. While a few scattered authors suggested a more pluralistic vision of the national community, such a vision was a distinctly minor presence in political debate.[72] The emphasis on the importance of political unanimity within the nation was certainly not unique to Prussia. Numerous historians have pointed to the centrality of this ideal in the French Revolution,[73] as well as in nationalist movements throughout the modern world. Yet, this ideological tendency may have become especially pronounced in Napoleonic Prussia because of the confluence of factors pointing in this direction.

While Prussian civil servants strongly emphasized the desirability of social rationalization, popular education, and domestic political harmony, other dimensions of the national community remained less well defined in their writings. For example, they expressed conflicting views over the proper degree of social equality within the nation: should the old corporate bodies be abolished altogether or simply redefined according to new principles? On the question of Jewish citizenship, they sought a compromise solution.[74]

Just as important as the disagreements among the bureaucratic nationalists were the ambiguities and shared silences. During the Napoleonic period, Prussia's reform-minded civil servants avoided addressing two political questions of monumental import: first, whether the nation was Prussia or Germany; and second, how sovereign authority should be distributed between the monarch and the nation. They sought to link Prussia to Germany without explicitly supporting German national unification. This conceptual ambivalence was reflected in their political program: just as the reformers refused to identify the nation as Germany, they also devoted little effort to asserting the linguistic, religious, and territorial unity of the national community. Stein and Hardenberg's initial plans for constitutional reform were similarly sketchy: they called for the nation's participation in politics without advocating any specific legislative role for the new representative assemblies.

The next three chapters explore the evolution of the concept "nation" in Prussia during the fifteen years between 1806 and 1820. These chapters show that the fundamental silences within bureaucratic nationalist discourse proved impossible to sustain. Chapter 4 examines how Prussian aristocrats appropriated the new nationalist rhetoric in order to defend their traditional privileges. Chapter 5 analyzes the rhetoric of bourgeois political activists who demanded German national unification. These individuals forced Prussian officials to abandon their efforts to equivocate over whether the true nation was Prussia or Germany. Chapter 6 focuses on a series of political controversies that highlighted the problem of sovereignty. The heated conflicts between Prussian state officials and self-proclaimed representatives of the "nation" began to call into question the most basic claim of the reform movement: namely, that the will of the king and his people were one and indivisible.

II

THE CONCEPT IN PLAY

Four

A NATION OF ARISTOCRATS

When King Frederick William III dismissed Freiherr Karl vom Stein from office in November 1808, he approved his first minister's final wish for a decree reorganizing the Prussian administration. Stein hoped that the edict, which concentrated supreme administrative authority in a new Council of State (*Staatsrat*) and called for a national representative assembly, would carry forward the reform movement by instilling in the government the "greatest possible unity, force, and responsiveness . . . and laying claim to the energies of the entire nation and of the individual in the most practical and simple way."[1] This decree, issued on 24 November 1808 but never implemented, linked all the elements of Stein's great reform memoranda of the previous two years. By establishing popular "participation in the administration," it sought to mold the nation and forge a common spirit, thus fortifying and unifying the state. Through this plan Stein believed that "the cultivation of the nation will be furthered, common spirit awakened, and the entire conduct of business become simpler, more forceful, and less costly."[2]

Yet how different were Stein's words less than two years later! In June 1810, Hardenberg took office as Prussian state chancellor, unifying the departments of finance and interior, which had been divided between Stein's immediate successors Altenstein and Dohna. In August and September of that year, Stein (living in exile in Prague to avoid an arrest order of Napoleon's) wrote two memoranda concerning Hardenberg's plans for financial reform. Incensed by the Brandenburg nobility's recalcitrance toward the adoption of an income tax, Stein counseled Hardenberg to pursue his reform plan whatever the resistance:

In Prussia one should pay little attention to opinion. Deep-rooted egotism, incomplete cultivation [*halbe Bildung*], and licentiousness dominate here, coupled with the northern callousness and crudeness. This barbarous public opinion must be corrected through rigorous means, not confirmed in its confusion through indulgence and deference.[3]

Stein's anger intensified six weeks later, after he learned that the noble opposition had led Hardenberg to suspend the new income tax in Brandenburg's Kurmark:

Insubordination, indifference to the good of the whole, insolence in speech and writing, and gross egotism have taken hold of all of the estates, especially the civil servants and the nobles. Discipline and obedience can be reestablished only through rigorous measures.[4]

Only by resorting to the "maxims applied by Richelieu," Stein declared, could Hardenberg control a "disobedient, degenerate, scheming nation." Among the measures Stein considered necessary were surveillance of leading figures among the nobility and bureaucracy, "sudden dismissals from service, arrests, exile to small towns where the prisoner will be isolated and live under control."[5]

In the same letter, however, Stein argued that the maxims of Richelieu must be supplemented by the enlightened methods of the Swiss educational reformer, Pestalozzi. Children must be schooled in a way that would foster their "spontaneity of spirit . . . and nobler human feelings," countering the tendency to lead a "hedonistic, self-seeking life." Writers must be subjected to a governmental "leadership of literature," which would "keep public opinion pure and strong." Finally, the country must be granted a "national representation," which would contribute to the formation of a "public and common spirit."[6]

Stein was not alone in praising the principle of political representation but excoriating its practice. His collaborators Ludwig von Vincke and Johann August Sack, both strong proponents of a constitution, also railed against the selfishness of the Kurmark estates in 1810. The nobility of the Kurmark, Sack complained, wanted to "immortalize all differences between provinces and castes"; it was willing to "move heaven and earth in order to preserve itself in its ancient egotism."[7] Another illuminating example is that of Theodor Gottlieb von Hippel, director of the West Prussian *Landschaft* and another of Stein's advisers. Hippel argued in a constitutional proposal of 1808 that it was unnecessary to resolve whether the king had the right to veto legislation, because "in a state such as ours, where the regent and the people have good intentions toward each other," the need for a veto would never arise. In September

1811, he heralded the convocation of a "provisional national representation" as a measure "which will tighten the bond of mutual trust between king and people."[8] By December 1812, however, after the new
assembly had spent eight months in session, he demanded "still narrower
limits" on its already tightly circumscribed jurisdiction because of "the
experience that the representatives are not what they are supposed to
be, and the concern that they will go even further in their oppositional
spirit against the government, which they manifest at every opportunity."[9]

Between 1808 and 1815, Prussia's rulers created a series of experimental representative institutions, all of which were intended to harness
the energies of the nation and to forge a public spirit. As the complaints
by Stein and his associates attest, however, the ideals of national representation and participation in the administration proved far more problematic in practice than anticipated by the bold memoranda of 1807–
1808. Rather than supporting the government's reform initiatives, the
new representative assemblies aroused, in Altenstein's expression, a "hy-
dra" of entrenched, inflexible interests.[10] Yet the ideal of participatory
politics continued to exercise a powerful grip over the imaginations of
Prussian leaders despite the difficulties in its implementation.

Prussia's rulers sought to use the ideas of nationhood and popular
representation in the service of the monarchy. Yet, once introduced into
Prussian political discourse, the concept "nation" proved capable of being manipulated by other groups with widely varying agendas. Opponents of social reform, including aristocrats and members of the urban
elites, used the idea of the nation in a rallying cry for the defense of the
traditional social order. The aristocratic nationalism of this era was
marked by a peculiar tension: Prussian nobles sought to defend their
private corporate interests by employing universalistic rhetoric that emphasized the national interest.

Although, to a great extent, this aristocratic rhetorical strategy proved
successful, it was not without cost. In the aftermath of the Napoleonic
era, Prussian nobles found it difficult to reassert their traditional claims
that a special contractual relationship existed between the nobility and
the crown.[11] Moreover, by insisting on the political rights of the nation,
aristocratic activists made it more difficult to banish this concept from
Prussian political debate during the era of the Restoration after 1815.
Although the reform optimism of the Napoleonic period was followed
by decades of deep suspicion toward a politically active *Volk*, the experiments in national politics during the reform period irrevocably transformed the conceptual framework of Prussian political debate.

Learning to Speak Nationally

At the beginning of the nineteenth century, the Prussian aristocracy confronted serious challenges to its social identity and prestige. Traditionally, the aristocracy had been defined as a warrior class, and in the late eighteenth century, nobles had held a near monopoly over positions in the Prussian officer corps. The military disasters of 1806–1807 humiliated the leadership of the Prussian army, inspiring Scharnhorst and Gneisenau's plans for a citizen militia in which members of the bourgeoisie would be free to serve as officers. In the countryside, fundamental social and legal dislocations were undermining the nobility's traditional role as well. Beginning in the last quarter of the eighteenth century, a wave of land speculation swept Prussia, resulting in numerous sales of noble properties, especially in the eastern provinces. The increasing fluidity of estate ownership made it more difficult to sustain the plausibility of one of the guiding principles of the old social order, namely, that the noble was like the father of his serfs and that this role gave him both absolute authority to rule his estate and the responsibility to care for those in his charge.[12] Legal reforms enacted during the Stein ministry, such as the abolition of serfdom, added to the challenge of reasserting the nobility's traditional paternalistic role. Hardenberg's plans went even further, attacking the very principle of a social order based on estates. Proclaiming the precept of equality before the law, he systematically attacked the web of legal distinctions that defined the Prussian estates, such as the monopoly rights of the guilds, the nobility's tax exemptions and rural administrative powers, and the peasantry's compulsory labor obligations.

All of these factors contributed to a deep legitimation crisis for the Prussian nobility and other traditional social elites. Forced to justify the legal privileges that were under assault by the reformers, members of these groups experimented with various rhetorical strategies. Some of them launched impassioned defenses of the preexisting "contracts" between the king and the estates, declaring that the government's legal innovations violated the traditional constitution of the realm. Others adopted a more novel strategy, invoking the new concept of national representation as a means of defending their old prerogatives. Like the bureaucratic reformers, they identified the nation as an ideally harmonious and unitary political community, but they appropriated the reformers' political symbols and rhetoric for their own purposes.

During the Napoleonic era, the Prussian government established a series of representative assemblies, initially for the purpose of raising funds to pay the country's war tribute to France. Between 1808 and 1810,

during Stein's ministry and the eighteen-month interim ministry of Altenstein and Dohna, the government convened assemblies in three of the
four rump Prussian provinces—East Prussia, Pomerania, and Brandenburg—and attempted unsuccessfully to establish a provincial diet in Silesia. Altenstein and Dohna also experimented, with little success, with
Stein's plan to select representatives to serve directly in the provincial
administrative departments.[13] In 1811, Hardenberg called together an Assembly of Notables, whose members were appointed by the king. In
1812–1813, an elective Provisional National Representation (*interimistische Nationalrepräsentation*) met in Berlin, and it reconvened under a
different name in 1814–1815.

The story of how Prussian aristocrats manipulated these new experimental parliamentary bodies has been ably told in previous historical
works. Reinhart Koselleck, for example, has demonstrated how nobles
used their dominant position in these assemblies to block many of Hardenberg's fiscal and administrative reforms.[14] Likewise, Herbert Obenaus
has spoken of the emergence of "two reform movements" that were at
cross purposes with each other: "a *ständisch* one and a state one."[15]
Whereas the bureaucratic reformers viewed representative institutions as
a means of overcoming corporate allegiances, aristocrats saw these assemblies as vehicles for reasserting their particularistic interests against the
state's totalizing claims. What has been less thoroughly analyzed by historians, however, is how this aristocratic activism shaped the evolution
of the concept "nation" and how Prussian nobles' use of this concept
affected their own self-understanding as a political interest group.

The aristocratic nationalism discussed in this chapter, like the bureaucratic nationalism analyzed in chapter 3, is an ideal type. In practice,
Prussian aristocrats expressed widely varying political views, reflecting
both geographic and social differences. For example, nobles from Brandenburg, one of the original provinces of the monarchy, defended the
traditional provincial constitution far more zealously than those from
Silesia, where Frederick the Great had dismantled the old provincial governing bodies after annexing this territory in 1740. In East Prussia, a
history of close trading relationships with England and Holland exposed
the social elites to Western economic ideas, stimulating the emergence of
what some scholars have termed "aristocratic liberalism." Likewise, in
the Rhenish territories annexed by Prussia in 1815, nobles' political
views were influenced by their close contact with France during the
revolutionary and Napoleonic eras, as well as by the Rhineland's relatively strong tradition of regional self-rule. (This chapter, which focuses
on political debates within the rump Prussian states of 1807–1815, ex-
cludes the Rhineland from consideration.)[16] Differences in social and legal

status also affected aristocrats' attitudes toward state authority and constitutional reform. For example, members of the former imperial (*reichsunmittelbare*) nobility, who had previously owed allegiance to the Holy Roman emperor alone, often took a more fiercely oppositional stance toward the Prussian state than did the less elevated members of the "knights" (*Ritterschaft*) of Prussia's core provinces, who had traditionally played prominent roles in the military and state administration.[17] Despite the wide variations in the political views of Prussian aristocrats, it is possible to identify certain broad lines of consensus and conflict within their discourse, an essential step in tracing the evolution of the concept "nation" and the impact of this concept on Prussian political culture.

The German word *Repräsentation* possesses a double sense: it can mean either *Vertretung* (advocacy) or *Darstellung* (portrayal). Traditionally, representative institutions in Prussia had performed the first role: the estates had been viewed not as public but as private corporations, which were charged with upholding the preexisting fabric of privileges that defined the social order. The members of these corporations chose delegates who would most effectively advocate their own interests to the government.[18] The Prussian reformers, on the other hand, sought delegates who were representative of the population, who would portray the condition of the realm. Such a portrayal would help identify problems that required government action and also aid in identifying the most rational solution.

The reformers' innovative theory of representation reflected the political theories of Enlightenment philosophers such as Rousseau, Kant, and Svarez, all of whom held that the purpose of politics was to identify and act on the "common interest" of the people. In *The Social Contract*, Rousseau distinguished the common interest from "private interests." To determine the true "general will," he argued, it is essential to prevent participants in politics from expressing the interests of particular factions or "partial associations."[19] Similarly, Kant maintained that the original civil constitution of society arose "from the general, united will of the people." Under despotic rule, Kant argued, the sovereign sought to enforce "his own private will," whereas the republican legislator made "his laws as if they *could* have arisen out of the united will of an entire people."[20] The Prussian reformers concurred with these views: in the new era, they declared, all citizens must look past their private interests, devoting themselves solely to the common good.

Broadly speaking, Prussian aristocrats and members of other traditional elites had two rhetorical options in seeking to defend their privileges against encroachment by the Prussian ministry, first, to appeal to tradition, reasserting the inviolability of their private rights, or second, to invoke the new political theories of their opponents, arguing that the preservation of these rights, was essential to the national interest. During the Napoleonic era, the protests of Prussia's social elites reflected both of these rhetorical strategies. After 1807, the estates' demands for representation intensified, partly because their social position had been threatened by the massive physical and economic damage from the French invasion. In 1810, when Hardenberg further undermined their status with radical social and economic reforms, these pleas ascended to a fever pitch.

In December 1810, responding to the wave of protests unleashed by the Finance Edict and the *Gewerbesteueredikt*, Hardenberg announced that an Assembly of Notables would convene in Berlin the following February. This assembly was to consist of sixty-four delegates to be appointed by the king, thirty of them noble estate owners. Hardenberg hoped that this assembly would assist the government in implementing his economic reforms. His announcement, however, provoked numerous petitions from nobles and members of other estates that demanded modifications to the reform legislation and the expansion of representative institutions.[21] These petitions surrounding the formation of the Assembly of Notables revealed a distinctive blend of traditional and innovative rhetorical strategies.

Some Prussian aristocrats, above all those from the province of Brandenburg, sought to legitimate their cause by appealing to Prussia's constitutional traditions—even as they reinterpreted those traditions to suit their own purposes. In January 1811, for example, thirteen prominent nobles representing the estates of Brandenburg's Kurmark petitioned the king concerning Hardenberg's economic decrees. They insisted that the "proper and constitutional path" for any financial or tax reforms was through "consultation, negotiation, and contract with the estates, assembled in a diet." To bolster their claims, the nobles cited passages from several royal proclamations of the seventeenth and eighteenth centuries, which confirmed the political rights and social privileges of the estates. The king, they maintained, was contractually bound to these traditional agreements:

> This *ständische* constitution, founded on inviolably preserved contracts, was the most precious bond between the sovereign and the nation; it gave rise to the nation's unshakable devotion, which in earlier times sustained our state in the most dangerous crises.

Only by continuing to observe these established contracts would it be possible to "secure the state credit, guarantee the durability and effectiveness of the new laws, and prevent the dangerous fluctuation of legal provisions, which has so often brought about the overthrow of all state constitutions."[22]

By equating the constitution with the traditional "contracts" between the king and the estates, the Brandenburg nobility did more than simply reassert its customary social privileges. Rather, it represented itself as an equal partner in the governance of the realm. Strikingly, none of the traditional documents cited by the petition justified such a bold formulation of the estates' legislative role. In the Recess of the Diet of 1653, for example, the king had pledged that when important interests of the country were at stake, he would "neither conclude nor undertake anything without the foreknowledge and counsel of our loyal estates." He had not granted the estates a deciding vote, however, on any issue except the formation of military alliances.[23] Thus the petition did not just rearticulate, but it significantly extended traditional assertions concerning the political role of the estates.

Not only did this petition insist on political parity between the monarchy and the estates, it also refused to elevate the authority of the nation above that of the individual provinces. In order to safeguard traditional rights, the petitioners requested that "if the formation of a national representation should entail changes in our provincial constitution and *ständischen* rights, these changes should ensue only by way of the contract with the estates of the Kurmark."[24] The nobles of the Kurmark displayed a cautious attitude toward the idea of national representation: they seemed to regard it as a possible political benefit, but they were unwilling to grant it any power superior to that of provincial institutions.

The government responded to the petitioners' display of constitutional erudition with deeds rather than words. One of Hardenberg's reforms of October 1810 had eliminated the estates' control over the provincial poor relief funds (*Landarmenkassen*). Friedrich August Ludwig von der Marwitz, a tempestuous champion of traditional social privileges, who administered the fund for the Kurmark estates, defied the chancellor's order to surrender its receipts to the government. Hence, on 13 February 1811, when Marwitz was away, government agents forced the safe in which this money was kept and removed the 25,000 talers it contained. The estates of the Kurmark immediately protested this act of force, but the government responded coldly. Several weeks later, a second episode occurred that added to Marwitz's outrage. Again during his absence, a government official appeared on his estate and ordered the village mayor to begin collecting taxes there, in accordance with the tax laws of October 1810. Insulted by these two challenges to traditional noble prerogatives, Marwitz composed a lengthy plea to the king denouncing the arbitrariness of Hardenberg's measures.[25]

This remonstrance, which was signed by twenty-two nobles from the Kurmark counties Lebus, Beeskow, and Storkow and sent to the king on 10 June 1811, rejected the most basic premises of the reform movement.[26] Marwitz returned to a more traditional political metaphor: the Prussian state, he argued, had formerly been "like a great family, in which the father enjoyed the utmost trust of all family members, and in which everyone strove to establish the prosperity of the house." Hardenberg's methods, however, threatened to turn Prussia into "an Indian plantation, where the slaves are forced to work."[27] The metaphor portraying the king as the father of the realm was a venerable one in Prussian politics. In Marwitz's petition, it served two purposes, first, to emphasize the king's obligations to his subjects, and second, to legitimate other patriarchal hierarchies, such as the one between nobles and their peasants.[28] Marwitz attacked the government's abrogation of "the most sacred contracts" with the estates, and he scorned its promise to establish a national representation because

> the issue is not having a representation under any circumstances, but rather having *a lawful one.*
>
> A representation which is *given* is none at all, because just as it is given, so can it be *taken away* again, and no one will believe himself to be represented through it.

The petition warned that "calamity and ruin" would result from the "introduction of the alien principles of arbitrariness and force" in Prussia. Hardenberg's legislation would contribute toward the "leveling of all estates." Marwitz reserved particular vitriol for Jews, who under the new laws were permitted to purchase estates. Depicting them as "the necessary enemies of every existing state," he claimed that they would soon buy up all the land. As estate owners, Jews would then become "the principal representatives of the state, and so our venerable old Brandenburg-Prussia will become a newfangled Jew state."[29]

It is not surprising that Hardenberg took offense at this petition, though it is hard to say which upset him more: its inflammatory tone or its pessimistic observations about the chancellor's proposals for popular representation. In a report to the king of 23 June, Hardenberg observed that if the petition's constitutional claims were accepted, "then practically everything that has been done by the glorious rulers of Prussia since the Great Elector would be invalid."[30] Calling the petition a grave affront to royal authority, he recommended jailing Marwitz, along with

Friedrich Ludwig Karl Finck von Finckenstein, whose name appeared at the top of the list of signatures on the document. The following day, the king accepted Hardenberg's recommendation, and the two nobles spent the next five weeks under guard in the fortress of Spandau. Perhaps more striking than Hardenberg's response was that of the other Kurmark nobles, who made only halfhearted attempts to secure the release of Marwitz and Finckenstein from prison. In the view of many Brandenburg aristocrats, Marwitz's position was too extreme for the current age: most nobles no longer supported the indiscriminate defense of all traditional privileges.[31]

Such skirmishes with royal authority occurred elsewhere in the Prussian provinces as well. In East Prussia, for example, the estates of Tapiau County complained that Hardenberg's legislation violated the "constitution" of the state. "[W]ith the stroke of a pen," they declared, "the welfare of thousands of families is destroyed," and if the Finance Edict were implemented, "nine out of ten of the present estate owners will become beggars." The assembly of Sehesten County, also in East Prussia, resolved to suspend collecting any taxes under the new law until the king justified the need for these extraordinary demands. Hardenberg, acting in keeping with Stein's advice to apply the "maxims of Richelieu," retaliated by jailing two leaders of this disobedient group of nobles for more than a month.[32]

Alongside such appeals to the authority of Prussia's constitutional tradition, which earned harsh rebukes from the government, some aristocrats began to develop an innovative rhetorical strategy that embraced the principle of national representation. This strategy was evident in petitions composed by the Committee of East Prussian and Lithuanian Estates, which spearheaded a massive wave of East Prussian protests against Hardenberg's reforms in 1811. This committee, established in 1808, consisted initially of four nobles and one non-noble landowner; later it was expanded to include representatives of the towns as well. On 9 January 1811, the committee wrote to the king declaring its disappointment with the proclamations of the autumn of 1810:

> The new legislation, from which we expected deliverance and salvation, has increased our misfortune and brought us more quickly to ruin. The first pillar of the state, the sanctity of law [*Recht*], is demolished; as rights [*Rechte*] whose maintenance was sworn by our kings, whose protection was promised by our laws, have been annihilated with the stroke of a pen.[33]

Like the nobles of Brandenburg's Kurmark, the East Prussians associated the welfare of the state with the preservation of traditional rights. By abolishing these rights, they implied, the state risked its own destruction.

In the view of the East Prussians, however, the best defense of these old rights lay in the formation of new representative institutions:

> [U]rgent is the wish that Your Royal Majesty may deign to convoke a General Diet, granting admission to deputies from all estates and provinces, who will be trustingly elected by the nation itself. Through the union of a regent, acting as the father of the land, and a faithful nation, much good could happen and the unfortunate state could perhaps be helped.[34]

Here the East Prussians parted company from the Kurmark nobles by arguing that the status of the national representation should exceed that of any individual province or estate. The deputies of the Kurmark insisted that no national representation be created except with their own approval, thus arrogating to the provincial nobility a political authority equal to that of the nation. The East Prussian petition, in contrast, demanded that deputies "from all estates and provinces" be elected to serve in a general diet. Not only did the authors include all of the estates in the nation, but they also implied that the nation was a higher political entity than any of its geographical or social components. In effect, the East Prussians aimed to forestall the potential criticism that they were egotistically defending the rights of the provincial nobility by appealing to the common good of the nation. Their petition established a model for aristocratic protest rhetoric that would be refined in subsequent years.

The nobility was not alone in demanding recognition of its political rights; the other estates joined the fray as well. Representatives of the municipalities, like the nobles, sought the restoration of the traditional legal order. During the winter of 1810–1811, the cities (primarily those of Silesia and East Prussia) protested vehemently against the *Gewerbesteueredikt* of November 1810, which abolished the monopoly rights of the guilds and made the payment of an annual "tax on occupations" the sole condition for the practice of most trades. In the Silesian city of Glogau, the shoemakers, bakers, and butchers refused to obey the new regulations. In Breslau, the elders of various guilds staged a boisterous protest against the edict in front of the city hall, with the support of the local merchants' association. The city councils of both Breslau and Königsberg petitioned the king for the repeal of this law. In the words of the Breslau council, the abolition of the guilds' rights (*Gerechtigkeiten*) had led to "desperation" and "disruption in our community." The king himself, they observed, had confirmed these rights upon his accession

to the throne in 1797; and in "the eyes of the public," they were so
inviolable "that the maxim became generally established among our citizens: The house can burn down and be destroyed, but never the *Gerechtigkeit*." If the government insisted on abolishing these rights, it
would have to pay "full compensation" to the guilds: "Only in this way
is it possible to avert the ruin of our community." Likewise, in the Assembly of Notables in Berlin, the deputy from Königsberg declared that
the *Gewerbesteueredikt* would lead to the "complete downfall of the cities" and that members of the guilds must be compensated for any loss
of rights.[35]

But the government displayed less indulgence toward the cities' protests than toward those of the nobility (the imprisonment of Marwitz
and Finckenstein notwithstanding). The ministry rejected the guilds' demands for compensation; it instructed district authorities to take a firm
hand against craftsmen who refused to pay the occupation tax; and it
even banned an association that had been formed to lobby against the
new trade legislation.[36] Though Hardenberg backpedaled from his initial
plans to abolish aristocratic privileges, he remained steadfast in his insistence on urban economic reform.

Historians have identified several reasons why Hardenberg was more
responsive to aristocratic protests than to the complaints of the municipalities. For example, he was convinced of the efficiency of large-estate
agriculture, while he considered guild craft production outmoded. Moreover, unlike the leaders of the guilds, Prussian nobles had close personal
ties at court, and they exercised influence as guarantors of the state
debt.[37] The analysis here, however, suggests a further reason for this
striking phenomenon: the municipal representatives may have failed to
persuade Hardenberg of the justice of their cause in part because they
failed to invoke the new principle of the national interest. Their una-
pologetic defense of traditional corporate privileges exposed them to the
fatal accusation of egotism.

Hardenberg initially envisioned the purpose of national representation
in highly restrictive terms. Indeed, he declared that the main goal of
convening the Assembly of Notables in 1811 was "to explain the internal
coherence of the measures taken,"[38] rather than to deliberate over how
his reform legislation might be improved. As one historian has observed,
Hardenberg initially believed that the representatives should serve "less
as spokesmen toward above than as a mouthpiece toward below."[39] Nonetheless, he proved responsive to complaints, particularly when they were
framed in public-spirited rather than in egotistical terms. The next section explores how representatives of the Prussian estates came to master

the new idiom of nationalist political rhetoric during the early years of Hardenberg's ministry.

The Politics of Privilege, 1811–1815

In an edict of 7 September 1811, Frederick William III announced his intention to create a "general commission for the regulation of provincial and communal war debts," whose members would "also, for the time being, constitute the national representation."[40] Through the wording of this edict, the king and his ministers displayed once again their ambivalence toward popular political participation. While declaring their allegiance to the principle of national representation, they were careful to limit its purview to the narrow context of supervising government debt. Government leaders sought always to contain the activity of these assemblies within predetermined boundaries: to involve the people in politics without undermining monarchical authority. Yet the new assemblies chafed at these restrictions. Created for the purpose of representing the nation, they considered themselves entitled to deliberate freely concerning all political matters of national import.

In the Provisional National Representation (*interimistische National-repräsentation*), which gathered in Berlin in April 1812, the incompatibility of these two visions of political participation became painfully apparent. The earlier representative institutions of the reform period had been either provincial ones or, in the case of the Assembly of Notables, composed of delegates appointed by the crown to carry out a clearly restricted mandate. The new assembly (though containing only forty-two members) was an elected one and a national representation in name. Its members hoped to play a vital role in Prussian politics, and when their hopes were disappointed, they expressed anger and bitterness at Hardenberg's regime.

The Provisional National Representation remained in session for ten months, from April 1812 until February 1813, when it was suspended because of the outbreak of war with France. In February 1814, it reconvened under a new name, the Provisional Representation of the Land (*interimistische Landesrepräsentation*). The second session lasted until July 1815, when the king disbanded the assembly, announcing his intention to establish a permanent one in its place. The session of 1812–1813 was particularly eventful; major legislative battles over several issues sparked vehement debates over the character and political role of the nation. During these disputes, much of the hesitation about national representation that had characterized the petitions of 1811 fell away. Deputies of all estates and all provinces called for a constitution guaranteeing national representation. Yet their vision of the nation as a union of the traditional estates had little in common with Hardenberg's political program.

Though the government had announced its plan to convene a Provisional National Representation in September 1811, it waited until the following February to make public details about its organization and to provide instructions to the district administrative departments concerning the election of deputies. Like the Assembly of Notables, the new institution consisted of a single chamber, with delegates drawn from each of the three estates. Eighteen of the forty-two representatives were noble owners of landed estates; the other twenty-four came from the peasantry and the municipalities.[41] Only landowners were permitted to serve as deputies, even from the municipalities. As in the previous assemblies, the representatives were supposed to serve as individuals rather than as advocates for their particular estate. Additionally, the local authorities who supervised the elections were instructed to ensure "that only irreproachable, insightful, . . . unprejudiced men whose faithful devotion to the royal house and their fatherland is unquestionable" be elected.[42]

The ministry's extensive prescripts about the procedures for electing representatives contrasted with its almost total lack of attention to the substantive issues that the assembly would discuss. When the assembly met for its first session on 10 April 1812, its responsibilities and rules of procedure remained completely undefined. No one had even prepared an order of business, the most elementary requirement for beginning deliberations. In the absence of any direction from above, members of the assembly began preparing their own legislative proposals, calling for the introduction of a national paper currency, the establishment of a national bank, and so forth. They also asked Hardenberg for the right to deliberate over one of his own financial plans: a tax on income and capital assets. The chancellor agreed to show them the draft of this law and permitted them to discuss it, but then, on 24 May, he submitted the law to be signed by the king without having received the assembly's opinion.[43]

The representatives, unhappy from the beginning about the lack of clarity concerning their position, took this legislative fiat as an affront to their dignity and clamored for the clarification of their responsibilities. On 2 June, Justice Commissioner Bock, the representative of the Lithuanian towns, delivered a bombastic speech to the assembly in which he called on the king to establish a "formal constitution" as soon as possible. The government, he argued, should be required to inform the Provisional National Representation in writing of all legislative proposals, and the assembly must be permitted to vote on and to modify laws, including measures involving taxation and government spending. Bock scoffed at the suggestion

> that the representation of the nation could be disadvantageous for our beloved monarch, or perhaps for the honored men who should take, and will take, the rudder of our ship of state, which remains on stormy waves, amidst reefs, sand banks, and sharks.

No one in Prussia, he declared, desired the "exchange of the throne"; on the contrary, everyone "will gladly sacrifice treasure and blood to see the happiness of the whole of the nation, and in it the royal house of the Hohenzollerns."[44]

The assembly as a whole took a less adamant line than Bock; nonetheless, on 4 June it resolved, with only one dissenting vote, to petition Hardenberg about the constitution. Describing themselves as "elected by the nation," the representatives pointed out that

> through us, the bond between the monarch and the nation, as well as between the individual provinces, is supposed to become more tightly woven; therefore, everything depends upon our retaining the lasting trust of the nation. This can only fully be the case, however, if our associates know the exact relationship in which the National Representation will come to stand to the monarch, and to his administration.

To remedy the current situation, they asked Hardenberg to publish a brief notice confirming the king's "definitive" plan to grant a constitution, promising to make the details of it "generally known."[45]

At the time of this petition, Hardenberg had been in Dresden with the king for a meeting with Napoleon. He saw little urgency in answering the assembly's request, and the representatives received only an indirect response. In late May, one of the delegates had written to Hardenberg asking him to clarify the assembly's rules of procedure. On 6 June, the chancellor replied that for the time being, the form of the assembly's deliberations was "quite inconsequential." The king, he observed, had no intention of giving up either the right of legislative initiative or the right to ratify the laws. The assembly's role extended "only to consultation over matters that are submitted to it for consideration." More specific stipulations concerning the organization of the assembly, he promised, would be provided soon.[46]

Not surprisingly, the representatives took Hardenberg's brusque response as an insult. On 23 June, two delegates moved that the assembly refuse to consider any additional legislative proposals until the government had clarified its status and powers. The ministry, they charged, had given the assembly "no firm goal"; the representatives were "consulted today, ignored tomorrow, so their responsibility has no boundaries and their effort no use." Rather than performing an honorable service, the delegates risked becoming "laughing-stock" by appearing to be "a machine employed for amusement" by the government.[47] The following day, the assembly repeated its earlier petition to Hardenberg, complaining of the "uncertain position . . . in which we still find ourselves as the representatives [of our fellow citizens]."[48]

This time Hardenberg's reply was even frostier. "The members of the various estates," he observed, who were currently meeting as the "General Commission for the Regulation of Provincial and Communal War Debts," only constituted a "preliminary" national representation. Only after the commission's dissolution, he declared, would the government take further steps toward clarifying this matter.[49] The administration did, however, adopt one of the assembly's recommendations. In August 1812, the king named Count Friedrich August Burchard von Hardenberg, a Silesian estate owner who was both a relative of the chancellor and a respected delegate, as "a commissioner, who for the time being will take the presidency" of the assembly.[50] Additionally, the king had issued an order that sought to clarify the legal status of the representatives. "The members of the commission," he declared, "although they are initially to be viewed as the proxies [Stellvertreter] and spokesmen of their electors, they are not permitted to make decisions on the basis of instructions [from their constituents]." The delegates were responsible "not to the province and the community that elected them, but rather to me and to the entire state."[51]

Just a month later, the controversy over the assembly's status erupted again, with the enactment of the Gendarmerie Edict. This decree, which mandated radical changes in local administration, was published in August 1812, several weeks after being signed into law on 30 July, without the slightest advance notice to the representatives. The edict divided Prussia into new administrative districts; within these districts it established 164 counties, according to size and population, with no regard for the traditional boundaries. Except for the seven largest cities, which formed individual administrative units, the municipalities were included in the new counties. In place of the traditional county assembly (Kreistag), in which the nobles dominated, the law mandated the creation of a new representative institution with equal representation for the towns, estate owners, and the peasantry. Likewise, the Landrat, an official elected by the Kreistag, was to be replaced by a county director appointed by the crown, and the nobles' patrimonial courts were to be abolished in favor of centrally administered county courts.[52]

The national representatives, especially those from the nobility, were incensed both by the content of the new law and by the dictatorial method of its enactment. The noble delegate Gerlach declared, "Through the new constitution, the last remnant of political freedom is destroyed."[53] Another noble, Sanden, protested primarily on procedural grounds. "The state has formally committed itself to give the nation an appropriate representation," he argued; thus the assembly must be permitted to deliberate on the new law and to propose modifications.[54] The representative from Breslau, Lange, concurred: "Either our advice and judgment are considered to be of value or they are not; if of value, they should be made use of; if of no value, it must be demonstrated why not."[55]

On 26 September, the assembly sent a detailed memorandum to Hardenberg that protested the provisions of the Gendarmerie Edict.[56] Six weeks later, still having received no satisfactory response, the representatives finally resolved to petition the king directly, this time asking for a constitution. The representatives argued that if they were to prove themselves "worthy of the trust of Your Royal Majesty and of the nation," their authority and their relationship to the administration needed to be clarified. In a petition sent on 28 November 1812, they noted that the king had "wisely and generously" promised

> to give our fatherland a constitution founded on representation. May Your Royal Majesty therefore deign to take the requested step toward the further execution of the initiated work, a work which will unite the interest of the regent and the nation even more intimately, and which will elevate the credit of the state and give the laws stability and duration.[57]

The debates of 1812 represent a fascinating moment in Prussian history: representatives from all estates and all provinces appeared to agree on a basic political agenda. Though bourgeois and noble delegates disagreed over certain substantive policy issues, such as whether aristocrats should retain their patrimonial police and justice powers over their estates,[58] a strong majority of both groups favored the adoption of a constitution providing for national representation. In November 1812, for example, the assembly voted by an 18–12 margin to petition the king for a constitution. Seven of the twelve dissenters were nonaristocratic delegates, six of them from the *Bauernstand*. The assembly selected a committee composed of three nobles—Quast, Bredow, and Burgsdorf—to draft the petition.[59] Strikingly, in 1815, Burgsdorf would be one of the most outspoken opponents of the assembly's resolution, which passed by a vote of 22–13, to send another similar petition to the king. By that time, he had come to believe that the difficult work of a "state constitution" (*Staatsverfassung*) needed to be "prepared" through the development of provincial constitutions.[60] A number of other delegates also voted against the 1815 petition, despite their support for a constitution, because they believed that the decision to grant one was solely a royal prerogative.[61]

Even the nobles of Brandenburg's Kurmark, who had earlier expressed deep reservations about national representation, were nearly unanimous in their support for such an assembly. One of the delegates from the Kurmark, Otto Christoph Leopold von Quast-Garz, proclaimed enthusiastically in February 1812 that a national representative assembly would contribute to "the most forceful and beautiful animation of the national spirit."[62] Marwitz, though a steadfast opponent of Hardenberg's social reforms, embraced the idea of national unification. In the summer of 1806 (several months before the French attack on Prussia), he had proposed a patriotic war against Napoleon.[63] In September 1814, after France had been defeated, he wrote to Hardenberg proposing the establishment of a "common German fatherland" under Prussian leadership.[64] Though Marwitz largely equated the nation with the nobility, the idea of a nationally united aristocracy was a new one. According to traditional theory, the nobility was a particularistic institution rooted in provincial law.[65] This effervescent patriotism proved short-lived: less than a decade later, most Kurmark nobles would again vehemently reject the idea of a politically active nation.

Strikingly, the representatives from the peasantry appear to have displayed less vocal support for a constitution than did the nobility. This did not hold true, however, for the municipal delegates. Representatives such as Bock (from Lithuania) and Elsner (from Silesia) presented bold calls for constitutional government and legal equality. The *Stadtrat* Poselger, the West Prussian representative from Elbing, was virtually the only delegate from any estate who explicitly demanded that the assembly be given a deciding vote over some legislative matters. He also noted that because "monarchical power would be restricted in certain cases through the conferring of this authority," it could be granted only by the direct decision of the king.[66]

The boldness of these municipal delegates may have resulted less from their bourgeois economic interests than from the enactment of the *Städteordnung* four years earlier. This law granted the Prussian towns extensive rights of self-government. The delegates from the municipalities, therefore, were the only members of the assembly with practical governing experience. Thus, they may have viewed local self-rule as an example for the entire realm. This experience, however, had not transformed them into radical republicans. Even Poselger asked for limits on monarchical power only "in certain cases." Bock, who maintained that the assembly itself had the right to draft a constitution, argued that its goal should be to "secure the monarch and the people, and to forever banish and restrain every conflict between His servants."[67] Only if the national representation were given an "adequate" constitution, he claimed, could it serve as "the mainstay of the throne of the House of the Hohenzollerns, and of the united Prussian people"[68]

The above words of the delegate Bock illustrate a striking tendency of Prussian oppositional rhetoric during the reform period. Bock suggested that the future national representation should serve as the "mainstay of the throne . . . and of the united Prussian people." Similarly, the assembly's petition of 28 November 1812 claimed that a constitution would "unite the interest of the regent and the nation." Both of these passages portrayed the nation (or the *Volk*) as possessing a unanimous and harmonious will; more significantly, both of them drew a parallel between the political authority of the king and that of the people. To declare allegiance to both the monarch and the nation was to raise the question: did the king stand above the nation, or vice versa? And whose will should prevail in the event of a conflict between the two? Prussian proponents of a constitution consistently avoided taking a stand on this issue, in part because they viewed the political process as ideally harmonious, rather than contestatory. Yet as popular political participation moved from the realm of theory to that of practice, this question became increasingly unavoidable.

The Intensification of Aristocratic Nationalism during the War of Liberation

With Napoleon's army in retreat from Moscow in December 1812, General Yorck von Wartenburg switched the Prussian troops under his command from the French to the Russian side. In response, King Frederick William III stripped the general of his command and ordered his immediate arrest. Nonetheless, by mid–January, Hardenberg also had concluded that the time had come to change sides in the war. On 22 January, the king moved away from the French garrison that occupied Berlin and established his court in Breslau.

The War of Liberation of 1813–1814 raised the temperature of political discourse in Prussia. Now, the nation stood united not against a usurping bureaucracy but against a foreign enemy. Prussians boldly proclaimed their loyalty to king and fatherland. And the king, recalling the ardent patriotism of the French revolutionaries, began to become nervous at their enthusiasm.

Upon learning of the king's decision to move his court to Breslau, the bourgeois delegate Elsner proposed that the representative assembly move with him. The "pure preservation of the concept of monarchy," he argued, required "the inseparability of the monarch and the national representation."[69] Other delegates, such as Quast, disagreed: the spectacle of forty-two representatives joining the king's retinue, he said, "would undoubtedly create a sensation which might not be useful."[70] Two days later, the king decided the matter for them, ordering that the assembly remain in Berlin under the direction of a government commission.[71] The delegates had to content themselves with composing, on 13 February, an "Appeal to Our Fellow Citizens," which declared, "The fatherland is in danger!" It called for popular sacrifice in support of the military effort:

> Joyfully will the youths and the able-bodied men of the nation follow
> [the king's] call, which has been longed for. *Märker* and Silesians, Pom-
> eranians and Prussians, united through the common bond of loyalty for
> the king and the national honor, will vie with each other in streaming to
> the colors. With the war–cry "Frederick William" and "Prussian father-
> land," they will defy every danger.[72]

The following day, the king ordered the Provisional National Representation to adjourn but kept a small group of delegates in session for possible wartime consultations. In a letter accompanying these instructions, Hardenberg added: "I hope that a less stormy time than the present one will soon allow us to organize definitively a national representation, which will correspond to the wishes of all estates."[73]

In March 1813, Frederick William III formally agreed to join a campaign with Russia for the liberation of Europe. On 17 March, he issued a proclamation calling on his soldiers to "fight for the independence and the honor of the *Volk*." Every "son of the fatherland," he declared, must participate "in this battle for honor and freedom. . . . My cause is the cause of my *Volk*, and of all well-intentioned Europeans."[74] In April, the offensive began, with the Prussian and Russian armies backed by a Swedish force in the north and by British naval and economic power in the west. Austria entered the war on the allied side in August. Metternich secured the cooperation of most of the major middle-sized German states, including Bavaria, Württemberg, Baden, and Hesse-Darmstadt, between October and December 1813. The decisive allied victory came at the battle of Leipzig on 16–18 October 1813. The French lost 38,000 troops in combat and another 30,000 who were taken prisoner, and they were forced to withdraw from the field. By early November, Napoleon's troops had retreated across the Rhine, and on 31 March 1814, the victorious allied monarchs entered Paris. Except for a brief final act the following year, when the captured French emperor escaped from the island of Elba and mounted a last military assault at Waterloo in June 1815, the Napoleonic era was over.[75]

On 17 November 1813, after the French army had been expelled from German soil, King Frederick William III sent a cabinet order from Frankfurt-am-Main that ordered the Prussian representative assembly to reconvene for a second session. Despite the enthusiasm he had exhibited for "the cause of my *Volk*" in his proclamation eight months before, he insisted that the new assembly operate under even tighter government control than the first. Its deliberations were to be supervised by a four-member royal commission, and it would be authorized to discuss only two issues: proposals for the "preservation of landowners" and the "appropriate equalization of the burdens of war."[76] Unlike the first assembly, the new one was permitted to publish the results of its deliberations. Only two numbers of this publication would appear, however, in part because some of the delegates had begun to worry about the "inflamed" emotions of the public.[77]

The assembly gathered for the first time on 21 February 1814. An episode from this meeting illustrates just how sensitive the issue of representation had become for the king. The royal commission, in its report on the session, used the name "National Assembly" (*National-Versammlung*) several times. It also reported that the delegates twice broke into a spontaneous cheer:

Hail and blessing to our worthy and righteous nation!
Hail and blessing to our good, worthy, and just king![78]

Two weeks later, Frederick William sent a curt message back from his headquarters at Chaumont, indicating that "under no circumstances" did he want the institution called a "National Assembly" (a name that evoked frightening memories of the French Revolution). The king knew that the revolution of 1789 in France had begun with salutations to the king and to the nation. He recognized that the delegates, through their words of praise for both him and for the nation, were helping establish the nation as a potential rival to his own sovereign authority. In response to this order, the royal commission renamed the assembly the Provisional Representation of the Land (*interimistische Landesrepräsentation*), a title that carried no such fearful connotations.[79]

Despite the tight rein on the assembly's deliberations in 1814–1815, frictions between government and representatives still occurred. On 16 February 1814 (five days before the second session officially opened), the delegates sent a petition to Hardenberg asking that the implementation of the Gendarmerie Edict be deferred until the "general peace," in order that a representative assembly could deliberate over its provisions.[80] This request, in conjunction with a series of petitions from East Prussia, persuaded Frederick William to suspend the law indefinitely in March 1814, even though the king criticized the East Prussians for their protests.[81]

The constitutional question also continued to resurface in the representatives' deliberations. The topic emerged repeatedly during the debates of 1814; and in April 1815, the assembly resolved by a large majority to address another petition to Hardenberg, asking once again for a constitution and thus the fulfillment of the king's two previous promises to grant a national representation (in the edicts of 27 October 1810 and 7 September 1811). A constitution, the delegates claimed, would secure "true civil freedom and all purposes of the social union," thus contributing to the king's own glory. Although the representatives professed to believe that the state intended to grant a constitution soon on its own initiative, they still considered it their duty to ask, "in the name of the nation," for the "acceleration of that great work, which has been yearned for so long and so universally." The new "representation of the land," they wrote, should be "organically joined" to a "constitution of the provinces, to be based on appropriate representation of all classes of citizens [Staatsbürger]." Such a constitution, they declared, would enhance the "unshakable loyalty" of the traditional Prussian provinces "for the cherished king, for the inexpressibly beloved fatherland." It would also offer "a principle of vitality and cultivation [Bildung]" for the newly acquired lands (the Rhine territories and part of Saxony). In this way, the new provinces would not simply be annexed by Prussia but rather united into "one true great family."[82]

As this petition illustrates, the liberalization of aristocratic rhetoric during the reform period had definite limits. The noble delegates (as well as those of the other traditional estates) adopted some of the concepts associated with reform, such as "citizen" (Staatsbürger), "civil freedom" (bürgerliche Freiheit), and Bildung. They also accepted the ideal of a unified nation, in whose name they claimed to speak; and professed their ardent love for the fatherland and for the king. But the nation, in their view, was still Prussia, not Germany; and within that nation, they jealously insisted upon the preservation of provincial rights. Count Dönhoff, a member of the Committee of East Prussian and Lithuanian Estates, declared in March 1815 that "salutary provincialism" was a necessary condition for "true nationality." He condemned the principle "that the majority of votes in a general representative national assembly must be viewed as the expression of the general national desire [Nationalwunsch] of all provinces."[83] Similarly, a petition of the East Prussian Committee of April 1815 called for the "reanimation of the provincial estates," which would function in interaction with the "general estates." Such a system of representation, "supported by freedom of the press, along with publicity and freedom of deliberations" would foster the formation of a "truly venerable public voice [öffentliche Stimme]."[84]

If the East Prussian nobility at least paid homage to the liberal principles of freedom of the press and of parliamentary deliberations, not so the nobles of Brandenburg. With the end of the war, the Kurmark estates quickly resumed their defense of the gamut of traditional privileges. In August 1814, the Kurmärkische Ritterschaft wrote to the king extolling the "sacrifice" that they had "willingly offered, along with the whole nation," during the war and asking that their patriotic contributions be acknowledged through "the restoration of our former constitution." They thanked the king for his promise "to grant the whole monarchy a representation" but noted that

> for the completion of this beneficial deed, a provincial constitution is an essential requirement. Without this, the representatives have no legal association with the province; they remain unacquainted with its wishes, and therefore cannot be the true organ of the province.[85]

The nobles of the Kurmark, in other words, still viewed a national representative assembly as an instrument for advocating provincial interests—just as in their petition of January 1811. Their primary loyalty was still not to the nation but to the province.

On 22 May 1815, the king published a decree that promised to establish a "representation of the Volk," which would consist of both a central representative assembly and a system of provincial estates.[86] Seven weeks later, Hardenberg dissolved the provisional assembly, declaring that "the duties assigned to it by His Majesty have been completed, and the organization of a complete [vollständigen] representation of the land has been ordered by the decree of 22 May."[87] With the adjournment of this assembly, no elected institution representing the entire realm would again assemble in Prussia until 1847. During the intervening years, the public debates over a Prussian constitution would be waged either through provincial institutions or outside official channels.

Conclusion: The Ideal of Harmony in Aristocratic Nationalist Discourse

Words have consequences and, as the representatives of Prussia's privileged elites discovered during the Napoleonic era, the defense of their corporate interests depended on their ability to manipulate the new language of national politics. A new historical a priori had emerged in Prussia (for at least the brief moment in which Napoleon reigned supreme). To participate effectively in legitimate political discourse, one needed to claim to speak on behalf of the national interest rather than for the egotistical interests of one's own estate. To fail to pay homage to these principles, as the aristocrats Marwitz and Finckenstein ruefully discovered during their row with Hardenberg in 1811, could jeopardize not only one's cause but also one's own liberty.

According to the prevailing interpretation of this era of Prussian history, the aristocratic opposition to Hardenberg's social and economic reforms forced the government to abandon its plans for political liberalization.[88] Because the experimental representative assemblies established during the Napoleonic era sought to derail Hardenberg's reform program, the chancellor chose to enact these measures by fiat, giving up his ambition to create a parliamentary system of rule in Prussia. Therefore, historians have argued, during the early nineteenth century, Prussia developed liberal social and economic institutions, but its political system remained a bureaucratic dictatorship.

Through a close analysis of the political debates of 1810–1815, this chapter has demonstrated the inadequacy of this conventional interpretation of the Prussian reform movement. Rather than abandoning the idea of creating a national representation, Hardenberg significantly expanded his constitutional plans over this period. In October 1810, Hardenberg had insisted that the new central representative institution must serve as a purely consultative body whose members would be appointed by the king rather than elected. Coming down as a "gift from above," the assembly's role was to help with the implementation of Hardenberg's reform legislation rather than to deliberate over its provisions. In September 1811, the Provisional National Representation was charged only with regulating "provincial and communal war debts," and in June 1812, Hardenberg brusquely denied that the king had any obligation to submit a legislative proposal to this assembly for its opinion before signing the measure into law. Yet, ultimately, Hardenberg and the king heeded many of the assembly's demands for a greater political voice. By 1815, Hardenberg was calling for the establishment of a "representation of the *Volk*," involving both a central representative assembly and a system of provincial diets, and in later years, he advocated granting these bodies broad authority over legislative and fiscal matters.[89]

In the face of concerted opposition to social and economic reform, Hardenberg did not retreat from his plans for a national representation. Nor did he generally disregard the protests of Prussia's privileged elites against his reform proposals. Beginning in 1810, he backed off from his proposal for an income tax, and, subsequently, he complied with aristocratic demands for the preservation of their police and judicial powers on their estates, as well as for the maintenance of the traditional system of local administration in the countryside. With respect to the legislation establishing free trade, however, which affected primarily Prussia's municipalities, Hardenberg took a harder line, simply ignoring the complaints of the representative assembly.

Hardenberg's conduct thus followed a perplexing pattern. Rather than—like Napoleon—rigging representative institutions that possessed authority in theory alone,[90] he created assemblies that in theory had little authority but in practice exercised ever-greater power even as they worked to undermine his program of social and economic reform. The explanation for this curious phenomenon lies partly in the realm of political rhetoric. To the extent that Prussia's privileged elites mastered a new idiom by learning to "speak nationally," they were able to persuade Hardenberg and the king to expand the domain of the new representative institutions. Thus, for example, in 1814 Frederick William III suspended the Gendarmerie Edict indefinitely, in order that a representative assembly might deliberate over its provisions before its implementation. Conversely, those groups that failed to invoke the principle of the national interest, such as the urban guilds, enjoyed little success in their efforts to lobby the Prussian ministry, perhaps in part because they employed rather traditional rhetoric in defense of their legal privileges. The claims about the nation analyzed in this chapter are summarized in table 4.1.

As table 4.1 illustrates, noble activists based their political arguments on some of the same premises as the bureaucratic nationalists, for example, they argued that the nation was an ideally unified and harmonious community and that the nation's political interests coincided with the king's. Yet they articulated this claim for a very different purpose

4.1 The Concept "Nation" in Prussian Aristocratic Discourse, 1810–1815

Consensual features	Contested features
The nation is a harmonious community possessing one unified interest and will.	Can Jews be citizens?
Old corporate bodies such as the aristocracy and the guilds must be preserved.	What degree of legal hierarchy should be maintained?
Traditional property rights must be protected.	
The nation's interest is identical to the king's interest.	Is the king sovereign, or is his authority limited by "contracts" with the nation?
	How much political authority should be vested in the nation vs. in the provinces?

than the Stein-Hardenberg party. Whereas the leading reformers sought to compel the nation to cooperate with the king, Prussian aristocrats invoked the ideal of harmony as a means of persuading the king to respect the wishes of the nation. This novel logic about the need for national harmony coexisted with a more traditional line of reasoning in aristocratic rhetoric. Many Prussian nobles challenged the principle of monarchical sovereignty, arguing that the king's authority was limited by his "contracts" with the estates. These customary contracts, they maintained, had to serve as the starting point for any new system of representative rule. Many aristocrats (above all in the province of Brandenburg) also interwove their arguments in favor of national representation with calls for the preservation of the traditional provincial constitution, along with the retention of old corporate distinctions and property rights.

While invoking the authority of the nation proved—in the short term—an effective means of defending aristocratic privileges, the use of this rhetorical strategy also had two broader consequences. First, by mastering the idiom of speaking nationally, Prussian nobles reinforced the civil servants' definition of the nation as an ideally unitary and harmonious body. Second, by proclaiming the need for unity between the nation and the monarchical state, aristocrats subtly transformed their own social and political identities, for example, by conceiving of the nobility as a national, rather than a provincial, institution and by starting to back away from some traditional claims about the contractual nature of sovereign authority. Thus, the advent of national politics exercised a powerful effect on conservative political theory in Prussia. The implications of this transformation of Prussian nobles' social and political claims will be explored more fully in Chapter 7.

Like the bureaucratic reformers, most Prussian aristocrats expressed relatively little interest in establishing linguistic, ethnic, or cultural solidarity within the nation. A few exceptions, including Marwitz, called for "a common German fatherland" under Prussian leadership. The next chapter examines the rhetoric of bourgeois political writers and activists who made German national unification the centerpiece of their political program. This new popular nationalism presented a troubling spectacle to the king and the nobility alike. By challenging the boundaries of legitimate political discourse, these popular nationalists ultimately provoked a powerful reaction against the movement toward a constitutional system of government in Prussia.

Five

A NATION OF ROMANTICS

In the winter of 1807–1808, Johann Gottlieb Fichte presented his *Addresses to the German Nation* in a lecture hall in French-occupied Berlin. Germany had become corrupt, Fichte declared, because its people had become completely "self-seeking"; the "means of salvation" lay in the establishment of a program of "German national education" to forge new bonds between the people and their national community. Fichte waxed rhapsodic in contemplating the joys that awaited the Germans upon the reconstitution of their nation:

> Love that is truly love, and not a mere transitory lust, never clings to what is transient; only in the eternal does it awaken and become kindled, and there alone does it rest. . . . [H]e to whom a fatherland has been handed down, and in whose soul heaven and earth, visible and invisible meet and mingle, and thus, and only thus, create a true and enduring heaven—such a man fights to the last drop of his blood to hand on the precious possession unimpaired to his posterity.[1]

Though the immediate reception of Fichte's lectures was more modest than reported in patriotic legends, the philosopher may still have found cause to believe that the resurrection of the German nation could coincide with the resurrection of his own career. A student of Kant's in Königsberg, Fichte had won a chair in philosophy at the University of Jena in 1794 at the age of thirty-two, only to lose it five years later under the accusation of atheism. After several nomadic years, Fichte settled in Berlin; and by the eve of the Napoleonic invasion of Prussia, he had achieved renown as an independent scholar, lecturing to prominent members of Berlin's society and civil service. In 1810, on the force of the

Addresses and his earlier philosophical works, he was named rector of the new University of Berlin.[2]

The rhetoric of bourgeois intellectuals and popular activists in Napoleonic Prussia differed significantly from that of the civil servants and nobles discussed in the previous two chapters. For the most part excluded from the privileged institutions of the realm, these figures went outside official channels, addressing their appeals directly to the *Volk*. Moreover, unlike the bureaucratic and aristocratic nationalists, whose sober and abstract prose had remained signally vague in defining the nation, these bourgeois activists emphasized the cultural and ethnic foundations of national community.

Historians have often referred to these early nineteenth-century popular activists as "romantic nationalists," because they drew their inspiration in part from the culture of German romanticism, as represented by figures such as Friedrich Hölderlin, Friedrich and Wilhelm Schlegel, Novalis (Friedrich Hardenberg), and Heinrich von Kleist. While romanticism was an amorphous movement, notoriously difficult to define, its adherents shared certain concerns. Their writings highlighted the estrangement of the individual from the community. They often depicted modern life as corrupt and fragmented and idealized the medieval world as harmonious and pure. The romantics hoped to restore harmony and to reunite the individual with the community by recapturing "true feelings and authentic life."[3]

The world view of the romantic nationalists is frequently depicted as sharply opposed to the eighteenth-century values of the Enlightenment. Rather than articulating secular ideals, they presented an expressly Christian—and specifically Protestant pietist—vision of the national community.[4] In contrast to the rationalism characteristic of Enlightenment intellectuals, they adopted "the mentality of the miraculous," which celebrated passion and irrational desire.[5] Instead of valuing individual autonomy as the greatest good, the romantic nationalists believed that the individual could attain fulfillment only through immersion in collective life.[6] Each of these conventional judgments contains an important element of truth. The romantic nationalists' rhetoric was tinged with quasi–Christian elements, and they often portrayed the nation in those breathless tones usually reserved for descriptions of a lover. By denouncing the corruption of contemporary political life and by trumpeting the advent of a utopian order, these activists raised the temperature of Prussian and German political debate, alarming both the traditional social elites and leading members of the governments of most German states.

Nonetheless, it is too simplistic to hold that romantic nationalism represented a wholesale rejection of Enlightenment values. Though these popular activists' views cannot be located within the framework of enlightened nationalism, as defined earlier, they reinforced one of the key premises of enlightened nationalist rhetoric, namely, that the nation was an ideally harmonious and unified political community. Moreover, like the leading reformers within the Prussian civil service, many of these figures held that national harmony could be achieved only through a process of popular education. Fichte's intellectual biography illustrates the blurring of boundaries between the Enlightenment and romanticism in nineteenth-century Prussia. Scholars generally identify Fichte as a rationalist rather than as a romantic: in the words of James Sheehan, "Fichte never abandoned the *Aufklärung*'s commitment to philosophical analysis as the way to knowledge and morality."[7] Nonetheless, his denunciations of "self-seeking" and his paeans to national solidarity reveal a typically romantic preoccupation with the isolation of the individual in the modern world. By advocating a program of national education, Fichte sought to use the tools of the Enlightenment as a means of solving the dilemma of the romantics.

The socially marginalized status of many of the bourgeois activists led them to criticize existing social and political institutions in more radical terms than was the case with the civil servants and aristocrats discussed in previous chapters. Yet their movement represented a fractured and often self-contradictory set of political discourses and actions. Though many of these figures called for the preservation of traditional hierarchical institutions, the public political spectacles they staged were often relentlessly egalitarian in their implications. Moreover, while nearly all of these figures professed devotion to the principle of monarchical sovereignty, they both appealed to and helped constitute a public sphere autonomous from the will of the Prussian king and his ministers. Thus, the romantic nationalists provoked suspicions that they were secretly fomenting a revolution. Finally, while the bourgeois activists emphasized the ethnic and cultural foundations of nationhood, they often disagreed over the specific characteristics that defined the national community.

The Genesis of Romantic Nationalism

Despite the populist rhetoric of the romantic nationalists, which purported to represent the will of the entire *Volk*, this movement was confined to a narrow segment of the population during the Napoleonic era.

Throughout the German states, popular nationalism was an overwhelmingly urban phenomenon. Its adherents were primarily Protestant men who belonged to the literate bourgeoisie,[8] including students, professors, journalists, and freelance writers. They were relatively few in number and possessed little socioeconomic power, but they exercised a disproportionate influence on the political debates of this era.

That the early popular nationalist movement was centered in the literate bourgeoisie is unsurprising. As scholars such as Karl Deutsch and Miroslav Hroch have observed, increasing "social mobility and communication" have historically contributed to the emergence of nationalist movements.[9] Likewise, Benedict Anderson notes that the rise of print capitalism in Europe from the sixteenth century onward "laid the bases for national consciousnesses" by creating "unified fields of exchange and communications" in vernacular languages.[10] The invention of national identity, these scholars argue, provides a basis for unifying diverse regions that are increasingly linked both economically and through the exchange of ideas. In the German states at the beginning of the nineteenth century, groups such as students, professors, and freelance journalists were both relatively mobile, frequently moving from city to city for their studies or their work, and more capable than most of exchanging ideas beyond their own localities through the medium of print. Thus, these groups were one logical nexus for the formation of a nascent German national identity.

Numerous historians have observed that bourgeois popular nationalism in nineteenth-century Germany strongly emphasized the importance of collective solidarity within the nation.[11] This obsession with the reconstitution of a harmonious community may be explained both culturally and sociologically. As Anderson observes, nationalism possesses "a strong affinity with religious imaginings"; in the face of the "modern darkness" of "rationalist secularism," it aims to achieve "a secular transformation of fatality into continuity, contingency into meaning."[12] Many German romantic nationalists drew directly on the cultural legacy of the Protestant spiritual movement known as pietism. Initiated by Philip Spener (1635–1705) and August Hermann Francke (1663–1727), pietism emphasized the importance of a direct and powerfully emotional relationship between the individual believer and God. The pietists devalued dogma and external church authority, identifying Christian love as the central element of devotional experience. They envisioned a religious fellowship founded on spiritual communion and the equality of all believers.[13]

From a sociological standpoint, the radical temperament of many German romantic nationalists also reflected a response to the marginalization experienced by many members of the German educated middle classes during the late eighteenth and early nineteenth centuries which resulted in what one scholar has termed "an oppressive sense of status-inconsistency among those who eventually became the prime movers of German nationalism."[14] As Gordon Craig remarks of romanticism, "politically it was an escape from the bourgeois dilemma of powerlessness."[15] Over the course of the eighteenth century, the German states experienced substantial population growth, along with significant increases in literacy rates and in numbers of university graduates. This expanded educated class, however, was confronted by stagnant or declining numbers of positions in the traditional occupations for university graduates: the civil service, the church, and schools and universities. This squeeze gave rise to a growing "intellectual proletariat"—ambitious university graduates forced to endure a decade or more of humiliating work as tutors or apprentices before obtaining permanent positions.[16] During the late eighteenth and early nineteenth centuries, increasing numbers of young educated Germans turned to careers as freelance writers, a path that generally led to impoverishment, in part because the lack of adequate copyright protections led to widespread piracy in publishing, thus diminishing the royalties paid to authors.[17]

In certain respects, the plight of Prussia's literate bourgeoisie during this era mirrored the situation that had existed in late eighteenth-century France. Historians such as Robert Darnton have explored how the social marginalization of many French intellectuals during the decades preceding the revolution fostered the growth of a "Grub Street" literature by struggling and embittered writers, far more radical in tone than the High Enlightenment.[18] Likewise, Lynn Hunt has demonstrated that many of the most ardent participants in revolutionary politics in France were educated commoners who had failed to achieve advancement within the social hierarchies of the Old Regime.[19] In each of these cases, the repeated frustration of social ambitions among the members of the literate bourgeoisie contributed to the radicalization of their political views.

Like Fichte, most romantic nationalists developed their political theories as ambitious outsiders. Craving status and a sense of belonging, these activists projected their desires onto an ideally harmonious and unified national community. Excluded from the experimental representative institutions established during the Napoleonic era, the romantic nationalists appealed for legitimacy by attempting to constitute a space for public politics autonomous from the authority of the state. It was their claim that the authority of the nation was equal to that of the monarchical state, this ultimately proved most troubling to representatives of the established order.

Equality: Constituting the Public

Like the reform party in the Prussian civil service, the bourgeois popular nationalists cannot be pigeonholed either as a progressive or as a reactionary political force by twentieth-century standards. Their political views were simultaneously forward-looking and backward-looking. They were torn between the desire to forge a new egalitarian political community and the desire to recover the organic solidarity found in traditional hierarchical institutions. The lives of two of the most influential early nationalists, Joseph Görres and Friedrich Ludwig Jahn, illustrate these conflicting tendencies of romantic nationalism. Though both Görres and Jahn portrayed themselves partly as defenders of the traditional order, they both played an important role in constituting a politicized public sphere that came to challenge the monopoly over public life claimed by the monarchical state.

Joseph Görres was born to a Catholic family in Koblenz in 1776, the son of a prosperous wood merchant. Attending *Gymnasium* during the early 1790s, he was swept up in the enthusiasm for the French Revolution. In 1795, after the French invasion of the Rhineland, he published an article that celebrated the deeds of the "Frankish republic," which he predicted would liberate Europe from its tyrants and erect a temple of freedom on the rubble of despotism. Upon visiting Paris in 1799, however, Görres became disillusioned with revolutionary ideals. After a brief career as a journalist, he settled in Koblenz in 1800 as a teacher of physics and chemistry at the *école secondaire*, a post he held until 1814 (except for a two-year hiatus in Heidelberg, where he worked on a project to recover German folk art). Over the course of the Napoleonic occupation, Görres became increasingly frustrated and pessimistic. Though happy in his domestic life, his efforts to obtain a university professorship came to naught, and he found the French occupation increasingly burdensome. With the liberation of the Rhineland from Napoleonic rule in January 1814, he began publication of a newspaper, the *Rheinische Merkur*, which exultantly called for the unification of Germany under joint Austrian and Prussian leadership and the establishment of a constitution.[20]

By this time, Görres had long ago abandoned the centralizing and leveling ideals of the French Revolution. Too much centralization of power, he argued, would result in despotism; the best form of government for Germany would be "strong unity within free multiplicity." Just as the German people had a duty to obey their princes, the individual princes owed allegiance to the fatherland. It must be remembered, he declared, "that the freedom of the people finds its limits in the freedom of the princes—but also vice versa." Görres was thus no republican, nor did he believe in the abolition of legal differences between the estates. The new constitution (*ständische Verfassung*), he wrote, should be founded on "the three pillars" of the ancient "estates of the learned, the warriors, and the farmers" (*Lehrstand, Wehrstand, und Nährstand*), who would form a new "ruling contract" (*Staatsvertrag*) with the prince: "The heads of the three estates will stand around the prince as participants in his responsibility, . . . mediators between the people and the government."[21]

Though many German leaders had welcomed Görres's patriotic publications during the war of 1813–1814, the end of the war against Napoleon brought a sudden chill in rulers' attitudes toward popular nationalism. Concerns about the implications of the nationalist movement were especially pronounced in the states of southern and central Germany. Many of these states had substantially increased their territories during the Napoleonic era, but the leaders of these states recognized that national unification might mean their own absorption into a greater Germany. The abolition of the Holy Roman Empire in 1806 meant that the governments of these *Mittelstaaten* had to struggle to assert their legitimacy. The empire, despite its practical weakness, had provided an overarching constitutional structure that united the various German states. This unity was only partly reestablished in the new German confederation of 1815, a loose federal order that defined each territorial prince as the supreme sovereign within his territory. In the wake of the Vienna Settlement, a potentially explosive situation developed: the German princes nervously guarded their autonomy, while popular nationalists like Görres sought to establish a stronger political union that would serve as a more worthy replacement for the Old Reich.

Fearing that Görres's patriotic ardor might jeopardize their sovereignty, the rulers of Baden, Bavaria, and Württemberg had banned distribution of the *Rheinische Merkur* in the summer of 1814. The following year, under the terms of the Vienna Settlement, Koblenz (along with most of the rest of the Rhineland) came under Prussian rule. Facing pressure from other members of the German confederation, Hardenberg reluctantly agreed to shut down Görres's newspaper outright in January 1816.[22]

Görres, however, did not let this setback dissuade him from further political activism. In May 1815, King Frederick William III published a decree promising to establish a "representation of the *Volk*" in Prussia, which would consist of both a central representative assembly and a system of provincial estates.[23] Deliberations on this project, however, proceeded at a snail's pace. Thus, on 18 October 1817, at a celebration in Koblenz commemorating the German victory at Leipzig four years earlier, Görres took the opportunity to circulate a petition to the Prussian king that called for the fulfillment of the constitutional promise of 1815. During the following three months, the petition (which came to be known as the Koblenz Address) was passed around the city and its outlying areas. Having obtained 3,296 signatures, Görres presented it to Hardenberg in a ceremony held on 12 January 1818.

The Koblenz Address was remarkable for its blend of traditional and modern political logic. On the one hand, it explicitly disavowed any Jacobin ambitions, decrying "despotism coming up from below, as well as down from above." Rather than a republican form of government, the petition called for a state consisting of organically linked estates, founded on "eternal justice" (Gerechtigkeit), with an inviolable monarch at its peak.[24] The people of Koblenz, Görres declared, desired "the reestablishment of the freedoms of the land [Landschaft] and the ancient truly German constitution [wahrhaft teutschen Verfassung]." This ancient constitution had long been under assault by "foreign tyranny," which "for centuries, through its indirect and direct influence, has brought about the suppression and annihilation of those ancient freedoms, rights, and constitutions."

Yet these appeals to antiquity were wedded to an innovative logic about the nature of the German "public" and its relationship to royal authority. In justifying the decision to petition the king, Görres noted that Frederick William III had asked the provincial governors to survey local views concerning a constitution. To be successful, he argued, the survey must reflect not just the views of a few prominent citizens but "public opinion and the collective conviction of the great majority." For this reason, the signers of the petition considered it their "duty as citizens" (Bürgerpflicht) to "approach the throne" with their opinions on this subject. The signers of the petition viewed themselves "not only as citizens [Bürger] of the Prussian monarchy, but also as Germans"; as such, "the salvation of the entire Fatherland is a matter close to their hearts." The petition reminded the king of his constitutional promise and also asked him to use his influence in the Bundestag to ensure that all German states would receive constitutions, in accordance with Article 13 of the German Articles of Confederation of 1815.[25]

The Koblenz Address provides one fascinating glimpse at how the Prussian bourgeoisie learned to speak nationally during the early nineteenth century. The petition is fraught with internal tensions between egalitarian and hierarchical principles. Though Görres avowed the supremacy of the Prussian king, he also expressed allegiance to the higher goal of the "salvation of the entire [German] Fatherland." Görres demanded the reestablishment of the ancient constitution (which would have been based on limited political participation by legally privileged elites), but he justified the petition on the grounds that it expressed "public opinion" and the "collective conviction" of the majority of citizens. In stating this claim, he implicitly acknowledged the egalitarian principle of majority rule and the democratic premise that the citizenry possessed a unified collective voice. These ideals of equality and unity were hardly compatible with the traditional hierarchical institutions that were lauded elsewhere in the petition.

For Görres, public opinion was no mere abstraction. By circulating his petition for signatures, he literally helped constitute the politicized public sphere to which he appealed. Even as he called for the reestablishment of the traditional corporate order, he transcended the boundaries of the old estates by seeking an expression of the desires of the citizenry as a whole. Through this act of political communication, the nation began to take on reality as an entity at least partly autonomous from the royal will.

A more colorful figure than Görres was Friedrich Ludwig Jahn, who founded both the gymnastics movement (*Turnerschaft*) among the German youth in 1811 and the first nationalist student organization (*Burschenschaft*), which he established in Jena in 1815. Jahn was the son of a Lutheran minister, born in Prussia's heartland, the Kurmark of Brandenburg, in 1778. Initially educated at home by his father, Jahn attended *Gymnasium* in Berlin, then studied theology at the Universities of Halle and Greifswald without completing a degree. Throughout most of his twenties, Jahn led an itinerant existence as a private tutor and freelance political publicist. During the Napoleonic invasion of 1806, he became a camp follower of the Prussian army, and, in the wake of Prussia's defeat, he wandered throughout the country for several years attempting to stir German nationalist sentiment against the French.

Unlike Görres, Jahn never went through a Jacobin stage. He came to German nationalism after expressing ideals of Prussian patriotism. Jahn's first book, written at the age of twenty-one in 1799, appealed for Prussian rather than German patriotism. Jahn declared in this tract that in hand-to-hand combat, "one Prussian defeats three Saxons, Hanoverians, Mecklenburgians, or Swedes."[26] After 1806, however, influenced by the nascent nationalism of figures such as Fichte and Ernst Moritz Arndt, Jahn began to shift his allegiances to an imagined pan–German collectivity that included Switzerland, Denmark, the Low Countries, Prussia, and Austria.[27] Like Görres, Jahn believed that Germany possessed a glorious past, but that it had fallen from greatness in recent times. Jahn maintained that the German *Volk* had "never overcome" the "wretched,

5.1 Friedrich Ludwig Jahn's gymnastics ground on the Hasenheide in Berlin, 1818. Staatsbibliothek zu Berlin—Preußischer Kulturbesitz— Handschriftenabteilung, YB 14220 m.

shameful Peace of Westphalia" of 1648. A powerful German empire, he argued, could be reestablished only through the unification of the *Volk*: "A state is nothing without a *Volk*—a soulless artifact. A *Volk* is nothing without a state—a bodiless phantom, like the wandering gypsies and Jews. Only the unity of state and *Volk* makes a *Reich*."[28]

Jahn was not content to confine his nationalism to the realm of theory. In 1809, he finally achieved a secure position as a schoolteacher at the *Gymnasium* in Berlin-Kölln that he himself had attended. There, in collaboration with a fellow instructor, Friedrich Friesen, he devised a plan for martial training inspired partly by Greek ideals of harmony of body and spirit and partly by Fichte's idea for a German national education. In 1811, the two teachers opened the first gymnastics ground (*Turnplatz*) on the Hasenheide, in front of the gates of Berlin, deriving the word *turnen* from the medieval tournaments, which for Jahn symbolized the ancient German spirit.[29]

In part, Jahn envisioned the *Turnerschaft* as a training ground for the new national militia, which he hoped would soon overthrow the French occupation of Germany. By performing gymnastic exercises, Jahn wrote, the "entire *Volk* will become manly and patriotic, and, feeling its power, will be reborn."[30] Yet Jahn's gymnastics movement also served as a visual emblem of the unity and equality of the German nation itself. He and Friesen began with a group of 200 youths, whom he instructed in games, gymnastic drills, and other athletics. The gymnastics movement, like the

Burschenschaft organization Jahn subsequently founded, attempted to break down the social differences among its adherents. Both students and workers participated, all of them wearing an identical gray linen uniform. All of them employed rough and familiar speech (which Jahn considered authentically German), addressing each other with the informal *Du*. They sang songs, which likewise emphasized the equality of all Germans:

> So hegen wir ein freies Reich,
> An Rang und Stand sind alle gleich!
> Freies Reich! Alles gleich! heissa juchhe![31]

The *Turner* movement, in other words, was intended to function as a public spectacle, as a festival that would constitute the nation as a fraternity of equals.[32] Franz Schnabel describes the exercises of the *Turner* as follows:

> From all occupations, they stood here in rank and file, addressed each other as "Du," wore the same clothes, performed the same gymnastic exercises, and raved in the same way about *Volk* and fatherland. The community of the *Turner* was also supposed to be the germ-cell of the *Volksgemeinschaft*.

Jahn, declares Schnabel, would have "happily put the entire *Volk* in the *Turner* uniform [*Turntracht*] and urged them to perform exercises."[33]

Both Görres's petition campaign and Jahn's gymnastics movement represented attempts to define a new public space. Their efforts illustrate some of the complexities and ambiguities that attended the birth of popular politics during the Napoleonic era. Neither demanded the abolition of the monarchy nor the creation of a republic. Moreover, though both men offered a more egalitarian vision of the nation than was evident in the aristocratic rhetoric discussed in Chapter 4, neither called for the outright elimination of the traditional corporate social order. In this respect, the nomadic Jahn was more radical than Görres, who had spent much of his life as a pillar of the Koblenz bourgeoisie and who demanded the restoration of the "ancient truly German constitution" in the Rhenish provinces. Even Jahn's egalitarianism, however, was tempered by deference to the aristocracy and Germany's royal houses; estates, he declared, were "natural divisions of the *Volk*."[34] In the *Burschenschaft* movement initiated by Jahn, a continuing dispute existed over whether the future constitution should build on old German institutions or whether it should begin from new egalitarian premises, and, in this argument, the "olds" held the upper hand.[35]

Thus, even for those at the vanguard of the popular nationalist movement in Germany during the 1810s, the notion of full social equality remained beyond the pale of discussion. Nonetheless, their ideas represented a serious potential threat to the legitimacy of existing social hierarchies. Jahn's gymnastics movement, by eliminating distinctions in costume and forms of polite address, inevitably called into question the system of social ranks symbolized by these distinctions. Likewise, by insisting that the nation was Germany, rather than Prussia, and by beginning to mobilize mass movements of self-identified "Germans," Görres and Jahn began to forge new spaces for political activism independent of the Prussian monarchy. Unlike the aristocratic activism of the Napoleonic era, which had been expressed through channels formally established by the monarchy, these new bourgeois movements claimed to have emerged spontaneously from the nation itself. Consequently, many civil servants and aristocrats, along with the king, soon would come to view the new popular nationalism as a dire threat to all existing social and political hierarchies.

Harmony: The Reconciliation of King and People

The popular nationalists' arguments about the proper foundations of sovereign authority, like their notions about traditional social hierarchies, were highly ambivalent. On the one hand, few of these activists explicitly challenged royal authority; indeed, they generally assumed that Germany would retain monarchical rule. In all of the German states, only Karl Follen, a university lecturer and *Burschenschaft* leader in Jena, called for the overthrow of Germany's kings and the founding of a unified "ethical republic," and he never attracted more than two dozen followers. Indeed, even Follen's constitutional plan called for the election of a king by the governing council of the realm.[36]

Popular nationalism may be viewed as *potentially* democratic in nature, however, because these activists envisioned an entirely new relationship between the monarch and the people. This shifting attitude toward monarchical authority is illustrated by the writings of Ernst Moritz Arndt (1769–1860), whose early works inspired Jahn's discovery of German nationalism. During the French occupation, Arndt wrote numerous patriotic pamphlets and songs; he was also the author of several longer treatises, including the four-volume *Geist der Zeit*, which celebrated the rise of national consciousness in Germany. In July 1815, Arndt declared that "princes are there only as servants and officials of the *Volk*, and they must cease to exist as soon as the *Volk* does not need them anymore, or as soon as they actually become the ruin of the *Volk*."[37] Arndt's own political program was tamer than his rhetoric suggests; in Ernst Müsebeck's words, he favored "the foundation of a monarchical-democratic unity under Prussia's leadership."[38] Arndt intended his criticisms not for the idea of monarchy per se but for some of the princes of the *Mittelstaaten*, who he thought were obstructing German unity.

Nonetheless, Arndt's attacks suggested the possibility of a more far-reaching critique of monarchical sovereignty. Lamenting that the words "democrat" and "democracy" had become vilified as "rat poison" as a result of the upheavals of the revolutionary era, Arndt declared that "all states, even those that are not yet democracies, will become from century to century more democratic." In the true sense, he wrote, these words implied only "what the best kings and emperors have always known," namely, that "they are there for the people and that they rule for and with the people. The people are just as holy as the mob is unholy; anyone who wishes for the people to be ruled for and through the people is a democrat."[39] At one level, Arndt's manifesto echoed the words of Hardenberg's Riga Memorandum of 1807. "Democratic principles in a monarchical government," Hardenberg had written, was the appropriate ruling formula "for the present age," but gradually (perhaps by the year 2440, he declared) a true democracy might evolve in Prussia. Arndt, however, also radicalized Hardenberg's formula: he made it abundantly clear that the duty of kings was to do the people's bidding and not vice versa.

Like Arndt, Friedrich Ludwig Jahn argued for a fusion of the principles of monarchical and democratic sovereignty. He eagerly anticipated the day when "the German nation will be unified through wise laws under a powerful monarch." For Jahn, however, the monarch served primarily as an official representative of the sovereignty of the state: "Only one is lord—the state; and the residents of the state are subject only to it." Jahn did not favor simply imposing a unitary state upon the *Volk*. Rather, he argued for a gradual organic fusion of the two through the "cultivation of the *Volk*" (*Volkserziehung*), which he said would "innoculate the ancient race" against "all future epidemics" and "breed a new ennobled *Volk* within the *Volk*." As a result of this *Volkserziehung*, "the citizen [*Bürger*] will feel, think, and act *with* the state, *through* it, *for* it, and *in* it. He will become one with it, and with the *Volk*, in life, passion, and love."[40] Jahn's ideas, as this passage indicates, were "democratic" more in the sense of Rousseau's *volonté générale* than in the sense of modern parliamentary republicanism. In Jahn's view, the *Volk* could

5.2 Procession of the *Turner* at the Wartburg, 18 October 1817. Bildarchiv Preußischer Kulturbesitz, Berlin.

achieve self-determination only through absolute unity. He wanted the *Volk* to live and act as a single organism, pure and strong.

Thus, though the romantic nationalists generally claimed that they favored the principle of monarchical sovereignty, the princes of the German states might be forgiven if they were nervous about the potential implications of these new doctrines. These nationalists all concurred that the *Volk* existed as an organism autonomous from the monarchy and other political institutions; they also insisted that kings were bound to rule for the benefit of the *Volk*. Moreover, while some of these figures lauded Prussia as the vessel of the future nation, they were far more antagonistic toward the leaders of the other German states.

The tensions between the monarchical and democratic tendencies of romantic nationalist thought exploded into full view on 18 and 19 October 1817, when 468 members of *Burschenschaften* from various German universities gathered at the Wartburg, the castle in Eisenach where Luther had translated the Bible, to call for constitutional government and German unification. The date marked not only the fourth anniversary of the victory at Leipzig but also the tricentenary of the Reformation. In keeping with the occasion, the order of the service at the Wartburg was patterned on the Christian liturgy: the festival opened with a hymn (Luther's "Eine feste Burg ist unser Gott") sung around a fire, then came more songs and "patriotic sermons," and the service closed with a prayer of thanksgiving.[41] Jena theology student Heinrich Hermann Riemann, who gave the opening speech at the Wartburg Festival, cited Luther as a national hero, sent by God "out of the dark walls of an Augustine monastery . . . to . . . free the world from the worst of all bondages, that of the spirit." Jakob Friedrich Fries, a philosophy professor at Jena, attended the Wartburg Festival and preached to the students that they must remain "inviolably united" through the "holy chain of friend-ship,"[42] a sentiment echoed by other speakers.

Several of the speakers at the Wartburg framed their political demands in highly inflammatory terms, exciting the wrath of rulers throughout the German states. Riemann's speech alluded to the patriotic spirit displayed at the battle of Leipzig four years earlier:

> Then the German people had high hopes. Now these hopes have all been frustrated. Everything turned out differently than we expected. Many grand and noble dreams that could have happened—that had to happen!—were treated with scorn and derision!

Only one German ruler, Riemann observed, Duke Karl-August of Saxe-Weimar, where the Wartburg was located, had so far kept his promise to establish a constitution. Riemann admonished the other German princes by invoking the memory of Luther: "Thoughts of thee shall give us strength in every struggle and make us able for every sacrifice. Hatred of the righteous and damnation to those who forget in their lowly, dirty selfishness the common good!"[43] Ludwig Rödiger, another student leader from Jena, declared that the princes of the *Mittelstaaten* "shamelessly destroyed" Germany during the Napoleonic era, when its people were "under the iron yoke of the destroyer." Speaking in the name of the veterans of the War of Liberation, Rödiger demanded a greater popular voice in domestic politics:

> Those who are allowed to bleed for the fatherland also have the right to speak about how they can best serve the fatherland in peacetime. . . . For, thank goodness, the time has come when Germans need no longer fear the poison pen of spies and the executioner's axe of tyrants.[44]

Another element of the ceremony at the Wartburg that created particular consternation among the rulers of the German states was a book burning staged at the end of the festival, after most of the students had left. Imitating Luther's public burning of the papal bull "Exsurge Domine" in 1520, the students consecrated to the flames various books they denounced as "un-German"; they also burned three symbols of the military authoritarian state: an Austrian corporal's cane, a uniform from the

5.3 Book burning at the Wartburg Festival, 18 October 1817. Woodcut by F. Hottenroth, 19th century. Bildarchiv Preußischer Kulturbesitz, Berlin.

Prussian Ulanen cavalry, and a pigtail from a Hessian officer's wig.[45] One of the immolated works was Saul Ascher's pamphlet *Die Germanomie*, which criticized the anti–Semitism of the student movement. It was thrown into the fire accompanied by calls of mockery against the Jews. This ritual of book burning, chillingly imitated by later nationalist movements, including the National Socialists, had a biblical foundation in Acts 19:19–20, in which Paul, preaching to the Ephesians, induced practitioners of the magic arts to burn their books publicly, thereby demonstrating the power of the Lord's word. Thus, this event provides a further illustration of how the rhetoric and rituals of the popular nationalists drew on a Christian vocabulary.

Shortly before the close of the festivities at the Wartburg, an argument erupted between two factions of the *Burschenschaft* of Giessen over whether Germany should receive an "old" or a "new" constitution. An account by one of the participants describes the crowd's response to the dispute:

> A cry arose as from *one* soul, *one* voice: "Pardon each other! Forgive each other!" And since they were standing there in doubt of what to do, the leader of the Jena *Burschenschaft* came forth and said: "Listen, brothers! Forget what's past! Let's not inquire here who is right and who is wrong—

but he is wrong, who here follows the voice of discord; he is wrong, who disdains the word of his brothers."

The leader from Jena called on the parties to the controversy to join their hands in friendship, then shouted out to all the assembled students to extend their hands to one another "and promise and swear, in this holy place, to adhere to the *Bund* to the end!" The chronicler continued:

> And then the youths reached out their hands to each other and fell in each other's arms and pressed against each other in inward love. The silence continued—only single words or broken sentences could be heard, being passed softly from soul to soul. "To the future!"—"For now and forever"—"Until death!"—"Never forget this moment!"—"Never! Never!"[46]

Episodes such as these illustrate not only the youthful exuberance and utopian hopes of the celebrants at the Wartburg but also the precariousness of the balance of monarchical and democratic principles in romantic nationalist rhetoric. Even though most of the student activists professed to accept the principle of monarchical sovereignty, their words and deeds emphasized the primacy of the brotherhood of the nation. This balance would prove increasingly difficult to sustain over the course of the decade after the end of the Napoleonic wars.

Unity: The Communion of the German Nation

In public spectacles such as the Wartburg Festival, the nation was made manifest as a fellowship of equals. Yet the activities of figures such as Görres, Jahn, and the *Burschenschaft* leaders, by putting the nation on display through petitions and festivals, inevitably gave rise to the question of how membership in the nation should be determined. Who would be admitted to the fellowship, and what sources of political and social cohesion would bind the nation together? Görres defined Germany in territorial and institutional terms—as the land covered by the "ancient truly German constitution." Other authors offered cultural or racial definitions of the nation. Arndt, whose early works inspired Jahn's discovery of German nationalism, linked national identity to the mobilization of a common spirit. In volume 3 of *Geist der Zeit*, published in 1813, he declared:

> From the North Sea to the Carpathians, from the Baltic to the Alps, from the Vistula to the Schelde, *one* belief, *one* love, *one* spirit, and *one* passion must again bring together the whole German *Volk* in brotherly union.

They must learn to feel how great, powerful, and fortunate their fathers were in obedience to *one* German emperor and *one Reich*, when the many feuds had not yet incited them against one another.

This imagined past bore little relation to the actual historical Holy Roman Empire, which had always been a diverse and fragmented political entity. Nonetheless, Arndt's historical vision provided a powerful model for future efforts at political reform. The German people, he proclaimed, must "no longer [be] Catholics and Protestants, no longer Prussians and Austrians, Saxons and Bavarians, Silesians and Hanoverians." He called on them to "be Germans, be *one*, desire to be *one* through love and faith; and no devil will defeat you."[47]

Like Görres, Arndt invoked the notion of an original state of grace in which Germany was unified both politically and spiritually. He blamed the nation's current fallen condition on "feuds" between different factions of the *Volk*. Divisions had erupted, he argued, both between territorial states and between the Catholic and Protestant confessions. In his view, all Christian Germans belonged to a greater spiritual and political whole. By recognizing their common membership in the German nation, they could reestablish the ancient union. Arndt wrote:

> Like other men I am egoistic and sinful but in my exaltation I am freed at once from all my sins, I am no longer a single suffering individual, I am one with the *Volk* and God. In such a moment any doubts about my life and work vanish.

The "highest form of religion," he maintained, "is to love the fatherland more passionately than laws and princes, fathers and mothers, wives and children."[48]

For Jahn, racial purity defined the nation. In *Deutsches Volkstum*, Jahn defined nationality on the basis of a blend of religious, racial, and cultural elements. Like Arndt, Jahn identified Christianity as a key attribute of German national identity. But Jahn placed far more emphasis than Arndt on the need to recapture Germany's racial purity.[49] "Mixed-breed animals," he wrote, "have no true power of propagation; and just as little do mongrel peoples achieve national [*volkstümliches*] survival." Jahn continued:

> The Spanish proverb "Trust no mule and no mulatto" is quite apt; and the German "neither fish nor fowl" is a warning. The purer the *Volk*, the better; the more mixed, the more it resembles a horde [*je bandenmäßiger*]. . . . The founding day of the universal monarchy will be the final moment of humanity.[50]

As these examples illustrate, romantic nationalist writers concurred that the nation must be a unified community of all Germans—whether that unity derived primarily from territory, laws, moral commitment, language, race, or religion. In large part a movement of young people and social outsiders, it centered around an effort to reconstitute what was imagined to be a lost original community—or, in stronger terms, an original *communion* of believers. Though employing the rhetoric of a return to the past, these activists' logic was thoroughly modern: they insisted on cultural and social uniformity and on the civic equality of all citizens, unlike the multiplicity of hierarchical orders that had characterized the traditional world. It was their very insistence on uniformity that made their quest to identify the true characteristics of the national community so urgently pressing. It is worth emphasizing, however, the fractured and contested nature of these claims about the sources of this communion: there were always numerous strands in the popular nationalists' arguments, rather than one single characteristic vision of the national community. The contested character of German identity may be illustrated by exploring the images of two potential out-groups—Jews and Poles—that met with strikingly different treatment in the popular nationalist rhetoric of this era.

Jews, Poles, and the Limits of National Community

In 1819, a series of anti–Jewish uprisings broke out throughout the German states. These riots, motivated partly by a postwar economic downturn, represented the culmination of a backlash against Jewish emancipation that had been building for several years. Some historians, referring to these incidents, have concluded that anti–Semitism became a dominant "axiomatic" element of nineteenth-century German political culture. In an iconoclastic history of the Holocaust, Daniel Jonah Goldhagen declares: "From the beginning of the nineteenth century, anti–Semitism was ubiquitous in Germany. . . . Jews came to be identified with and symbolic of anything and everything which was deemed awry in German society."[51] This view is an exaggeration. As with other issues, substantial disagreements existed, even among nationalists themselves, over the significance and centrality of religion in defining the national community. Nonetheless, Goldhagen rightly identifies a disturbing tendency of German romantic nationalism. In the aftermath of the Napoleonic era, a number of prominent German intellectuals articulated anti–Semitic ideas that anticipated subsequent Nazi racial doctrine. This new political anti–Semitism was qualitatively different from traditional anti–Jewish thought of the premodern era. Nationalists' arguments about the need for religious purity should be understood as one disturbing dimension of a larger project of "imagining the nation" that took place in the German states during the early nineteenth century.

During the Napoleonic era, the German states of the Confederation of the Rhine had adopted the Code Napoléon, thus granting for the first time full civic equality to Jews. In 1812, Prussia had implemented a more limited edict that eliminated most of the social and economic restrictions on Prussian Jews, though it still denied them active political rights and excluded them from government service.[52] This legislation was consistent with the broader spirit of Hardenberg's reform program, which rejected the traditional legal distinctions between estates, favoring a social order based on equality of citizens before the law. In his Riga Memorandum, Hardenberg had argued that the "only effective means to improve" the Jews was "the appropriate instruction of their children and their participation in freedom of trade and civic burdens."[53]

The immediate impulse for the Prussian Emancipation Edict, however, came not from Hardenberg but from the progressive minister Friedrich Leopold von Schrötter. In the autumn of 1808, Schrötter asked the *Kriminalrat* Brand, the legal adviser for the city of Königsberg, if he knew of a means "to slay [the Jews] all at once, though of course without bloodshed." Brand replied that he was "in possession of an effective method of slaying not the Jews, but Judaism." Brand proceeded to draft a law that mandated "equal rights and equal duties" for Jews living in Prussia, which became the basis for the edict of 1812.[54]

The use of this astonishingly bloody language to describe a liberal piece of legislation highlights one of the central dilemmas of the Prussian reform movement. As the above exchange illustrates, both Schrötter and Brand found the juridical distinctions between Jews and other Prussian subjects intolerable. In order to forge a unitary Prussian state, they believed, all citizens must have the same legal status. For many centuries, Jews had lived under tight restrictions in most European countries: governments imposed limitations on Jews' choice of occupation and place of residence and subjected them to special taxes. In the particularistic social structure of the premodern period, however, Jews had constituted only one of many individual corporate groups, each of which possessed its own unique juridical and social status. As non–Christians, Jewish residents had long been attacked as a threat to the religious integrity of the realm, but their special system of laws had not been considered a social or political "problem," because *all* social groups were differentiated on the basis of their particular legal status.[55]

At the end of the eighteenth century, with the emergence of the ideas of the unitary state and the politically unified nation, this way of thinking began to change. Christian Wilhelm von Dohm's 1781 treatise, *On the Civic Improvement of the Jews*, anticipated subsequent arguments for Jewish emancipation. Dohm declared that centuries of oppression had rendered the Jews "morally corrupt"; the abolition of these oppressive conditions would facilitate the *Bildung* of the Jews, enabling them to participate in society as full equals.[56] In proposing to "slay Judaism," Brand was building on Dohm's logic: he emphasized the need to eradicate the juridical distinctions that inhibited the formation of a common public spirit among the citizenry.

In France during the revolution, the question of Jewish rights had been decided with the stroke of a pen in September 1791 with the passage of a decree securing full civic equality for Jews. Under the terms of this decree, Jews were entitled to active citizenship upon swearing a "civic oath" and renouncing the "privileges and exceptions" that had previously been granted to members of autonomous Jewish communities in France.[57] This unambivalent approach was consistent with the radical spirit of the French Revolution as a whole, in which virtually the entire fabric of feudalism was abolished on the night of 4 August 1789, and aristocratic titles were legally eradicated by decree in June 1790. The Prussian reform movement, by contrast, followed a more gradualist approach. For example, rather than abolishing the aristocracy, the reformers sought to transform it from an egotistical into a public-spirited class. The adoption of this incrementalist strategy in the sphere of religious policy ensured that the question of Jews' legal and social status would become a long-running controversy in nineteenth-century Prussia. Dissatisfied with Hardenberg's compromises, purists argued that a true unity of the nation could only be attained by establishing full equality of conditions among the citizenry. Some argued that the "Jewish problem" could be solved by assimilation (i.e., by abolishing the differences between Jews and Christians); others claimed that only the elimination of the Jews could make the nation pure.

After the end of the Napoleonic wars, chillingly anti–Jewish rhetoric appeared in the German press, some of it penned by "respectable" authors. In 1815, Christian Friedrich Rühs, a professor of history at the newly founded University of Berlin, who later became the official historian of the Prussian state, published a tract entitled *The Demands of the Jews for German Citizenship*. Rühs rejected Jewish claims to become German citizens, maintaining that Jews constituted a separate nation of their own by virtue of their system of law, which was both religious and political. Rühs viewed conversion to Christianity as the sole means of integrating Jews into the state. Jews who refused to convert, he argued, should be treated only as a "tolerated people," and they should be excluded from public offices, the army, guilds, and corporations. Rühs also proposed that Jews be required to wear a yellow badge, so that Germans could recognize immediately the "Hebrew enemy."[58]

Jakob Friedrich Fries, one of Germany's leading Kantians and a professor of philosophy at the University of Jena, published an even more virulent attack on Judaism the following year, in the form of a review of Rühs's tract. Fries called the Jews "junk dealers and pillagers of the *Volk*"; he labeled Judaism a "people's disease" (*Völkerkrankheit*) and a "plague." Fries wrote: "We declare war *not on the Jews*, our brothers, but rather on Jewry [*Judenschaft*]." Fries thus drew a distinction between individual Jews, against whom he claimed to harbor no animus, and the collectivity of Jews as a corporatively constituted institution. Possessing their own "theocratic state constitution," the Jews could be "*subjects* of our government" but never "*citizens* in our *Volk*." Indeed, Jews "form not just a *Volk*, they also form a *state*."[59]

Not only did the Jews form "a separate nation," according to Fries, they were also "a political association" and a "religious party," which possessed a "strictly aristocratic constitution" that stemmed from the power of the rabbis. Motivated by "caste spirit," their activities had a "terribly demoralizing power" on the entire *Volk*. It was of utmost importance, concluded Fries, "that this caste be exterminated root and branch, as it is manifestly the most dangerous of all the secret and public political societies and states within the state."[60] To this end, he argued for the prohibition of Jewish immigration into Germany and the encouragement of Jews' emigration, as well as for further restrictions on Jewish marriages. Jews should be banned from living in the countryside, wrote Fries, "because their influence is much too quickly pernicious there"; they should be permitted to live only in towns, under restricted conditions. Jews, he maintained, should also be required to send their children to Christian schools.[61] Fries's pamphlet was read aloud in beerhouses after its publication in 1816, and its ideas even provoked a response from Hegel, who criticized the "brew and stew" of Fries's German philosophy.[62]

Though political anti–Semitism became widespread in early nineteenth-century Germany, it was far from ubiquitous. A few examples will serve to illustrate the complexity of the religious issue in the German states during this period. In 1816, two proconstitutional journals in the Rhineland, the *Hermann* and the *Westfälische Anzeiger*, defended Jews against the attacks by Rühs and Fries. Arnold Mallinckrodt, the editor of the *Westfälische Anzeiger*, declared: "The struggle against the Jews is a truly peculiar spectacle of our convulsive time," and he argued that Jews should be granted the same legal rights as Christians.[63] Other authors had no love for Judaism but all the same criticized the virulent spirit of the student movement. In 1817, for example, historian Karl Adolf Menzel of Breslau published a tract chastising Jahn and his associates for their "cannibalistic war songs" and for their "un–German" egalitarianism, which threatened to annihilate the existing social order. "All this," he concluded, "is not Christian and German, but pagan and Jewish, Jewish in the worst sense of the word, in spite of the haughtiness with which you look down from your German superiority upon Jews and Judaism."[64] Menzel attacked the nationalists' anti–Semitic agitation as a symptom of their troubling egalitarianism, which sought to abolish all distinctions in the social order.

Other figures, however, took precisely the opposite tack, criticizing anti–Jewish sentiment as an obstacle to achieving a truly rational egalitarian order. In 1817, the young scholar Friedrich Wilhelm Carové (1789–1852), Hegel's assistant in Berlin and one of the early leaders of the *Burschenschaft* movement, wrote a plan for transforming the *Burschenschaft* into a truly universal community that would facilitate the education of its members as free and autonomous individuals. Carové argued that prohibitions on the membership of Jews and foreigners in German student organizations prevented them from becoming associations of rational beings. In the words of one of Carové's allies, "the main goal of the *Burschenschaft* should be considered patriotic [*vaterländische*] education, but not German patriotic education; instead, for each according to his own way."[65] Carové's views won him no love from his former compatriots in the student organization: he was attacked as a betrayer of the nationalist cause, and his program was easily defeated at the *Burschenschaft* congress in Jena in the autumn of 1818.[66]

One final example illustrating the complexity of this issue may be found in the pamphlets of Saul Ascher (1767–1822), a Jewish publicist, who argued against the extremes of anti–Semitism. In *Die Germanomie*, conceived in part as a response to Rühs's diatribe against Jewish citizenship, Ascher denied that Germany possessed or should seek to attain "an original state, an original *Volk*, and an original language." Ascher argued that the division of humans into "isolated nations" reflected the "lower stage of formation in which humans formerly found themselves." In the nineteenth century, he contended, a new cosmopolitan identity was rendering obsolete the more primitive divisions of humanity into races and nations:

We have, thank heaven!, come so far that we do not divide humans into tribes and races and deduce dissimilarities within the human race from territorial distinctions. From a legal perspective, the human race is now conceived in its full magnitude by the name *Humanity* . . . Gradually, in all regions of the world, every human individual will be assured an equal latitude for the exercise of his energies.[67]

In this manner, Ascher sought to refute religious bigotry with radiant optimism about the potential for universal enlightenment and human progress.

This brief survey of literature on the "Jewish question" in the early nineteenth century suggests two conclusions about the nature of romantic nationalism. First, nationalist anti–Semitism was both more extreme and different in character from earlier anti–Jewish thought. The new nationalist theory held that Germany must be unified not only religiously but also socially and politically. This new totalizing vision, which insisted on the cultural and social homogeneity of the nation, encouraged the formation of a new view of Judaism. No longer were Jews simply "a quasi-autonomous estate on the margins of society"; now they were seen as a threat to the very integrity of the nation.[68] Second, for many romantic nationalists, religious purity served as a vital source of cultural and social cohesion for the new community. It is striking that Menzel, a defender of traditional hierarchies, chastised the nationalists for their anti–Semitic ardor, viewing it as gratuitous and irrational. More egalitarian authors, such as Jahn and Fries, on the other hand, argued that the nation could achieve spiritual and political unity only through forging a specifically Protestant identity. Follen, the leader of the most radically democratic faction in the *Burschenschaft*, was also one of the most fanatical opponents of Jewish inclusion, arguing that "religious and national [*volksthümliches*] struggle are profoundly unified."[69] For most members of the *Burschenschaft*, Carové's arid rationalism (not to mention Ascher's cosmopolitan ideals) appeared insufficient for nurturing the community that they craved.

While popular nationalists of the 1810s focused intense scrutiny on the relationship between German and Jewish identity, they hardly even alluded to the status of the ethnic Poles living within Prussia's boundaries. Prussia's Polish minority was rarely, if ever, mentioned in early nationalist tracts, such as Jahn's *Deutsches Volkstum*, Arndt's *Geist der Zeit*, and Görres's *Teutschland und die Revolution*. Another telling example of this omission was found in a report on the Wartburg Festival composed in

1817 by the nationalist professor Lorenz Oken and published in the Weimar journal *Isis*. Along with a list of the books burned at the festival,
Oken provided illustrations, including a goose, a donkey, a caricature of
a Jew's head with a hooked nose, and a Star of David.[70] While employing
these anti–Semitic images, Oken remained silent on the status of Poles.
In addressing the students at the Wartburg, he described them as a "universal" group, who would be entitled to live and work in any of the
German states. At the same time, he insisted:

> This universality does not extend to the entire world. At the university,
> you do not learn French, English, Spanish, Russian, Turkish ethics and
> science. You can become, and desire to become, . . . nothing other than
> educated *Germans*, who are all equal, and who are all free to do business
> everywhere.[71]

In this passage, Oken demarcated Germans from Spaniards, Russians,
Turks, and so forth; but he apparently did not think to distinguish Germans from Poles.

The relative absence of the "Polish question" from early popular nationalist discourse is surprising. Prussia had long contained a substantial
Polish minority, and figures such as Frederick the Great had expressed
blatantly anti–Polish sentiments long before the Napoleonic era. After
the founding of the German Empire in 1871, the policy toward Poles
would become a question of burning concern for German nationalists.[72]
During the Napoleonic era, the bureaucratic reformers sometimes referred
to Prussia's Polish minority as an ethnic nation in its own right: Stein,
for example, declared in his Nassau Memorandum: "The Polish nation
. . . possesses a noble pride, energy, courage, nobility, and willingness to
sacrifice itself for fatherland and freedom." Similarly, in a memorandum
of March 1807, Altenstein lauded the Poles' "national pride" and proposed that the Polish gentry participate in Prussia's local and central
administration.[73]

Yet this issue was a decidedly subordinate theme in German popular
nationalist literature at least until 1830, the year in which a popular
uprising in Russia's Polish territories called new attention to this region.
Indeed, during the 1830s and 1840s, many German nationalists supported the cause of Polish unification. At the German national festival
in Hambach in 1832, for example, speaker Johann Georg August Wirth
demanded "freedom, enlightenment, nationality, and popular sovereignty [*Volkshoheit*]" not only for Germans but also for the "brother
peoples" of Poland, Hungary, Italy, and Spain.[74] Likewise, in the Frankfurt National Assembly of 1848, the radical delegate Arnold Ruge de-

picted Poles as the "element of freedom in the Slavic peoples," and he called for the "reestablishment of a free and independent Poland."[75]

The Revolution of 1848, however, marked a turning point in the relations between the German and Polish nationalist movements. During the initial uprising in March of that year, revolutionary leaders in Berlin freed several leaders of the Polish independence movement from a Moabit prison and led them in a triumphal parade through the city. In a cabinet order of 24 March 1848, King Frederick William IV promised a "national reorganization" of the grand duchy of Posen, whose population was of mixed German and Polish ethnicity. Yet, over the next few months, most of the revolutionaries in the German states took a less generous stance toward the Polish national movement, and "friends of Poland" like Ruge found themselves in a distinct minority. In July 1848, the Frankfurt National Assembly rejected a resolution calling for the reestablishment of an independent Polish state, and it voted by a 342–31 majority to absorb the predominantly German-speaking territories of Posen into the German Confederation.[76] This new harsher line toward Polish independence foreshadowed the rise of anti–Slavic sentiment in Germany during the late nineteenth century.

Two provisional explanations may be advanced for the early popular nationalists' lack of concern for Poland. First, during the economic depression that struck the German states in the aftermath of the Napoleonic wars, Jews may have served more easily as scapegoats than Poles. Prussia's Polish population was overwhelmingly agrarian: it consisted largely of peasants and aristocrats living on the land. Thus, direct social contacts between ethnic Poles and ethnic Germans would have been limited in most regions. Throughout the German states, however, Jews lived mainly in urban areas, and historically, they had been legally restricted to occupations in trade and finance. The Jewish economic elite, who were financiers and large merchants, attracted resentment from Christian debtors and competitors. Poor Jewish peddlers, who traveled from village to village, often generated hostility from local artisans.[77] Thus, early popular nationalism in Germany may have been more anti–Semitic than anti–Polish in part because of the higher degree of economic friction between Germans and Jews than between Germans and Poles.

A second likely reason why the early nationalists attacked Jews more than Poles is that these activists drew their inspiration from a religious rather than a racial model of thought. Only during the latter half of the nineteenth century did racialist theories of national identity become highly developed in Europe, making it easier to conceive of a permanent and unalterable opposition between Germans and Poles.[78] At the beginning of the nineteenth century, this ethnic boundary may still have appeared more permeable and less absolute than it became in subsequent generations. In contrast, many romantic nationalists viewed Christianity as the keystone of German national identity, and they labored vigilantly to defend this religious frontier.

Conclusion: The Clash of Symbolic Economies

This chapter has explored the political discourses and practices of bourgeois popular activists in the German states during and immediately after the Napoleonic era. Unlike the enlightened nationalists within the Prussian civil service, who built on eighteenth-century theories of rational administration, these activists drew their inspiration partly from the culture of romanticism and from pietist spirituality. Moreover, unlike the bureaucratic reformers, whose primary goal in mobilizing the nation was to enhance the authority of the state, these romantic nationalists viewed the nation as an object of quasi-religious devotion, a communion of souls that accorded its citizens an earthly link to the eternal.

For all of the differences between these two strands of nationalism, they proved to be mutually reinforcing in certain critical respects. Like the Stein-Hardenberg party, the romantics stressed the ideally harmonious and unitary character of the national community. Furthermore, these popular activists generally favored monarchical sovereignty, at least in principle. They contended that many of the smaller German states would need to be absorbed by Prussia, but most argued that the Prussian monarch himself should remain in power. Virtually all of these figures called for cooperation between the nation and its king; outright republicanism was not yet a serious option (except for Karl Follen and his tiny band of followers).

Thus, an uneasy balance existed between the enlightened nationalism of Prussian officialdom and the romantic nationalism of the bourgeois popular activists. Several findings of my analysis are summarized in table 5.1.

As this table indicates, important ambivalences existed within German bourgeois nationalist discourse during this era. For example, these figures were far from united in demanding the abolition of aristocratic privilege. Most of them agreed on the desirability of "equality before the law." Nonetheless, many popular nationalists also hoped to preserve elements of the old corporate order. Even as enthusiastic a leveler as Friedrich Ludwig Jahn supported the preservation of some remnants of the traditional estates, and the question of whether economic classes should be

5.1 The Concept "Nation" in Romantic Nationalist Discourse, c. 1815

Consensual features	Contested features
The nation is a harmonious community possessing one unified interest and will.	Can Jews be citizens?
The nation is Germany not Prussia.	
The nation must possess one contiguous territory.	
The nation must be linguistically and culturally unified.	
All citizens must be equal before the law.	Must the old corporate bodies (e.g., the aristocracy) be abolished?
The nation's interest is compatible with the Prussian king's interest.	What is the relationship between the other German states and the nation?

abolished was not yet an issue open to debate. Though all of the popular nationalists agreed on the need for German unification, there was little consensus about the primary characteristics that defined that unity. Some figures, such as Görres, defined "Germany" in primarily institutional and cultural terms; others, such as Jahn, emphasized race and ethnicity. Religion served as an important marker of national identity, but not everyone agreed that Jews must be excluded from the nation. The question of the relationship between Protestants and Catholics in the national community (which would become so central in the *Kulturkampf* later in the century) was as yet little discussed. Nor did these activists devote much attention to the status of ethnic Poles in the German nation. In their writings, female citizenship remained out of the question.

Bourgeois popular nationalism was marked by contention over the proper mix of new and old institutions and over the proper relationship between the people and their princes. On these issues, the arguments offered by the popular nationalists often resembled those of reform-minded ministers, such as Stein and Hardenberg. In one vital respect, however, the romantic nationalists both moved beyond and challenged the conceptions of the reform party within the Prussian ministry. The bureaucratic reformers always envisioned the nation as existing in tandem with and in support of state institutions. The romantic nationalists, by contrast, labored to forge a national community as an organic entity autonomous from the state. Since they viewed the people as the highest court of appeal, they saw no need for official sanction for launching a petition drive or for holding a festival on behalf of national unity. Thus, while not explicitly antimonarchical, the popular nationalist movement played an important role in politicizing the public sphere in Prussia and the other German states during the early nineteenth century and, consequently, in challenging the symbolic centrality of the king and his ministers in the political process. The next chapter traces the Prussian government's response to this challenge during the initial years after the Vienna Congress.

Six

A NATION OF REVOLUTIONARIES

In March 1819, alarmed by the spread of nationalist activism among young people, the Prussian government closed Jahn's gymnastics ground on the Hasenheide in Berlin. The following evening, about fifty youths gathered in front of Jahn's house. Lighting two torches, they proceeded to sing Luther's "Eine feste Burg" and then cheered Jahn three times with a *Lebehoch*. Jahn, it turned out, was not at home, so the group quietly withdrew. Two days later, Berlin's police inspector filed a report on this incident with Hardenberg. Over the next month, the inspector identified and interrogated several of the participants, at least one of whom professed not to know that "political demonstrations" had been prohibited in Prussia since 1815.[1]

One of the youths who had joined in saluting Jahn was a twenty-four-year-old army captain by the name of Hans Rudolph von Plehwe. At the beginning of April, Plehwe came under additional suspicion when he insulted a Berlin innkeeper, who had condemned the assassination of the conservative publicist and playwright August von Kotzebue. Consequently, Plehwe was arrested, and he was denied the right to have visitors in jail.[2] During his imprisonment, the young captain wrote a series of bizarre letters both to the king's adjutant and to the king himself. Plehwe addressed both the adjutant and the king with the familiar *Du*, and his letters intertwined German and Christian images in a most unsettling way. One of Plehwe's letters to Frederick William III read as follows:

My King and Lord, God's anointed: Take me to thee [*Nimm mich zu dir*]: I have seen thee pray and kneel down among thy *Volk*, which made my heart so soft that I cannot leave thee in eternity. Thou dost an injustice before God and men; of such terrible sins there is nothing to say—that is why thy heart is so heavy. Let me be with thee in a German frock; then thou wilt tell if I am a fool: as thou desirest, for worldly wisdom is foolishness to God. Dear King and Lord, take me to thee—I want to tell thee everything: I have received it all from Christ, who is the savior of us both, before whom we are brothers; but on earth I want to be thy servant [*Knecht*] and son. Take me on, for it is high time. God in high heaven has received thy tears and thy prayer for thy *Volk*; hear my true voice—thou wilt lead thy *Volk* to the Lord.

I will pray for thee; I cannot do more. Christ, thou Lamb of God, thou who carriest the sins of the world, forgive us ours. Christ, thou Lamb of God, thou who carriest the sins of the world, give us thy peace of the Lord.

Ruler, rule! Conqueror, conquer! King, use thy regiment, lead thy realm to war, make an end to slavery.[3]

The letter was signed, "Thy servant and son, Hans Rudolf [sic] Plehwe."

Having read Plehwe's letters, Hardenberg called him a "crazy religious fanatic" who was "ripe for the madhouse" and recommended that he be dismissed from the army.[4] The chancellor's judgment of Plehwe's mental state may well have been justified, but the young army officer's ravings reflected the logic of romantic nationalism. To call the king *Du* was outrageous, yet this pronominal usage only extended the practice of the *Turner* and the *Burschenschaftler*, who used the familiar form of address toward members of all estates. Plehwe's language also echoed the enthusiastic spirituality of the pietists, who proclaimed the equality of all believers and who emphasized the existence of a direct bond between the individual Christian and God. Some of the letter's passages invoked the Bible: for example, the claim that "worldly wisdom is foolishness to God" is a paraphrase of I Corinthians 1:20. A particularly fascinating aspect of the letter was its portrayal of the triangular relationship between the king, his subjects (as embodied by Plehwe), and God. Plehwe wrote that on earth, he was the king's "servant and son," but before Christ they were both brothers. He described the king as the leader of the *Volk* ("Ruler, rule! . . . King, use thy regiment, lead thy realm to war"), but he also said that the king had done "an injustice before God and men"—thus, in effect, placing the people on the same level as God. Indeed, Plehwe's use of the pronoun *Du* was itself ambiguous: in German one employs this pronominal form not only with one's familiars but also when addressing God. It was thus unclear whether Plehwe was portraying the king as his own equal or as God's representative on earth ("My King and Lord, God's anointed").

In Plehwe's letter, every hierarchical relationship (whether political, social, or religious) was in flux. Plehwe was both the king's servant and his brother. The king was both the leader of the *Volk* and a sinner "before God and men." Moreover, though the king was "God's anointed," Plehwe portrayed himself as a prophet who must convey Christ's word to the king. The degree of confusion in Plehwe's letter was extreme; yet this tendency to confuse or obscure fundamental political and social relationships appeared in many of the writings by the romantic nationalists. Political authority depends upon political legitimacy, and, in the years after 1815, German leaders came to fear that the moral foundations of monarchical rule might crumble under the assault of the new nationalist ideas.

At the conclusion of the Napoleonic wars, deep ambivalences and ambiguities existed within the concept "nation." For example, while the romantic nationalists insisted that the nation was Germany, not Prussia, both the bureaucratic and the aristocratic nationalists generally avoided committing themselves one way or the other on this issue.[5] While the aristocratic nationalists insisted that the Prussian nobility preserve its privileged status in the new nation, both the bureaucratic and the romantic nationalists were divided over the proper balance of egalitarian and hierarchical social principles. Indeed, many bourgeois popular nationalists, despite their reputation as radical egalitarians, favored the preservation of the aristocracy and other traditional corporate elites. Finally, the nature of sovereign authority within the nation remained ill-defined. On the one hand, nearly all participants in Prussian politics agreed that the nation was an ideally harmonious and unified political community, and virtually no one had yet developed a systematic critique of monarchical sovereignty. On the other hand, both the aristocratic and the romantic nationalists were advancing claims about their political rights that proved troubling to Prussia's leading civil servants and to King Frederick William III.

The present chapter, which focuses mainly on the rhetoric of a small group of leading civil servants and aristocrats who were influential advisers to Frederick William III, has two objectives. First, it examines the crystallization of the concept "nation" during the years immediately following Napoleon's final defeat in 1815, analyzing how the range of ambiguity within this concept narrowed in this period. In particular, it examines why two definitions of this concept that had been employed during the Napoleonic era—the "Prussian nation" and the hierarchical "nation of aristocrats"—began to disappear from use. Second, this chapter analyzes how certain consensual features of the concept "nation" shaped Prussian political culture during this era.

Despite the many differences among civil servants, aristocrats, and bourgeois popular activists, these groups all concurred about the ideally harmonious and unanimous character of the national will. Thus, the volatile internal conflicts of the years after 1815 proved highly troubling to Prussia's political elite. Some figures interpreted this turbulence as merely a temporary setback on the path to a future utopian order; others responded more pessimistically, rejecting the ideal of a politically active nation altogether. Neither side, however, acknowledged that intense domestic disputes might be an acceptable feature of a viable constitutional government.

Drawing on previously unpublished documents, I show how these semantic struggles over the concept "nation" influenced King Frederick William III's decision against the adoption of a Prussian constitution. Though historians have often depicted the Prussian king as having capitulated to the forces of an aristocratic "Reaction" after Napoleon's fall, this view is too simplistic. Frederick William III decisively dismissed the possibility of fully restoring Prussia's traditional political and social hierarchies; nonetheless, he came to believe that a politically active nation would inevitably challenge monarchical sovereignty. Ultimately, the king's political imagination proved as powerful as his material interests: he sought to forge a new defensive alliance, along with leading civil servants and aristocrats, to fend off what he perceived as an imminent revolutionary threat.

The Perils of Speaking Nationally in the Post–Napoleonic Era

Napoleon's final defeat in 1815 had profound effects on nationalist discourse in Prussia. The advent of peace, along with the end of the Prussian ministry's aggressive efforts at domestic social reform, diminished the motivation of civil servants and aristocrats alike to appeal for the mobilization of the nation. The Prussian government no longer needed to mobilize the populace in order to fend off the French military threat. Likewise, by 1815, the aristocracy had coopted or defeated some of the Prussian ministry's more onerous reform proposals. For example, many nobles had turned the liberation of the serfs to their own economic advantage, and aristocrats had successfully resisted the implementation of various measures, such as the income tax, the Gendarmerie Edict, and the abolition of patrimonial justice and police powers.[6] Hence, Prussian nobles had less urgent motives than before to demand a national representation that would protect them against the arbitrary power of the state.

While the intensity of bureaucratic nationalist and aristocratic nationalist rhetoric in Prussia generally declined after 1815, the opposite was true of bourgeois romantic nationalism. The patriotic war of 1813–1814 had stimulated popular demands for political liberalization and German national unification. The Vienna Settlement, however, produced no substantial progress toward either of these objectives. Thus, after 1815, bourgeois activists increasingly invoked the authority of the nation for the purpose of compelling the leaders of the German states to fulfill the political desires of their people. During this period, in other words, nationalism became increasingly an oppositional ideology rather than a source of legitimation for the state.

The abandonment of the concept "nation" by Prussia's ruling elites, however, was neither sudden nor complete. In the aftermath of the Napoleonic Wars, the lines of political debate in the German states remained blurred and indistinct. The complexity of the national question was evident at the Vienna Congress of 1814–1815, which brought together the four leaders of the alliance against Napoleon (Britain, Russia, Austria, and Prussia), along with representatives of France, Spain, and the smaller German states. The statesmen who gathered there faced a complex chain of interconnected problems. At the international level, they needed to resolve the territorial claims of various powers and to forge a permanent alliance that would restrain French expansionism in the future; within Central Europe, they needed to forge a viable plan for reorganizing the German states.

The twenty-five-year upheaval following the French Revolution had resulted in a massive reorganization of the German political order. Not only was the Holy Roman Empire abolished in 1806, but many of its smaller constituent states were absorbed during this period by their larger neighbors. Independently governed church lands were secularized, and the so-called imperial (*reichsunmittelbare*) nobility, who had previously owed allegiance to the emperor alone, were subjected to princely authority. In addition, all but a handful of the autonomous *Reichsstädte* were absorbed into the territorial states. Prior to the French Revolution, close to 1,800 distinct political units had existed in German-speaking Europe; in 1815, the German Confederation counted only thirty-nine members.[7]

These massive political changes had produced a volatile situation in Germany, and the representatives of the various German states came to the Vienna Congress with significantly differing agendas. For example, numerous groups that had lost traditional rights during the period of

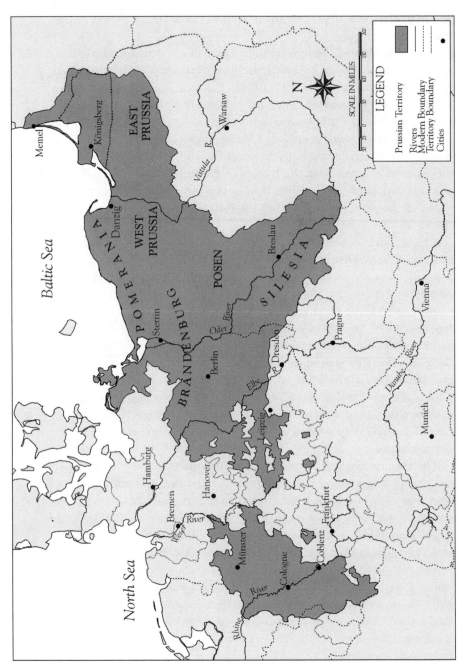

Prussia in 1815

Napoleonic domination, such as the imperial nobility and the Catholic church, sent delegates to Vienna to lobby (generally in vain) for the restoration of their special status. A number of small and middle-sized states in southern and central Germany, in contrast, had substantially increased their territories as a result of the political reorganization under Napoleon. Baden, for example, had quadrupled its holdings since the French Revolution; Bavaria and Württemberg had also significantly expanded. In order to consolidate and legitimate their gains, these states needed to establish their political authority over their new holdings, while at the same time fending off the expansionist urges of larger German powers. These states were thus forced to strike a delicate balance: they had to justify their internal consolidation of political power but to reject demands for more extensive centralization of powers within a greater Germany. In order to anchor their political authority, many of these states enacted constitutions. Nassau, for example, had established a constitution in 1814; Bavaria, Baden, and Württemberg all declared such intentions by January 1815 (though each of these states issued its constitution only several years later).[8] Yet these south German states, which led the movement toward constitutional government, would also be among the first to denounce the popular German nationalism of the postwar era.

Austrian and Prussian objectives at the Vienna Congress were somewhat less clear-cut than those of the smaller states. Prussia had significant territorial ambitions. In addition, Hardenberg wanted to establish a closely knit league of German states, within which Prussia and Austria would play the leading roles. In the initial stages of the Vienna deliberations, Metternich supported Hardenberg's plan, which, in the words of one historian, would have converted the smaller German states to a "double-headed protectorate" under Austrian and Prussian domination.[9] Metternich, however, was more concerned with forging a stable system of European alliances than with increasing Austrian influence over domestic affairs in Germany. By 1815, he had backed off from the goal of achieving a more unified German order, instead applying his energies to strengthening Austrian influence in northern Italy and consolidating the dynastic Habsburg lands. The Vienna Settlement of June 1815 thus created not a *Bundesstaat* but a loosely federated *Staatenbund*, which possessed little authority over its members. Austria's decision against a more united Germany also signaled a turn away from the principle of constitutional government. Article 13 of the Vienna Settlement of 1815 stipulated that "in every federal state there will be a constitution [*landständische Verfassung*]," but this provision was left wide open to interpretation. Within its own territories, Austria created a series of regional diets, but it rejected calls for a central representative institution. For a multiethnic empire bound together by dynastic loyalty, Metternich realized, the idea of a united and politically active nation posed a potentially fatal threat.[10]

As Austria turned its attention away from the German Confederation, however, Prussia was thrust into closer involvement with it. At the Vienna Congress, Russia demanded control over a new Polish protectorate, to be created partly out of lands acquired by Prussia in the 1790s through the second and third Polish partitions. As compensation, Prussia wanted to annex Saxony, which had remained allied to France throughout the war; but instead it was forced to accept the former French satellite state of Westphalia, along with most of the Left Rhine territories that had been annexed by France during the war. This territorial acquisition posed significant problems for Prussia: although the Rhine possessions were among the most prosperous lands in Germany, they were not contiguous with the rest of Prussia's holdings, and they would force the country into the front lines of any future war with France. Additionally, the Rhineland was predominately Catholic, in contrast to the Lutheran majority in the other Prussian provinces.

In seeking to integrate the new Rhenish possessions into the existing state, the Prussian government confronted a difficult challenge. One potential strategy for legitimating its dominion over these lands was for the Prussian government to associate itself with the twin principles of German unity and constitutional rule. Initially, Hardenberg and other leaders found this strategy attractive, partly because for Prussia, the nationalist movement posed a less imminent challenge than for many other German states. Unlike the ethnically splintered Habsburg Empire, Prussia was predominantly German, though it contained a substantial Polish minority; and unlike some of the smaller German states, Prussia was in no danger of being swallowed by an ambitious neighbor in the name of national unity. Moreover, the romantic nationalists themselves displayed more sympathy toward Prussia than toward other members of the German Confederation. Arndt, for example, derided the autonomy of the south German states (he argued that "princes . . . must cease to exist as soon as the *Volk* does not need them anymore") but proclaimed that Prussia's historical mission was to lead a united Germany.[11]

Yet the ideal of national unity also carried dangers. If Prussia advocated the creation of a unified "German" nation, it would endanger its alliances with the other German states and call into question the status of its predominantly Polish possessions in the east. To simply call for the union of the "Prussian" nation, on the other hand, might mean alienating the residents of the new Rhine territories, most of whom had no historical bond to Prussia. For these new subjects, an identity as Germans seemed far more natural. Finally, as Prussia's leaders were acutely aware, the idea of national sovereignty had fatally undermined the French monarchy. They wanted to avoid at all costs a German sequel to the revolution in France.

Prussian statesmen had begun to struggle with these dilemmas during the war. In December 1813, for example, Wilhelm von Humboldt (since 1810 the Prussian ambassador in Vienna) had sent a memorandum to Stein concerning the future German constitution.[12] Humboldt had no doubt that "Germany forms a whole"; all of its constituent states benefited from their association with each other, and Germans would always perceive it to be "one nation, one *Volk*, one state."[13] Both Stein and Hardenberg initially supported this plan for a closely bound confederation under joint Austrian-Prussian leadership, along with constitutional guarantees within the individual German states.[14] In 1815, after Metternich rejected this proposal, Hardenberg briefly flirted with the idea of attempting sole Prussian hegemony in the *Mittelstaaten*, secretly corresponding with a nationalist group under the leadership of Carl Hoffmann.[15] Any open discussions of German unification among the Prussian ruling elite, however, came to an abrupt halt in that year, and Hardenberg restricted his subsequent efforts at institutional reform to the Prussian context.

Even at the level of Prussia alone, the idea of national representation remained highly problematic. During the War of Liberation, King Frederick William III had expressed deep anxiety about the revolutionary potential of a national assembly. The monarch's ambivalence about constitutional rule was shared by royal advisers, including Johann Peter Friedrich Ancillon (1767–1837), the tutor of the crown prince and a former Huguenot pastor, who ultimately became one of Hardenberg's most influential opponents. Ancillon is often dismissed by historians as an "intriguer" or as a leader of the "court camarilla" in Prussia against a constitution.[16] This judgment is not entirely fair: Ancillon consistently favored the eventual adoption of a constitution, but he grasped more clearly than most of his contemporaries the difficulties of sharing sovereignty between the nation and the king. In the flush of victory after the battle of Leipzig of October 1813, Ancillon offered a depiction of the relationship between nation and king that was as ambiguous as Plehwe's. He declared in a letter to the crown prince:

> The nation stands as high as the army, and both of them as high as the King. This forms a glorious unity or trinity [*Dreieinigkeit*], unique in its

form. In this respect it is the ideal of a state: a true republican spirit under
true monarchical forms.[17]

By the spring of 1815, however, he was warning the king of the perils
of national representation and urging him to delay publication of the
edict promising a constitution:

> To desire to change the constitution of Prussia is to desire to impose limits
> and barriers on the existing sovereign authority; or rather, to introduce a
> division of sovereignty . . . , whereas up to the present it has emanated
> from one source alone.[18]

Only after a period of years, when Prussia's financial condition had improved and popular emotions had quieted would it be safe to establish
a national constitution.[19]

The tensions exhibited in Ancillon's writings inhibited the deliberations over a constitution from the outset. In January 1815, with news in
the air of proposed constitutions for Württemberg, Baden, Bavaria, and
Poland, Hardenberg appointed a four-member commission to draft a
Prussian constitution. By April, the commission had agreed on the responsibilities of the representative assembly but remained divided over
whether the assembly would have a deciding or only a consultative vote
and over the extent of the representatives' rights to propose and amend
laws. The commission agreed that the king should maintain control over
the army and foreign affairs, whereas the national representation would
deliberate over the creation of new state debts, the assessment of taxes,
and the passage of laws. One faction of the commission, in agreement
with Frederick William III, favored tightly restricting the assembly's
right to propose and modify legislation; Hardenberg and the other faction
argued for greater flexibility. Likewise, one faction argued along with
the king for a purely consultative vote; Hardenberg now held that the
estates of the realm (*Reichsstände*) should have at least a limited right of
decision over financial questions.[20]

In March, Napoleon had returned triumphantly to Paris after escaping
from the island of Elba; the Prussian king and his ministers had no time
to resolve their differences before mobilizing the country for war. Hardenberg and Frederick William agreed to publish, in place of an immediate constitution, a declaration of the king's intention to grant a constitution—a "second constitutional promise" that elaborated on the first
promise of October 1810. The page-long edict of 22 May 1815 expressed
in concentrated form the contradictions that would later doom the constitutional movement. Hardenberg insisted on opening the proclamation
with the sentence: "A representation of the people [*Repräsentation des
Volkes*] shall be established," but in section 3, the document retreated to

the less provocative term preferred by the king: "assembly of representatives of the land [*Versammlung der Landes-Repräsentanten*]."[21] Section
2 referred to the establishment of provincial assemblies in a manner "consistent with the needs of the time"—leaving untouched the question of
whether the historical claims of the nobles should be recognized or the
estates organized on a new rationalistic basis.[22] Finally, though the edict
specifically identified the assembly's role as one of "consultation" (*Ber-
atung*), this provision satisfied neither Hardenberg, who now preferred a
deciding vote in some matters, nor his opponents, who would come to
doubt that a national representative assembly could be confined within
a consultative role.

As the above discussion illustrates, the idea of a politically active
nation became highly problematic for German statesmen following the
Vienna Congress. In Austria, figures such as Metternich worried that
popular political mobilization had the potential to splinter the Habsburg
Empire along ethnic lines. The leaders of the *Mittelstaaten*, by contrast,
feared the loss of their states' political autonomy through their absorption into a unified Germany. Even Prussian leaders, such as Hardenberg,
who were initially optimistic about harnessing the idea of nationhood in
the service of their political objectives, soon adopted a more cautious
approach. After 1815, Hardenberg severed his ties with Carl Hoffmann's
secret nationalist association; and in his correspondence with King Frederick William III, Hardenberg stopped advocating the creation of a national representation because of the king's aversion to this term. Instead,
the chancellor spoke of establishing an "assembly of representatives of
the land" or a "constitution based on estates" (*landständische Verfassung*),
phrases that Frederick William found less alarming.

Yet these semantic acrobatics by Hardenberg and other proponents of
a constitution failed to resolve two fundamental dilemmas. First, how
could national spirit be fostered without reference to a German nation?
Second, how could the *Volk* participate in politics without challenging
monarchical sovereignty? Within a few years after the Vienna Congress,
one faction (identified by historians as the Reaction) began to argue that
both dilemmas were insoluble, that the ideas of nationhood and popular
representation were inherently incompatible with the existing social and
political order.

Contesting the Boundaries of the Public Sphere

Histories of Prussian politics during the era of the Restoration frequently
allude to the activities of an archconservative court camarilla surrounding Frederick William III, plotting first secretly, then openly, to overturn

the legislative accomplishments of the Stein-Hardenberg party and to block any movement toward political liberalization. Political alignments during this period, however, were more fluid than this conventional interpretation suggests. Leading figures in the supposed camarilla, such as Ancillon and Prince Wittgenstein, Prussia's police minister, were slow to clarify their ideas concerning a constitution in the wake of the Vienna Congress. Indeed, even Metternich flirted with the idea of establishing a constitutional system of government in the Habsburg Empire for a year or two after Napoleon's demise. On the other side of the political spectrum, some figures generally identified as progressives, most notably Hardenberg, embraced the cause of press censorship in 1819 because they were concerned about the destabilizing potential of popular nationalist agitation.[23]

Rather than speaking of a struggle between rigidly defined parties, it is more productive to analyze Restoration politics as motivated by the *common* struggle to reconcile two principles, first, an increasingly politicized public sphere, and second, the sovereign authority of the monarchical state. Those figures who believed in the possibility of such a reconciliation have commonly been identified as progressives, whereas those who came to doubt the wisdom or desirability of such a political balancing act have become known to posterity as reactionaries.

Between 1815 and 1820, a series of events in Prussia and elsewhere in Europe created challenges for those who hoped for a harmonious relationship between a politically active populace and a sovereign monarch. In March 1815, elections were held in Württemberg for a unicameral assembly whose first task was to approve a constitution proposed by the king. These elections produced a fractious assembly composed of members of the old imperial nobility, who demanded the restoration of their traditional rights; lawyers, who wanted greater representation for the towns; and radicals, who were dissatisfied with the powers granted to the parliament. The delegates were united only in their contempt for the king's constitutional proposal, and the Württemberg assembly's rejection of this document created a sobering example for other German monarchs who were also considering establishing constitutions.[24]

The events at the Wartburg Festival in October 1817 and the Koblenz Address of January 1818 presented more alarming challenges to the authority of the Prussian king. In the aftermath of the Wartburg Festival, Frederick William III demanded that his ministry take swift action: "It is an urgent duty," he declared, "to counteract vigorously the highly dangerous and criminal state of mind which has gained ascendancy among the inexperienced youth of the German universities."[25] Even Hardenberg, who had long supported the principle of freedom of the press,[26] wrote to Metternich in December 1817 concerning the need to "suppress the revolutionary tendency . . . and Jacobinism, which is almost everywhere raising its head." Hardenberg argued that "firm measures" were essential in order to "prevent the evil which threatens us," specifically: "A common law for all of Germany is absolutely indispensable in order to put limits to the unbridled license of our gazetteers and journalists, who are protected by the small sovereigns and the city of Bremen."[27]

While Hardenberg and Frederick William III were equally exercised over the outbursts of romantic nationalism at the Wartburg, the two men reacted in strikingly different ways to Görres's Koblenz Address. On 12 January 1818, Hardenberg (who was then traveling in Prussia's new Rhenish provinces to gather opinions about a constitution) met with Görres and other citizens to receive the address, which was signed by more than 3,000 residents of the Rhineland. The petition reminded the king of his constitutional promise and also requested him to use his influence in the *Bundestag* to ensure that *all* German states would receive constitutions, in accordance with Article 13 of the German Articles of Confederation of 1815.[28] On 30 January, Görres followed the petition with the publication of a pamphlet, *The Delivery of the Address of the City Koblenz*, which described his audience with Hardenberg.

Hardenberg, who had remained on cordial terms with Görres despite having banned the *Rheinische Merkur* two years earlier, forwarded the petition to Frederick William III on 19 February, observing: "It is composed in a deferential tone, and contains in itself nothing objectionable." Nonetheless, Hardenberg felt that the very act of collecting so many signatures presented the "appearance of distrust in Your Highness's promise."[29] He drafted a royal response to the petition that acknowledged the right of "immediate access to the throne" in the Prussian monarchy but criticized this "appearance of distrust." The Rhinelanders had no grounds for "the slightest doubt" that the king intended to grant a constitution, Hardenberg wrote, the constitutional deliberations were proceeding at a careful pace rather than in "detrimental and wholly unacceptable precipitance."[30]

Some of the king's advisers in the Prussian court, however, viewed this affair with alarm, and they compared the signers of the Rhenish petitions to the French mob that assembled in front of the Tuileries on 10 August 1792.[31] On 23 February Frederick William III wrote to Hardenberg, pointing to Görres's pamphlet as new evidence of the "utmost pernicious intrigues in the Rhine provinces." The petition was an intolerable affront to royal authority: "It is impossible to permit and condone that one or several individuals collect signatures in such a manner, even if the petition itself is acceptable." The king demanded that Görres be removed from the Rhineland and ordered Hardenberg to reprimand the local administrative authorities for allowing the petition to circulate.[32]

Stung by the royal rebuke, Hardenberg replied to the king on 10 March by defending the right of subjects to petition the monarch: "In the Prussian state, access to the throne is open to every man. . . . The bond of trust between the sovereign and the subjects cannot be drawn tightly enough."[33] Though Hardenberg viewed the Koblenz Address itself as blameless, he now condemned Görres's pamphlet, which he had earlier described with qualified approval.[34] Hardenberg agreed that Görres should be removed from the Rhineland—though he recommended accomplishing this by appointing the activist to a post in the Ministry of Education and Religious Affairs in Berlin—and he proposed publishing an open response to the Görres pamphlet.

Hardenberg's draft of an open letter to Görres dated 10 March 1818 (which was never sent) provides a fascinating glimpse of the uneasy balance between the democratic and monarchical elements in Hardenberg's political thought. He accused Görres of publicizing "dangerous errors concerning the spirit [Geist] and conduct of the Prussian government"; the pamphlet depicted the government "as if it had been and still were in conflict with Prussia's Volk." Nothing could be further from the truth, claimed Hardenberg: the Prussian king had freely granted the constitutional promise of 22 May 1815; the Prussian government had supported the stipulation in the Articles of Confederation of 1815 that all German states would receive a constitution; and a constitutional commission was currently at work. The Rhinelanders had no right to question the sincerity of the royal promise: "It is blasphemy to doubt the Royal word; it is duty to trustingly await its fulfillment."[35] Hardenberg criticized especially harshly Görres's suggestion that a Reaction in Prussia was working against a constitution:

> Everything that you say about a Reaction in Prussia is thoroughly unfounded. One cannot speak of the opinions of particular parties and their activities. The government stands impartially [unpartheyisch] above everyone. It tolerates all, as long as they do not become dangerous and do not overstep the boundaries given to them by the nature of the matter and the welfare of the state. It will know how to restrain and chasten those who overstep these bounds.[36]

Hardenberg depicted the Prussian government as impartial and enlightened, tolerating free expression of opinion—as long as it did not threaten the "welfare of the state." But the government stood ready to "restrain and chasten" any subject who overstepped the proper "boundaries" by expressing "dangerous" ideas.

Frederick William III rejected Hardenberg's distinction between a petition that properly expressed public opinion and a pamphlet that endangered the monarchy. On 21 March the king issued his abrupt response to the residents of Koblenz:

> I will determine when the promise of a constitution [*landständische Verfassung*] shall be fulfilled. The subjects' duty is to await in trust my free resolution, which gave this pledge and which occasioned the corresponding article of the Articles of Confederation. Guided by a view of the whole, I will choose the proper moment for the fulfillment of this promise.[37]

The king's rebuke to the Rhinelanders discouraged his first minister as well. Despite a request from the king of the same day to continue work on a constitution,[38] Hardenberg dropped this project entirely for almost half a year.[39]

The debate between Hardenberg and Frederick William III over the significance of the Koblenz Address reflected a larger controversy about the nature of the Prussian public and its relationship to the state. Frederick William III objected primarily not to the content of the Koblenz Address but to the method of its circulation. Though, as Hardenberg observed, Prussian subjects had traditionally possessed the right of "access to the throne," this access was provided only via officially sanctioned channels, for example, to royally chartered associations of nobles communicating directly to the king. Görres, by openly distributing his petition for signatures, both appealed to and helped constitute a public that existed entirely independently of the royal will. This invocation of a principle of political authority parallel to—but autonomous from—monarchical authority was deeply disturbing to Frederick William III, because he saw the potential for this new public to rival his own claims to sovereignty.

The final event that catalyzed support for stringent censorship measures in the German states was the assassination of August von Kotzebue on 23 March 1819. Kotzebue was a playwright, a reactionary publicist, and a sometime political agent of the Russian government. His assassin, twenty-three-year-old Karl Ludwig Sand, was a theology student and a *Burschenschaftler* who was a fringe member of Karl Follen's radical political group in Jena. Sand, however, apparently acted on his own initiative. Traveling to Kotzebue's home in Mannheim, he found the author in his study and plunged a dagger into his chest, crying: "Here, you traitor to the fatherland!" Outside the house, Sand left a manifesto explaining the bloody deed; and then, thanking God for his "triumph," he stabbed himself with a second dagger. Sand's suicide attempt was unsuccessful: he survived to stand trial and to be executed fourteen months later.[40]

It was not only the assassination itself that alarmed German officials; they were equally shocked by the subsequent attempts of various figures to justify Sand's deed. A week after the murder, Wilhelm de Wette, a professor of theology at the University of Berlin, wrote a letter of consolation to Sand's mother, copies of which were circulated within the student movement. Praising her "excellent son," de Wette conceded that Sand's act was "unlawful and punishable by the worldly magistrate"; nonetheless, he argued that Sand should be judged not by the "error" of his deed but by the purity of his convictions:

> Error is excused and to some extent absolved by steadfastness and sincerity of conviction, and passion is sanctified by the good source from which it flows. I am firmly convinced that both of these were the case with your pious and virtuous son. He was certain of his cause; he believed it was right to do what he did, *and so he did right*.[41]

Because Sand's act was motivated by the "purest inspiration," de Wette considered it a "beautiful sign of the time,"[42] and he was not alone in offering apologies for the assassination of Kotzebue. The contemporary depiction of "Sand the free" portrays this youth as pure and slightly otherworldly, bidding farewell to the beloved mountains and valleys of his homeland as he sets out on the path to Mannheim. He clutches a walking stick in one hand, and a dagger is tucked into his tunic.

When the Prussian Police Ministry intercepted a copy of de Wette's letter, Wittgenstein circulated it to receive expert opinions. Most striking was the response of the court bishop, Rulemann Friedrich Eylert. Eylert was outraged by de Wette's argument, which he said replaced an objective moral standard with a purely subjective one; according to de Wette, "murder is no longer a sin if he who commits it intends well by it." If this teaching were accepted, Eylert warned:

> not only will every moral law be invalidated, but respect *for authority and for legal power* [*gesetzlichen Gewalt*] *will be undermined.* . . . From then on there will be no more talk of what a person *should* do according to the law; everyone can do what *he* wants to, and he has done the best if he has acted "according to his conviction."[43]

The spread of this doctrine would mean that "no regent in his land, no father of a family in his house, will any longer be sure of his life." De Wette's moral teaching, Eylert concluded:

> comes not from heaven but from hell; it is the birth of an overexcited fantasy which obtains its unclean destructive fire from egotism and pas-

6.1 "Sand the free": Karl Sand on his way to Mannheim to assassinate August von Kotzebue (1819). Staatsbibliothek zu Berlin—Preußischer Kulturbesitz—Handschriftenabteilung, YB 14260 kl.

sion. In the turbid intoxication of political-mystical feeling, it fancies itself to be serving God, while becoming a tool of the devil.[44]

Frederick William III, not surprisingly, agreed with Bishop Eylert, and on 30 September 1819, the king summarily dismissed de Wette from his teaching post.[45] But the tale of de Wette also had a tragicomic counterpart, one involving the young philosopher Friedrich Wilhelm Carové. Carové was a former activist in the Heidelberg *Burschenschaft*, who was serving as Hegel's assistant in Berlin. In June 1819, he sent Altenstein (now Prussia's minister of education and religion) a long tract denouncing the assassination of Kotzebue. Carové hoped to impress Altenstein with his learned discourse, but unfortunately, he employed such an esoteric Hegelian style that the minister interpreted it as a *defense* of Sand's act. According to one hostile reviewer of the tract, Carové argued that "only Sand's outer deed was bad; the inner deed, which expressed itself through such an infamous act, was that of a pure youth."[46] Though Carové attacked the "Jacobin swindle of freedom and equality,"[47] he lauded Sand's energy and virtue, and he declared that the murder was a "necessary" object lesson for the development of the German people, because it revealed the corruption that afflicted the German national spirit.[48] Carové offered the following bafflingly ambivalent assessment of the assassination:

> That Kotzebue had not entirely corrupted the popular spirit was demonstrated by the deed itself. That, over the past four years, ideas, language, history, and the youth had become confused, and the popular spirit corrupted, was demonstrated by Sand's deed and the excuses, even the defenses, offered for it.[49]

During the next eleven months, many of Prussia's leading government officials exchanged letters and reports debating how to interpret Carové's pamphlet. Not only did Altenstein and Wittgenstein become involved but so did Wittgenstein's deputy Karl von Kamptz, Justice Minister Kircheisen, Interior Minister Schuckmann, and even Hardenberg. Carové was interrogated by the German censorship commission (*Untersuchungskommission*) in Mainz; his movements were restricted; and even after the matter was finally resolved in his favor, he was banned from any future academic employment in Germany.[50]

Most histories of the early Restoration period in Germany dismiss the notion that the popular nationalist movement posed a potential "revolutionary threat."[51] The entire movement, scholars note, was quite small, and most of its adherents supported not revolution but constitutional monarchy. The *Demagogenverfolgung*, most historians argue, was a plot by aristocratic reactionaries, such as Metternich and Wittgenstein, to turn back the German states' progress toward political liberalization.

This standard interpretation oversimplifies the German political situation in 1819. During the post–Napoleonic period, German leaders were acutely aware of the unpredictability and the potential fury of revolutionary politics. In 1819, Europe had just endured almost three decades of cataclysmic political upheavals. Moreover, these leaders recognized that the French Revolution of 1789 had begun not with demands for a republic but with calls for the "regeneration" of the French state through the establishment of a constitutional monarchy. Many contemporary observers believed that an analogous progression of events was conceivable in the German states as well.

Germany's rulers were disturbed both by the content of the nationalists' attack on the principles of the traditional social and political order and the channels via which the popular nationalists chose to communicate their "subversive" ideas. Jahn's gymnasts, for example, all wore identical uniforms and addressed each other as *Du*, thus obliterating the social distinctions between estates. Moreover, they performed their ex-

ercises as a public spectacle on a gymnastics ground in the heart of
Berlin: Jahn believed that the fortitude and purity of the individual
gymnasts would serve as an example to help strengthen and purify the
national body at large. De Wette, in justifying Kotzebue's assassination,
argued that Sand's act was morally right because it was motivated by
the "purest inspiration." He permitted copies of his letter to Sand's
mother to be circulated within the student movement, thus helping constitute another public space autonomous from state control. Bishop
Eylert's outrage at de Wette's claim was understandable: if the traditional
religious and social moral codes were replaced by a purely subjective
morality, then the privileged status of kings, fathers, and other authority
figures might all be thrown into doubt. In this sense, the nationalist
movement was indeed a potentially subversive social force.

Yet German rulers failed to respond to this potential threat in a nuanced way. Beginning in 1819, they resorted to massive repressive measures, including press censorship, surveillance, interrogations, and imprisonment of suspicious figures. The fear of revolution became
remarkably widespread during that year. Hardenberg wrote to Wittgenstein in April: "I am quite fearful that the malignant spirits here are in
union [with the assassination of Kotzebue]."[52] Wittgenstein, in turn,
warned the king in June of the existence of a secret association of
German students, government officials, military officers, and others

> whose goal is to change the present public constitution both of the whole
> of Germany and of the individual federated states, in part through the
> dissemination of demagogical principles among the youth and the Volk,
> in part through force; and to introduce a new constitution based on unity,
> tribalism [Volksthumlichkeit] and freedom.[53]

Such a dire warning was not unexpected from Wittgenstein; but in the
summer of 1819 Karl vom Stein too became alarmed at the radical threat.
That July, he wrote to Görres, "It is the duty of every moral and religious
man to insist that this accursed sect be punished and that it become the
object of public repugnance."[54] Even General von Gneisenau, who had
himself been accused in 1815 of being a Jacobin and in 1819 was still
under suspicion, defended the necessity of the Karlsbad Decrees after
their publication.[55] In Austria, Metternich began referring to the revolutionary threat as a malignant "cancer," a theme he would sound with
ever-increasing alarm throughout the next thirty years.[56] Yet not all of
Prussia's statesmen supported these policies. Wilhelm von Humboldt opposed the Karlsbad Decrees and was therefore forced out of the government in December 1819.

Motivating all of these fears was one underlying concern: that the newly emerging public sphere had somehow exceeded the ability of the state to control it and was poisoning rather than nurturing rational public discourse. Both the romantic nationalists and their opponents envisioned sovereign authority as ideally unanimous, rather than as shared between competing factions. Thus, neither side saw the possibility of mediating between the monarchical state and the popular activists. The explosion of the traditional boundaries of political expression, both in terms of ideological content and in terms of channels of communication, forced the leaders of Prussia and the other German states to reevaluate the relationship between state authority and the populace at large. One possible approach to this challenge, the tack taken at Karlsbad, was to attempt to tame the public sphere by severely limiting the scope of popular political expression. Censorship, however, offered only a partial solution to the dilemma. German leaders also needed to find new ways of articulating the legitimacy of monarchical sovereignty, taking into account the dramatic social and political transformations that had occurred in Europe over the previous thirty years.

1819: The Year of Indecision

According to the prevailing interpretation of this period of Prussian history, the events of the summer of 1819 marked a decisive defeat for the cause of political reform. Already in January of that year, King Frederick William III had signed a cabinet order (drafted by Altenstein and Hardenberg) that had called for restrictions on the *Turner* movement and the preparation of press censorship legislation.[57] During the last days of July, Frederick William III and Hardenberg met with Metternich in the Bohemian resort town of Teplitz to plan for the Karlsbad Conference, which would begin the following week. In the Teplitz Accord of 1 August 1819, Austria and Prussia agreed to support stringent press censorship measures and controls over the schools and universities throughout the German Confederation. The Karlsbad Decrees subjected all works less than twenty sheets (320 pages) long to censorship prior to their publication.[58] On its part, Prussia pledged that it would adopt a constitution "only after completely settling its internal and financial arrangements." Moreover, Prussia declared that it would "establish no general popular representation [*allgemeine Volksvertretung*]" but rather merely a "central committee of representatives of the land," which would be selected by provincial representative bodies.[59]

Yet the debate over a Prussian constitution remained far from resolved in August 1819. It is true that Metternich had become a strong opponent of constitutional government by this time,[60] but the Austrian chancellor apparently shied from expressing these views openly to Frederick William III.[61] Within the Prussian ministry, virtually no one expressed unequivocal opposition to a constitution as late as the summer of 1819. Hardenberg, who had made little progress toward framing a constitution between 1815 and 1818,[62] took up this cause with great urgency during the final four years of his life. On 3 May 1819, six weeks after the assassination of Kotzebue, Hardenberg sent the king a draft of a constitutional proposal. In a letter to Frederick William that accompanied this plan, Hardenberg argued that the government must act boldly to quell popular unrest rather than remain passively silent. "The yearning for representative constitutions is becoming constantly more vociferous and traverses all estates," wrote Hardenberg: this demand was an expression of the "truly general spirit of the age, brought forth through the occurrences of the last fifty years." The government could not hope to resist the tide of history, rather the "wisdom of a ruler" consisted of the ability "to meet the true *Zeitgeist* halfway with appropriate measures, to steer it for the happiness of his subjects."[63]

Hardenberg's plan called for the establishment of a Prussian General Assembly (*allgemeine Landtagsversammlung*) in conjunction with a network of provincial and county assemblies. The members of the county assemblies were to be elected by the estate owners (*Rittergutsbesitzer*) of each district, whether noble or bourgeois. These county assemblies would choose delegates to the provincial diets (*Provinzialstände*), which would assemble in a single chamber. In addition to the representatives from the county assemblies, the provincial estates would include the former imperial nobles residing in each province—now known as the *Standesherren*—along with a delegate from each town that was large enough to constitute its own county (*Kreis*). The General Assembly, which would convene annually, was to consist of two chambers somewhat analogous to the English Houses of Lords and Commons. The first chamber would include the princes of the royal house; the heads of the families of the former imperial nobility in Prussia (*Häupter der standesherrlichen Familien*), the country's archbishops, bishops, and prelates (both Catholic and Lutheran), and representatives from Prussia's universities. The second chamber would consist of delegates elected by the provincial assemblies, along with some others elected directly by the large towns. Hardenberg's plan left open the question of whether the delegates elected to serve in the General Assembly must themselves be members of the provincial diets.[64]

Though Hardenberg billed his constitutional proposal as a means of securing and enhancing monarchical authority, the plan avoided clarifying the exact nature of the relationship between the king and the General Assembly. On the one hand, Hardenberg included several provisions that restricted the assembly's power. His plan reserved to the king the right to introduce legislative proposals before the assembly; furthermore, no proposal could become law without the royal sanction, along with the approval of both chambers of the assembly. Yet Hardenberg refused to state explicitly whether the assembly should possess a deciding vote over legislation or only a purely consultative one. In his letter of 3 May 1819 to the king, the chancellor declared that it was of "no practical use" to address this issue, rather, he thought that this topic was "one of those things that it is better not to bring up at all." Hardenberg explained his reasoning:

> The monarch will not lightly proceed against an opinion of the estates, even if it were merely consultative; if he finds the case such that it must happen, if he has the courage and strength to proceed against such an opinion, then he will not lack means to do so even against an opinion not explicitly declared to be merely consultative.[65]

In other words, it was unnecessary to determine the status of the assembly's vote because conflicts between king and assembly would be rare and because the king could if necessary prevail against any opposition.

The wording of Hardenberg's letter to the king suggests that in 1819, the Prussian chancellor still remained convinced that a fundamentally cooperative, rather than contestatory, relationship could be forged between the monarch and the national representatives. To the modern observer, Hardenberg's belief in the possibility of conflict-free representative politics may appear baffling—especially in light of Hardenberg's own serious difficulties with the experimental Prussian assemblies established between 1811 and 1815. Yet Prussian political leaders did not initially recognize any fundamental incompatibility between monarchical and parliamentary rule. Indeed, as late as the summer of 1819, even many of the most "reactionary" Prussian political figures still supported the principle of constitutional government.

In May 1819, apparently at the king's request, Police Minister Wittgenstein circulated copies of Hardenberg's constitutional proposal to at least four leading ministers, all of whom have generally been identified by scholars as staunch opponents of a constitution. These ministers included Ancillon, Interior Minister Kaspar Friedrich von Schuckmann, *Kabinettsrat* Daniel Ludwig Albrecht (the king's secretary), and the Prussian foreign minister, Count Albrecht von Bernstorff. Of the four ministers polled by Wittgenstein, only Bernstorff (a Danish noble, who had joined the Prussian ministry only in 1817) unequivocally opposed the adoption of a constitution.[66] The other so-called reactionaries who reviewed Hardenberg's plan all assessed it in more ambivalent terms. Though all of them expressed concern about the danger of ceding too much power (such as budgetary authority) to a representative assembly, each of these men favored the eventual establishment of a constitution. Ancillon, for example, observed that the government had formally promised to establish a constitution. Hence, he argued, it had imposed "duties upon itself that it cannot cast off without losing face, and without exposing itself to the suspicion of [ruling by] fear or the reproach that it has broken its word."[67] Albrecht agreed that, given the "prevailing sentiment of the nation in favor of a constitution [landständische Verfassung]," the king must eventually fulfill his pledge—even though he was not legally bound to do so.[68] Schuckmann declared (with greater optimism than the others): "My opinion on the matter is that consultation with representatives and publicity in the administration, if intelligently conducted, would be truly beneficial."[69]

Frederick William III, who bore the ultimate responsibility for deciding whether Prussia would receive a constitution, vacillated between the impulses of Hardenberg and those of Metternich. In August 1819, Frederick William still hoped to reconcile monarchical sovereignty with at least a small central representative assembly. Then, in January 1820, he urged Hardenberg to accelerate his work on the constitution, demanding that it be completed by the end of the year.[70] In the same month, Frederick William approved Hardenberg's proposal for the State Debt Law, which provided a plan for amortizing the debts that Prussia had accumulated in order to pay indemnities to Napoleon and to fight the War of Liberation. The law also mandated that, henceforth, the Prussian government would be allowed to accumulate new debts "only upon consultation with and coguarantee by the future estates of the realm."[71] By December 1820, however, Frederick William III had come to view the establishment of a central representative assembly as impossible—at least under the then-existing conditions in Prussia.

The Monarchical Principle and the Rejection of Constitutionalism

In order to understand the king's change of heart, it is necessary to examine the concept of the "monarchical principle," an idea that first appeared in Germany around the time of the Karlsbad Conference and that quickly became a nearly universally accepted axiom in German political debate. The term "monarchical principle" originated in France during the deliberations over that country's *charte constitutionelle* of June 1814; it was transmitted to Germany through the writings of French royalists, such as Louis de Bonald and Joseph de Maistre.[72] The term received a formal definition in the Vienna Final Acts of June 1820. Article 57 of this document declared: "The entire state power [*Staatsgewalt*] must remain united in the supreme head of the state. Only in the exercise of certain rights can the sovereign be bound to the participation of the Estates through a *landständische* constitution."[73]

In Germany, the monarchical principle was first articulated in the Bavarian constitutional charter of 1818,[74] and it was further elaborated the following year in an influential essay by Friedrich von Gentz, a renowned political theorist who was Metternich's closest adviser. Circulated at the opening of the Karlsbad Conference in August 1819,[75] Gentz's essay was entitled "Concerning the Difference between Constitutions Based on Estates and Representative Constitutions." The essay presented a new interpretation of Article 13 of the German *Bundesakte* of 1815, in which all German states had pledged to establish constitutions. Gentz argued that German leaders must distinguish between two types of constitutions. The first type, he wrote, were those based on the estates of the country (*landständische Verfassungen*). Under such constitutions, Gentz declared:

> [M]embers or delegates of existing corporate bodies exercise a right of participation in either part or all of a state's legislative process [*Staatsgesetzgebung*], whether through consultation, consent, remonstrance, or through some other constitutionally determined form.

Quite different from this first type were "representative constitutions," where the delegates were expected to "represent not the privilege [*Gerechtsame*] and the interest of individual estates . . . but rather the *entire mass* of the *Volk*."

According to Gentz, the first type of constitution would tend to stabilize and protect the traditional social and political order, whereas the second type would result in rebellion and chaos. *Landständische* constitutions, he argued, existed "on the natural foundation of a well-ordered civil society," which recognized the "*ständische* relationships and *ständische* rights" of particular "classes and corporations." Consequently, they naturally tended to preserve "all *true* positive rights and all *true* freedoms which are possible in the state." Representative constitutions, on the other hand, were founded on "the perverted concept of the *supreme sovereignty* of the *Volk*." Thus, they had the constant tendency to set the phantom of so-called *freedom of the people* (i.e., universal arbitrariness) in the place of civil order and subordination; and to set the *delusion* of *equality of rights*, or (what is no better) universal *equality before the law*, in the place of the ineradicable distinctions between the estates that were established by God Himself.

Not only did representative constitutions undermine the status of the privileged estates, argued Gentz, they also had catastrophic consequences for monarchical authority. Under a *landständische* constitution, the king remained the "supreme legislator" and the "recognized organ of the state." Representative constitutions, in contrast, derived from the principle of "division of powers—an axiom which . . . always and everywhere must lead to the complete destruction of all power, and hence to pure *anarchy*."[76]

Gentz was hardly the first German to express misgivings about popular representation. Figures such as Ancillon had been worried about the results of a constitution since 1815. By November 1818, Metternich had warned Prussian police minister Wittgenstein: "Central representation through deputies of the people means the dissolution of the Prussian state." Metternich had urged that the Prussian king "never go further than the establishment of provincial diets," which he considered less dangerous than a central representative body.[77] Yet Gentz's essay of 1819 played a key role in crystallizing German anticonstitutional theory. This essay was among the first German documents to argue that a unified and politically active *Volk* was inherently incompatible with monarchical sovereignty; it also presented the clearest argument of any so far that monarchical sovereignty depended upon the preservation of aristocratic privileges.

Beginning at the Karlsbad Conference, the monarchical principle quickly gained wide acceptance in German political debate. Many advocates of a constitution, not just opponents like Gentz and Metternich, enlisted this concept in support of their views. Hardenberg, for example, wrote in his constitutional proposal of August 1819: "Everything must be directed toward the proper reinforcement of the monarchical principle, which is completely consistent with the true freedom and security of the individual and his property."[78] Similarly, Humboldt declared in a memorandum of October 1819: "The constitution, which the Prussian state requires, must serve to support and complete the monarchical principle. . . . The force and authority of the government must not be diminished, but rather enhanced, through [the constitution]."[79]

As Heinrich Otto Meisner observes, a distinction must be drawn between the monarchical principle and the theory of unlimited or absolute monarchical sovereignty. The monarchical principle implied "not the reestablishment of an unlimited governing power for the ruler; nor the greatest possible expansion of his authority. Rather it involved the "primarily defensive assertion and demarcation of a clear sacrosanct area of royal rights against the onslaught of the masses."[80] But the nature of these sacrosanct royal prerogatives was a hotly contested issue. Austrian statesmen, such as Gentz and Metternich, viewed the king as the "supreme legislator" in a hierarchical "well-ordered civil society." Prussian leaders, by contrast, offered more ambiguous interpretations of the monarchical principle. Even the leading opponents of constitutional rule accepted the modern political principles of freedom and legal equality, at least in part. Proponents of a constitution held even more complex views: they hoped to preserve a strong monarchy, even though they unabashedly supported many of the principles of a modern liberal social and political order. The terms "Restoration" and "Reaction" are misleading characterizations of Prussian politics after 1819. Figures such as Frederick William III had no ambition to overturn the major social reforms of the Napoleonic era; rather, their overwhelming concern was simply to stabilize the authority of the state in the face of potential popular unrest.

As late as February 1820, six months after the adoption of the Karlsbad Decrees, the king still expressed clear support for a constitution. By December of that year, however, he had concluded that the establishment of a central representative assembly must be indefinitely postponed. The key events during the intervening months were a series of revolutions that swept southern Europe, beginning in Spain and quickly spreading to Portugal and Italy, in the spring and summer of 1820. During the previous decade, national liberation movements had erupted in Spanish colonies throughout Latin America, initially in Mexico (1810), then in Venezuela (1811), Chile (1817), and Colombia (1819). With Russian assistance, King Ferdinand of Spain built a navy and assembled an army, which he intended to send to quell the American rebellions. But on New Year's Day 1820, a mutiny broke out within the troops near Cadiz. The uprising soon spread throughout Spain, and on 9 March King Ferdinand bowed to popular pressure by accepting the Cortes constitution of 1812. This constitution, which had first been enacted after the Spanish victory over Napoleon, preserved the monarchy but severely restricted the king's authority. It established a unicameral representative assembly whose members were to be popularly elected every two years and granted the king only a limited veto right over legislative proposals.

Inspired by the Spaniards, the Portuguese army also mutinied, rebel-ling against the English dominion over the country. In July, the move-ment jumped to Italy, where the Neapolitan army revolted, and from Naples to Sicily. Everywhere, the revolutionaries triumphed easily over a weak and dispirited opposition; everywhere, they proclaimed versions of the Cortes constitution—even in Sicily, where no complete reprint of this document could be located anywhere in the country. In Germany and other northern European lands, the educated public reacted enthu-siastically to these liberation movements. But in Vienna, Berlin, and St. Petersburg, the monarchs and their leading ministers viewed the chal-lenges to monarchical authority abroad as omens of potential insurrection at home.[81]

From late October through December 1820, representatives of the Eu-ropean Great Powers (Russia, Austria, Prussia, France, and Britain) as-sembled in Troppau, the capital of Austrian Silesia, to determine a re-sponse to the uprisings in southern Europe.[82] After several weeks of deliberations at Troppau, the three eastern powers arrived at a provi-sional agreement (later rejected by Britain and France) that: "States in which a change of government has taken place in consequence of revolt, and when the consequences of this change threaten other states, spon-taneously cease to participate in the European alliance."[83] The conference adjourned at Christmas, with no final resolution having been reached on a course of action. In January, representatives of the five powers recon-vened in Laibach, the capital of Slovenia. There Metternich won approval for his plan to send an Austrian force to restore the original governments on the Italian peninsula, a task that was accomplished with surprising ease in March and April 1821.[84]

Historians have always faced difficulties in deciphering King Frederick William III's views concerning the constitutional question—partly be-cause he wrote so little on the subject and partly because he vacillated so much. Frederick William III repeatedly expressed support for the prin-ciple of a constitution—for example, in decrees published in 1810, 1811, and 1815—but he worried from the start that a Prussian national assem-bly might submit him to the same fate as Louis XVI, and his fears inten-sified after the end of the War of Liberation. With a few exceptions, scholars have generally portrayed the king as being firmly within the clutches of the Prussian Reaction by 1819.[85]

The Prussian State Archive contains several previously unpublished documents that shed important new light on the questions of when and why Frederick William III ultimately decided not to establish a consti-tution. The documents consist of three letters and two memoranda exchanged between an aide to the king, Friedrich von Schilden, and a former minister who had bitterly opposed the reform movement, Otto von Voß-Buch. This correspondence proves that Frederick William III made his final choice against a constitution between October and December 1820, during the congress of Troppau. More significantly, these documents give us a much clearer and more detailed view of the king's thoughts about the constitutional question during this period than any materials previously published.

In early October 1820, Frederick William III wrote to Hardenberg asking him to prepare a short essay summarizing the principles of the proposed constitution for Prussia, to be completed before the chancellor's departure for Troppau.[86] Hardenberg responded by repeating his earlier ideas on this subject. He declared that "the state will consist of free persons" and that "each community and corporation has the right to manage its own affairs." He observed, however, that the constitution must be regarded as the "free and spontaneous gift of the sovereign," and he claimed that his plan would "preserve the monarchical principle in all its purity."[87]

In addition to consulting Hardenberg, the king also asked for an opinion on the constitutional question from Voß-Buch. A *Junker* from the Kurmark, Voß had long been an implacable foe of both Stein and Hardenberg. He had served under Stein in the Prussian ministry, but the king had dismissed him in February 1809 because of his resistance to the reforms. Since that year, he had remained in private life, though he had joined in some of the protests by the *Kurmärkische Ritterschaft* against Hardenberg's reforms.[88] Voß's isolation from public affairs ended in the autumn of 1820, when Frederick William III asked him to write an essay summarizing his views on "the appropriate establishment of a constitution [*ständische Verfassung*]." Schilden, who was master of the royal house [*Obenhofmeister*], had apparently discussed this issue with Voß in late September or early October 1820. The king was intrigued by the former minister's ideas, and he wanted Voß to explain them in more detail.[89]

Schilden's first note to Voß, written under the heading "Remarks of the King concerning the Establishment of a Constitution," offers a detailed summary of Frederick William III's opinions on this subject just prior to the congress of Troppau. The king expressed profound ambivalence about a central representative assembly but apparently still considered himself bound by his earlier promises to establish such an institution. He observed, however, that "nothing has been determined about the manner and method of fulfillment" of these promises, so that the obligation could be met through a constitution that would restrict monarchical authority "to the least possible extent." To this end, the king favored the establishment of "consultative provincial estates, which would assemble in small committees in a manner most appropriate to the condition of the state. These provincial estates would concern themselves only with matters laid before them for consultation by the king."

Frederick William III expressed "great anxiety concerning an assembly of *Reichsstände*," which he considered a "dangerous central point in which revolutionary views could quietly develop." He declared that he "could never resolve himself to swear [an oath to] a constitution," and he roundly criticized the new constitutions of Bavaria and Württemberg. The king said he was pleased by the loyal sentiments "of the greatest part of the royal subjects," but he declared that "much had occurred from the side of the administration to corrupt these sentiments" and that "this negative influence would not be very easy to eliminate."

One of the most interesting aspects of this document is that Frederick William III repeatedly rejected the notion of a return to Prussia's feudal past. Though the king refused to grant "a constitution based on the new political [*staatsrechtlichen*] theories," he also believed it would be impossible to "reestablish the old estates in their earlier great rights and grounded relations." He declared:

> The laws of recent years were written partly in the new spirit. A formal reversal would not be possible, but rather an expedient guidance and application of these laws in order to prevent greater damage.

The king was particularly eager to hear Voß's views because he believed the former minister understood the need to avoid both "the entirely old and the entirely new in matter of the estates." Apart from a few people (including Prince Metternich), the king said that virtually everyone advised positions belonging either to "the one or the other extreme on this subject." Unable to resolve these dilemmas on his own, the king was easily swayed by Voß's urgently worded reply, which counseled in the strongest possible terms against the adoption of a constitution.

According to Voß, proponents of constitutional rule were motivated not by the "good of the land" but rather by a "factious spirit" that sought the "restriction of the monarchs." Voß warned that a constitution could only result in "internal discord" and Prussia's "loss of political greatness" as a European power. It was a "delusion" to think that the king might be able to "guide a central assembly." Voß declared:

> How easily this center will seize unauthorized powers; then those who are well and justly intentioned will withdraw from it. The king will be abandoned (as examples have already taught), and he will be carried away

against his will toward *revolutionary* measures, and compelled to do what he does not desire!

A constitution was both unnecessary and dangerous, argued Voß. Prussia owed its greatness not to republican institutions but rather to "the force, the courage, the wisdom—in short, to the personality of its regents." Thus the king should seek to consolidate his own power, not to give it away to his political opponents.[90]

From Troppau, again via Schilden, Frederick William III replied to Voß on 9 November 1820. The king had read Voß's memorandum with "true pleasure and just appreciation." Frederick William expressed the view that "the Minister von Voß is correct, but the matter has already gone too far." Therefore the king had decided on behalf of "consultative estates, and [he] sometimes also speaks of a small Central Committee, which would convene on his authority alone." In addition to conveying the king's response to Voß's memorandum, Schilden also sent a copy of the plan for the communal and county estates, which had been written by the third constituent committee. The king had requested Voß's opinion on this matter as well.[91]

As this letter shows, Frederick William III still had not firmly decided against establishing a central representative assembly as late as November 1820. But this changed during his sojourn in Troppau. At the congress, the king kept his distance from Hardenberg, holding many long conversations with Wittgenstein and Metternich. According to Wittgenstein, he had become so anxious over the constitutional question that he considered abdicating.[92] Finally, Frederick William III decided to stay on the throne but to follow the advice of Metternich, Wittgenstein, and Voß, namely, to establish provincial estates but to avoid creating any central representative assembly.

In early December 1820, the king returned to Berlin. Awaiting him was a new memorandum from Voß, which harshly criticized the report of the third constituent committee concerning the local assemblies. The committee's proposals, Voß argued, were nothing but an "artificial fabric of democratic maxims" that provided "the first building blocks for a complete transformation of the governing constitution that has existed up to now in the Prussian state."[93] Schilden replied on 3 December that the king agreed with Voß, but that Frederick William had observed that "not everyone shared these views."[94] On 19 December 1820, Frederick William III appointed yet a fourth constituent committee, which he ordered to review and revise the proposals for the communal and county estates. The new committee, which was chaired by the crown prince, consisted entirely of ministers who were deeply critical of Hardenberg's constitutional plans. Meanwhile, the king sent his chancellor to the congress of Laibach, in distant Slovenia, to prevent him from interfering with the new committee's work.[95] By the time Hardenberg returned to Potsdam in April 1821, his struggle for the adoption of a Prussian constitution had been lost.

These newly discovered letters not only reveal a strikingly different image of King Frederick William III's political views after 1819 than is found in the existing scholarly literature but also indicate the inadequacy of conventional interpretations of the "reactionary" movement in post– Napoleonic Prussia. This correspondence provides two particularly significant revelations about the king's state of mind during the year after the adoption of the Karlsbad Decrees. First, it demonstrates that, for Frederick William III, as for Hardenberg, the acceptance of press censorship legislation was not synonymous with the rejection of a constitution. The king continued seriously to consider establishing a central representative assembly in Prussia for more than a year after agreeing to strict censorship measures for the German states. Second, these letters show that fear of a revolution, rather than the desire to placate Prussia's privileged elites, proved the decisive factor in the king's decision against the adoption of a constitution. Frederick William III decisively rejected the possibility of fully restoring the nobility's traditional privileges, insisting instead on a fusion of old and new political and social principles.[96] But he remained terrified that an assembly of estates of the realm would become a "dangerous central point" for the formation of revolutionary sentiments—a fear that Voß eagerly reinforced.

That Frederick William III continued so long to weigh the adoption of a constitution, despite his long-standing concerns about political upheaval, is evidence of the power of discourse to transform the landscape of Prussian political debate. By 1820, the king saw no compelling rationale for the establishment of representative institutions of government, and he expressed powerful arguments against such a move. Nonetheless, he found it difficult to justify abandoning his earlier pledges on behalf of a constitution, and he was unable fully to dismiss Hardenberg's claims that the *Zeitgeist* was ineluctably propelling Prussia toward a system of parliamentary rule. In effect, Frederick William remained at least partially convinced by the argument that the legitimacy of monarchical authority depended upon the consent of the people. While figures such as Gentz, Metternich, and Voß worked feverishly to exorcise the demons of this new thinking, ultimately this proved to be an impossible task.

Conclusion: The Crystallization of the Concept
"Nation"

This chapter has illustrated the intimate connection between political and conceptual history in Prussia during the Restoration era. Scholars have often explained the events of this period in terms of an implacable opposition between the forces of progress and reaction, in which the latter side ultimately prevailed. As the analysis here has demonstrated, however, political alignments were fluid and ill-defined in the aftermath of the Vienna Congress. "Progressives," such as Hardenberg and Gneisenau, worried seriously about the threat of political subversion posed by the popular nationalist movement, and they favored strict measures to counteract this danger. Conversely, a number of leading "reactionaries" initially supported the creation of representative assemblies, and Frederick William III seriously considered establishing a constitution for a full year after the adoption of the Karlsbad Decrees.

Between 1815 and 1820, however, political discourse in Prussia became increasingly polarized. At the heart of this division was a disagreement over the nature and proclivities of a politically active nation. Hardenberg and his compatriots believed institutions for popular self-government could coexist harmoniously with a sovereign monarch. Even though Hardenberg forcefully supported the Karlsbad Decrees in 1819, he envisioned these laws as interim measures that would become superfluous as soon as the citizenry had achieved a higher level of maturity. Hardenberg's opponents, however, came to believe that a politically active nation would necessarily become a rival center of political authority to the king. Put in different terms, members of the reform party believed that the creation of a self-regulating and self-determining national community would enhance the authority of the Prussian monarchy, whereas conservatives thought that the emergence of an autonomous public sphere would destabilize the monarchical state.

The outcome of this struggle over the concept "nation" had important consequences both at the level of practice and at the level of discourse. The immediate practical result was that the party of fear triumphed over the party of hope. The popular nationalist movement was effectively driven underground by punitive censorship measures, and the Prussian king rejected moves toward political liberalization. Moreover, fearing a revolution, many Prussian nobles also backed away from their traditional arguments against royal absolutism: by the 1820s, allegiance to the monarchical principle became nearly universal among the traditional elites. In the absence of any serious challenge either from the left or the right, the monarchical state consolidated its political authority to a greater extent than ever before. Indeed, some scholars have suggested that the project of absolute monarchy was fulfilled in Prussia not during the era of Frederick the Great but only in the aftermath of the Napoleonic Wars.[97]

Discursively, however, the political developments of the Restoration era had a strikingly different result. Because the opponents of national representation often denied the very existence of the nation, the work of defining this concept was to a great extent left to bourgeois popular activists and their compatriots. Since these figures supported German unification, the idea of the Prussian nation largely disappeared from use after 1820;[98] as did the idea of the nation of aristocrats, which had been championed by Marwitz and other stalwarts of the Prussian nobility. From the 1820s onward, most Prussians who wrote of the nation used this term to indicate a harmonious pan–German community organized according to the principle of civil equality. The next two chapters explore the impact of this conceptual development on Prussian political debate between 1820 and 1848.

III

LEGACIES

Seven

EXPERIMENTS IN CONSERVATISM

"The people will never attain maturity," declared Otto von Voß-Buch in January 1821.[1] This statement, as clearly as any other, signaled the end of the era of reform in Prussia. Dismissed from the Prussian ministry in 1809 because of his bitter opposition to Stein and Hardenberg, Voß reentered the inner circle of the king's advisers in the autumn of 1820. Upon Hardenberg's death in November 1822, Voß became the new head of the Prussian ministry—though he died within two months of assuming his new post.[2]

The Prussian reformers, for all their differences, shared a commitment to the same central Enlightenment ideal: they believed that Prussia's populace could be educated and its laws perfected, in order that the people could assist in governing themselves. Stein's Municipal Ordinance and Hardenberg's provisional representative assemblies both constituted attempts to establish channels for popular participation in the Prussian government. Likewise, their social and economic reforms—from the abolition of serfdom to the establishment of a free market economy—sought to create a common Prussian citizenry by eliminating the legal barriers between estates. Voß's claim represented a direct challenge to this basic premise of the reform movement. By denying that the Prussian people could ever attain maturity (*Mündigkeit*), Voß rejected not only the notion of national representation but also the Enlightenment ideal of human perfectibility. Against the concept of a unified nation composed of free and equal citizens, Voß and his allies presented a hierarchical social vision, arguing that order could be preserved only by authority.

The years between Napoleon's defeat in 1815 and the Revolution of 1848 are commonly designated the era of Restoration or Reaction in Prussia. Both of these terms suggest that a fundamental reversal of the Stein-

Hardenberg reforms occurred during this period. This conventional interpretation, however, both underestimates the creativity of Prussian
conservatives and overestimates their success. Though figures such as
Voß portrayed themselves as staunch traditionalists, they in fact sought
to fashion a fundamentally new social and political order in response to
two ongoing challenges. First, the dramatic socioeconomic changes in
Prussia since 1806—including the abolition of serfdom, the elimination
of restrictions on the sale of noble estates, and the establishment of a
free market economy—had rendered increasingly problematic the traditional vision of a paternalistic social order dominated by an aristocratic
elite. Thus, conservatives had to find new ways of defining and justifying social hierarchies to replace the traditional distinctions that were
becoming ever more blurred. Second, in the wake of twenty-six years
of political upheaval in Europe, from the fall of the Bastille to the fall of
Napoleon, conservatives considered it urgently necessary to neutralize
the danger of a German revolution by reasserting the legitimacy of monarchical and aristocratic authority. Prussian conservatism thus involved
not a simple return to the past but rather a series of experiments that
sought to re-create traditional forms of rule within a new social and
political universe.

This chapter reassesses the evolution of conservative theory and practice during the early nineteenth century, focusing primarily on one specific dimension of this movement, namely, how did Prussian aristocrats
grapple with the implications of the concept "nation" during the decades
leading up to 1848? Parts I and II of this study explored the impact of
material interests on political concepts, analyzing how, between 1806 and
1820, the "nation" came to be defined as a harmonious and politically
unified pan–German community, organized according to the principle of
civil equality. In this chapter the logic of the inquiry is reversed: I concentrate less on how the clash of interests among competing constituencies shaped the concept "nation" than on how this concept itself influenced conservatives' political strategies. An abbreviated account of
Prussian conservatism, as the one here, cannot aim at comprehensiveness.
For example, my analysis is confined primarily to Prussia's older East
Elbian territories,[3] and while the chapter makes some references to the
ideas of conservative civil servants and academic theorists, the bulk of
it is devoted to the rhetoric of aristocrats.[4] The goal of this chapter is to
illustrate certain ways in which the rhetoric employed by various conservative activists played a role in defining the political possibilities of
this era.

Many historians have viewed conservatism primarily as "traditionalism made articulate." I conclude, however, that Prussian conservatism

was a highly fluid and experimental phenomenon during the decades leading up to the Revolution of 1848. Efforts to reestablish traditional social hierarchies after 1815 frequently proved unsuccessful, forcing aristocrats to reevaluate their identities and interests. Likewise, conservative theories of sovereignty cannot be easily pigeonholed as traditionalist in character. Some conservatives, fearing a revolution, went so far as to deny the political rights—and even the very existence—of the nation; yet these efforts to "dis-invent" the nation undermined aristocrats' own claims to political authority. Other conservative activists, troubled by their waning influence in public affairs, sought to recast the rhetoric of aristocratic nationalism in order to claim a more active political role. While this second strategy proved more effective than the first in reasserting the authority of the Prussian nobility, it also reinforced fundamental changes in aristocrats' social and political identities. Thus, during the decades leading up to the Revolution of 1848, Prussian conservatism must be understood not simply as a reaction against, but also as an integral element of, the country's process of modernization.

Traditionalism and Conservatism

In the landmark essay "Conservative Thought," Karl Mannheim distinguished between two forms of political behavior, which he termed "traditionalism" and "conservatism." Mannheim viewed traditionalism as a "general psychological attitude" that reflected the fear of innovation. "Almost purely reactive in nature," traditionalism signified "a tendency to cling to vegetative patterns, to old ways of life." Conservatism, by contrast, was both creative and articulate, and it emerged as a specific historical response to the "natural law thought" of the Enlightenment and the French Revolution. Conservatism, wrote Mannheim, "grew out of traditionalism: indeed, it is after all primarily nothing more than traditionalism become conscious." But paradoxically, the self-conscious conservatism of the nineteenth century appeared precisely at the moment when much of the traditional social order had been irrevocably undermined:

> [C]onservatism first becomes conscious and reflective when other ways of life and thought appear on the scene, against which it is compelled to take up arms in the ideological struggle. . . . The simple habit of living more or less unconsciously, as though the old ways of life were still appropriate, gradually gives way to a deliberate effort to maintain them under the new conditions, and they are raised to the level of conscious reflection, of deliberate "recollection." Conservative thought thus saves itself, so to speak, by raising to the level of reflection and conscious ma-

nipulation those forms of experience which can no longer be had in an authentic way.[5]

In the scholarly literature on German conservatism, at least until recently, a broad consensus has existed that this political movement must be understood in large part as a reaction to the rationalistic and egalitarian impulses of eighteenth-century politics and philosophy.[6] Some historians portray conservatism primarily as a response to the French Revolution[7]; others view it as an answer to the Enlightenment.[8] Still other scholars emphasize that conservatism evolved in the context of the German nobility's struggle against the ambitions of the absolutist state.[9]

Yet, in contending that conservatism represented "the elevation of traditional patterns of authority to a conscious and formal level of articulation,"[10] many historians have underestimated a key dimension of this movement identified by Mannheim, namely, that German conservatives did not so much restore old ways of life as create a convincing *memory* of tradition.[11] At heart, the project of conservatism was to retrieve the irretrievable, to construct the illusion that the present was seamlessly bound to an organic past.

A pair of examples may help illustrate this point. The Prussian kings Frederick William III and Frederick William IV were both conservatives, but they displayed strikingly different attitudes toward many fundamental social and political questions. Frederick William III, rejected the possibility of reversing most of the social and economic reforms of the Napoleonic era, and he adopted the new rationalistic definition of sovereignty reflected in the monarchical principle. When the first railroads were constructed in Prussia during the 1830s, however, Frederick William III was deeply suspicious. He feared that the advent of rapid intercity travel, by increasing the mobility of the Prussian population, would break down traditional social distinctions and contribute to the rise of democratic sentiments. Frederick William IV possessed a far more romantic sensibility than his father: he glorified the medieval world, insisting that monarchical sovereignty derived from the "grace of God." But the younger Frederick William was also a railroad enthusiast. Indeed, it was his support for a government bond issue to finance a railway from Berlin to Königsberg that forced him to convene the United Diet of 1847, an event that helped precipitate the Prussian Revolution of 1848.[12]

Along with railroads, nineteenth-century conservatives were forced to grapple with a wide variety of other radical changes in Prussia's social and political landscape. The abolition of the Holy Roman Empire in 1806 marked the end of a governing structure that had been uniquely congenial to the independence and political authority of the nobility. The empire had provided an overarching constitutional framework that provided extensive autonomy for local rulers and protected smaller lords from their ambitious neighbors. The new German Confederation, established at the Vienna Congress in 1815, created a loose federal structure that linked the various German states, but each territorial prince was formally defined as the supreme sovereign within his borders.[13] Thus, the political events of the Napoleonic era contributed to the consolidation of the authority of the territorial states and the decline of the independence of the aristocracy. The traditional authority of the nobility was rendered even more problematic by legal reforms, such as the abolition of serfdom and the loosening of restrictions on the sale of *Rittergüter*, as well as by economic and social changes, such as the rise of free market capitalism and rapid population growth, which led to increasing urbanization.

To preserve intact the traditional social order in the face of all these assaults was an impossible task. Thus, rather than resisting all changes, conservatives sought to identify and fortify those elements of the old order that were critical to maintaining their own authority and prestige. In this sense, conservatism was a reinvention of tradition.[14] What remained unclear in the aftermath of the Vienna Congress, however, was precisely which elements of the traditional order were capable of being salvaged, and how. For example, to what extent could the landed nobility continue to play its traditional paternalistic role, and to what extent would it have to accommodate the new principle of civil equality? Could the nobility successfully manipulate a system of popular representation in order to serve its political goals, or would it need to deny the political rights of the nation in order to defend old social hierarchies?

The Impossibility of a Restoration

In 1820, King Frederick William III decided against the establishment of a central representative assembly in Prussia, concluding that such an assembly would be a "dangerous central point" for the nourishment of revolutionary views.[15] As a compromise solution, however, he decided to proceed with the establishment of representative assemblies in each of the eight Prussian provinces. For this purpose, he convened a commission under the chairmanship of Crown Prince Frederick William. The so-called Crown Prince's Commission, (*Kronprinzenkommission*) was initially appointed in December 1820 and deliberated until March 1821, reviewing (and rejecting) Hardenberg's proposals for communal and county representative assemblies, which will be discussed in Chapter 8. It reconvened from late 1821 through 1824, drafting plans for the new provincial representative assemblies. The nine-member commission included old-line nobles, such as Otto von Voß-Buch, along with career civil servants of both aristocratic and bourgeois extraction, including Wittgenstein, Ancillon, and Vincke.[16]

In January 1822, the commission sent its preliminary report regarding the new provincial diets to Frederick William III. In a cover letter to the king, the commission declared:

> [F]or the future everything depends upon the further separation, securing, and ordering of the different estates . . . ; if this structure should be effaced, then the entire *ständische* constitution would also vanish. . . . The preservation of the nobility is intimately linked with the preservation of the monarchy.

The monarchical principle and the aristocratic principle, in other words, were one and the same. To buttress the traditional order, the commission urged that the social and economic reforms enacted during the Napoleonic period be rescinded wherever possible. For example, Prussia's trade guilds should be reestablished, and the nobility should maintain ownership of the country's large landed estates.[17]

Though the notion that the interests of the monarchy coincided with those of the aristocracy may seem unremarkable, the commission's arguments were more novel than they appear. As late as 1819, the year of the Karlsbad Decrees, relations between the Prussian king and the nobility had often been highly contentious. From the time of Napoleon's defeat, for example, the nobles of Brandenburg had repeatedly petitioned the Prussian king for the "restoration of our former constitution."[18] In November 1819, the nobility of the Kurmark counties of Westhavelland and Zauche sent another such plea to Frederick William III. The petition criticized the new constitutions in other German states, such as Bavaria, Württemberg, and Baden, claiming that the "so-called popular representatives [*Volks Repräsentanten*] confuse all rights and interests, irreconcilably dividing the particular elements of the nation, [and] nourishing a fatal distrust between prince and people." For nearly half a millennium, the "*landständische* constitutions" of the German states had "precisely determined, by mutually inviolable promises, the rights and obligations of the prince and of the particular elements of the population." These traditional relationships could not legitimately be modified "except through the agreement of both sides—that is, by way of contract." After enumerating some of these ancient rights, the petition concluded by demanding the "restoration of the essence of our old provincial constitution."[19]

Despite having just agreed to stringent press censorship legislation intended to counter the revolutionary threat, Frederick William III contemptuously dismissed the plea by the nobles of Zauche and Westhavelland in December 1819 with a single brusque sentence:

> In response to your petition of 15 November, I inform you that your request for the restoration of the former provincial constitution cannot be granted; instead, you must await the general organization of estates of the land [*Landständen*], which is currently under way.[20]

Within the next few years, with the outbreak of revolutions throughout southern Europe, attitudes on both sides softened considerably. Prussian aristocrats began to back away from their claims about the contractual basis of monarchical authority,[21] and the king himself adopted a more conciliatory attitude toward the nobility than he had displayed in previous years.[22]

To proclaim the unity of interests between the monarchy and the aristocracy was one thing; to succeed in reestablishing the traditional social order was something else again. In analyzing the history of Prussian conservatism between 1815 and 1848, it is essential to distinguish between the rhetoric and the reality of Restoration. Though many historians have insisted that the Prussian aristocracy remained socially and politically dominant throughout the first half of the nineteenth century,[23] an equally persuasive case can be made that "the aristocratic position disintegrated" during the decades after 1815.[24] Patterns in the ownership of landed estates provide one barometer of the status of the aristocracy. By 1800, approximately two-thirds of the aristocracy owned no landed property, and about 10–15 percent of noble estates had been sold to members of the bourgeoisie. Following the adoption of the October Edict of 1807, which ended legal restrictions on the sale of *Rittergüter*, bourgeois ownership of estates rose higher—especially during the agricultural crisis of the 1820s, which resulted in numerous bankruptcies and forced sales. By 1842, one-third of noble estates had bourgeois owners, and this figure rose to 42 percent by 1856. This transfer of estates to members of the bourgeoisie proceeded rapidly despite the government's economic intervention to support aristocratic ownership of *Rittergüter*. Moreover, even those estates that remained in noble hands frequently had new owners, undermining the traditional patrimonial bond between lords and peasants; by 1856, only 16.4 percent of *Rittergüter* were still owned by the same family as in 1807.[25] If aristocrats' ownership of landed estates was in decline, so too was their position in the bureaucracy and army. In the mid–eighteenth century, under Frederick the Great, 95 percent of ministerial appointments had gone to *Junkers*, and the officer corps was almost exclusively aristocratic. By the 1820s, bourgeois appointees constituted three-quarters of the staff of the Prussian ministries and almost half of the military officers.[26] Some retrenchment occurred between 1820 and 1848. For example, in 1820, 59 percent of all provincial administrators in Prussia (including the *Landräte*) were commoners; by 1845 this proportion had declined to 53 percent.[27] The aristocracy, however, never fully recovered its previous position of dominance.

Not only was the preeminence of the nobility under assault in these purely quantitative terms, but the very nature of the aristocracy as a ruling estate was fundamentally redefined during this era. Though the First Estate was still called the *Ritterschaft* (the "knights"), commoners as well as nobles were entitled to membership in this estate upon purchasing a *Rittergut*. The Provincial Estates Law of 1823 confirmed this change by entitling bourgeois estate owners to be represented along with nobles in the First Estate. Procedures for deliberating and voting within the assemblies likewise reflected a hybrid of traditional and modern political logic. The Crown Prince's Commission adopted the general principle that "the municipalities and peasants together elect the same number of deputies as the *Ritterschaft*," thus attempting to strike a balance between the old principle of aristocratic preeminence and the new practice of allocating representatives in proportion to population.[28] In the assembly, the delegates were to sit in a block with the other members of their estate, but as a rule the whole body was to deliberate together. Voting in the assembly was generally by head, rather than by estate; and the traditional practice whereby constituents would give binding instructions to their representatives was forbidden.[29]

In the words of one contemporary observer, the new provincial diets provided for representation not for the traditional corporate entities of the realm but rather for "mere classes of the population."[30] As philosopher of law Eduard Gans noted, the growing permeability of the estates fundamentally undermined the old corporate order:

> The laws of 1807 dissolved the three *Stände* by permitting a nobleman to pursue a trade and a tradesman to own a noble estate. The provincial diets have called these *Stände* back from the dead. *Stände*, however, are only truly present when an individual can belong to only one *Stand*; if he can simultaneously belong to various *Stände*, the *ständisch* principle is merely an artifice, the acceptance of it arbitrary, and its inner truth is stripped away.[31]

By defining membership in an estate in purely functional terms, in other words, the old social hierarchy no longer appeared to reflect a natural and divinely ordained order. It was precisely this loss of the fixed and sacred character of the traditional order that Brandenburg *Junker* Adolf von Rochow had in mind when he declared that "the nobility in the Prussian state is to be considered as politically annihilated."[32]

Like the aristocracy, the peasantry and the guilds proved impossible to restore to their previous condition. By the end of the Napoleonic era, all but the staunchest conservatives viewed the liberation of the serfs as a fait accompli. A petition of 1818 by the nobles of Brandenburg's Kurmark and Neumark was characteristic in this regard. Though the nobles demanded the reestablishment of the traditional provincial constitution, they also declared: "By no means is it however the intention of the estates . . . to request the establishment of that which is incompatible with the rights and innate freedom of humanity, among which we count hereditary serfdom [*Leibeigenschaft*] and the subjection of the peasant estate."[33] This passage illustrates how Enlightenment premises concerning the desirability of universal human freedom penetrated the rhetoric of conservatives as well as liberals during this era. As for the urban guilds, the reestablishment of their trade monopolies proved impractical, despite the support of the Crown Prince's Commission and that of six of the eight Prussian provincial assemblies during the 1820s. Frederick William III rejected the idea of overturning Hardenberg's free trade legislation, arguing that "a rapid, forcible transition to a different legal order will only lead to new disturbances and destroy lawful relationships and procedures which have more or less put down roots." By the mid–1820s, the economic upturn in Prussia was widely attributed to Hardenberg's economic policies, and a government commission on guild reform subsequently confirmed the principles of the new economic order.[34]

However ardently Hardenberg's opponents denounced the reform movement and demanded the reestablishment of traditional institutions, many of the social and political changes that had occurred in Prussia since the Napoleonic period proved irreversible. Though some historians have claimed to find evidence of the "feudalization of the German bourgeoisie" during the nineteenth century, it is perhaps more accurate to speak of an "embourgeoisement of the aristocracy."[35] Hans Rosenberg has gone so far as to argue that a "pseudodemocratization" of the Prussian landholding nobility began during the reform period. Not only did members of the bourgeoisie gain control over many estates, observes Rosenberg, but the changing pattern of land ownership "accelerated the transition to 'rational agriculture.' The landholding nobility 'democratized' itself, in that it developed into a class of productive large land owners who operated more and more according to purely economic considerations."[36]

In the face of these dramatic social and political changes, Prussian aristocrats struggled to develop rhetorical strategies to defend their status. Some historians, in characterizing these strategies, have distinguished between old (*altständische*) conservatives, who rejected any modification of traditional social hierarchies, and new (*neuständische*) conservatives, who advocated a compromise between feudal and egalitarian social principles.[37] This divide between old and new conservatism manifested itself in debates over the theory of sovereignty as well. Some nobles, coming to believe that a politically active nation would inevitably threaten their own privileged status, attempted (with only partial success) to extinguish all elements of the new thinking from their political rhetoric. Others, however, tentatively embraced the principle of national representation, arguing that their political objectives would best be served through the adoption of a constitution.

Strategy 1: Dis-inventing the Nation

"The idea of a common German fatherland has irrevocably taken root. He who seizes this idea will rule in Germany." Thus wrote Brandenburg noble Friedrich August Ludwig von der Marwitz to Chancellor Hardenberg in 1814, in the first flush of the military victories over France.[38] During the Napoleonic era, many Prussian nobles had fervently supported the idea of a national representative assembly. In 1812, for example, Brandenburg *Junker* Otto von Quast had argued that such an institution would contribute "to the grand education [*Ausbildung*] of this general voice, and to the most forceful and beautiful animation of the national spirit."[39] Even Hardenberg's enemy Voß, who had refused to serve as a delegate to the Provisional National Representation in 1812, had proclaimed the importance of forging "national unity and a feeling for the interest of the whole" among the Prussian provinces.[40] A decade later, these and many other aristocrats had lost their ardor for participatory politics. Popular representative assemblies, they now believed, produced nothing but confusion and division, threatening the stability of the realm.

This rejection of popular politics corresponded with a new distrust for the very concept of the "nation." Marwitz, who had written with such passion about seizing the national idea,[41] now articulated his views more circumspectly, defending the rights of "the owners among the people, who hitherto, along with their king, had formed the *nation*."[42] The transformation of Quast's political thought was equally striking. Abandoning his ambition to animate the "national spirit," Quast's attitude became overwhelmingly defensive by the early 1820s. The estates of the province of Brandenburg, he insisted, comprised only the "*Ritterschaft* and the towns."[43] Asked for his advice on the organization of the new Brandenburg provincial assembly in 1822, Quast argued strenuously against the inclusion of representatives from the peasantry. Neither the traditional German constitution nor Prussian law permitted peasants "unrestricted participation" in the provincial estates, he claimed. To offer them such rights now would be risky, "because some demagogues would easily purchase peasant properties and thus achieve entry into the assembly, and then could become dangerous to the monarchy." Moreover, because the peasantry not only made up most of the population but also owned most of the land in Brandenburg, peasant representatives might be tempted to "strive for predominance" in the assembly, "which can lead to popular sovereignty [*Volkssouverainität*], particularly if secret influences interfere."[44]

The ideas expressed by Marwitz and Quast in the 1820s reflected the deep fear of revolution that gripped much of the Prussian political elite in the wake of Napoleon's defeat. Despite the virtual absence of republican sentiment in the German states during this era, many participants in political debate were convinced that the "spirit of destruction" threatened to annihilate all existing order. This attitude was particularly pronounced among the aristocrats of Brandenburg, who had been the most strenuous opponents of social reform during the Napoleonic era. In other provinces, such as East Prussia, where the nobility had willingly acceded to some of the Stein-Hardenberg reforms, suspicions about the revolutionary designs of the nation were less pronounced during the 1820s and 1830s.[45]

These fears were not limited to Prussia alone. The Austrian chancellor, Metternich, for example, warned obsessively of the danger of impending political chaos throughout the period between 1815 and 1848, employing a rich panoply of medical and geological metaphors: in his letters the revolution appeared variously as a cancer, a plague, a monster, an earthquake, and a volcano.[46] The adoption of a "representative constitution," warned Metternich's adviser Friedrich von Gentz, would "lead to the complete destruction of all power, and hence to pure *anarchy*." Not only did Gentz argue for the defense of the traditional hierarchical order, but he denied the very existence of the nation conceived as the "entire mass of the people."[47] Gentz's essay on *landständische* constitutions did not use the word "nation" even once, nor is this word to be found in the writings after 1819 by other leading conservatives, such as Metternich, Wittgenstein, Ancillon, Voß, and Adam Müller. To stem the tide of revolution, these figures believed it was necessary to "dis-invent" the nation.

The dis-invention of the nation, however, proved to be a problematic political strategy for aristocratic activists. In attempting to reassert the social preeminence of the traditional elites, conservatives often presented ideas that limited the political authority and independence of the nobility. These points may be illustrated by examining the political thought of three leading theorists of this era: Carl Ludwig von Haller (1768–1854), Ernst Ludwig von Gerlach (1795–1877), and Friedrich Julius Stahl (1802–1861), whose writings provide a sense of how some conservatives attempted to shore up existing hierarchies and to contain the destabilizing potential of a politically active populace.

Haller, who was born to a patrician family in the Swiss city of Bern, sought to answer this challenge in a six-volume work published between 1816 and 1834 entitled *Restauration der Staatswissenschaft*. Having begun his career in the civil service at age nineteen as a devotee of Enlightenment ideals, Haller became disillusioned by the revolutionary events both in France and in Bern during the 1790s. In his *Restauration*, he put forth a scathing critique of the liberal theory of the social contract, which he said had resulted in "nearly universal confusion" among Europe's educated classes during the eighteenth century. The true state of nature, he argued, was not characterized by the universal equality of all humans but rather by gradations of strength and weakness, of independence and dependence: "Where strength and need meet, a relationship develops in which the former acquires domination and the latter dependence. It is therefore the eternal law of God that the more powerful dominates, must dominate, and will always dominate."[48]

Haller's theory thus served to legitimate the full array of patrimonial relationships that characterized the traditional order, including the rule of husbands over their wives and children, of masters over their servants, and of lords over their peasants. His arguments were appealing to many Prussian aristocrats because he defended the indivisibility of sovereignty, arguing that nobles should continue to exercise unlimited police and judicial powers over their estates. Moreover, Haller denied that any fundamental difference existed between the public authority of the monarch and the private authority of the nobility. Rather, all power, including that of the prince, was essentially private in character: "Every family forms a small monarchy. . . . Every individual man is king and monarch in the circle of his realm, only smaller and less powerful, more or less subordinated, by nature or contract, to a higher authority." The prince, in other words, was distinguished from the smaller landlord only by the size of his realm and by the degree of his independence.

The insistence on the private character of monarchical authority had ambiguous consequences for Haller's theory of sovereignty. On the one hand, this principle imposed certain limits on the prince's rights with respect to his subjects, for example, the prince did not have the right to compel his subjects to perform military service, and subjects had the right to resist a prince who abused his authority (as a result of the natural law of self-defense). Moreover, if the prince wanted to impose any special tax on his subjects (for example to support a military campaign), he needed to consult his vassals, who acted through the *Landstände*. Yet, the delegates to the *Landstände* represented only themselves not the people as a whole. Because the rights of the nobility and other social elites, like those of the prince, were essentially private in character, these groups possessed no general right to participate in the exercise of sovereign authority. Instead, the prince was the sole legislator in the state, and law was "a binding expression of the will" of the monarch. Haller denounced the principle of separation of powers, articulated by Montesquieu and other authors, as the "first step toward a revolutionary system." Haller's political theory thus represented a curious hybrid of old and new legal principles. He developed a highly rationalistic argument against natural law rationalism. He also defended the traditional social privileges of the nobility but only by undermining their claims to participate in the exercise of public power.[49]

In contrast to Haller, who viewed absolute monarchical sovereignty as an essential bulwark against revolution, Gerlach depicted "royal absolutism and revolution" as "but different aspects of one and the same thing, twin children of the same mother."[50] Gerlach was the descendant of an old Brandenburg family ennobled in 1735 and the son of Berlin's first mayor. A veteran of the War of Liberation, he became active in the Awakening (*Erweckungsbewegung*), a revival of evangelical Christianity that spread throughout Germany after 1815, and he was one of the leading contributors to the *Berliner Politisches Wochenblatt*, an influential conservative journal founded in 1831. In 1848, he became one of the founders of the Prussian Conservative party. Though he spent his entire career as a bureaucrat, serving as a high-ranking official (*Gerichtspräsident*) in the judicial branch of the government, Gerlach glorified the medieval social order. He went even further than Haller in his defense of paternalistic institutions, decrying the rise of free market capitalism and arguing for the reestablishment of hereditary serfdom.[51]

Absolutism, argued Gerlach, was the most "able and fearful ally of revolution" because it robbed "the king of the brilliance of his majesty," stripping away the divine sanction for royal authority. Anticipating Tocqueville's interpretation of the French Revolution,[52] Gerlach contended that Europe's absolute monarchs, by leveling the social order and by annihilating the political authority of the aristocracy, had prepared the ground for the destruction of the monarchy itself. Moreover, those who made claims to "immoderate and boundless royal power" haughtily ignored the principle that the king ruled *only* by God's grace, *only* as God's servant." The "right of subjects [*der Untertanen Recht*]," Gerlach insisted, "is as holy as the right of the king, and his right is limited by ours."[53] Thus, in defending the religious foundation of the social order, Gerlach also sought to resuscitate the old contractual obligations between the king and his vassals, along with the entire web of rights and privileges that defined the old corporate order. This social philosophy left little room for accommodating the dramatic changes that had wracked Europe over the previous half century—or, indeed, since the rise of absolute monarchy in the late seventeenth century. Thus, Gerlach and his circle displayed an almost purely negative and defensive attitude toward contemporary historical events.

Stahl, while sharing elements of Haller's and Gerlach's critiques of modernity, expressed less hostile views toward recent historical developments in Prussia. Stahl was a converted Jew from a Bavarian merchant family who, as a professor of political philosophy at the University of Berlin, became the most influential Prussian conservative theorist of the mid–nineteenth century. Like Haller and Gerlach, Stahl attacked natural law rationalism as intrinsically revolutionary in character, both because it idealized social equality and because it sought to reconstruct the world purely from reason, rather than viewing the social order as divinely ordained. Like the other two theorists, Stahl articulated a hierarchical conception of civil society, defending paternalistic institutions, such as nobles' police and judicial powers over their estates, as traditional "organic" relations of authority. Yet, Stahl's political philosophy was grounded in a dynamic rather than a static conception of history. He directed his energy toward containing the revolutionary potential of the nation, instead of denying altogether the existence of such a political community.

In Stahl's view, his era was marked by an irreversible "progress from corporate particularism to national unity, from a patrimonial to a statist or constitutional system." Thus, though he denounced the "political system of the West," which was based on "popular sovereignty, the division of powers," and "simple numerical representation of the people," he argued that any viable system of government must acknowledge the growing unity of the realm as well as its traditional "corporate hierarchy."[54] Moreover, Stahl rejected Haller's theory of the private nature of princely authority and, more generally, Haller's claim that the true "law of nature was simply the domination of the stronger." Instead, the state was an "ethical kingdom" whose charge was to educate its citizens to become moral human beings. Within the state, the king embodied the "personality of *Herrschaft*." For the state to perform this moral mission, Stahl argued, the monarch had to exercise ultimate and undivided political authority.[55]

For Stahl, the monarchical principle denoted more than simply the "sovereignty of the king," rather, it meant that "the prince truly remains the center of gravity of the constitution, the positively shaping power in the state, the leader of development"—in other words, that "the prince has the right and the power to rule by himself."[56] This insistence on enhancing the powers of the monarch did not mean the rejection of constitutionalism. Indeed, Stahl called for the fulfillment of the Prussian king's promise to establish a constitution. In place of the traditional provincial diets, which had represented the interests of the individual estates, he advocated the creation of a "healthy representation" based on occupation or profession, which would illuminate both the particular needs of "the *Land*" and the general desires of "the *Volk*" as a whole. Such an institution would be almost purely advisory in nature, for example, it would have the right to approve taxes, but it would possess neither the authority to allocate taxes nor to deprive the government of the power to collect existing taxes. The representatives would have no right to initiate legislation nor would the king be obliged to consult the assembly over legislative proposals, except those affecting the "basic laws" of the realm. Stahl's watchword was "authority, not majority": representative institutions, by informing the king of public opinion, would help him rule more justly and efficiently—but they were not intended to challenge his rights as sovereign.[57]

The writings of Haller, Gerlach, and Stahl represented three attempts to develop new legitimacy for traditional ruling structures. Haller and Gerlach both avoided any reference to the nation, viewing this concept as intrinsically revolutionary in its implications. Stahl, while less alarmed by this concept and by the political developments of the modern era, insisted on the need to contain popular political activism through the unbending defense of monarchical sovereignty. None of these three theoretical approaches, however, provided an effective intellectual foundation for the revitalization of the nobility as a political elite. Haller's theory of private law sought to defend the rights of the nobility against encroachment by the absolutist state, arguing that the king was merely the largest landowner in the realm rather than the supreme overlord. But Haller's theory also depicted the nobility's authority as essentially private in nature. Thus, while justifying nobles' dominion over their own estates, he provided no theory that would legitimize aristocratic claims to public power. The writings of Gerlach and his collaborators on the *Ber-*

liner Politisches Wochenblatt presented the most explicit critique of absolute monarchical sovereignty voiced by Prussian conservatives during this era. "All absolutism," declared Gerlach, "is the service of idolatry."[58] He sought to overcome the "atomistic pulverization" of the people caused by absolutism and revolution, returning the realm to a feudal theocracy. But the *Wochenblatt*'s deep pessimism about the future and its unrelenting attacks on capitalism, railroads, and the "aristocracy of money" ultimately rendered it a marginal force in Prussian political debate.[59] Stahl's theory of the Christian state also sought to reconstitute a hierarchical social order based on the principle of paternalism. Unlike Haller and Gerlach, however, Stahl argued that the king embodied the "personality of *Herrschaft*." His theory of the monarchical principle thus undermined aristocratic claims for an independent political voice.

As the above analysis suggests, the dis-invention of the nation proved to be a counterproductive strategy for Prussian aristocrats seeking to organize politically and to articulate their claims. By denying the existence of the nation, the nobility deprived itself of the opportunity to redefine itself as a national institution rather than as a local or provincial one. Likewise, by rejecting the principle of popular representation, many nobles abandoned any attempt to strike alliances with other constituencies, such as the peasantry and the towns, against the ambitions of the absolutist state. The history of the provincial diets established in Prussia during the 1820s provides a further example of how conservatives' fears of a revolutionary nation impeded efforts toward an aristocratic renaissance. The Crown Prince's Commission, charged with designing these new assemblies, proclaimed in its initial report that its goal was to reinvigorate Prussia's traditional *landständische* constitution.[60] But the Provincial Estates Law of July 1823, which it drafted, resulted in a basic restructuring of the political process that severely limited the assemblies' capacity to act independently or to challenge the authority of the monarchical state.

The provisions of the Provincial Estates Law were tailored to restrict, rather than encourage, the free and open airing of political views in Prussia. The government closely monitored the deliberations of the provincial diets and placed tight restrictions on their activities. For example, a royal commissioner attended all of the sessions in order to ensure that proper procedures were followed. The assemblies were given the right to offer opinions concerning legislation that would affect the whole realm—but only if consulted by the king. They were granted a deciding vote only on legislative proposals concerning local and provincial affairs—but even these measures required royal approval in order to become law. The diets had the right to petition the king on issues affecting the "particular interest" of their province, but if the government rejected their petition, they were forbidden to renew their complaint. The members of the assemblies were strictly banned from publishing their minutes and from corresponding with the assemblies of other provinces, and even their correspondence with local governing bodies in their *own* province had to be approved by the royal commissioner.[61]

Not only did the provincial diets fail to provide an effective forum for aristocratic activism, but they also contributed to the decline of already existing representative institutions, such as the *Kurmärkische Ritterschaft* and the Committee of East Prussian and Lithuanian Estates. The law of July 1823 made no specific determination concerning the fate of these old regional corporate bodies, and initially their constituents attempted to preserve them. Between 1824 and 1827, for example, the East Prussian Committee continued to meet and correspond regularly during the periods between sessions of the new provincial assembly. Indeed, in 1824, the assembly of the province of Prussia voted unanimously in favor of maintaining the committee and for expanding it to include delegates from West Prussia as well. In 1828, however, Frederick William III decided to abolish the Committee of East Prussian and Lithuanian Estates, accepting his advisers' opinion that no need existed in this region for a separate committee concerned with communal affairs.[62]

Hampered by these severe limitations on their activities, the provincial diets played little meaningful role in Prussian politics during the pre–1848 era. The government frequently overruled resolutions passed by these assemblies, and it often delayed for as long as two years before responding to such resolutions. Moreover, many important laws were adopted without even being submitted to the diets for consideration. In other words, the provincial assemblies possessed the form, but few of the functions, of genuine representative institutions. In the words of one scholar, the assemblies served as "committees for rendering opinions on legislation" rather than as true parliamentary institutions—and even in this capacity their participation was not mandatory.[63]

Why did the delegates to the representative assemblies accede to this tight circumscription of their legislative role? Some historians have argued that Prussian nobles willingly accepted a diminished voice in politics for the simple reason that the government had already granted their most important demands. According to Rosenberg's classic interpretation, a new ruling compromise was established between the bureaucracy and the aristocracy in the aftermath of the Napoleonic Wars, resulting in a "streamlined system of political absolutism; a modified pattern of aristocratic privilege and social inequality; [and] a redistribution of oligarchical authority among the revitalized segments of the traditional master class."[64] Rosenberg argues that the bureaucracy and the landholding nobility created an alliance against the monarchy, whereby the nobility preserved its privileged social status and the bureaucracy tightened its control over state power. By 1820, the Prussian government had conceded to the nobles' demands on a wide variety of issues, for example, estate owners had achieved a favorable settlement with their former serfs, and they had retained many of their administrative rights, as well as their police and judicial powers, over their lands.[65] Hanna Schissler concurs, observing that the bureaucracy sacrificed its own "members who were unwilling to compromise" with the nobility, and the estate owners "transformed themselves into a class of noble and bourgeois agrarian capitalists."[66]

The Prussian state's increasingly accommodationist stance toward aristocratic privilege, along with the aristocrats' changing conceptions of their own self-interest, were undoubtedly important factors in transforming the dynamic of political debate after 1815. Nonetheless, it is essential to add two nuances to the interpretation of Prussian conservatism advanced by Rosenberg, Schissler, and other scholars. First, the motives for the new alliance between elements of the Prussian aristocracy and civil service were more complex than these historians suggest. Rather than simply seeking to enhance their own authority at the expense of the Prussian monarchy, leading civil servants were deeply troubled by the prospect of a revolutionary upheaval that might overthrow the state and the aristocracy alike. Indeed, it is not clear that any sharp schism existed between interests of the civil service and those of the royal family. It is true that the exercise of monarchical authority became increasingly regimented by bureaucratic procedure during the early nineteenth century, with the establishment of institutions such as the Council of State, which further formalized the legislative process.[67] Both the king and the crown prince, however, played extensive personal roles throughout the early nineteenth century in supervising the provincial estates and in other vital political deliberations, and leading civil servants and aristocrats alike continued to acknowledge the centrality of the monarch in political decision making.[68] Moreover, it is important to note that the increasing regimentation of political authority during the early nineteenth century imposed strict limits on the activities of the civil service itself, as well as on those of the monarch.[69] While there may be truth to the claim that Prussian civil servants struck bargains with aristocrats in hopes of containing the authority of the king, it is equally true that all three of these groups—aristocracy, civil service, and the royal family— made common cause with each other against the phantom of a revolution.

This shared fear of chaos was a powerful force in reshaping political alliances in Prussia during this era.

The notion that Prussian aristocrats accepted a diminished political role in exchange for the preservation of their social privileges must be qualified in a second way as well. Although certain elements of the nobility willingly acknowledged the supremacy of the state, others continued to lobby actively for the right to participate in the exercise of sovereign authority. The next section assesses various Prussian nobles' efforts to revitalize their status after 1820 by demanding a greater role for the "nation" or the "public" in political decision-making.

Strategy 2: Appealing to Public Opinion

Although the Provincial Estates Law of 1823 established a tightly circumscribed role for the new provincial diets, most Prussian nobles initially expressed satisfaction with this legislation. Under the new system, fully half of the delegates to the assemblies were reserved to the owners of landed estates (*Rittergutsbesitzer*), except in the Rhineland, where this class received one-third of the delegates. Some Rhenish aristocrats argued that greater barriers needed to be erected to differentiate the old landholding nobility from the new bourgeois estate owners. In the East Elbian provinces, however, even the most conservative aristocrats, such as Marwitz, accepted the organizational principles of the new diets.[70]

Yet, over the course of the 1820s and 1830s, as the relative impotence of the provincial diets became increasingly evident, both bourgeois and aristocratic delegates in various provinces began to campaign for the expansion of these institutions' political role. The diet of the province of Prussia (which combined the former provinces of East Prussia and West Prussia) petitioned the crown repeatedly, beginning already in its first session of 1824, for the right to publish the minutes of its deliberations. During the 1830s, the diets of Saxony and the Rhineland likewise petitioned for permission to publicize their proceedings, and the pressure for the loosening of censorship became more intense after Frederick William IV's accession to the throne in 1840.[71]

These demands for a closer bond between the provincial diets and the public were often combined with requests for the fulfillment of the king's pledge to establish a constitution. In 1824, Count Fabian Dohna wrote to the chair of the Committee of East Prussian and Lithuanian Estates, pondering whether a "German empire" was likely to be established in the near future. Dohna also referred to the need for internal political reform:

One appreciates how necessary it is to establish a bond that will unite the old and new provinces into a single state: in other words, a constitution. This will not be made by deputies of the nation, as would be appropriate; presumably it will simply be laid before them for their approval. . . . These hearings by the deputies would need to be public.[72]

Likewise, at the beginning of the second session of the diet of the province of Prussia in 1827, the delegate von Rosenberg requested that the assembly grant him permission to present a written petition calling for the "convening of General-Estates." The diet voted by a majority of 65–27 to delay taking up this petition, declaring that the time was not yet ripe for such a measure. Two aspects of the debate surrounding this petition are particularly noteworthy. First, support for Rosenberg's petition was stronger among the nobility than among either of the other two estates: of those who voted to take it up for consideration, sixteen were from the *Ritterschaft*, seven from the towns, and four from the peasantry (*Landgemeinden*). (Of those who voted against the petition, twenty-seven were from the *Ritterschaft*, twenty from the towns, and eighteen from the peasantry.) Second, Rosenberg himself was a West Prussian estate owner who subsequently established a reputation as one of the most conservative nobles of the province.[73] These facts suggest that support for a constitution during this era cannot be identified as an essentially bourgeois phenomenon.

Historians have puzzled over the reasons for the strong support for political reform among the nobles of East and West Prussia during the 1820s and 1830s, a phenomenon that was at odds with developments in Brandenburg and other provinces. Some scholars have argued that the high level of bourgeois ownership of *Rittergüter* during this era gradually converted the East and West Prussian aristocracy into a landed gentry, as existed in England, and that this class displayed progressive political attitudes that were elsewhere associated primarily with the bourgeoisie. Other historians have noted that the extensive grain trade between this region and other countries, especially Britain, inspired the rise of liberal economic ideas among aristocrats.[74] One especially intriguing interpretation holds that East and West Prussian nobles were deeply troubled by a series of disastrous harvests that threatened to undermine the stability of the social order. Serious crop failures occurred from 1819 through 1822 and again in 1826–1827, 1835, 1838, and 1844–1847, inspiring unrest and resentment within the agrarian population. According to this interpretation, East and West Prussian nobles sought to preserve their authority in the face of this crisis by making concessions to the peasantry and the towns—hence they developed more progressive social and political views than was the case elsewhere in the realm.[75]

To identify the reasons for the differences among the political views of Prussian nobles of various provinces is a project beyond the scope of the present inquiry. Rather, the objective of this chapter is to illustrate how the rhetorical strategies employed by Prussian aristocrats played a role in defining their political program. In this respect, two points are of particular significance. First, by appealing to the authority of the nation or of public opinion (*öffentliche Meinung*), nobles posited a vision of a homogeneous political community that was difficult to reconcile with support for a hierarchical *ständisch* social order. Second, such appeals had the potential to shift the symbolic locus of political authority away from the aristocracy and the monarchy and toward the nation as a whole.

A critical difference existed between the aristocratic nationalism of the Napoleonic era and that of the period after 1820, a difference related less to the content of the claims than to the audiences toward which they were directed. Between 1807 and 1815, Prussian aristocrats had taken advantage of new representative institutions, such as the Assembly of Notables and the Provisional National Representation, in order to advocate their political positions. Though many of these nobles had claimed to speak on behalf of the nation, they had presented their pleas as members of royally sanctioned institutions via petitions addressed to the king and his ministers. From the 1820s onward—and especially after 1840—petitioners both from the aristocracy and from other estates began to address public opinion as a second, parallel audience along with the monarchical state. For example, they began to publish their views in journals accessible to all literate Prussians, rather than directing them solely to the monarch. This rhetorical strategy tended to erode the very distinctions among estates on which the special status of the aristocracy rested.

The cadre of royal advisers who constituted the Special Commission for Estate Affairs (*Immediatkommission für ständische Angelegenheiten*), which supervised the provincial diets, was acutely aware of the dangers posed by this development. In 1832, the commission summarily rejected a request by one of the diets to admit observers to its sessions, arguing that "the publicity of deliberations would seduce the delegates into striving for the approval of the public, leading them away from a calm and thorough consideration" of the issues at stake.[76] Historian Heinrich von Treitschke, writing at the end of the nineteenth century, made a similar point:

> With the [end of] the secrecy of deliberations, a foundation pillar of the old order of estates [*alten Ständewesens*] collapsed. Diets that abandoned themselves to the judgment of public opinion could not long remain sat-

isfied with providing unbinding recommendations; instead, they had to lodge demands.[77]

The accession to the throne of Frederick William IV excited great hopes in Prussia. Many observers saw in this event the advent of a new age, and the king contributed to these expectations by temporarily easing press censorship and by promising to revisit the constitutional question. Frederick William's new minister for censorship declared in a memorandum of 1841 that the "bond of trust between the government and its own people" could no longer be preserved through instruction alone but only through insight and persuasion. Indeed, during the early 1840s, the government adopted several measures that eased restrictions on the provincial diets. Beginning in 1840, Prussian newspapers were permitted to report on the progress of bills submitted to the provincial diets. From 1843 onward, the press was also granted limited rights to discuss the substance of the delegates' deliberations, as well as to publish certain petitions that had been submitted to the diets for their consideration.[78]

During the early 1840s, provincial diets throughout the realm, particularly in the Rhineland and the province of Prussia, were flooded by petitions—most of them from the bourgeoisie and the peasantry but some from aristocrats as well. These petitions addressed a wide range of issues: some demanded social and economic reforms or changes to the legal code, others called for the lifting of press censorship and the establishment of a constitution. For example, in 1843, a group of seventeen residents of the Marienwerder region of East Prussia, among them eight *Rittergutsbesitzer*, called on the king to honor "the general desire of the people for the establishment of a legal state of affairs through the fulfillment of the contract of 1815 [to create a constitution]."[79] In the same year, a West Prussian estate owner petitioned the provincial diet to ask the king to grant "the most ardent desire of the nation," namely, "the General Constitution [*Allgemeine ständische Verfassung*] after the manner of the German *Bundesstaaten*," along with "freedom of the press without any censorship."[80]

During the 1840s, certain prominent conservative intellectuals and civil servants also began appealing to the authority of public opinion or of the nation. For these scholars and officials, this rhetoric served primarily a defensive purpose. In the words of one historian, conservative civil servants sought to "integrate publicity into the existing political order as a means of securing the domination of the state."[81] This strategy was evident in the writings of Friedrich Julius Stahl, who—despite his fierce defense of the monarchical principle—favored the establishment of representative institutions to communicate the desires of the people.

Stahl may be identified as a transitional figure in the history of Prussian conservatism: on the one hand, he was deeply suspicious of the revolutionary potential of the nation, but on the other hand, he was convinced of the need to respect the wishes of the populace in order to preserve the authority of the state.

Another such transitional figure was Viktor Aimé Huber, a Marburg literature professor and publisher of the conservative journal *Janus*. During the early 1840s, Huber composed two treatises in which he identified the need to fuse the "conservative elements" into "the *conservative party*" and in which he argued that Prussia should become the "*central point of all true conservative, national, Christian-monarchical forces in all of Germany.*"[82] Like Stahl, Huber supported the establishment of a central representative assembly as a means of distilling a true expression of public opinion, while insisting on the purely advisory capacity of such an assembly. "The political influence of the estates," Huber declared, "will go precisely *so far* as their political education [*Bildung*]." Indeed, he criticized Stahl for conceding too much authority to the parliamentary assembly by proposing that such an assembly have a deciding vote over new taxes.[83]

While conservative leaders hoped to fend off the revolution by reinvigorating traditional forms of authority, they found themselves obliged to make compromises with the new order. The disposition of the constitutional question between 1820 and 1848 provides perhaps the most telling illustration of how Prussian conservatism sought to balance old and new governing principles. Despite Frederick William III's deep fears about the revolutionary potential of a central representative assembly, he never formally repudiated the constitutional promise of 1815, even at the height of the Reaction during the 1820s and 1830s. The law of 5 June 1823, which established provincial assemblies in Prussia, remained signally vague on this subject. It declared simply: "The question of when a convocation of general estates will be required, and how they shall be established on the basis of the provincial estates, will be left to Our further determination."[84] The State Debt Law of January 1820, which stipulated that any new state debts must be approved by the Prussian *Reichsstände*, remained officially in force, and Frederick William IV honored its terms by convening the United Diet of 1847.

Many prominent conservatives during this era expressed intense ambivalence about representative politics. Consider the voices of two of Hardenberg's leading political opponents, Ancillon and Wittgenstein. Scholars have generally portrayed both of them as stalwart reactionaries who ardently opposed a constitution from the time of the Vienna Congress. As shown above, both men actually vacillated a great deal over the constitutional question.[85] A further illustration of this point comes from two memoranda of 1821 and 1822, which they wrote as members of the Crown Prince's Commission. Both of these memoranda were written in confidence to the other members of the commission, most of whom also strenuously opposed Hardenberg's constitutional plans. Yet both authors referred to the issue of a central representative assembly in remarkably equivocal tones. Ancillon, writing in January 1821, criticized Hardenberg's plan for the communal ordinance by arguing that it would transform a "monarchy with estates" into a "royal democracy." Nonetheless, he conceded that "in the important matter of the constitution, we are all convinced that something must *happen* and *happen soon*." Ancillon argued that "the beginning must be made with the provincial estates" and that these bodies should serve as the basis for further constitutional developments both at the local and at the central level.[86] Wittgenstein's remarks, in a memorandum of September 1822 that concerned the proposed Provincial Estates Law, were even more striking. Wittgenstein wrote that he "dare not express an opinion" on the question of whether the law should state that the provincial assemblies would eventually elect the delegates to the Prussian "general estates." The king, Wittgenstein noted, had already declared that any further pronouncements concerning the general estates would come only at his own discretion. In the draft of this memorandum, Wittgenstein wrote—and then crossed out—the following words:

> In expressing myself in this sense, I hope I may not be misunderstood by the High Commission as if I entertained the fear that the convening of general estates could become dangerous and detrimental to the monarchy. I am far from giving credence to this thought.[87]

Even though Wittgenstein excised this passage from the final version of the memorandum, it is striking that one of Prussia's leading "reactionaries," writing to an audience of his like-minded peers, should have felt compelled to avow his faith in the ideal of constitutional rule.[88]

"The storms of today must be met with the institutions of today," declared historian Leopold von Ranke in the aftermath of the Revolution of 1848.[89] Ranke's remark reflected the attitude of a growing number of Prussian conservatives during the mid–nineteenth century. Stahl, decrying the "negative spirit of the age," called for the establishment of "national unity" and parliamentary institutions.[90] Likewise, Joseph Maria von Radowitz, a close adviser of King Frederick William IV, concluded that "the monarchy based on estates [*die ständische Monarchie*] is extinct in the consciousness of the masses." The state, Radowitz contended, had "lost its foundation in public opinion," and it was essential to restore the loyalty of the people to their king through the establishment of a "constitutional monarchy." After the Revolution of 1848, Radowitz attempted to revitalize the monarchy through his unsuccessful union project, a precursor to Bismarck's program of German national unification under conservative auspices during the 1860s.[91]

King Frederick William IV declared in alarm in 1854 that his closest ideological allies had "may God have mercy!, suddenly become constitutional!!!"[92] Indeed, what one scholar has termed the "pseudoconstitutionalization" of the Prussian Right became a widespread tendency after the defeat of the revolutionary movement in 1848–1849.[93] Yet, as will be discussed further in Chapter 8, Frederick William IV had himself played a major role in creating a new popular form of monarchy.[94] Frederick William IV recognized that, in the new age of mass production and mass politics, it was essential to employ innovative methods for legitimating monarchical rule. To recast the form of the monarchy, however, inevitably meant to transform its substance as well. Despite conservatives' deep suspicion toward the idea of a politically active nation, the new political ideas exerted a profound influence over the thinking of even the most reactionary figures in Prussia. With the decline of the old agrarian corporate social order, appeals to the sanctity of the traditional *Stände* had lost much of their resonance, so it was essential to redefine the bonds of community that unified the realm.

Conclusion: Prussian Conservatism and the Dilemma of Nationhood

Most historical accounts of conservatism in nineteenth-century Prussia emphasize how aristocratic social interests shaped conservative political theory and rhetoric. This chapter has focused on the opposite phenomenon, analyzing how discursive conventions influenced the ways in which conservative nobles and civil servants conceived and articulated their own interests. During the decades leading up to 1848, Prussian aristocrats confronted a perplexing dilemma: by rejecting the ideas of nationhood and national representation, they limited their capacity to organize as a unified interest group vis-à-vis the monarchical state; by embracing these ideas, however, they undermined the theoretical basis for the traditional corporate privileges of the provincial nobility. Thus, a division emerged within the conservative movement of this era. One strand of conservative thought, motivated by the fear of revolution, was characterized by the effort to deny the existence of the nation, or, at least, to subordinate the nation's political rights unequivocally to the authority of the state. Other conservatives, however, were dissatisfied with this rejection of the principle of a politically active nation. Some aristocratic activists, particularly in Prussia's easternmost provinces, viewed the establishment of a constitution as the only viable means of achieving an active role in the exercise of sovereign authority. Some of these activists explicitly demanded a national representation; others employed a more diffuse vocabulary, calling on the government to heed the authority of public opinion. For some leading conservative civil servants and scholars, the appeal to public opinion served a different purpose: namely, to secure the legitimacy of the monarchical state by coopting popular demands for political representation.

This conservative dilemma concerning what stance to take toward the idea of the nation reflected the broader problem of how to respond to the epochal social and political transformations occurring across Europe during the late eighteenth and early nineteenth centuries. As a fluid and urbanized society emerged in place of the relatively stable, agrarian, and localized premodern order, the old legal fictions about natural social hierarchy and the paternalistic mission of the aristocracy proved increasingly difficult to sustain. During the Restoration, the government's efforts to revitalize Prussia's traditional *ständische* order met with only limited success. The reestablishment of the trade guilds proved impractical and unpopular, and the ongoing transformation of the agricultural sector was irreversible.

More important for our inquiry here, conservative leaders failed to reestablish the old symbolic ground of Prussian politics. Both of the conservative rhetorical strategies explored in this chapter had important transformative effects on Prussian political culture. Those aristocrats who sought to foil the revolutionary threat by dis-inventing the nation found it difficult to forge political coalitions with other classes in opposition to the state or to legitimate their own preeminence as a ruling elite. After 1820, most Prussian nobles declared their allegiance to the monarchical principle, thus in effect abandoning their claims that royal power was limited by a contract with the estates. As a result of this defensive attitude on the part of many aristocrats, the monarchical state succeeded in consolidating its political authority during this era to a greater extent than ever before. The second conservative strategy, the appeal to "public opinion," was equally disruptive of traditional ruling relationships. Aristocratic efforts to speak on behalf of the nation or the public tended to blur, rather than reinforce, the boundaries between estates.[95] As one historian observes, " 'Publicity' was tightly linked to parliamentarization and party formation, as well as to freedom of the press and access to information." Thus, an "insurmountable contradiction" marked the efforts of civil servants who sought to preserve the state's monopoly over political power by invoking the authority of "public opinion."[96] The next chapter carries this story further, examining how, during the years leading up to 1848, bourgeois liberals and radicals strove to balance the authority of the "nation" with that of the monarchical state.

Eight

TOWARD A DEMOCRATIC MONARCHY

With the adoption of the Karlsbad Decrees in 1819, the scope for the free expression of political ideas narrowed dramatically in Prussia and the other German states. These measures, which remained in effect until April 1848, not only established strict censorship of the popular press but also allowed for surveillance of the universities and civic life and the summary imprisonment of dissidents. An American observer offered the following portrait of public life in Berlin during the 1820s:

> Conscious as every Prussian is that the almost omniscient eye of the government, through the medium of its system of *espionage* is fixed upon him, and that a single word expressed with boldness, may furnish an occasion for transferring him to Koepnic or Spandau; he becomes of course, in every circle, suspicious of those around him, sustains a negative character in his conversation, advances those indefinite opinions which are harmless, and if he does not commend, he takes very good care never to censure the proceedings of government.[1]

Many historians have argued that these conditions of repression fatally handicapped Prussian liberalism throughout the first half of the nineteenth century. Under the weight of censorship and suspicion, declares one scholar, Berlin's "flowering Enlightenment culture . . . gradually lost its intellectual élan and social coherence." Prussian progressives expressed their political views through "resentment and passive resistance," but until the eve of the Revolution of 1848 they failed to form any "coherent political movement."[2]

Though the censorship measures adopted at Karlsbad were vital factors in inhibiting open political discourse, the existence of political repression alone does not explain the distinctive character of Prussian liberal thought after 1819. Prussian liberalism emerged as a legacy of the political struggles of the Napoleonic era. As such, it reflected some of the same basic impulses and internal tensions that had characterized the thought of Stein and Hardenberg.

Throughout the pre–1848 era, leading liberal activists—and even many radicals—struggled to reconcile the principles of democratic and monarchical sovereignty. Like the Prussian reformers of the Napoleonic era, these figures sought to establish a harmonious relationship between the nation and the monarchical state by rationalizing civil society, fostering public education, and establishing parliamentary political institutions. Although in the 1840s, a few radicals began calling for the outright abolition of the Prussian monarchy, this faction remained quite small even after the outbreak of the Revolution of 1848. A substantial majority of revolutionary leaders, including many who are often identified as radical republicans, favored the preservation of at least some elements of monarchical authority. Rather than seeking to abolish the monarchy, most of the revolutionaries hoped to achieve a union of the monarch and the people—a goal that ultimately proved impracticable. Historians have often blamed the failure of the German Revolution of 1848 on the fractured and indecisive character of its leadership. Yet it was this shared commitment to forging a democratic monarchy, as much as the infighting among competing factions, that sabotaged the revolutionary movement of 1848 in Germany.

Shifting Conceptions of State and Civil Society

Chapter 2 of this book identified two fundamental challenges that confronted Prussian leaders at the beginning of the nineteenth century: the problem of social cohesion and the problem of sovereignty. In certain critical respects, the agendas of Stein and Hardenberg continued to inform the writings of later theorists on both of these issues. Philosophers from Hegel to Marx, like the Prussian reformers, hoped to solve the problem of cohesion partly by establishing social harmony. If private interests could somehow be synchronized with the public good, they argued, then the latent destructive forces within civil society could be tamed. The harmonization of private and public interests, these philosophers believed, would also help resolve the problem of sovereignty. If the institutions of the state were sufficiently rational and impartial, and the populace sufficiently enlightened, any tensions between state and civil society would be diminished. In Hegel's view, the "general estate" of the civil service would ideally act solely for the benefit of society as a whole. Marx's theory went still further: he hoped that social life would ultimately become so harmonious that sovereign authority would ultimately "wither away."

While similarities existed between the thought of the Prussian reformers and that of subsequent theorists, there were profound differences as well. First and foremost, the emergence of the "social question" during the decades leading up to 1848 shifted the center of gravity of philosophical inquiry and political debate. For Stein and Hardenberg, the liberation of the Prussian state from French domination had been the paramount objective. Though Hardenberg's reform program had fundamentally recast Prussia's economic and social order, these reforms had been motivated by the desire to mobilize the energies of society on behalf of the monarchical state.

After 1815, the political constellation changed dramatically in Central Europe. The fall of Napoleon inaugurated a century of relative peace, diminishing the need for states to mobilize their populations for political and military objectives. Moreover, the dramatic expansion of the population, along with the initial stages of industrialization, resulted in widespread social dislocation and pauperization. Between 1815 and 1845, the population of non–Austrian Germany increased by 38.5 percent. These demographic pressures became especially pronounced during the two years before 1848, when poor harvests led to misery and starvation, fueling social discontent. Among the educated elites, widespread frustration existed as well. During the 1820s, university enrollments expanded significantly, nearly doubling the number of lawyers in some cities by the mid–1830s. The number of new university graduates exceeded the number of available positions. These structural conditions encouraged the radicalization of certain segments of the educated classes, as some disappointed jurists took up careers in journalism.[3]

These changing social and political conditions were reflected in the philosophy of the era. From 1820 onward, many publicists and political theorists placed increasing emphasis on social issues. Hegel's *Philosophy of Right* (1821), for example, portrayed civil society as a sphere of activity separate from the state, which warranted it being studied on its own terms. Earlier German political theorists, such as the eighteenth-century cameralists, had used "state" and "society" as identical categories. The state, according to their terminology, represented the sum of all social relations. Conversely, social order was constituted and maintained only by judicious government regulation. Even Prussian reformers, such as Hardenberg, who had sought to reduce government intervention in society, had still spoken in terms of creating a "state society" (*Staatsgesellschaft*) or "citizens' society" (*Staatsbürgergesellschaft*). As these terms suggest, Hardenberg intended that the populace be mobilized both by and on behalf of the state.[4]

Hegel's theory signaled the transition toward the concept of a "modern economic society, set free from *ständisch* corporate ties."[5] Hegel envisioned civil society as an autonomous sphere in which individuals acted according to "particular" goals and needs. The social principle of "particularity for itself," however, inevitably resulted in "selfish" activity, which, if unrestrained, would result in universal suffering and "ethical degeneration." The potentially destructive character of social behavior gave rise to a "system of complete interdependence," when members of society recognized that the good of the individual was intimately linked with the preservation of the "welfare and the rights of all."[6] This recognition of mutual dependence resulted in the foundation of the state.

The sphere of civil society, according to Hegel, was dominated by individualistic and self-seeking activity. The state, by contrast, was an impartial institution representing the common good. "The whole [*die Ganzheit*]," Hegel declared, "must preserve the strength to keep particularity in harmony with ethical unity," and this project could only be carried out by the institutions of the state. Hegel defined the civil service as the "general estate" that had the "general interests of the community as its business." The mission of the state was to preserve social harmony by working to overcome the conflict between private interests and the public good.[7]

Hegel's theory of the state was open to profoundly opposing interpretations, depending on whether he was understood as writing in a descriptive or in a prescriptive mode. If it were read as a description of the state in its present form, Hegel's account appeared to glorify Prussian absolutism. Conservative Right Hegelians, such as legal philosopher Karl Friedrich Sietze of Königsberg, celebrated the Prussian state as "a gigantic harp tuned in the garden of God to lead the world chorale."[8] Read as a prescription for the ideal government, however, Hegel's theory could be understood as a plea for radical political reform. This was the direction followed by the Left Hegelians, such as Arnold Ruge, Bruno Bauer, Ludwig Feuerbach, and Karl Marx, who employed Hegelian principles in order to justify social and political revolution.[9]

The same ambiguity that characterized Hegel's stance toward the absolutist state was found in the writings of other Prussian political and social theorists of this era as well. Jurist Karl Friedrich von Savigny, for example, has often been depicted as an archconservative whose "historical school of law" helped establish the juridical foundation for the Restoration in Prussia. This interpretation, however, is overly simplistic. As a recent study reveals, Savigny belonged to a group of "visionary con-

stitutional reformers," who sought to adopt Roman law in Germany "because they believed it carried within it the seeds of a rebirth of Rome."
Savigny and other "advocates of the *Rechtsstaat* offered their 'rule of
law' as a third way between *Volkssouveränität* and *Absolutismus*, between the absolutism of the popular revolutionaries and that of the
princes."[10]

On the left of the political spectrum as well, writers and activists
sought to navigate between the extremes of absolute monarchy and democracy. In the summer of 1841, Ruge became one of the founders of
the radical Left Hegelian movement in Germany. Becoming disillusioned
with the "Christian state" of Frederick William IV, who had ascended to
the Prussian throne the previous year, Ruge proclaimed the birth of a
"Jacobin" party on German soil.[11] Only months earlier, however, Ruge
had written a pamphlet in a far different tone. This pamphlet, entitled
Prussian Absolutism and its Development, had heralded the advent of a
"republican monarchy."[12] Ruge had distinguished the early stages of
monarchical rule in Prussia, which had been characterized by "egotism"
on the part of both princes and nobles, from a second era of absolute
monarchy, which had culminated during the reign of Frederick the Great.
Ruge had declared: "Frederick II was the fully realized absolute monarch
of the Protestant state, in that he acted entirely for the generality [*für's
Allgemeine*]," rather than on behalf of his private interests. Ruge had
praised Frederick the Great for having freed himself "inwardly" from
"egotism." Yet, only in the third and final historical stage, the "age of
revolution," would this transformation of government become complete.
As a result of the revolution, "the egotism of the absolute monarchs
would also be negated *in reality*, and the entire organism of the state
would be . . . permeated by a new life and . . . spirit."

The "revolution" in Germany, Ruge had argued in this pamphlet,
would not result in the abolition of monarchy. Rather, it would bring
about a new form of monarchical rule combining "*spiritual* and *political*
freedom." The "king of the future," Ruge had declared, would fulfill
Frederick the Great's mission of "abstracting himself from all private
dynastic interests, and directing the state toward the goal of establishing
the freedom of all."[13] Ruge's call for a "republican monarchy" was strikingly reminiscent of Kant's plea that monarchs, even if they "rule auto-
cratically," should "govern in a republican manner."[14] For Ruge in 1841,
as for Kant in the 1790s, republicanism still had more to do with the
spirit than with the institutional form of government.

With the emergence of the Left Hegelian movement, Ruge and his
collaborators abandoned any hope of reforming the monarchical state
from within, assuming an openly oppositional line. (This move to the

left, incidentally, alienated the majority of liberal Hegelians, so that Ruge's group represented only a tiny splinter party in Prussian politics.) A "true" and "free" state, wrote Ludwig Feuerbach, would need to be an egalitarian, democratic republic. In such a state, which would be a real "communal being [*Gemeinwesen*]," any difference between the communal will and the private will of individuals would be abolished.[15]

The most influential of the Prussian Left Hegelians was Karl Marx, who belonged briefly to the movement before becoming disenchanted with its idealist intellectual foundation. A systematic analysis of Marx lies beyond the scope of this study, but a few brief remarks concerning his thought are in order. The tradition of enlightened nationalism involved two intertwined projects, first, the effort to mobilize the nation politically, and second, the attempt to harmonize the will of the nation with that of the state. In one sense, both Left Hegelianism and Marxism represented radical ruptures with the legacy of enlightened nationalism, because both rejected the primacy of the nation as a political community. For Ruge, the "true nationality of the new Germany" lay in the "union of *political* and *spiritual* freedom," rather than in "raw tribalism [*rohe Volksthümlichkeit*]."[16] Marx went still further, denouncing nationalism as a form of "false consciousness" that obscured the universal unity of the proletariat.

Though Marx rejected nationalism, he embraced the ultimate goal of social harmony. "From each according to his abilities, to each according to his needs," Marx declared. This slogan reflected the premise that, in a communist society, the interests of the individual would be recognized as identical to those of the community as a whole. Likewise, Marx's notion that the state would eventually "wither away" was rooted in his belief that the abolition of "egotism" would render political authority superfluous. Like earlier Prussian theorists, Marx argued that the education of the populace was an essential precondition for overcoming egotism—though this education, he believed, would occur not in schools but in the daily brutalities of class struggle. As the contradictions inherent within the capitalist economy became ever more starkly obvious, the true unity of interests of all workers would gradually be revealed. The proletariat, Marx contended, would become capable of revolutionary action only when it attained "true consciousness"; and a successful revolution would in turn lead to the negation of antisocial, individualistic activity. In Marx's views regarding social harmony and popular education, striking parallels existed with the political tradition that is the subject of this book. Like the Prussian reformers of the Napoleonic era, Marx hoped to help forge a new rational social order that would overcome the conflict between private and public interests. In this rational society, the people would be energized, devoting their full efforts toward achieving the good of all.

If Prussian political theorists' arguments about social cohesion exhibited significant continuities throughout the first half of the nineteenth century, so too did their writings on the problem of sovereignty. Like the Stein-Hardenberg party, many subsequent authors argued that institutions for popular political representation would *enhance* the authority of the monarchical state. Up to the Revolution of 1848, nearly all German intellectuals and political activists, except for a small group of radicals, including the Left Hegelians, continued to accept the principle of monarchical sovereignty.[17] As Dieter Langewiesche observes, "For liberals, the governmental form that would bring about the society of the future, founded on reason and freedom, was a constitutional monarchy rather than a republic."[18]

The modern Western concept of the balance of powers was not entirely absent from Prussian political theory of the early nineteenth century, but it played a more minor role than in British or American constitutional political theory. During the Napoleonic era, for example, both Stein and Hardenberg favored the establishment of a Council of State (*Staatsrat*), partly in order to limit the king's capacity to act arbitrarily. The *Staatsrat*, finally established in 1817, came to play a decisive role in the Prussian legislative process.[19] Similarly, early nineteenth-century liberals, both in Prussia and in other German states, viewed parliamentary institutions as a necessary check on royal power. The Hanoverian Friedrich Dahlmann, for example, declared: "The chambers [of parliament] should cooperate in the legislative process, protecting the laws. They should, however, not be co-rulers or co-administrators [of the realm]."[20] This formula provided for a much weaker representative assembly and a much stronger monarchical executive than was found in other contemporary parliamentary systems, such as that of Britain. Dahlmann envisioned the parliamentary assembly mainly as a restraint on monarchical authority, rather than as the prime moving force in government.

Dahlmann's attitude toward the absolutist state was fundamentally ambivalent. Prussia, he declared, was a state "with the magic spear which heals as well as wounds."[21] This ambivalence was shared by many other German liberals throughout the period leading up to 1848. Rather than deciding between the stark alternatives of monarchy and democracy, or between corporatism and universal equality, their instinct was to try to find a means of balancing and integrating these disparate political and social principles. Like the earlier generation of Prussian reformers, they hoped to overcome the internal contradictions within their political philosophy through the rationalization of state authority and through the "education of the nation."

The Project of National Education

In historical accounts of nineteenth-century Europe, Prussia is conventionally portrayed as socioeconomically "backward" with respect to the countries of Western Europe. In its industrialization, Prussia lagged about two generations behind England and about one generation behind France and Belgium. In the development of public schooling, however, this pattern was reversed. Prussia was the first European country to develop a centralized, state-run network of schools for its youth, and during the nineteenth century, its educational system became a model for the Western world. During the first half of the nineteenth century, Prussia reformed and expanded its universities and classical *Gymnasien* for training the intellectual elites; it also embarked on a program of providing universal elementary instruction. By the 1840s, more than 80 percent of Prussian children between the ages of six and fourteen were attending primary schools, a figure far greater than for any other contemporary society, with the exception of Saxony and parts of Scotland and New England.[22]

The question of why Prussia was the first European country to develop such an extensive program of public education has been debated among historians. Ultimately, this "schooling revolution" must be understood as one integral element of the broader response to the crisis that confronted the Prussian state during the Napoleonic era. As one scholar has observed, the discussion about educational reform in the early nineteenth century was entwined with "a larger consideration of problems that were seen as dangers to Prussia's social cohesion." Perceiving that "society was in danger of coming apart," Prussian leaders sought to generate "new binding myths" that would restore a sense of "wholeness" in social and political life.[23] They perceived popular education as an instrument for establishing harmony and "national spirit."

As previous chapters have shown, in the wake of the military defeat of 1806–1807, nearly all of the leading bureaucratic reformers shared the conviction that Prussia faced a crisis of social cohesion. Altenstein, for example, lamented the absence of a unified "voice of the nation," which he claimed had contributed to the disaster. "What was heard," he wrote, "were one-sided insights of individuals, guided and limited by private interest."[24] Gneisenau denounced the "stupidity" and passivity of the

Germans. Stein lambasted the nobles of Brandenburg for their "deep-rooted egotism" and "incomplete education [*halbe Bildung*]."[25]

In the first years of the Prussian reform period, both Stein and Hardenberg composed memoranda that emphasized the importance of schooling for forging a unified national community. In October 1808, Stein proclaimed the commitment of his ministry to "the raising [*Erziehung*] of the youth into a powerful species [*Geschlechte*], in which the goals of the state will be preserved and developed." His plans for school reform, he declared, would be an essential step toward a "uniform national education [*Nationalbildung*]," which would reinvigorate the state.[26] Hardenberg described the links between schooling and his broader reform program in similar terms:

> In the interior of the state . . . a new constitution will take shape. The energies of individuals will be urgently demanded by the state, but these energies will not be used as a mere tool by others. Rather, they will be dedicated, through the highest freedom, and the freest use of these energies, to the attainment of the greatest good.[27]

The first generation of nineteenth-century educational reformers in Prussia expressed a highly idealistic vision of the techniques and ultimate ends of schooling. The goal of universal schooling, declared Johann Wilhelm Süvern, was to form Prussia into "an organism [*Organismus*] in which each of society's components, province, nobleman, vassal, or locality, is allowed to develop its life [while] allowing at the same time these components to grow together into a unified whole [*Ganzen*]."[28] The schools, he argued, should foster the "general education of humanity [*allgemeinen Bildung des Menschen*]" through the "education of the nation and the youth [*National- und Jugendbildung*]."[29] This goal was to be attained not through narrow occupational training but rather through a broader program of humanistic learning. Up through the 1820s, the methods of the Swiss educational reformer Johann Heinrich Pestalozzi (1746–1827) served as the pedagogical model for the Prussian elementary schools. Pestalozzi, whose work was applauded by Stein, Süvern, and other leading reformers, encouraged spontaneous and independent inquiry by students. He also emphasized the intimate link between the formation of intellect and character.[30]

Numerous observers have pondered the "irony of liberal England producing a rigid undemocratic school system while hierarchical Germany developed a fairly open one."[31] The American educational reformer Horace Mann, visiting Berlin in the 1840s, remarked in amazement that Prussian children were *"taught to think for themselves."* Another American observer remarked on the "extraordinary spectacle" of the combination of despotic government and a wise educational system in Prussia.[32] The existence of an open educational system, however, is fully consistent with the interpretation of the Prussian reform movement advanced in this book. The Prussian reformers hoped that the education of the nation would advance the cause of harmony and public spirit rather than undermine the authority of the monarchical state.

As with the proposals for political liberalization, the Prussian educational reforms came under heavy attack during the early 1820s. A conservative educational commission appointed by Frederick William III reported in 1821 that the new school system had contributed to "increasing moral corruption" in Prussia, as shown by "fantastic rawness in clothing" and "arrogant cheekiness in conduct" among the youth. The liberals' attempt to foster the "self-development of religion and ethics in young people," declared the commission, had contributed to a "lack of true Christian religious teaching" and to a "revolutionary tendency of the young." These dangerous developments could be countered only by a return to "the *one effective* method of instruction, whereby the teacher communicates his knowledge or the results of his experience as something *fixed* and *certain*, in a manner appropriate to the intellectual capacity of the pupil."[33]

Beginning in 1821, under the leadership of the conservative Ludolf von Beckedorff, the development of Prussian schools took a much different direction than in the previous decade. Beckedorff criticized the leveling tendencies of Pestalozzi's pedagogy, as adapted by Süvern and other Prussian educational reformers. "Society," he argued, "does not rest on the possession of equal rights or demands upon its members, but upon their division . . . into separate classes and estates." Süvern's reform proposals, he claimed, would lead to "insecurity for the individual and eternal turmoil for the society as a whole."[34] Rather than promoting an "artificial equality," wrote Beckedorff, the proper goal of schooling was "the creation of orders or estates [*Standes-Bildung*]." Thus, he advocated the formation of a rigidly separated system of schools for each individual estate: *Landschulen* for peasants; *Armenschulen* for the lower urban orders; *Bürger-* and *Hauptschulen* for the industrial and commercial estates; and, finally, *Gelehrtenschulen*, *Gymnasien*, and universities for training members of the learned estates.[35]

Though Beckedorff sought to re-create a hierarchical, particularist society, it is essential to recognize that his program cannot be understood as purely reactionary in character. No less than the liberal educational reformers like Süvern, Beckedorff recognized that the traditional social order in Prussia had been permanently disrupted. The older division of the population into "the estates of the peasants, the warriors, and the learned" (*Nähr-, Wehr-, und Lehr-Stand*), he declared, "was appropriate to the relations of the earlier age, but does not entirely match those of the present." Instead, schools should be designed to prepare children for each of the "main types of occupations": agriculture, industry, trade, and scholarship.[36] In the future, he observed, the Prussian state would "have to be molded with forethought and purpose, like a work of art."[37] Thus, rather than attempting to abolish the new public school system, he expanded it, seeking to infuse the Prussian populace with an anti-egalitarian consciousness based on the notion of a "positive Christianity."[38]

The debates in Prussia over education policy during the period 1815–1848 mirrored the broader political and social disputes between liberals and conservatives. The liberal program of national education was far from being anti-monarchical in intent. Rather, liberals sought to fuse together the Prussian populace into a living organism, to forge a unified national consciousness, and to eliminate "strife between estates." They considered *Bildung*—the cultivation of both intellect and character—to be an essential prerequisite for overcoming egotism, which they believed was a fundamental source of conflict between the populace and the state authorities. Thus, for liberals, school reform was a critical tool for ensuring the future viability of the Prussian monarchical state. For conservatives, schooling was equally important. In their case, however, the primary lessons to be conveyed were that social hierarchy was eternal and that monarchical sovereignty was guaranteed by the will of God. Conservatives, in other words, attempted to use the innovative institution of universal schooling to secure the legitimacy of traditional social and political hierarchies.

The Pedagogical Function of Participatory Politics

Universal schooling was but one of several elements of the broader program of national education favored by the Prussian reformers and their successors in the liberal movement. As previous chapters have shown, the Stein-Hardenberg party believed that popular participation in politics would also serve a vital pedagogical role. For example, in the Nassau Memorandum of 1807, Stein argued that local and provincial assemblies would promote "the awakening of a spirit of community and civic pride, the employment of dormant or misapplied energies and of unused knowledge," along with "harmony between the views and desires of the nation and those of the administrative authorities of the state."[39] Stein's Municipal Ordinance, as well as Hardenberg's experimental representative assemblies of 1810–1815, were organized with this pedagogical function in mind. A brief discussion of two additional proposals for political reform will be useful in illustrating this connection between the goals of popular representation and national education. These proposals were the plans for a communal ordinance and for a general representative assembly for the Prussian state. Hardenberg lobbied fiercely for both of these measures between 1819 and 1822, during the final three years of his life, but ultimately neither proposal was adopted before the Revolution of 1848.

Plans for a Prussian communal and county ordinance went through several incarnations between 1808 and 1820. Stein originally proposed these measures as a counterpart to his Municipal Ordinance, to allow for political representation for residents of the Prussian countryside, as well as the towns. Stein's associates prepared drafts for such a law in 1808 and 1810, but neither was enacted.[40] In February 1820, Frederick William III ordered the formation of yet a third committee charged with drafting plans for the local and county representative assemblies.[41] Six months later, the committee completed a 240-page report, which included detailed legislative proposals for the communal and county estates. The committee envisioned these institutions as the first steps toward a "general representation of the state," which would "awaken a vigorous common spirit in the *Volk*" and move the citizenry to "forget individual and particular concerns on behalf of common goals." These local representative bodies would play a vital role in educating the Prussian populace for self-government. The committee observed: "In order to be released from guardianship and administer one's own affairs, one must be mature." To this end, the local assemblies were designed "not only to accord with a future higher level of popular cultivation [*Volksbildung*], but also to prepare it."[42] Kant had defined Enlightenment as "man's emergence from his self-imposed immaturity."[43] The constituent committee directed its legislative proposals toward precisely this goal.

Strikingly, the committee's lofty vision of Germans' capacity for self-government did not extend to Prussians of Polish ethnicity. The committee's report claimed that Stein's Municipal Ordinance had been a rousing success "even in the smallest agricultural villages" of the German provinces. Thus, the "differing levels of education" should not prove to be an obstacle to self-government in the countryside. Nonetheless, "everyone who had the opportunity to become familiar with the non–German provinces acknowledges that the rural communities of these territories cannot be recognized as mature."[44] The diametrically opposed perceptions of German and Polish villagers point to a much larger controversy, which lay at the heart of the project of national education, namely, whether to seek to Germanize Prussia's Polish territories or to respect non–German language and culture.

Like the "Jewish question," the status of the Prussian Poles would remain hotly contested throughout the nineteenth century and beyond. Karl von Altenstein, who served as minister of education and religion from 1817 until his death in 1840, took a relatively conciliatory attitude toward Polish culture. He declared in 1822: "Religion and mother tongue are the most sacred possessions of a nation," warning that "a government which shows itself indifferent to them, or even allows attacks upon them, embitters and dishonors a nation and makes of its members untrue and bad subjects." For Altenstein, in other words, the existence of an autonomous Polish cultural nation presented no threat to the integrity of the Prussian state. Under Altenstein's ministry, elementary education in the Polish territories was conducted in the pupils' mother tongue, though most advanced courses at the *Gymnasium* level were taught in German. As the century progressed, however, the Prussian government came to place increasing pressure on Polish culture, emphasizing the use of the German language in education and government.[45] This repressive activity stemmed in large part from the conviction that the political unity of the nation required cultural unity as well.

Like the plans for communal and county assemblies, the Prussian reformers' proposals for a general representative assembly were intended partly to further the political education of the populace. Before 1815, Hardenberg had used the term "national representation" to describe this new political body, but in the climate of growing suspicion toward popular nationalism, he subsequently employed less-threatening names such as "representatives of the land" (*Landesrepräsentanten*) or "estates of the realm" (*Reichsstände*).[46] In 1819, shortly before the adoption of the Karlsbad Decrees, both Hardenberg and Wilhelm von Humboldt presented proposals for a Prussian constitution to Frederick William III. These outlines, which were similar in their basic features, illustrate how progressive Prussian statesmen of this era sought to harmonize monarchical sovereignty with parliamentary institutions.

Both Hardenberg and Humboldt favored establishing the *Reichsstände* in connection with a network of local, county, and provincial representative assemblies. By requiring the citizenry to participate in governing itself, Humboldt hoped to stimulate the moral development of the individual and to forge a living bond between the state and the national spirit. Like Hardenberg, Humboldt argued for a two-chamber central representative assembly; in the upper chamber, representation would be granted on a hereditary basis to members of the privileged estates, whereas delegates to the lower chamber would be elected by the nobility, the non-noble landowners, and the citizens of the towns. Unlike Hardenberg, Humboldt insisted that the delegates to the central assembly be elected directly by the Prussian citizenry rather than indirectly by the members of the local and provincial assemblies. Though Humboldt claimed that national elections were essential in order to overcome the "corporative spirit," he also (like Stein) emphasized more than Hardenberg the need to preserve the traditional estates.[47]

Apart from these minor differences over the details of their constitutional plans, Hardenberg and Humboldt also clashed with each other over political tactics. For example, Humboldt insisted that the central representative body should convene no later than 1822 or 1823, whereas Hardenberg was too wary to propose a definite timetable. Humboldt also demanded that the central estates be granted a deciding vote over legislation and the right to initiate legislative proposals, while Hardenberg knew that Frederick William III would only accept an assembly with a purely consultative role.[48] Hardenberg was willing to work within the constraints dictated by the king; Humboldt preferred to stand on principle.

Historians have often portrayed Humboldt as a far more liberal and laudable character than Hardenberg. Indeed, in the autumn of 1819, Humboldt's principled stance against the Karlsbad Decrees earned him expulsion from the Prussian government. Yet, regarding monarchical sovereignty, the two men held remarkably similar views. When Hardenberg presented his constitutional proposal to King Frederick William III in August 1819, he declared:

> All necessary steps must be taken to ensure that the monarchical principle shall be firmly established, that true freedom and security of person and property shall harmonize with that principle, and that in this way freedom and security may best and most enduringly persist in conjunction with order and energy. Thus the principle will be maintained: *Salus publica suprema lex esto!*[49]

Hardenberg hoped that the monarch and the estates would cooperate harmoniously on behalf of the public good. Likewise, Humboldt argued in October 1819: "The constitution, which the Prussian state requires, must serve to support and complete the monarchical principle. . . . The force and authority of the government must not be diminished, but rather enhanced, through [the constitution]."[50]

Hardenberg and Humboldt shared a deep faith in the capacity of an enlightened nation to coexist harmoniously with a sovereign monarch.

Because of this faith, Hardenberg included in the State Debt Law of January 1820 a provision mandating that, henceforth, the Prussian government would be allowed to accumulate new debts "only upon consultation with and co-guarantee by the future estates of the realm."[51] Abiding by this requirement, Prussian leaders refrained from issuing any new state bonds until 1847. In that year, King Frederick William IV, seeking funds for the construction of a Berlin-Königsberg railroad, revived the public debate over a Prussian constitution.

Frederick William IV's Monarchical Offensive, 1840–1847

The final two decades of the reign of King Frederick William III, from 1820 to 1840, were characterized by a highly rigid and defensive political stance. In his Last Testament of 1827, Frederick William III declared: "Prussia's position in the general state system depends above all on the unlimited character of royal power." He strongly counseled his successors against any measure that would alter this "foundation pillar of the monarchy," thus weakening the Prussian state.[52] Frederick William IV, who ascended to the throne in 1840, shared his father's suspicion of the revolutionary potential of a politically active populace. Nonetheless, the younger Frederick was convinced that the Prussian monarchy needed to secure new sources of legitimacy in order to survive and flourish. It was impossible, he declared early in his reign, "to come up with any kind of concept that could describe the political entity called Prussia. This thing has no historical basis; it consists of an agglomeration of territories, which themselves once had such a basis and then lost them."[53] Frederick William's remark about the artificial character of the Prussian state was strikingly reminiscent of Karl vom Stein's 1806 observation that Prussia was merely an "aggregation of many individual provinces brought together through inheritance, purchase, and conquest" and that it lacked any "state constitution."[54]

While Stein had sought to establish unity among the Prussian provinces by rationalizing the exercise of sovereign authority and by establishing representative institutions, Frederick William IV took a very different approach: he asserted that the Prussian monarchy was divinely ordained and that he was king "by the grace of God." As David Barclay notes, Frederick William IV was thus "breaking with the actual traditions of his own state," which had long emphasized the legal rather than the sacred foundations of monarchical authority.[55] These theological appeals, however, were only one element of Frederick William IV's effort to revitalize the Prussian monarchy: he also sought to legitimate his rule on the basis of popular support, using public speeches and mass gatherings in order to secure the loyalty of his subjects. In effect, Frederick William IV sought to portray himself as a representative both of God *and* of the people. These two dimensions of his monarchical project are neatly captured by illustration 8.1, which depicts the "ceremonial entry of Their Majesties the King and Queen into Breslau" in September 1841. Here, Frederick William appears (at the bottom center of the frame) riding on horseback in military uniform, with the queen at his side. He is surrounded by his subjects rather than addressing them from a distance— a king *of* the people, not apart from them. At the same time, the ceremonial gate behind the king emphasizes the link between royalty and divinity. This edifice, whose spires resemble those of a cathedral, is capped by several ornate crowns. The design vividly depicts the principle of *Gottesgnadentum*—Frederick William's claim that he ruled "by the grace of God." Thus, this image associated the Prussian king equally closely with God and the *Volk*.[56]

In seeking to inspire popular allegiance, Frederick William IV often portrayed Prussia as the vessel for a greater German identity. In 1842,

8.1 "Ceremonial entry of Their Majesties the King and Queen of Prussia into Breslau on 13 September 1841." Staatsbibliothek zu Berlin— Preußischer Kulturbesitz—Handschriftenabteilung, YB 15476 m.

for example, at an event that celebrated the resumption of construction of the unfinished Cologne Cathedral, he saluted the "spirit of German unity and strength" in front of an ecstatic crowd. Frederick William envisioned that union quite differently than did the bourgeois popular nationalists of his day. In Barclay's words:

> Germany was, to his mind, a medieval world of corporative or *ständisch* freedom, based on a hierarchical and paternalistic social order, infused with Christian humility, and sustained by a harmonious union of prince and people.[57]

Nonetheless, his listeners may not have caught all of these nuances. Chancellor Metternich of Austria, who also attended the Cologne event, warned that the king's "artistic" tendencies would inevitably lead him and his subjects "in new directions invented only by themselves."[58] One such direction is captured by the ominous image in illustration 8.2, which the anonymous artist entitled simply "1942." In the background of this engraving, produced around the time of the 1842 celebration, a circle of men dances around a liberty tree while the Cologne Cathedral burns. In the foreground, a German (appearing as the mythic figure Hermann, dressed in a bear pelt and a crown of oak leaves) and a Frenchman wearing a laurel wreath grasp each other's hands while straddling the Rhine River. This image was intended as a radical fantasy of the future, in which French and German citizens would unite in peace, liberated from what the artist saw as the reactionary tyranny of the church. (Chillingly, the prophecy proved half right: the first bombing raids on Cologne during World War II occurred in 1942, but these fires were the product of continuing enmity rather than newfound peace between Germany and France.) As this engraving shows, popular support for the notion of a sacralized German-Christian monarchy modeled on the medieval order was by no means universal during this era.[59]

In defining himself as king by grace of both God and the Prussian people, Frederick William IV attempted a difficult balancing act. During the first years of his reign, Frederick William vacillated between two contradictory impulses: on the one hand, to create a more open political process, thus binding the monarchy more tightly to the populace, and on the other hand, to suppress any potentially revolutionary activities. Within a few days of becoming king, he began to discuss the possibility of convening representatives from the Prussian provinces in Berlin. He also abolished most press censorship, granted amnesty to political prisoners, and allowed the provincial assemblies to publish the results of their deliberations. Yet, at the same time, he jealously guarded his government's monopoly over sovereign authority. For example, when the

8.2 "1942": Prophecy of the burning of the Cologne Cathedral
(1842). In the foreground, the German mythic hero Hermann,
dressed in a bear pelt and a crown of oak leaves, grasps the
hand of a Frenchman wearing a laurel wreath. Staatsbibliothek
zu Berlin—Preußischer Kulturbesitz—Handschriftenabteilung,
YB 15511 gr.

easing of press censorship measures in Prussia resulted in open criticism
of the monarchy, the king reacted by reinstating the earlier restrictions.
Likewise, the decision to allow the provincial estates to publish their
deliberations quickened the pulse of political life in Prussia. The delegates to the assemblies began to stake bolder claims about their own role
as guardians of the public interest, and they campaigned openly for
expanding the role of representative institutions.[60]

Frederick William's ideas concerning the establishment of parliamentary institutions reflect this tension between the desires to secure popular support and to maintain a monopoly on political power. In 1840, for example, he toyed with a proposal for convening a central assembly of representatives in Prussia, modeled on his father's idea of bringing together thirty-two delegates from the various provinces along with an equal number of delegates drawn from the Council of State. By stipulating that half of the delegates in the assembly would be appointed directly by the king, this plan sought to ensure that the representative body would support rather than undermine the monarchy.[61] Four years later, in 1844, Frederick William IV returned to the project of constitutional reform with greater seriousness. The king was becoming increasingly frustrated over his government's inability to raise money for building railroads and highways; moreover, delegates to the eight provincial diets were taking an increasingly oppositional stance because of their desire for a Prussian constitution. Frederick William decided that the best solution to this dilemma would be to call together all of the delegates from the various provincial diets in Berlin. The activities of this assembly would be strictly limited to guaranteeing state debts and raising taxes. Moreover, the king was adamant that there should be "no national representation," no direct elections of delegates, and no stipulation of a regular interval between meetings of the assembly, which would stimulate a "periodic fever" of public opinion in Prussia. He insisted: "I will not drop the sceptre from my hands, I will not issue a Charter, I will *never* share my sovereign powers with the estates."[62] After more than two years of deliberations involving the king's ministers and members of the royal family, this plan became the basis of the Patent of 3 February 1847, which announced that the provincial diets of the country would convene as a United Diet whenever the state needed to secure new loans or additional taxes.

The first meeting of the United Diet was scheduled for 11 April 1847, and in the two months leading up to the opening session, political activists on both the right and the left of the political spectrum expressed intense disappointment with the February Patent. For conservatives, this document represented the first step on the slippery slope toward a constitution. Some leading liberals, however, threatened to boycott the assembly because the king's plan defined the diet's legislative role in such narrow terms.[63] The king's opening address to the United Diet only increased the unhappiness on all sides. Frederick William IV spoke to the assembled delegates from the throne in the White Hall of the royal palace in Berlin. The physical organization of the assembly—the delegates arranged in orderly rows with the king seated on a high platform in the

8.3 The opening session of the United Diet in Berlin, 11 April 1847.
Staatsbibliothek zu Berlin—Preußischer Kulturbesitz—Handschriftenabteilung, YB 15912 m.

center—reflected the monarch's own view of the proceedings. He described himself as the "inheritor of an *undiminished* crown, which I *must*
and *will* pass on undiminished to my successors." He dismissed out of
hand the notion of the "division of sovereignty" or the "breaking of the
full authority [*Vollgewalt*] of kings." Frederick William IV said that he
regarded the assembly as "German estates in the ancient sense." By this,
he meant that the delegates should serve as "representatives and protec-
tors of particular rights [*eigenen Rechte*], the rights of the estates." Frederick William, in other words, defined the role of the delegates in exactly
the opposite sense from Stein and Hardenberg, who had demanded that
representatives act on behalf of the "good of the whole" rather than
expressing their own "private perspective." Frederick William declared
that the deputies also had the right to offer conscientious advice to the
king on issues concerning which he requested their counsel. They possessed no brief, however, to "represent opinions." Rather, their role was
confined to helping the king rule "according to the law of God and of
the land."[64]

Despite the king's highly restrictive vision of representation, the very
act of publicly convening a central representative assembly in Prussia
made it possible for the delegates to demand a broader political role.

Frederick William IV pledged: "From this time on, every man in the land will know that I . . . will negotiate no state bond measure, that I will increase no tax, and establish no new tax without the free consent of all the estates."[65] Like Hardenberg before him, Frederick William IV sought to expand the role of representative institutions in Prussia, while still preserving the principle of absolute monarchical sovereignty. This balance, however, proved impossible to sustain.

Frederick William's opening address of 11 April provoked consternation among the delegates to the assembly: in the words of the Austrian observer Count Trauttmansdorff, the speech "hit the assembly like a thunderbolt. . . . With one blow the *Stände* have seen their hopes and desires obliterated; not one happy face left the assembly."[66] On 20 April, the delegates to the United Diet voted to send the king a formal reply. Their petition thanked Frederick William for convening the diet, which they said represented "a great step" toward the "development of the life of the nation [*National-Lebens*]"; however, they admonished the king that the responsibilities of this assembly fell short of what had been articulated by the State Debt Law of 1820 and the Provincial Estates Law of 1823. The petition declared that the viability of the Prussian monarchy depended upon the further involvement of the Prussian people in political decision making:

> The power of the throne is firmly grounded when it is rooted in the ethical consciousness of the nation. . . . Under the blessings of a powerful monarchical government, [the Prussian people] will share the benefits of a free and open public life [*Staatslebens*], which will elevate all classes of the people; and, rallying around its royal leader in love and faithfulness, face the great destiny, to which Providence has called the Prussian state and with it the entire German fatherland.[67]

While acknowledging the principle of monarchical sovereignty, the delegates demanded a clarification of the diet's legislative role. In particular, they were concerned that the king guarantee regular meetings of the assembly, rather than convening it solely at his own discretion.

In replying to the assembly's address, Frederick William IV dismissed the delegates' objections by insisting that the Patent of 3 February was "inviolable in its foundations"; nonetheless, he allowed, "We do not regard it for that reason as fully completed, but rather as capable of further development."[68] The king's ambivalent response inspired a group of dissidents within the diet to obtain the signatures of 138 delegates on a letter that protested the lack of "complete conformity" between the Patent of 3 February 1847 and the "older laws guaranteeing the rights of the estates."[69] The continuing wrangling over procedure stymied the

United Diet's work. The delegates to the assembly, bridling at the limitations imposed on them and at the government's rejection of their request for regularly scheduled meetings, refused to approve the bond measure or the tax reform proposals brought before them.

While the deliberations of the United Diet ended on 26 June 1847 with little having been achieved, this episode planted the seeds for the revolutionary movement that erupted in March of the following year. Metternich had warned Frederick William in advance against convening a United Diet: "Your majesty will bring together eight separate representative bodies and they will return home as a national parliament."[70] Indeed, the failure of the diet contributed to a heightened level of political activism throughout the remainder of the year. Liberals circulated petitions demanding constitutional reform and lobbied publicly at the meetings of city councils in Prussia. By early March 1848, inspired by the eruption of revolutionary events in Paris, mass demonstrations occurred in Cologne, Breslau, and Königsberg. On 14 March 1848, the king reluctantly agreed to reconvene the United Diet the following month to discuss the adoption of a constitution. Within four days of this decision, however, Berlin itself was swept up in revolutionary violence.[71]

In the midst of all this upheaval, the premises of enlightened nationalism continued to shape the views of politically active Prussians. Explicitly antimonarchical sentiment was virtually nonexistent among the delegates to the United Diet of 1847[72]; and even at the height of the political turmoil of the following year, few revolutionary leaders called for the outright abolition of the monarchy. Illustration 8.4, which dates from 1848, shows how liberal revolutionaries both built on and transformed the king's self-image as a popular sovereign. This engraving depicts the "ceremonial procession of His Majesty Frederick William IV . . . on 21 March 1848 in Berlin," the day on which the Prussian king issued a proclamation "to my people and the German nation," announcing that "Prussia will henceforth merge into Germany."[73] In many respects the composition of this engraving parallels that of illustration 8.1, from 1841. As in the earlier picture, the king is pictured on horseback in military dress, riding among his people. The (largely bourgeois) citizens, however, are much more clearly drawn than in the earlier picture, where they are depicted as indistinct forms and faces. In the 1848 picture, the members of the crowd are shown to be as fully human, and as fully individualized, as the king himself. Strikingly, numerous women are present in this crowd, suggesting that the national community was not exclusively male.[74] Just as in the picture of 1841, an edifice stands behind the king, but this time it is the State Opera in Berlin, above whose portal is inscribed "Fridericus Rex Apollini et Musis" (Frederick the King for Apollo

8.4 The king recrowned: "Ceremonial procession of His Majesty Frederick William IV, King of Prussia on 21 March 1848 in Berlin." Staatsbibliothek zu Berlin—Preußischer Kulturbesitz—Handschriftenabteilung, YB 17110 m.

and the Muses). This visual reference seems to associate Frederick William IV less with God than with *Kultur*. To the extent that he helped educate and civilize the Prussian people, preparing them for the task of self-determination, he would earne the enduring loyalty and love of his citizens.

In illustration 8.4, Frederick William IV is preceded by an officer on horseback, who carries the black-red-gold flag of the German nationalist movement. At the bottom of the frame, the artist has paraphrased the Prussian king's proclamation of 21 March: "I have adopted the German colors not in order to usurp crowns, but to join myself, along with my people, to the German nations, in order to be able to work in union with them against all storms from within and from without." Surrounding a depiction of two clasped hands is the slogan: "Union of the German nations."[75] Thus, in this picture, as in the revolutionary movement itself, the themes of unity, harmony, and *Bildung* are fused. The joint projects of national unification and national education, the artist suggests, will allow Germany to overcome the "storms" of social unrest and political dissension.

Revolutionary Ambitions of 1848

In early 1848, a constellation of factors, including famine, high urban unemployment, and long-simmering political discontent, combined to set off a wave of revolutions across Europe. The first uprising occurred in Palermo, Sicily, in January of that year. In February, a revolution in Paris toppled the reign of King Louis-Philippe of France, and within the next two months, more than forty revolutions erupted in the Italian states and throughout Central Europe.

After the outbreak of revolutionary events in Baden in April 1848, an anonymous caricaturist drew a scathing comparison of the political spirit in southern and northern Germany. Entitled "The German Michael has trouble deciding between a sleeping cap and a Jacobin cap," the picture contrasts the southern republican on the left, bearing a sword, with the northern monarchist on the right, carrying an olive branch.[76] This illustration, while exaggerating the political differences between northerners and southerners, effectively captures the powerful tensions within the revolutionary movement of 1848 in Germany. The 1848 revolutionaries, both in Prussia and in the other German states, were deeply divided both socially and politically. In their program for social reform, many revolutionaries desired both to establish equality and to preserve certain traditional hierarchies. In their political program, many revolutionaries sought both a democratic constitution and the preservation of the monarchy.

The views of Friedrich Ludwig Jahn point out some of these internal tensions of the revolutionary movement. Elected as a deputy to the Frankfurt National Assembly in 1848 at the age of sixty-nine, Jahn considered this honor the crowning achievement of his career. Having suffered years of persecution for his role in founding the gymnasts' movement and the *Burschenschaft*, he relished the opportunity finally to "speak in a public assembly as a representative of the German people on behalf of the unity and freedom of Germany." Jahn cautioned, however, that "by unity I do not mean leveling [*Einerleiheit*], by freedom I do not mean boundless arbitrariness." In August 1848, Jahn voted against the abolition of the nobility; in January 1849, he advocated the establishment of a hereditary emperor in Germany.[77]

On 25 August 1848, Jahn took the floor of the assembly to warn against the "subversive activities of the communist associations of the so-called radical democrats." The plotting of these groups, Jahn declared, threatened to plunge Germany into a "bloody civil war."[78] The manifest irony of this speech was not lost on an anonymous caricaturist, who

8.5 "The German Michael has trouble deciding between a sleeping cap and a Jacobin cap" (1848). The southern republican on
the left wears the Jacobin cap; the northern monarchist on the
right wears the sleeping cap. Staatsbibliothek zu Berlin—
Preußischer Kulturbesitz—Handschriftenabteilung, YB 16262 kl.

portrayed Jahn sardonically as the "exterminator of democrats," standing like Robespierre in front of the guillotine. Having himself long been
suspected of harboring subversive intentions, Jahn now leveled the same
exaggerated warnings about a "revolutionary threat" against his own
foes.

Jahn's political views placed him toward the right of the political
spectrum among delegates to the Frankfurt Assembly.[79] For example, the
proposal to establish a hereditary emperor in Germany was initially rejected by a vote of 263 to 211. (The assembly subsequently reversed its
decision on this matter in March 1849, voting by a narrow margin to

8.6 Friedrich Ludwig Jahn, "The exterminator of democrats" (1848). Staatsbibliothek zu Berlin—Preußischer Kulturbesitz—Handschriftenabteilung, YB 18041 m.

create a hereditary title of Kaiser.)[80] Jahn's conception of the ideal nature of political authority, however, had much in common with that of even the most radical German revolutionaries.

Histories of the Revolution of 1848 customarily draw sharp distinctions among the various revolutionary factions, for example, socialists versus liberals, monarchists versus democrats. While these labels provide a useful starting point for analysis, they tend to obscure the conceptual continuities that existed across the revolutionary movement. Jahn, despite his support for aristocracy and hereditary monarchy, expressed anti-elitist sentiments that resonated with those of the socialists. Money, he argued, was the source of "evil" and corruption. The "upper estates," he declared, had "destroyed Germany" by abandoning authentic German language and culture.[81]

If radicals and moderates both criticized excessive social hierarchy, important similarities also existed in their political views. A recent study of the democratic movement in the Prussian Rhineland examined the editorial content of the *Trier'sche Zeitung*, one of the most radical socialist newspapers in the Rhineland before 1848. Reviewing more than 300 incidents of censorship in 1846 and 1847, the author found that "explicitly communistic ideas made up only a small portion of the offending material." Far more common were attacks on the Prussian government, individual officials, censorship, and the church. Significantly, only 4 percent of the incidents of censorship were motivated by direct "attacks on monarchy."[82] Thus, even on the eve of the Revolution of 1848, many Prussian radicals continued to follow a venerable oppositional strategy of the premodern world: rather than criticizing the king himself, radicals decried the shortsightedness of royal officials and their policies.

Even for committed democrats of the 1848 era, the concept of a republic remained an abstraction. In the words of one historian, "The 'democratic republic' meant . . . a 'constitution in which the [people as a] whole assumed responsibility for the freedom and well-being of the individual.' "[83] Many democratic activists supported the preservation of the monarchy in some form. For example, a group of Düsseldorf radicals founded a new political club in April 1848, which they called the Association for Democratic Monarchy.[84] The prominent Rhenish labor leader Andreas Gottschalk, while calling for the founding of a "workers' republic," also opposed any agitation against the Prussian royal family. In May 1848, he refused to join a campaign that condemned the return from exile of Prince Wilhelm, the heir to the throne, who had advocated using artillery against the revolutionary crowds in Berlin—though it must be noted that Gottschalk's position on this question provoked a hostile reaction from nearly all of the city's other radical leaders.[85]

An examination of the rhetoric of two of the more radical delegates to the revolutionary assemblies, Friedrich Wilhelm Carové and Christian Gottfried Nees von Esenbeck, will help illustrate the ambiguous nature of democratic ideology in 1848. Carové, in his youth, had been one of the founders of the *Burschenschaft* movement and had served as an assistant to Hegel at the University of Berlin. In 1819, he had run afoul of the Prussian authorities for his ambiguous pamphlet discussing the assassination of Kotzebue.[86] Banned from subsequent university employment, he led a nomadic existence as an independent scholar. Upon the outbreak of the Revolution of 1848, Carové was elected as a delegate to the preliminary parliament (*Vorparlament*) in Frankfurt. In this capacity, he wrote a pamphlet entitled *The Sovereignty of the German Nation and the Competence of Its Constituent Assembly*, which was published in July 1848.

Carové's pamphlet defended both the principle of national sovereignty and the right of the *Vorparlament* to compose a German constitution. The "true democrat," Carové declared, desired the "freedom of every individual." In a democracy, the principle of sovereignty meant simply that "the state, consisting of free individuals, was dependent on no external power." Whether Germany called itself a republic by name was unimportant, he argued; the most fundamental political principle was that "in the state as in every organism," the good of the individual was linked to that of the whole. Thus, all members of the state must dedicate themselves to the "preservation of the commonweal [*Gesammtwesens*]," and moreover, "whoever wants to be the highest, must serve all the others to the greatest extent."[87]

The goal of the 1848 revolutionaries, wrote Carové, was the "struggle for rational freedom [*vernunftrechtlichen Freiheitsstrebens*]." This struggle was being waged against the "absolutism of the monarchical principle." Its goal, however, was not to replace absolute monarchy with a new "abstract absolutism . . . of the so-called democratic principle or of a doctrinaire contract theory." Rather, it was to forge an "ethical communal being [*Gemeinwesen*]," in which all individuals would recognize their duties to the whole. The fulfillment of the revolutionary project, therefore, required more than just the establishment of new laws and new political institutions. Carové envisioned the revolutionary process in Kantian terms, describing national sovereignty as the ultimate stage of a process of popular *Bildung*:

> For the individual human being, the release from guardianship [*Vormund-schaft*] and the achievement of rational law [*Vernunftrecht*] is conditional upon his being capable of and willing for self-determination. Thus, as we have also shown, a *Volk* is only fully entitled to constitute and govern itself when it truly wants to be a free nation, and when it also wills the conditions that are essential for this end.[88]

For Carové, in other words, the goal of political self-determination was inseparable from that of ethical self-determination. As for Kant, the term "republican" referred less to the form than to the spirit of government. Carové's ideal was a political community that would dedicate itself to justice and the common good. Whether or not this community retained a monarch as its chief executive was a question of secondary importance.

Christian Gottfried Nees von Esenbeck (1776–1858) entered politics along a different path than Carové. Born in Hesse, he attended the University of Jena, studying medicine, natural history, and philosophy.

While at the university, he also became a member of the Weimar circle, developing a friendship with Goethe. Until the age of forty-two, Nees lived as a country gentleman on a small estate left to him by his first wife, who had died in childbirth. He devoted himself to the study of European languages and to assembling natural history collections. In 1818, finally running short of money, he obtained an appointment as professor of botany, first at the University of Erlangen and then at Bonn. In 1830, he moved to the University of Breslau. In Breslau, Nees became active in civic causes, cofounding a health insurance plan and, in 1845, becoming the leader of a community of "Christian Catholics." In 1848, Nees helped found the Breslau Workers' Club, and upon the outbreak of the revolution, he was elected a delegate from Breslau to the Prussian National Assembly in Berlin.[89]

Nees's pamphlet *Die demokratische Monarchie*, which he presented to the Berlin Assembly in July 1848, articulated a constitutional plan based on radically democratic views. "The *Volk* is the sole legislative power in the state and the sole object of its legislation," Nees declared. "The *Volk* is lord, and the concept 'subject' [*Unterthan*] is struck from the life of the state for all time."[90] Even Nees's compatriots on the left of the Berlin Assembly were shocked by the "extremism" of his constitutional plan. After the collapse of the revolutionary movement, Nees was dismissed without pension from his professorship and permanently banned from Berlin.[91]

Nees favored the establishment of a unicameral legislative assembly that would exercise sovereign authority. His plan preserved the monarchy but offered a severely constricted vision of the monarch's political rights. Within the legislative assembly, the monarch would possess a single vote, but he would have no special power to veto legislation. The king was to be president of the ministerial council (*Ministerrath*), and he would also have the power to choose government ministers and other officials. He would open the sessions of the legislative assemblies and "sanction their decisions through his signature." Moreover, Nees declared that "if the legislative assembly injures the constitution," the king would be bound to dissolve the body and call for new elections. All in all, under this proposal, the rights of the king would have resembled those of a twentieth-century European prime minister.

Though Nees insisted on the principle of democratic sovereignty, his constitutional plan reserved a central role for the king as the "personal organ of the legislative . . . will of the *Volk*." He strenuously denied that he wanted to make the Prussian king a "puppet" of the national assembly. The institution of monarchy, he declared, was essential for distilling the thoughts and desires of the nation as a whole:

The king is the Volk in the form of a person. He has adopted all of the thoughts, all of the perceptions, all of the resolutions of the entire *Volk,* so that they are *his* thoughts, *his* perceptions, *his* resolutions. . . . Thus, the democratic-monarchical state presupposes the king to be a great, wise, powerful, and humanitarian man. It assists him through its basic law, in order that, in his elevated position, he may act without falling prey to pernicious swindles.[92]

As one scholar has observed, the term "republican" is somewhat of a misnomer for the radical faction among the German revolutionaries of 1848. Though many democratic activists supported the principle of a republic as the "ideal form of government," in practice they sought to establish a "parliamentary monarchy." Nonetheless, the radicals'

theoretical affirmation of the republic sufficed, in the perception of liberals and conservatives, to brand them as social revolutionaries. That is why the battle cry "republic or constitutional monarchy" was able to divide the organized revolutionary movement into two hostile camps, even though there were hardly any determined republicans in Germany.[93]

In other words, in Germany during the Revolution of 1848, even most of the republicans were monarchists, at least in terms of their immediate political objectives.

Over the course of the revolutionary events of 1848–1849, however, the possibility of a more categorical critique of monarchical sovereignty began to emerge. This process of political radicalization is illustrated by the history of the Democratic Club (*Demokratischer Klub*) of Berlin, which was the largest democratic political association in Prussia during 1848. Founded as the Political Club (*Politischer Klub*) on 23 March 1848, only days after the outbreak of the revolution, this association was initially open to progressives of every stripe, from socialists to liberals, and was intended to safeguard the achievements of the revolution. The club's early meetings, which were held every evening, often dissolved into an "extraordinary confusion" of political views, according to a contemporary observer.[94]

By May 1848, frustrated by the club's ineffectuality as a political force, its members decided to reorganize it under the name Democratic Club, publishing a statement of principles that read: "The goal of the club is the propagation and implementation of the democratic principle," which it defined as the "full guarantee" of political freedoms "through a constitution which secures for the people its sovereignty and the right of self-rule" at every level of society. Even so, this initial manifesto stopped short of declaring whether the Prussian state should take the form of a monarchy or a republic, because the club's members considered other issues, such as suffrage qualifications, more pressing ones to resolve. The Democratic Club attracted a large and growing following over the spring and summer of 1848. By June it had more than a thousand formal members, and some of its sessions attracted an audience of several thousand listeners. The leadership of the club consisted primarily of students and members of the academic proletariat (freelance journalists, private tutors, etc.), but the rank and file was increasingly dominated by Berliners from the working classes. Only men were permitted to become members, although women were allowed to attend meetings as guests. Over the course of 1848, female participation in the club's activities expanded steadily: more than 300 women were reported to have attended one session in August.[95]

A pivotal event in polarizing the revolutionary movement in Prussia was the storming of the Berlin arsenal on 14 June 1848. Alarmed by rumors that the king was plotting to suppress the revolution, a group of workers surrounded the arsenal, demanding weapons in order to defend their cause. Members of the bourgeois citizen militia guarding the arsenal opened fire on the crowd, killing two demonstrators and severely wounding two others. This event sparked a full-scale riot: barricades were thrown up in the streets, the arsenal was overrun and plundered, and groups of workers flew red flags, shouting, *"Es lebe die Republik!"* As Rüdiger Hachtmann observes, the word "republic" remained for many of its advocates merely "a slogan that was associated with no precise political conceptions, rather, it was a synonym for diffuse social demands, overfreighted with chiliastic hopes."[96] Nonetheless, this violence (which occurred almost simultaneously with the bloody June Days in Paris) terrified not only conservatives but also bourgeois liberals, providing a political opening for opponents of the revolution, who warned of the danger of impending anarchy.

While the violence of June 1848 drove Prussia's moderates into closer collaboration with the monarchy, it also radicalized many members of the democratic faction. During the late summer and fall of 1848, red flags were displayed at many popular demonstrations of the working classes, and speakers displayed a "revolutionary nostalgia" for the events of the French Terror of 1793–1794. The Democratic Club of Berlin intensified its rhetoric concerning the "social question," and at the end of June, Berlin's radical leaders formed the new Republican Club, which was intended to "strive openly for the goal of a republic." Though this club convened only a few times over the subsequent months, a number of its members played leading roles in the democratic movement during the remainder of the revolution.[97]

Despite the progressive radicalization of some left-wing revolutionary leaders, the majority of delegates to both the Berlin and the Frankfurt assembly remained unconvinced by the rhetoric of the democratic faction. Rather than calling for the abolition of monarchical sovereignty, they favored the "union [*Vereinbarung*] of the monarch and the people." The national representatives, wrote one liberal Prussian pamphleteer, should serve as "advisers to the king" and as "mediators between king and people."[98] Another author declared his desire to "unite, as much as possible, the two elements of monarchy and democracy" in the new constitution.[99]

A study of voting patterns in the Frankfurt National Assembly concluded that the moderate delegates broadly supported the "individualist dogmas of nineteenth-century liberalism." They voted by overwhelming majorities in favor of principles such as equality before the law, freedom of the press, the "career open to talent," and the "inviolability of personal liberty." Their liberalism, however, "faded at the point of abridging the rights of the sovereign or of specifically attacking an aristocracy that was associated with traditional monarchical sovereignty. . . . The truth is that they were at least as strongly opposed to democracy as they were to the old regime, and their challenge to the latter should not be overrated."[100]

Many historians have argued that the fear of socialism inhibited liberals' ability to organize effectively against monarchical authority in 1848. As had been the case among their conservative opponents during the previous decades, liberals became terrified of the danger of an unchecked revolution. In their view, writes one scholar, the republic came to mean "civil war, anarchy, mob rule, the ruin of all civilization and culture, the overthrow of any rational order in society."[101] In March 1848, Otto Camphausen, the brother of the minister president of the new liberal Prussian government, declared: "Never in the history of the world has there been an epoch in which dangers mounted up from so many sides." It was vital, he argued, to erect "dams" against the "wild flood of spirits" that had been unleashed upon the outbreak of the revolution.[102] This terror of social upheaval, historians have observed, dampened liberals' enthusiasm for challenging the authority of the monarchical state. Viewing a strong monarchical executive as a necessary stabilizing factor in politics, liberals made common cause with "the old powers, the dynasties." They thus rendered themselves "the subordinate partner of an illiberal system of governance."[103]

These arguments about the defensive character of German liberalism in 1848 have merit. It is essential to recognize, however, that liberals were not motivated to support a strong monarchy solely for tactical reasons. During this era, strong pro-monarchical sentiment persisted among many sectors of the populace at large. Between 1847 and 1849, for example, a series of riots broke out in the Prussian provinces on behalf of "church and king."[104] For liberal activists as well, the monarchy fulfilled critical symbolic and political functions. Symbolically, as Nees von Esenbeck observed, the monarch personified the nation. This was a particularly important function in the context of the national unification movement. If Germany were to be unified, it would need both symbols and institutions that would manifest the unity of the *Volk*. A "democratic monarch" would perform precisely this role. Politically, the monarch would serve as the chief executive of the state, as well as carrying out certain responsibilities in the legislative process. The institution of monarchy, liberals believed, would help clarify and unify the exercise of sovereign authority in the new pan–German state.

Conclusion: The Persistence of Enlightenment in Nineteenth-century Prussia

The Frankfurt National Assembly of 1848–1849 has often been ridiculed as a "professors' parliament" that held interminable philosophical discussions, rather than acting decisively to forge a new constitution for Germany. As table 8.1 indicates, however, there were good reasons why the delegates to this assembly were unable to stop talking.

During the Revolution of 1848, fundamental debates about the nature of the nation were occurring along many disparate axes. The column "Contested features" in table 8.1 indicates several points of controversy that divided the revolutionary movement. First and foremost, delegates to the Frankfurt Assembly argued over the borders of the new Germany, specifically over whether Austria should be included in the new nation-state. A *Großdeutschland* or "large Germany," would include the German-speaking territories of the Austrian Habsburg Empire. A *Kleindeutschland*, or "small Germany," would exclude Austria and center around Prussia.

The argument over whether to establish a *großdeutsch* or a *kleindeutsch* nation proved to be one of the most intractable dilemmas for the 1848 revolutionaries, in large part because of the Habsburg rulers' intense opposition to national unification. But the question of borders was only one of a number of basic rifts regarding the composition of the national community. Without Austria, the German nation would be primarily Protestant; with Austria, it would be predominately Catholic. Thus, this dispute over Germany's borders was intimately linked to another controversy over national religion. Moreover, the earlier arguments within

8.1 The Concept "Nation" in the German Revolution of 1848

Consensual features	Contested features
The nation is a harmonious community possessing one unified interest and will.	Is the nation *Großdeutschland* or *Kleindeutschland?*
The nation is Germany.	Is it predominately Catholic or Protestant?
The nation must possess one contiguous territory.	
	Can Poles and Jews be citizens?
The nation must be linguistically and culturally unified.	Can women be citizens?
The nation must be politically educated.	
All citizens must be equal before the law.	Must the old corporate bodies (e.g., the aristocracy) be abolished?
	Must all economic inequality and private property be abolished?
	Is the nation's interest identical to the king's interest?
	Who is sovereign: the nation or the king? or, can sovereignty peacefully be shared between the nation and the monarch?
	What relationship should exist between the German nation and the territorial states?
	Are the individual territorial states (e.g., Prussia, Bavaria) also "nations"?

the nationalist movement over religion and ethnicity were still very much unresolved. The extension of citizenship to Jews remained controversial; likewise, nationalists argued over whether the "Polish question" should be handled through the Germanization of territories of mixed German and Polish population. None of the leading revolutionaries of 1848 yet proposed extending voting rights to women. Nonetheless, the question of female citizenship, which had been rarely discussed in Prussia or in the other German states before that year, now emerged from time to time in public debate. While women were excluded from membership in associations such as the Democratic Club, they attended meetings in large numbers as guests, and organizations such as the Democratic Women's Association (*Demokratischer Frauenverein*), founded in September 1848, provided a forum for limited participation in revolutionary politics.[105]

If the boundaries and membership of the national community were hotly contested in 1848, so too were the principles of its social composition. Many—though far from all—liberals argued for the abolition of the traditional estates, claiming that the existence of privileged classes prevented the formation of a truly unified nation and that universal equality was a fundamental prerequisite for the achievement of national consciousness. The most radical of the socialist revolutionaries carried this view to its logical conclusion, demanding the abolition of private property. So long as economic inequalities existed within the populace, they claimed, a true unity of the people was impossible.

A further set of issues that caused controversy during the Revolution of 1848 pertained to the problem of sovereignty. On the extreme left of the national assemblies, both in Frankfurt and Berlin, were republican activists, who demanded the outright abolition of the monarchy. Far more numerous, however, were those who sought a means of redistributing sovereign authority between the monarch and the nation. Another problem for the revolutionaries of 1848, as for subsequent generations of German political leaders, was the proper distribution of sovereign authority between the nation and the territorial states. Though the leading revolutionaries concurred that Germany should be unified, many believed that significant authority should remain vested within the individual territorial states. Indeed, many Germans would continue to use the word "nation" to describe Germany's constituent states, such as Bavaria and Württemberg, through the decade of the 1860s. Even Prussia had its own "national assembly" in 1848–1849. In Prussia, however, this usage of the word "nation" seems to have been an anomaly of the 1848 Revolution. The term "Prussian nation" had appeared quite rarely in public discourse since the Napoleonic era, and it virtually disappeared after 1850.

With all of these political and social controversies in play, German public discourse remained highly fractured and diffuse during the Revolution of 1848. The revolutionary movement failed to crystallize around a single central project, such as the abolition of monarchy or the redistribution of wealth. This deeply divided revolutionary movement ultimately proved no match for the conservative forces, which were determined to reassert monarchical authority in the German states. Thus, the failure of the 1848 Revolution stemmed in part from the intensely contested character of the concept "nation."

Though the revolutionary movement of 1848 displayed fundamental internal divisions, it was also handicapped by the very elements of consensus that existed across the spectrum of the revolutionary movement. Like earlier generations of political progressives, virtually all participants in the revolution believed that the nation was an ideally harmonious community, possessing a unified interest and will. Moreover, the revolutionaries of 1848 emphasized the need to educate the nation in order to prepare it for self-government. The ideal of political harmony had been a fundamental element of the political thought of Enlightenment philosophers, such as Turgot and Kant, as well as for the Prussian reformers of the Napoleonic era. All of these philosophers and political leaders had emphasized the importance of reconciling monarchical sovereignty with the new principle of popular self-rule. All of them had also argued that the education of the populace was an essential precondition for overcoming the contradiction between these two models of government.

Enlightened nationalism initially appeared in Prussia as a response to the challenges of the Napoleonic era. Through a program of social rationalization and popular education, the Prussian reformers hoped to mobilize the populace politically without provoking a revolution on German soil. Long after Napoleon's demise, this agenda continued to shape the political program of progressives in Prussia and other German states. The establishment of rational administration, a rational social order, and a reasonable citizenry, progressives argued, would make it possible to eliminate internal strife within the polity. In an enlightened nation, they believed, public spirit would supplant egotism. Cooperation among the citizenry would render unnecessary the arbitrary exercise of political power from above.

The Prussian Revolution of 1848 must not be regarded as an unmitigated failure. Indeed, in December 1848, Frederick William IV decreed on his own initiative a constitution that included many of the measures proposed by Prussian liberals. For example, this constitution established protections for the liberties of all Prussian subjects, and it guaranteed annual sessions of a bicameral legislature, though its suffrage provisions heavily favored the upper classes.[106] In 1848, Prussia was thus transformed into a constitutional monarchy, a situation that endured until the dissolution of the German Empire in 1918.

Even during the decades after the establishment of a constitution in Prussia, however, the principle of monarchical sovereignty remained largely unchallenged. The persistence of a strong monarchy in Prussia, this study has shown, cannot be understood solely on the basis of the purported backwardness of the bourgeoisie or the feudalization of the capitalist elites. Rather than simply seeking to understand political behavior based on socioeconomic forces, it is essential to analyze the interactions of these forces with the underlying discursive patterns that frame and channel political debate.

Nine

CONCLUSION

This study has addressed two questions. First, can Prussian political culture of the early nineteenth century rightly be said to
have followed a *Sonderweg*, or special path, of historical development? Second, to what extent were the political struggles in Prussia
during this era shaped by ideological as opposed to material forces?
Though the analysis here is confined to Prussia, it has important implications for understanding not only the history of nineteenth-century
Germany at large but also the evolution of modern political culture elsewhere in Europe and the world.

The Distinctiveness of Nineteenth-century
Prussian Political Culture

Whereas many historians have argued that nineteenth-century Prussia
failed to modernize politically,[1] I have shown that a profound and irreversible political transformation occurred in Prussia beginning in the
Napoleonic era. As a result of the humiliating military defeat of 1806–
1807, a group of leading civil servants sought to defend the Prussian
state against the threat of annihilation by mobilizing the nation. Over
the ensuing decades, the genie of nationalism proved impossible to return
to its bottle. I have analyzed how the political discourses and practices
of various groups—civil servants, aristocrats, bourgeois activists, and the
Hohenzollern kings—changed in response to the principle of a politically
active nation. All of these groups initially embraced this principle, be-
lieving that it would prove useful in furthering their own political agendas. Many of these initial hopes turned out to be ill-founded. Nonetheless, both the conservative and liberal movements in Prussia during the

period 1815–1848 reflected the influence of these early experiments in national politics. A true restoration of the old political and social order was ultimately impossible to attain.

Although Prussian political culture of the early nineteenth century cannot be understood as having been rooted in the feudal past, it may be regarded as distinctive in two important respects. First, while most members of Prussia's educated elites favored some measure of social and political reform during this era, virtually no one supported sudden and drastic internal change. Unlike the French revolutionaries of 1789, who sought to build an entirely new world on the ashes of the old, Prussian political leaders consistently sought to reconcile new universalistic, egalitarian governing principles with older corporatist, hierarchical ones. Civil servants, bourgeois activists, and even many aristocrats sought to transform the traditional corporate social order but not to abolish it altogether. Hardenberg, for example, favored the creation of a "rational order of ranks" based on functional social distinctions, and even many bourgeois popular nationalists, such as Görres and Jahn, supported the preservation of the traditional estates in a modified form. A second noteworthy feature of Prussian political culture involved the theory of sovereignty. Rather than perceiving a sharp duality between monarchical and popular sovereignty, politically active Prussians of the early nineteenth century sought to fuse together these two principles of government.

Three factors explain these distinctive characteristics of nineteenth-century Prussian political culture:

The eighteenth-century philosophical legacy. The absence of a systematic critique of monarchical sovereignty in Prussia in the wake of the French Revolution is partly attributable to the moderate character of the German Enlightenment. Because the German states lacked a metropolis like Paris, intellectual life in German-speaking Europe was more decentralized and more deeply embedded in the structures of traditional society than was the case in France. While the French revolutionaries derived their inspiration from independent iconoclasts, like Rousseau, the Prussian reformers built on the theories of more cautious figures, such as Kant, who was a professor and a civil servant.

In addition to invoking Kantian philosophy, the Prussian reformers drew on indigenous German governing traditions, such as cameralism, as well as on the theories of eighteenth-century intellectuals elsewhere in Europe, including the French physiocrats and the Scottish economist Adam Smith. Through the adoption of rational governing principles, they hoped to abolish the need for arbitrary acts of sovereign will. They believed that, ideally, civil society would become largely self-regulating, requiring little interference by state authorities. Political decisions, they thought, would ultimately be made by deriving an informed consensus of the citizenry and the government authorities concerning the public good. In such a rational governing system, they believed, a sovereign monarch could peacefully coexist with a politically active populace.

Prussia's conquest by Napoleon. In France, the mobilization of the nation initially occurred in the context of a revolutionary struggle to destroy the power of old social and political elites. In Prussia, by contrast, national mobilization was a response to the country's conquest by an external enemy. Moreover, the military defeat of 1806–1807 adversely affected all segments of the Prussian population. The status of the monarchy and civil service was jeopardized as Napoleon threatened to abolish Prussia's independence. Aristocrats lost land, money, and prestige; peasants lost livestock and crops; and residents of the towns and the countryside alike suffered from food shortages and epidemics. Thus, early nationalist rhetoric in Prussia called for solidarity of the entire population against a foreign foe. The nation was originally mobilized *for* the king, not against him. "With God for King and Fatherland!" was the rallying cry of Prussian patriots during the War of Liberation of 1813–1814. This early ideal of solidarity between nation and king continued to shape Prussian political culture long after Napoleon's fall.

The challenge of national unification. The absence of any unified German state before 1871 created distinctive challenges for German liberals. The establishment of national unity, they recognized, would require both symbols and political institutions around which the nation could be organized. During the Revolution of 1848, most delegates to the revolutionary assemblies both in Frankfurt and in Berlin supported the preservation of monarchical authority. In part, this was because they believed that a monarch would provide a necessary symbolic and institutional center for the new unified German nation.

The three factors identified above meant that the nationalist movement in nineteenth-century Prussia attempted to organize around a "high center,"[2] that political activists strove to unify the nation in conjunction with rather than in opposition to the monarchical state. The culture of enlightened nationalism in Prussia was a product of this struggle to reconcile a politically active nation with a sovereign monarch. This form of nationalism was "enlightened" in the sense that it sought to educate the nation for rational self-determination. In other words, it projected onto the collectivity certain attributes that, in eighteenth-century philosophy, had been applied mainly to the individual human being. Whether or not the Prussian reformers actually succeeded in enlightening the nation is another issue; the term is meant to characterize their political ambitions rather than their political achievements.

Enlightened nationalism manifested itself both at the level of political discourse and at the level of political practice. Discursively, it involved two fundamental premises, first, that the nation must be mobilized politically, and second, that the will of the nation must be harmonized with the will of the monarch. This harmonization was to be achieved both through the education of the populace and through the rationalization of political and social institutions. At the level of practice, enlightened nationalism was reflected in various reform efforts, both successful and unsuccessful, intended to accomplish the above objectives. These reform efforts included the liberation of the serfs, Stein's Municipal Ordinance, Hardenberg's free trade legislation, the establishment of universal public schooling, and the various plans for a Prussian constitution.

The primary exponents of enlightened nationalist ideas in Prussia were the reform-minded civil servants of the Napoleonic era and subsequent generations of bourgeois liberals. The aristocratic nationalists and romantic nationalists discussed in chapters 4 and 5 cannot be regarded as fitting neatly within the category of enlightened nationalism. Neither of these two groups placed as much emphasis as the bureaucratic reformers on the rationalization of social and administrative institutions or on the necessity for harmony between the nation and the state. Many aristocratic nationalists were concerned primarily with finding a new language for justifying the preservation of their traditional social and political prerogatives. Most romantic nationalists were influenced more by Protestant pietism and the culture of romanticism than by the tutelary ideals of the *Aufklärung*. Nonetheless, some common conceptual ground existed across the spectrum of political debate in Prussia. Thus, for example, the fervent anti–Semite Friedrich Ludwig Jahn articulated some of the premises of enlightened nationalism: his teachings stressed the ideals of political harmony, national education (*Volkserziehung*), and popular self-determination. Likewise, aristocratic activists who experimented with speaking nationally generally depicted themselves as allies rather than as antagonists of the monarchical state: they proclaimed their desire for a cooperative relationship between the nation and its king. Certain resonances of enlightened nationalist ideals were also evident in the speeches and deeds of King Frederick William IV, who is often depicted simply as a romantic reactionary. For example, by lifting press censorship restrictions in the early 1840s and by convening the United Diet of 1847,

Frederick William IV sought to forge a popular monarchy, linking together his own will with the desires of the *Volk*.

The quest for a rational and harmonious national community had both positive and negative consequences for Prussian political culture. On the one hand, it gave birth to an intensely utopian strain of thinking that persisted throughout the nineteenth century and beyond. Proponents of national education, administrative rationalization, and constitutional rule believed that these measures would help mobilize the citizenry while averting the upheavals that had afflicted France during the revolutionary era. "In the nineteenth century Germany became a land of schools," writes one historian, and within the German states, "Prussia was the model country for educational reform."[3] As Stein argued, the mission of the state was to make possible the "religious-moral, intellectual, and political perfection" of its people. The establishment of a system of national schooling was an essential instrument toward this end.[4] Likewise, the reformers' calls for administrative reform, which sought to transform the civil service into a rational and politically impartial general estate, were motivated by the desire to forge a durable union between an enlightened nation and its enlightened government. One might disparage as naïve the bureaucratic reformers' dream of a harmonious national community. These leaders, however, grasped an essential truth about participatory politics, namely, that parliamentary institutions alone cannot provide the basis for a vibrant public life. They recognized the need to foster a commitment to the good of the whole community among the populace at large.

While the culture of enlightened nationalism encouraged an admirable commitment to developing public spirit, it also resulted in a problematic tendency to avoid or suppress internal political conflict. During the Napoleonic era, for example, proponents of a constitution consistently avoided specifying whether the new national representation would have a deciding or merely a consultative role in the legislative process. Likewise, during the Revolution of 1848, Prussian liberals called for the "union" of the monarchy and the *Volk*. Thus, they avoided defining the precise distribution of sovereign authority within the polity. In the words of one scholar, many German liberals longed for an "unpolitical politics" that would move beyond partisan strife.[5]

The ideal of political harmony inhibited the effectiveness of the liberal movement in nineteenth-century Prussia by making it difficult to form a loyal opposition, as was traditional in England and elsewhere. The quest for harmony also hindered efforts to develop a legitimate critique of monarchical sovereignty. Indeed, most Prussian liberals remained staunch monarchists until the collapse of the German Empire in 1918.[6]

A parallel to this phenomenon may perhaps be found in contemporary Germany: some political scientists and sociologists have remarked on the continuing weakness of the "culture of political conflict" (*politische Streitkultur*), especially in the lands of the former German Democratic Republic. The desire to maintain consensus in political life, scholars have argued, discourages the open expression of conflict and thereby inhibits effective democratic decision making.[7]

The culture of enlightened nationalism also contributed to a far more dangerous tendency in Prussian and German political life, namely, the forcible suppression of internal conflict. Having postulated a utopian condition of national unity and harmony, Prussian political leaders became deeply disappointed by the failure to attain this ideal. Their disappointment gave birth to fears of a potentially revolutionary and anarchic nation; in effect, the dark side of the enlightened nationalists' utopianism was a pervasive tendency to exaggerate the negative effects of political strife. Such negative images of the nation were a dominant element of conservative rhetoric during the 1820s and 1830s. It was not only the members of a reactionary court camarilla, however, who expressed concern about a politically mobilized populace. In 1810, frustrated by aristocratic opposition to an income tax, Stein had lambasted the "disobedient, degenerate, scheming nation."[8] In 1819, Hardenberg called for the establishment of strict censorship measures in Prussia and the other German states, decrying the "incomplete cultivation [*halbe Bildung*]" of the Prussian population that led to "abuses" and "deformities" of public opinion.[9]

This tendency to exaggerate the danger posed by domestic political conflict manifested itself in subsequent German history as well. During the late nineteenth century, for example, Chancellor Bismarck unleashed blistering diatribes against the "red menace."[10] Likewise, during the Weimar era, many Germans were deeply unsettled by the pluralistic character of parliamentary politics. Rejecting the Anglo-American constitutional principle of the balance of powers, German political theorists and activists often argued that strong government required the concentration of supreme authority in a single individual or institution.[11] Such continuing fears of internal strife may have weakened the legitimacy of the Weimar Republic and contributed to the rise of the Nazi regime in 1933.

The introduction to this study identified three logical flaws associated with the *Sonderweg* thesis: the essentialist, the teleological, and the normative fallacies. My analytical framework avoids each of these pitfalls. The phrase "enlightened nationalism" is not intended to indicate a singularly Prussian or German phenomenon. The discursive patterns described here had little to do with the "Prussian character." Rather, they resulted from specific dimensions of Prussia's historical experience, for example, its distinctive political situation following the defeats at Auerstädt and Jena in 1806 and the decentralized nature of the German state system throughout the early nineteenth century. Nor have I argued that the rise of enlightened nationalism condemned Prussia and Germany to the political disasters of the twentieth century. The discursive formations of nineteenth-century political debate never provided more than an intellectual framework for the articulation and negotiation of competing interests. Ideas took shape in the play of everyday events, even as they shaped perceptions of the meaning and significance of events. Finally, I have not claimed that Prussia's political development was pathologically aberrant because it failed to conform to the French or British path of constitutional evolution. Prussian political culture displayed notable strengths, as well as notable weaknesses. Moreover, strong parallels existed between the way in which the nation came to be imagined as a harmonious and unified community in both revolutionary France and Napoleonic Prussia.

While enlightened nationalism was not a singularly Prussian or German phenomenon, it is important to recognize that significant differences existed between nineteenth-century Prussian political culture and that of many Western countries. Although the impulse to overcome internal strife through the rationalization of political life was hardly a uniquely Prussian phenomenon, the Prussian government carried out a more sustained experiment along these lines than most of its peers. For example, the Stein-Hardenberg reforms were in some ways reminiscent of the legislative initiatives of Louis XVI's minister Turgot in France during the 1770s. Seeking to unite a productive and patriotic citizenry with an enlightened monarchy, Turgot proposed a wide variety of measures, including tax reforms, the abolition of the guilds, the adoption of free trade, and the establishment of a system of local and provincial representative assemblies. These French experiments in monarchical reform, however, ended abruptly with Turgot's dismissal in 1776 and with greater finality in 1789 upon the outbreak of the French Revolution. In Prussia, by contrast, many profound legislative changes were successfully enacted while the monarchical state remained intact.

One need only turn to the writings of an American political theorist of this period, James Madison, to perceive the distinctiveness of the Prussian reformers' project. Defending the new U.S. Constitution in 1787, Madison declared:

> As long as the reason of man continues fallible, and he is at liberty to exercise it, different opinions will be formed. . . . The latent causes of faction are thus sown in the nature of man; and we see them everywhere brought into different degrees of activity, according to the different circumstances of civil society. . . . It is in vain to say, that enlightened statesmen will be able to adjust these clashing interests, and render them all subservient to the public good.[12]

Because Madison viewed faction as an inevitable feature of any free society, he argued that an effective government must be organized so as to limit the negative effects of partisan strife. He thus argued that it was vital to establish a balance of powers, a principle that has come to undergird American constitutional theory.

The Prussian reformers, by contrast, focused less on controlling the *effects* of faction than on eliminating its *causes*. They regarded themselves as precisely those "enlightened statesmen" about whom Madison expressed such skepticism: they sought to adjust the "clashing interests" of civil society in order to "render them all subservient to the public good."

The Anglo-American constitutional tradition, based on the balance of powers, and the Prussian tradition of enlightened nationalism may profitably be regarded as two ideal types of modern political culture. Many twentieth-century historians and political scientists have presumed that political modernization ideally entails the establishment of a pluralistic system of parliamentary rule.[13] Yet, there are good reasons to believe that this vision of modernity is excessively restrictive. For example, communist political leaders around the world, inspired by the Prussian social theorist Karl Marx, have generally emphasized the value of attaining social harmony and political consensus within the nation, more so than the value of fostering the free exchange of opposing views. Furthermore, some of the conditions that gave birth to enlightened nationalism in Prussia have existed in numerous regions of the world over the past two centuries, so it is likely that elements of enlightened nationalist culture may be identified there, as well as in Prussia. In response to domination by a foreign power, many countries have embarked on programs of social modernization and popular political mobilization. It would be worthwhile to conduct comparative studies of the political culture in Prussia and in some of these other states, for example, Russia, Spain, Italy, Japan, China, and the newly independent nation-states in Latin America during the early nineteenth century, and in postcolonial Africa and Asia during the mid–twentieth century.

Further comparative studies of Prussia and the other German states would also be useful.[14] Certain conditions that shaped nineteenth-century

Prussian political culture existed elsewhere in German-speaking Europe as well. For example, these regions shared a common cultural heritage, and political activists throughout Germany had to contend with the absence of a unified nation-state before 1871. In other respects, however, Prussia's history differed from that of the rest of German-speaking Europe. In particular, its experience during the Napoleonic era was unique. Unlike the states of the Rhine Confederation, Prussia was conquered by France and faced the possibility of annihilation for several years after 1806. Therefore, the impulse toward fundamental political and social reform was far stronger in Prussia than in most of the rest of Germany. Unlike other regions, such as Westphalia, Prussia retained its independence throughout the Napoleonic era, which made such a reform movement possible. Between 1806 and 1815, Prussia adopted more dramatic social reforms, such as Hardenberg's free trade legislation, than the other German states. Politically, the Prussian government also worked more aggressively to establish public spirit among the populace than was the case elsewhere in Germany. Because of this early commitment to popular political mobilization, the tensions resulting from the effort to fuse monarchical and democratic forms of government may have become sharper in Prussia than elsewhere in German-speaking Europe.

The Interdependence of Discourse and Action

Equally important as the substantive findings of this study are the methodological foundations on which they rest. This book seeks to navigate between the Scylla of socioeconomic determinism and the Charybdis of idealism, exploring the ways in which interests and ideas mutually condition each other. By confining the focus to a single concept—the nation—in one German state over the years 1806–1848, my study illuminates the complexity and fluidity of political discourses during this pivotal era.

The initial chapters of this book depict the formation of the concept nation as a process of intellectual patchwork, or *bricolage*. Theorists of "national" politics drew their inspiration from a variety of cultural and political traditions: the constitutional structure of the Holy Roman Empire, the Kantian ideal of the rational republic, the cameralists' theories of the well-ordered state, the literature of romanticism, the religious revivalism of the pietists, and the mysticism of the Freemasons, along with the rhetoric of the French revolutionaries and Napoleon. The discourses of bureaucratic nationalism, aristocratic nationalism, and romantic nationalism emphasized certain elements of these traditions and deemphasized others, depending on the nature of each group's political objectives. The writings of Prussian civil servants, for example, reflected the ideas of Kant and the cameralists, among other sources; bourgeois popular activists, by contrast, tended to invoke romantic and pietist ideals more than arid theories of administrative practice.

My analysis of these diverse political discourses of the Napoleonic era has yielded several findings about the concept "nation." First, certain features of this concept were strongly *contested* in Prussia during this period. Second, there were persistent *ambiguities* in the usage of this concept, although the range of ambiguity varied over time. Third, elements of *consensus* about the nation existed across the spectrum of political debate. Each of these dimensions of the concept was shaped by the struggle between competing interest groups; thus, the history of this idea is inseparable from the political and social history of the era.

The *contested* features of the concept "nation" reflected the wide range of purposes for which various constituencies invoked this term. For example, intense conflicts occurred over whether, and to what extent, legal and social hierarchies were compatible with the existence of a national community. The bureaucratic reformers believed that it was essential to create a degree of legal uniformity among all citizens in order to maximize their productivity, as well as to mobilize their energies most effectively on behalf of the state. At the same time, these civil servants wanted to enlist the support of Prussia's privileged elites in the effort against France, a necessity that dictated against taking an overly antagonistic line toward the aristocracy. Partly for these reasons, there were ongoing debates among the bureaucratic reformers over whether universal civil equality was an essential feature of the nation. Aristocratic nationalists, by contrast, generally held that the nation should be a hierarchical association that preserved the social and political prerogatives of the landed elites. Nonetheless, Prussian aristocrats were far from unanimous about precisely which traditional privileges were essential to maintain. For example, few nobles strenuously opposed the abolition of serfdom after Stein's October Edict of 1807, in part because they recognized the potential economic advantages that this legislation afforded them. In both of these cases, the ways in which these groups defined the nation corresponded to the ways in which they perceived their own self-interest.

The persistent *ambiguities* within the concept "nation" resulted from the efforts of Prussian leaders to pitch their rhetoric to disparate audiences or to obscure potential conflicts or contradictions within their political program. This discursive phenomenon—the systematic use of ambiguity—has attracted relatively little attention by students of political rhetoric. Nonetheless, it is a phenomenon of tremendous importance, because new political ideas often receive their initial articulation not as full-blown doctrine but in the form of a tentative counterpoint to arguments based on safer and more widely accepted premises.[15] It is impossible to determine precisely to what extent such discursive ambivalences are intentional and to what extent they are unconscious or accidental. Regardless of the authors' intentions, however, the presence of these ambiguities or ambivalences can be a signal of deep-seated tensions within a political system.

My analysis has focused primarily on two discursive ambiguities: first, whether the nation was Germany or Prussia, and second, whether ultimate sovereign authority resided in the nation or in the king. During the Napoleonic era, the leading bureaucratic reformers rarely characterized the nation either as Germany or as Prussia. By refusing to specify one or the other, they were able to pitch their rhetorical appeals as broadly as possible without explicitly challenging the sovereign authority of the other German states. Likewise, Hardenberg and other political leaders frequently avoided indicating whether the new national representation should have a deciding or merely a consultative vote in the legislative process. As the king's first minister, Hardenberg was in no position to advocate the diminution of monarchical authority; by the same token, however, he did not want to limit the new representative assembly to a merely symbolic role. The romantic nationalists, for their part, also generally steered clear of direct attacks on the principle of monarchical sovereignty; instead, their rhetoric usually called for the harmonious coexistence of a sovereign nation and its sovereign monarch. In the discourse of romantic nationalism, one might identify radical republicanism as the tentative counterpoint cropping up in the midst of patriotic pledges of loyalty to the monarchical state.

While ambiguous rhetoric may be a universal feature of political debate, at certain times the range of acceptable ambiguity concerning a given issue can narrow dramatically. During such historical moments, as concepts become clarified, the available choices for political action may also become more sharply delineated.[16] In this sense, the crystallization of ideas can be an important force in driving historical change. This is the phenomenon analyzed in chapter 6, which focuses on the years immediately following the Vienna Settlement of 1815. Most historians have described the triumph of the so-called Reaction between 1815 and 1820 as reflecting the dominance of the aristocracy and the monarchy over the nascent bourgeoisie. At the level of discourse, however, this development can be understood in terms of the sharpening of the conceptual framework of political debate, specifically: (1) the identification of the nation

as Germany, rather than Prussia, which made the concept "nation" problematic for Prussian political leaders; (2) the attenuation of aristocratic
rhetoric that depicted the nation as a hierarchical community, a development that decreased the appeal of this concept for many members of
the privileged elites; and (3) the loss of ambiguity over the question of
whether the national representation should play a consultative or a deciding role in politics, which made the king and other conservatives
highly fearful of a revolution.

Each of these three conceptual clarifications resulted from the interaction of competing political interests in Prussia following the Vienna
Congress. On the one hand, both bureaucrats and aristocrats possessed
less pressing motives to invoke the concept "nation" after 1815 than
during the previous decade. Prussian government officials no longer
needed to mobilize the populace against the French threat, and, by 1815,
Prussian aristocrats had succeeded in coopting or defeating some of the
reformers' most serious challenges to their social privileges. On the other
hand, civil servants, aristocrats, and members of the royal family all
became acutely aware of the destabilizing potential of romantic nationalism. Not only was popular political activism causing difficulties for the
state's efforts to assimilate the new territories of the Prussian Rhineland,
but government officials feared that the national unification movement
could undermine the Vienna Settlement by challenging the sovereignty
of the other German states. Likewise, many nobles came to fear that a
politically active nation would inevitably become a revolutionary force
that would destroy the aristocracy, as in France.

The political struggles of 1815–1820 culminated in an ironic result:
the conservative faction within the civil service and the aristocracy won
the immediate struggle over political policy, successfully suppressing the
popular nationalist movement by imposing stringent censorship measures. Yet this faction also effectively abandoned the struggle to define
the nation, which ultimately allowed elements of the popular nationalists'
definition of the nation to prevail. Thus, by the early 1820s, the ideas
of the "Prussian nation" and the hierarchical "nation of aristocrats" had
for the most part disappeared from mainstream political debate. The nation had come to be widely understood as a pan–German community
organized according to the principle of universal civil equality.

While significant conflicts and ambiguities surrounded the concept "nation," the *consensual* features of this idea were equally important. For a
variety of reasons, virtually all politically active Prussians during the
Napoleonic era portrayed the nation as a harmonious community possessing a single unified interest and will. The premise that the nation

should be a harmonious and unified community was overdetermined, in the sense that it was the product of a wide range of mutually reinforcing causes. These causes were rooted both in elements of Prussia's cultural heritage, such as pietist spirituality, and in immediate political exigencies, such as the need to present a united front against Napoleon. The Prussians were not alone in imagining the nation in this way, indeed, one important inspiration for their political theories was the rhetoric of the French revolutionaries, who also emphasized the ideally unanimous and harmonious character of the national will. Nonetheless, it is important to recognize that there existed a variety of roads not taken in Prussian political theory of the early nineteenth century. For example, the "nation" could conceivably have been imagined along the lines of the medieval *societas civilis*, in which the king ruled in concert with his nobles as "first among equals."[17] Alternatively, it could have been modeled on the Holy Roman Empire, which had a fragmented political structure based on multiple overlapping jurisdictions.[18] Or, it could have been envisioned as possessing a "mixed constitution," such as those depicted by Cicero, Montesquieu, or Burke, designed to temper the effects of vigorous partisan struggle among competing factions. In point of fact, however, each of these political traditions came to be overshadowed by a vision of the nation that emphasized the importance of harmony and internal unanimity.

This emphasis on the ideally harmonious nature of the national community remained a central feature of Prussian political culture well after Napoleon's final defeat in 1815. Although many conservatives came to reject the principle of national representation altogether during this era, others continued to lobby for the adoption of a constitution. Conservative activists between 1815 and 1848 tended to pursue one of two discursive options: either they attempted to dis-invent the nation (by denying its very existence or by narrowly circumscribing its political rights) or they recast their aristocratic nationalism in a new form. The first approach made it difficult for conservatives to legitimate themselves as a unified interest group possessing rights vis-à-vis the monarchical state; the second approach created pressure to adopt new positions on important social issues, for example, to acknowledge the principle of universal civil equality.

Liberals during the period 1815–1848 faced a different set of challenges. Unlike conservatives, many of whom held strong reservations concerning national unity and constitutional politics, liberals generally embraced the ideals of national unification and constitutional rule. But their insistence on the harmonious character of the national community made it difficult for them to mount successful challenges to the unbridled authority of the monarchical state. Liberal discourse of the pre–1848 era, and even of the Revolution of 1848 itself, tended to emphasize the importance of popular education and the rationalization of state institutions, and it acknowledged the legitimacy of the monarchical principle.

In sum, this study illuminates the highly complex relations that existed between class interests and political ideology in early nineteenth-century Prussia. *Pace* Karl Marx, this was a time in which the ruling ideas were *not* always the ideas of the ruling class. Indeed, ideas often proved to be constitutive of class interests, as much as the converse, because they composed the framework within which interests were conceived and articulated. The intellectual framework of enlightened nationalism did not foreclose the possibility of challenging the authority of Prussia's monarchical state. Nonetheless, it produced discursive conventions that played a key role in structuring the political choices that were feasible at a given time and in influencing the degree to which a given argument was likely to persuade its intended audience. Thus, during the Napoleonic era, only a tiny group of radicals, including Karl Follen, demanded the establishment of a republic in Germany—and even Follen hedged his bets by supporting the retention of an elected king along with a legislative assembly. During the Revolution of 1848, while a variety of democratic clubs demanded the establishment of a constitution based on popular sovereignty, these activists remained internally divided over the details of constitutional and social reform, and they were never able to rally the majority of Prussian revolutionaries around the anti-monarchical cause.

Not only has this study emphasized the central importance of discursive conventions in politics, it has also stressed the diverse nature of the material interests that motivate various political constituencies. It is essential to avoid making global normative assumptions about how a given class should speak or act politically; instead, one must attend to the specific, contingent situations in which political rhetoric is deployed. For example, Prussia's East Elbian aristocrats—often identified by historians as a notoriously conservative class—expressed a wide range of views concerning the establishment of a national representation during the early nineteenth century. The political attitudes of nobles in Brandenburg's Kurmark differed significantly from those of nobles in Silesia or East Prussia. Moreover, these attitudes also changed dramatically over brief spans of time. Between 1810 and 1815, chafing under French domination and alarmed by the assaults on their privileges by an aggressive Prussian bureaucracy, many nobles embraced the cause of national representation as a means of defending their traditional status. By 1820, no longer as worried about the leveling designs of the Prussian state, but newly fearful of the revolutionary threat, many of these same nobles became staunch opponents of constitutional reform.

Although Prussian political discourse of the early nineteenth century was highly fluid and complex, one overarching characteristic of this rhetoric was of critical importance. Unlike in certain other countries, such as France, where nationalism initially emerged primarily out of internal political struggles, in Prussia nationalism was first motivated by an external political threat. The culture of enlightened nationalism was in large part the product of the Prussian monarchy's effort to balance two potentially contradictory goals: first, to mobilize the populace politically to repel the Napoleonic threat, and second, to preserve the sovereign authority of the Prussian state. The internal harmony of the nation assumed paramount importance partly because it appeared to offer a means of reconciling these two objectives.

Rather than viewing nineteenth-century Prussian history as a special case of pathological historical development, the Prussian experience is best understood as a specific example of a more general phenomenon in the modern world. Over the past two centuries, political leaders around the globe have grappled with the implications of nationalism and popular demands for political participation. Everywhere, governments have striven to exploit and to channel the energies of their citizens so as to enhance rather than undermine constituted political authority. The course of Prussian history illuminates the volatile and unpredictable political forces that are unleashed by such efforts to utilize a politically mobilized populace to secure the supremacy of the state.

NOTES

Abbreviations

ADB   *Allgemeine deutsche Biographie*

BLHA   Brandenburgisches Landeshauptarchiv Potsdam (formerly Staatsarchiv Potsdam)

CEH   *Central European History*

FBPG   *Forschungen zur Brandenburgischen und Preußischen Geschichte*

GG   *Geschichte und Gesellschaft*

GStA BPH   Brandenburg-Preußisches Hausarchiv (in the Geheimes Staatsarchiv, Berlin)

GStA PK   Geheimes Staatsarchiv Preußischer Kulturbesitz, Berlin-Dahlem (Note: The designation "(M)" at the end of a citation indicates materials formerly held in the Zentrales Staatsarchiv, Dienststelle Merseburg)

HZ   *Historische Zeitschrift*

JMH   *Journal of Modern History*

Chapter 1

1. Wehler 1987, 1:398–405; Münchow-Pohl 1987, 49, 51, 55–56; Berdahl 1988, 107–08.

2. French political and administrative models had a greater direct impact on some areas of western Germany, which would base their legal systems on the Code Napoléon until the end of the nineteenth century. In those regions, however, Napoleon either annexed the territory outright or replaced traditional ruling structures with puppet regimes that did not seek to mount an indigenous opposition. Berding 1973; Fehrenbach 1974 and 1979; Blanning 1983; Weis 1984.

3. See, for example, Wehler 1987, 1:57–58, 1:363–485; Nipperdey 1983, 31–32. The phrase "revolution from above" apparently originated with the Prussian minister Johann Struensee, who told the French *chargé d'affaires* in 1799: "The creative revolution was made in France from below; in Prussia it will be made slowly and from

above." Hardenberg subsequently called for a "revolution in a positive sense," to be made "through the wisdom of the government," in his Riga Memorandum of 1807. (Sheehan 1989, 294, 305).

4. Koselleck 1981. An excellent summary and critique of Koselleck's analysis is found in Sperber 1985, 278–96. Other scholars who present interpretations similar to Koselleck's include Simon [1955] 1971; Fehrenbach 1979; Münchow-Pohl 1987.

5. Rosenberg [1958] 1966, 204, 203, 226. Analogous views are articulated by Kehr 1965 and Klein 1965.

6. Obenaus 1984; Vogel 1983a; Wehler 1987, 1:397–485. See also Vogel 1980; Scheel 1982; Gray 1986; Blanning 1986 and 1989; Berdahl 1988; Nolte 1990; Büsch and Neugebauer-Wölk 1991; Stamm-Kuhlmann 1992; Sösemann 1993; Brose 1993; Dunlavy 1994; Barclay 1995.

7. Kohn 1960, 69–98.

8. Krieger 1957, 4, 3, 5.

9. Dahrendorf 1967.

10. For an assessment of old and new versions of the Sonderweg, see Blackbourn and Eley 1984, 1–61; Faulenbach 1980; Stürmer 1983; Augustine 1994; Mommsen 1981; Groh 1983; Evans 1985; Grebing 1986; Kocka 1988; Hagen 1991; Beck 1995; Wehler 1995; Blackbourn 1998; Brophy 1998; Rürup 2000.

11. France's economic development during the eighteenth century is discussed in Asselain 1984; Gayot and Hirsch 1989; Bergeron 1991; Colin Jones 1991 and 1996; P. M. Jones 1995. On the vibrancy of the "public sphere" in the German states in the late eighteenth century, see Bödeker and Herrmann 1987; Hellmuth 1990; La Vopa 1992. The development of the German bourgeoisie during the nineteenth century is analyzed in Blackbourn and Eley 1984; Kocka and Mitchell 1993; Langewiesche 1993a; Wehler 1987 and 1995.

12. One prominent recent example of the essentialist fallacy is Daniel Jonah Goldhagen's argument in Hitler's Willing Executioners: Ordinary Germans and the Holocaust (1996). According to Goldhagen's analysis, anti–Semitism became a central element of German culture at the beginning of the nineteenth century, and the Holocaust was the logical consequence of Germans' intense hatred for Jews, which had been building for more than a hundred years. (After World War II, for mysterious reasons, German culture was suddenly purged of its anti–Semitic tendencies, Goldhagen maintains.)

13. McGovern 1941.

14. Blackbourn and Eley 1984, 10.

15. See, for example, Hintze 1962, 379; Brandt 1968, 5–7, 280–81. Jürgen Kocka notes: "[O]ne can hardly overestimate the importance of the specific continuity of the bureaucratic tradition in Germany: a strong and efficient Beamtentum; a long record of reform from above; a strong Obrigkeitsstaat which could achieve much, and which was widely admired (not without cause), but which had to be paid for with a weakness of civic virtues and liberal practices" (1988, 13).

16. For example, Meinecke [1906] 1977 and 1911. For a more general account of the idealist tradition in German historiography, see Iggers 1983.

17. Geertz 1973b, 218. See also Sahlins 1985, 153.

18. Hunt 1984, 10. (The quote is modified here from the past to the present tense.) Keith Michael Baker defines political culture as "the set of discourses or symbolic practices" through which "individuals and groups in any society articulate, nego-

tiate, implement, and enforce the competing claims they make upon one another and upon the whole" (1990, 4).

19. See, for example, Koselleck 1972 and 1985; Gumbrecht 1978; Reichardt and Schmitt 1985, 1:64–70.

20. Eugenio Cosieru, "System, Norm, Rede," in *Sprachtheorie und allgemeine Sprachwissenschaft: 5 studien* (Munich: Fink, 1975), 88, quoted in Reichardt and Schmitt 1985, 1:65.

21. Koselleck 1985, 90.

22. Canning 1996, 6.

23. To cite just a few of the many publications on this subject, see Toews 1987; Geyer and Jarausch 1989; Childers 1989; Ankersmit 1989; Vernon 1994; Iggers 1995; Jelavich 1995; Smith 1996; Schröttler 1997.

24. For example, Furet 1981; Hunt 1984; Baker 1990; Sewell 1994.

25. E. P. Thompson's *The Making of the English Working Class* (New York: Vintage, 1963), while predating the debates over the linguistic turn, displays a great sensitivity toward the linguistic dimensions of identity formation. More recent works, which emphasize discourse more explicitly, include Wahrman 1995; Sewell 1980; Stedman Jones 1983; Canning 1996.

26. For example, Landes 1988; Herzog 1996; Hull 1996; Scott 1996; Frader and Rose 1996.

27. Benedict Anderson's seminal work *Imagined Communities: Reflections on the Origin and Spread of Nationalism* (1983) has been an important inspiration for the anthropological study of nationalist movements. Anderson's analysis, however, focuses less on nationalist discourse per se than on epochal shifts in consciousness caused, for example, by the emergence of print capitalism in early modern Europe. Works that explore the discursive dimensions of nationalist movements more explicitly include Bhabha 1990; Anthony Smith 1986 and 1991; Dubois 1991; Link and Wülfing 1991; Kedourie 1993; Eley and Suny 1996; Pickett 1996; Brubaker 1996; Calhoun 1998; Hall 1998; Levinger and Lytle, forthcoming 2000. The 1990s saw a wave of scholarship on German nationalism in particular, much of which has also emphasized the linguistic dimensions of this movement. See, for example, Schulze 1985 and 1996; James 1990; Brubaker 1992; Schieder 1992; Jeismann 1992; François, Siegrist, and Vogel 1995; Helmut Smith 1995; Hettling and Nolte 1996; Dann 1996; Burger, Klein, and Schrader 1996; Echternkamp 1998; Giesen 1998.

28. Koselleck 1985, 74.

29. Baker 1990, 13, 24.

30. Ibid., 8.

31. Koselleck notes that because of the complexity of the project, "*Begriffsgeschichte* . . . in its reflection on concepts and their change, must initially disregard their extralinguistic content—the specific sphere of social history" (1985, 81).

32. For a sympathetic but trenchant critique of Baker's work along these lines, see the introduction to Sewell 1994.

33. Baker 1990, 14.

34. Foucault 1972, 31–38, 126–31, 166–77.

35. Jürgen Habermas's concept of "communicative action" reflects an analytical approach somewhat analogous to Foucault's notion of the historical a priori. Habermas notes that "symbolic interaction . . . is governed by binding *consensual norms*, which define reciprocal expectations about behavior and which must be understood and recognized by at least two acting subjects. Social norms are enforced through

sanctions. Their meaning is objectified in ordinary language communication" (1970, 92). See also Habermas 1979, 187, 182–83.

36. On this point, see Levinger 1990b.

Chapter 2

1. Frederick II, *L'Antimachiavel* (1740), quoted in Klassen 1929, 115.

2. Vierhaus 1987, 33–49.

3. Brunner 1968, 160–78; Lovejoy 1950. In Prussia, it should be noted, the theory of divine-right monarchy was never as fully developed as in many Western European states (Barclay 1995, 51).

4. Brunner 1968, 179; Klassen 1929, 115–19.

5. Koselleck 1972, 1:xiii–xxvii.

6. The dissolution of the *société d'ordres* in France and the *Ständegesellschaft* in Prussia is a central theme of Behrens 1985, esp. 7–23, 199–205. See also Raeff 1983, 174, 252–56.

7. My phrase "politics of harmony" is derived from the title of Lee 1980.

8. The figures for France and England are for the year 1800, from Wehler 1987, 1:69–70. The figure for Prussia is for the year 1816, from Rürup 1992, 32.

9. Wehler 1987, 1:180; Rürup 1992, 32; Sheehan 1989, 105, 115–16. Sheehan gives the figure for Berlin's population in 1800 as 150,000. The statistics on Paris and London are from Mitchell 1992, 72–75.

10. Wehler (1987, 1:70) gives the population for Prussian territories within the 1688 boundaries as 2.3 million in 1750 and 3.2 million in 1800. Within the boundaries of 1846, the population was 6.4 million in 1740 and 8.8 million in 1800. The other figures are from Rürup 1992, 22, 32.

11. Knudsen 1986, 4, 186.

12. Rürup 1992, 60–84. For example, per capita annual economic production in the territory of the future German Empire increased only 7 percent (from 250 marks to 268 marks) between 1800 and 1850, but nearly 30 percent (to 347 marks) between 1850 and 1870 (65).

13. Sheehan 1989, 121–22, 498–501; Wehler 1987, 1:81–118.

14. Hartung 1954, 63–65, 93–99; Vierhaus 1984, 133–34.

15. The largest Spanish army of the mid–sixteenth century numbered between 100,000 and 150,000 soldiers. Frederick the Great's army had about 150,000 soldiers during the Seven Years' War (1756–1763) and about 200,000 soldiers by his death in 1786. Parker 1996, 24, 147.

16. Behrens 1985, 38. On the intellectual and political background for the rise of the absolutist state, see Raeff 1983, 1–42.

17. Vierhaus 1987, 33–34; Vierhaus 1984, 133–34; Behrens 1985, 32, 60.

18. Koselleck writes, "The sum of all princes, the imperial diet, and the emperor never became a unified agent (*Handlungseinheit*) which, like the 'King in Parliament,' acted as sovereign. The empire never became a state in the French sense of the word" (Koselleck et al. 1990, 1; see also 2, 25–26). On the constitutional arrangements of the Reich, see also Sheehan 1989, 14–24.

19. Pufendorf, *Ueber die Verfassung des deutschen Reiches*, chap. 6, par. 9, 94, quoted in Knudsen 1986, 100. The first quote in this paragraph is from Eberhard August Wilhelm von Zimmermann, *A Political Survey of the Present State of Europe* (London: C. Dilly, 1787), quoted in Sheehan 1989, 15.

20. Quoted in Walker 1971, 195.

21. Sheehan 1989, 18–20. Walker (1987) emphasizes that the Holy Roman Empire served as an "incubator" for the freedoms of Germany's municipalities.

22. Sheehan 1989, 14.

23. [*eine vernünftige Rangordnung*] Hardenberg, "Über die Reorganisation des Preußischen Staats, verfaßt auf höchsten Befehl Sr. Majestät des Königs" (Riga Memorandum), 12 Sept. 1807, in Winter 1931, 316.

24. Justi 1760, *Vorrede*; quoted in Walker 1971, 164. Concerning eighteenth-century views of government, Keith Tribe writes:

> [T]his process of regulation cannot be conceived in terms of state intervention in the economy since the state and the economy have no independent existence—or put another way, they are the same thing. . . . *Staat* and *bürgerliche Gesellschaft* are alternative ways of designating the same political order, governed according to rules of prudence by a ruler. (1984, 266, 273)

See also Lindenfeld 1997, 1–45; Walker 1971, 161; Riedel 1975, 2:252–54. Definitions of these terms are slippery: Walker defines cameralism as a separate enterprise from *Polizei;* for Tribe, cameralism embraces *Polizei.*

25. Justi 1758, 1:65–66, quoted in Walker 1971, 164.

26. Quoted in Walker 1971, 164.

27. Tocqueville [1856] 1955, 227–28. On the provisions of the *Allgemeines Landrecht*, see Koselleck 1981, 23–149.

28. For a discussion of traditional visions of the monarchical order in France, see Baker 1990, 113–17.

29. Koselleck 1981, 70–77; Hintze 1896, 413–43; Müsebeck 1917, 115–46.

30. Tribe 1984, 282–83; Behrens 1985, 133–35, 159–60.

31. Behrens 1985, 150–51, 187; Tribe 1988, 133–48, 157–59; Treue 1951, 101–33; Kühn 1902–03. On Kraus's reworking of Smith's doctrines, see Lindenfeld 1997, 62–67.

32. Quoted in Behrens 1985, 187.

33. F. J. H. von Soden, *Die Nazional-Oekonomie* (Leipzig: J. A. Barth, 1805), 1:14, 18–19, quoted in Tribe 1988, 173.

34. Quoted in Behrens 1985, 160.

35. Humboldt [1791] 1969, 16; see also vii–viii, xxxvii–xxxviii; 28. On Humboldt's understanding of the concept *Bildung*, see Marchand 1996, 24–31.

36. Hellmuth 1982, 315–45; Dülmen 1977, 251–75.

37. See, for example, Makowski 1988; Janson 1963, 9–11.

38. Marchand 1996, xvii–xxiv, 3–35.

39. Koselleck 1973, 55–81; Krüger 1978, esp. 12–13, 34–38; Brose 1997, 19–21; Reinalter 1986 (esp. the essays by Reinalter, Vierhaus, Schindler, and Mühlpfordt).

40. Krüger 1978, esp. 12–13, 34–38; Koselleck 1973, 74–80, 110–15; Brose 1997, 20.

41. Turgot, "Mémoire au Roi, sur les municipalités, sur la hiérarchie qu'on pourrait établir entre elles, et sur les services que le gouvernement en pourrait tirer," in Turgot 1844, 2:504. This memorandum was drafted by Turgot's confidant Dupont de Nemours. Also quoted in Baker 1990, 120.

42. Turgot 1844, 2:508; Baker 1990, 120.

43. My discussion of Turgot's theory of representation follows Baker's distinction between the discourse of "reason" and the discourse of "will" in the debate over sovereignty in prerevolutionary France (Baker 1990, 126, 162–66).

44. On Turgot's term as controller general, see Baker 1990, 112, 120–23, 162–66;

Schama 1989, 81–88. Schama in particular focuses on the question of whether Turgot's proposals could have provided a viable path toward political and social modernization in France, averting the need for a revolution.

45. Stein, "Darstellung der fehlerhaften Organisation des Kabinetts und der Notwendigkeit einer Ministerialkonferenz," 26–27 Apr. 1806, in Botzenhart and Hubatsch 1957–74, 2:208–10, 213–14.

46. On the importance of Turgot's ideas as a model for the Prussian reformers, see esp. Adalbert Wahl, 1908; Heffter 1950, 91–92.

47. Kant's influence on the Prussian reform movement is explored in Levinger 1998; Wagner [1922] 1956; and Lindenfeld 1997, 55–59, 84–85.

48. Hubatsch 1975, 48–63; Sheehan 1989, 342–46; Krüger 1978, 35–39; Sweet 1978, 1:38.

49. Kant, "An Answer to the Question: 'What Is Enlightenment?' " in Reiss 1991, 55.

50. Krieger 1957, 124. Similar interpretations of Kant as an "apolitical German" appear in the works of Aris (1936) and Droz (1949), among others. Aris, for example, declares: "When he first discussed political problems, sixty fruitful years lay behind him, and neither his letters nor his great philosophic writings reveal that he had been specially interested in political questions" (73). In recent years, Kant has received more favorable reviews from scholars who have explored how he sought to develop a liberal political theory within the highly constrained, fracturing intellectual world of the Prussian Enlightenment during the 1780s and 1790s. Even this newer scholarship, however, still generally holds that the Königsberg philosopher exercised little practical effect on contemporary Prussian political leaders and that, at best, his political theory should be read as evidence of a road not taken toward the evolution of a German liberal tradition. See, for example, Beiser 1992, 8, 37, 364–65; Lestition 1993; Stedman Jones 1994; Beiner and Booth 1993. A discussion of recent literature on Kant's political theory is found in Levinger 1998.

51. Among the most important of these essays were "An Answer to the Question: 'What Is Enlightenment?' " (1784), On the Common Saying: "This May Be True in Theory, but It Does Not Apply in Practice" (1792), Perpetual Peace (1795), and The Contest of the Faculties (1798).

52. Kant, "Der Streit der Facultäten in drey Abschnitten," in Kant 1968, 11:364–65. See also Krieger 1957, 122–23.

53. Kant, Perpetual Peace, in Reiss 1991, 100–101.

54. Kant, "Über den Gemeinspruch: Das mag in Theorie richtig sein, taugt aber nicht für die Praxis," in Kant 1968, 11:145.

55. Kant, Perpetual Peace, in Reiss 1991, 101.

56. Kant, The Contest of the Faculties, quoted in Stedman Jones 1994, 159.

57. Kant, Perpetual Peace, in Reiss 1991, 101

58. Beiser 1992, 36–38. For Kant's refutation of the charge of Jacobinism, see The Contest of the Faculties, in Reiss 1991, 182–83.

59. Kant, "Was ist Aufklärung?" in Kant 1968, 11:55. See also Beiser 1992, 44–48.

60. See, esp., Beiser 1992, 48–53; and Lestition 1993.

61. Kant, "Über den Gemeinspruch," in Kant 1968, 11:151, 143–44, 156.

62. Ibid., 11:161–62, 153.

63. Patrick Riley (1983) offers an insightful discussion of how Kant views the republic as the culmination of an evolutionary process of moral and political development.

64. Jonathan Knudsen writes:

Against the omnipotence of the ruler Kant could only offer palliatives . . . : the pressure of public opinion, the power of the pen, freedom of thought, public education, and a belief in the gradual progress of the entire species. Stressing these 'civil rights,' he argued for gradual justice through law: once the state is constitutional, founded on public law, and once its citizens instill the moral law in themselves, an enlightened public will achieve what revolution cannot. (1986, 181)

65. Fichte, "Einige Vorlesungen über die Bestimmung des Gelehrten 2" (1794), quoted in Koselleck et al. 1990, 6:43–44.

66. ["Demokratische Grundsätze in einer monarchischen Regierung: dieses scheint mir die angemessene Form für den gegenwärtigen Zeitgeist"]. Hardenberg, Riga Memorandum, in Winter 1931, 306.

67. Frederick II, "Regierungsform und Herrscherpflichten," quoted in Koselleck et al. 1990, 6:27.

68. Svarez [1791–92] 1960, 12, 475.

69. Ibid., 12, 17.

70. Lehmann 1889, 444.

71. Svarez [1791–92] 1960, 218, 586, quoted in Koselleck 1981, 27.

72. Koselleck 1981, 26–28.

73. Fichte, *Reden an die deutsche Nation*, no. 11 (1808), quoted in Koselleck et al. 1990, 6:33. Concerning Fichte's intellectual development, see also Meinecke 1911; Neuhouser 1990; Schnabel [1929] 1987, 1:293–98; Schuurmans 1995, 347–52.

74. Quoted in Walker 1971, 149.

75. Sellin 1978, 4:831. See also Tribe 1984; Schuurmans 1995, 56–57.

Chapter 3

1. Gneisenau, letter to Heinrich von Beguelin, 27 May 1807, in Gneisenau 1911, 51; see also Hubatsch 1975, 55.

2. Wagner [1922] 1956, 137, 139; see also Hubatsch 1975, 55.

3. Sheehan 1989, 235–36, 246–50.

4. Stamm-Kuhlmann 1992, 267–311; Wehler 1987, 1:398; Münchow-Pohl 1987, 49, 51, 55–56; Behrens 1985, 190–91; Berdahl 1988, 107–8. The Clausewitz quote is from Behrens 1985, 191.

5. A detailed discussion of the political dynamics within the Prussian government during the decade leading up to 1806 is found in Simms 1997. See also Sheehan 1989, 295–99; Gray, 47–58; Stamm-Kuhlmann 1992, 207–14.

6. Sheehan 1989, 297, 303–5; Stamm-Kuhlmann 1992, 267–363; Brose 1993, 26–71; Schuurmans 1995, 367–68.

7. On Hardenberg's role in Prussian foreign policy deliberations before 1806, see Simms 1997, esp. 142, 154–55, 222–24, 240–43, 264–65.

8. See, for example, Meinecke [1906] 1977.

9. Zeeden 1940, 88–89. For similar arguments, see Meinecke [1906] 1977, 53; Klein 1965, 313; Simon [1955] 1971, 52; Obenaus 1980, 252; and to some extent Wehler 1987, 1:446–53. More positive assessments of Hardenberg's accomplishments include Vogel 1983a; Stamm-Kuhlmann 1992; Hofmeister-Hunger 1994; Brose 1993 and 1997.

10. Obenaus 1984, 12. Other recent studies that suggest that the Prussian government sought to preserve monarchical power through the adoption of limited representative institutions include Gray 1986 and Berdahl 1988, esp. 112, 126–32.

11. Klein 1965, 173–76, 313–17. See also Koselleck 1981, 170–71, 181–87; Rosenberg [1958] 1966, 203–4, 226; Kehr 1965.

12. Hardenberg, Riga Memorandum, in Winter 1931, 306.

13. Stein to Hardenberg, 7 Dec. 1807, in Botzenhart and Hubatsch 1957–74, 2/2: 562. See also Ritter [1958] 1983, 275.

14. Lévi-Strauss 1962, 18–19, 21. Regarding Lévi-Strauss's concept of *bricolage*, see Geertz 1973a; Koshar 1989.

15. For example, in Freud's "The Aetiology of Hysteria" (1896), *On Dreams* (1901), and *Fragment of an Analysis of a Case of Hysteria ("Dora")* (1905). Freud applies the concept of overdetermination not only in characterizing the symptoms of hysteria but also in analyzing dreams: "[E]ach element in the content of a dream is 'overdetermined' by material in the dream-thoughts; it is not derived from a *single* element in the dream-thoughts, but may be traced back to a whole number" (Freud 1989, 154). A slightly earlier usage of the concept overdetermination occurs in Friedrich Nietzsche's *Genealogy of Morals*, in which he argues that "punishment is overdetermined," because it reflects a variety of impulses: the desire to render the offender harmless, the desire for reparations, the desire for revenge, the desire to deter future crimes by inspiring fear, the desire to mock an enemy, etc. ([1887] 1989, 80–81). More recent scholarly works employing the concept of overdetermination include Althusser 1969; Lacan 1977, 59; Harootunian 1988, 226–28; Guha 1997, 60–63.

16. Quoted in Sheehan 1989, 165. See also Gschnitzer et al. 1992, 7:316–19; Schulze 1996, 156–57; Wehler 1987, 511, 514–15.

17. Quoted in Schulze 1996, 156.

18. Furet 1981, 33.

19. "Denkschrift Steins über den Finanzplan Hardenbergs von Sommer 1810," 12–13 Sept. 1810, in Botzenhart and Hubatsch 1957–74, 3:407.

20. Stein, Nassau Memorandum, in Botzenhart and Hubatsch 1957–74, 2/1:394. (Stein is referring here to the formation of local and provincial assemblies, rather than to a national representative assembly.)

21. Stein's "Political Testament," 24 Nov. 1808 (drafted by Schön, signed by Stein on 5 Dec. 1808), in Scheel and Schmidt 1968, 3:1136–38. Concerning Schön's role in drafting this document, see Ritter [1958] 1983, 360. For a discussion of the evolution of Hardenberg's views on political reform, see Levinger 1990a, 257–77; Levinger 1992.

22. Ritter [1958] 1983, 145–55; Sheehan 1989, 233–34, 297–98.

23. Hardenberg, Riga Memorandum, in Winter 1931, 318.

24. Zeeden 1940, 64; Berdahl 1988, 107; Schönbeck 1907, 3–6.

25. Gray 1977, 133–34.

26. Cabinet order to the *Generallandschaftsdirektion*, 10 Sept. 1807, quoted in Gray 1977, 134.

27. Zeeden 1940, 65; Gray 1977, 135, 138; Berdahl 1988, 113–14.

28. Frederick William III, cabinet order to Auerswald, 31 Jan. 1808, quoted in Lehmann 1902–5, 2:204.

29. Auerswald, quoted in Lehmann 1902–5, 2:208.

30. [*Nationalwohlstand*]. Cabinet order to Auerswald, 31 Jan. 1808, in Scheel and Schmidt 1966, 1:363.

31. Stein, cabinet order to Auerswald, 27 Feb. 1808, in Botzenhart and Hubatsch 1957–74, 2/2:673.

32. Auerswald, "Plan zur Organisierung eines jährlichen Generallandtages für Ostpreuen und Litauen," in Scheel and Schmidt 1966–68, 2:573, 574–80, 572.

33. Zeeden 1940, 85–86, 88, 90.

34. "Auszug aus dem Finanzplan Hardenbergs," 28 May 1810, in Botzenhart and Hubatsch 1957–74, 3:376.

35. Quoted in Botzenhart and Hubatsch 1957–74, 3:385, 388.

36. Raumer, "Pro Memoria über den Finanzplan des vorigen und jetzigen Ministerii," 11 Sept. 1810, quoted in Stern 1885, 167–68.

37. Huber 1978, 46.

38. Stein, Nassau Memorandum, in Botzenhart and Hubatsch 1957–74, 2/1:397.

39. Altenstein, Riga Memorandum, 1807, in Winter 1931, 403, quoted in Schuurmans 1995, 391–92. (Altenstein's memorandum was intended as a draft for Hardenberg's use, but Hardenberg sent it, along with his own memorandum, to the king.)

40. Edict of 9 Oct. 1807, in Huber 1978, 38, quoted in Sheehan 1989, 299–300.

41. "Edikt den erleichterten Besitz und den freien Gebrauch des Grundeigentums sowie die persönlichen Verhältnisse der Landbewohner betreffend," 9 Oct. 1807, in Botzenhart and Hubatsch 1957–74, 2/1:458. See also Ritter [1958] 1983, 220.

42. Koselleck 1981, 140–42; Hintze 1896, 419–21.

43. Botzenhart and Hubatsch 1957–74, 2/2:458; Ritter [1958] 1983, 227–31.

44. Quoted in Ritter [1958] 1983, 227.

45. Ritter [1958] 1983, 228–29; Schissler 1978, 107–12; Stein 1918–34, 2:274–306.

46. Botzenhart 1928, 218–24, 233–34; Ritter 1928, 31–32; Sheehan 1989, 300–301. An analysis of recent scholarly perspectives on the October Edict is found in Clemens Zimmermann, "Preußische Agrarreform in neuer Sicht: Kommentar zum Beitrag von Helmut Bleiber," in Sösemann 1993, 127–36. Zimmermann emphasizes the importance of domestic pressures, such as peasant revolts, as an additional motivating factor for the liberation of the serfs.

47. Ritter [1958] 1983, 258.

48. "Ordnung für sämtliche Städte der preußischen Monarchie...," 19 Nov. 1808, in Botzenhart and Hubatsch 1957–74, 2/2:947–79; Ritter [1958] 1983, 256–70; Koselleck 1981, 565; Ziekursch 1908.

49. Obenaus 1969, 135–36. See also Heffter 1950, 84–103; Ilja Mieck, "Die verschlungenen Wege der Städtereform in Preußen (1806–1856)," in Sösemann 1993, 53–84.

50. Koselleck 1981, 75–76; Koselleck 1985, 75–79. Recent scholarly approaches to Hardenberg's economic reforms are discussed in the articles by Kaufhold and by Baar in Sösemann 1993.

51. Vogel 1983a, 165–87; Koselleck 1981, 169, 189; Berdahl 1988, 124–25; Bornhak 1890, 590–93; Sheehan 1989, 306.

52. Berdahl 1988, 107–23; Koselleck 1981, 169.

53. See chapter 4 below.

54. Two authors who have explored aspects of this link between the emergence of a commercial economy and new conceptions of public virtue are Pocock (1985) and Dickey (1987).

55. Soden, *Die Nazional-Oekonomie*, 1:14, 18–19, quoted in Tribe 1988, 173.

56. Hardenberg to Frederick William III, 17 June 1810, quoted in Zeeden 1940, 89.

57. See, for example, Berdahl 1988, 3–76; Vierhaus 1987, 33–49; Bornhak 1890, 555–68; Schönbeck 1912–13, 120–25; Schönbeck 1907, 62–103.

58. Quoted in Schönbeck 1912–13, 170; for Dohna's views, see ibid., 173–74.

59. For example, Zeeden 1940, 86 (footnote); Ritter [1958] 1983, 377–85.

60. See, for example, "Bemerkungen Steins über den Finanzplan Hardenbergs vom 28 Mai 1810," 1–2 Aug. 1810, in Botzenhart and Hubatsch 1957–74, 3:377–80.

61. ["weil wir den *Provinzialismus* nicht verewigen, sondern *Nationalismus* einführen wollen"]. Hardenberg, "Finanzplan nach den neueren Erwägungen," [Aug.] 1810, in Botzenhart and Hubatsch 1957–74, 3:385.

62. Koselleck 1981, 185. (Koselleck is referring here to Hardenberg's plan for the state to unify the provincial debts.)

63. Gschnitzer et al. 1992, 7:316–19; Schulze 1996, 156–60.

64. Quoted in Krieger 1957, 489; see also Krieger 1957, 170–71; Jochen Hennigfeld, "Volk, Staat und Nation bei Wilhelm von Humboldt," in Burger, Klein, and Schrader 1996, 77–90.

65. Frederick William III, "An Mein Volk," 17 Mar. 1813, GStA PK, XII. HA, IV, Nr. 5, Bl. 1 (printed copy); see also Huber 1978, 49.

66. Koselleck 1981, 58.

67. Quoted in Göbel et al. 1989, 46.

68. On the role of women in the new political order, see Hagemann 1996, 562–91; Reder 1998; Hull 1996, 333–411. Hagemann argues that the nationalist movement during the War of Liberation intensified the polarization of gender roles in Prussia by defining the nation as a "family of the *Volk* [*Volks-Familie*] organized in a patriarchal, hierarchical manner with a gender-specific division of labor" (1996, 588).

69. See chapter 5 below, esp. pp. 115–17.

70. See chapter 6 below, as well as Sheehan 1989, 398–400; Nipperdey 1983, 93–94.

71. Quoted in Meusel 1908–13, 2/2:137–38.

72. For example, Stein's close associate August Wilhelm Rehberg argued for fusing elements of the pluralistic British constitution with the more unitary German model. Even Rehberg, however, claimed that representative institutions in the German states "can never become what Parliament is for the English nation." Rather than granting parliamentary bodies a "part in the government," the new constitutional system in the German states should serve to "bind the interests of the peoples and their regents intimately together, to secure the power and prestige of the princes, and thus to further the common good" (1807, 207–8).

73. For example, Furet 1981.

74. See chapter 5 below.

Chapter 4

1. "Verordnung, die veränderte Verfassung der obersten Verwaltungsbehörden in der Preußischen Monarchie betreffend," in Scheel and Schmidt 1968, 3:1089.

2. Ibid., 3:1089–90.

3. "Bemerkungen Steins über den Finanzplan Hardenbergs vom 28 Mai 1810," 1–2 Aug. 1810, in Botzenhart and Hubatsch 1957–74, 3:380.

4. "Denkschrift Steins über den Finanzplan Hardenbergs vom Sommer 1810," 12–13 Sept. 1810, in Botzenhart and Hubatsch 1957–74, 3:402–3. See also Vincke to Stein, 26 Aug. 1810, ibid., 3:345; Sack to Stein, 31 Aug. 1810, ibid., 3:348–49.

5. Botzenhart and Hubatsch 1957–74, 3:405. See also Ritter [1958] 1983, 381–82.

6. Botzenhart and Hubatsch 1957–74, 3:406, 405, 407.

7. Sack to Stein, 31 Aug. 1810, in Botzenhart and Hubatsch 1957–74, 3:348–49. See also Vincke to Stein, 26 Aug. 1810, ibid., 3:345. Compare Sack's views of 26 Oct. 1808, in Scheel and Schmidt 1968, 3:958, and Vincke [1808] 1848.

8. Stern 1885, 151, 197; see also Zeeden 1940, 152.

9. Stern 1885, 196–97.

10. Altenstein to Sack, 20 Mar. 1809, quoted in Zeeden 1940, 71–72.

11. See chapter 7 below, as well as Kondylis 1986, 63–206.

12. Behrens 1985, 150; Berdahl 1988, 77–90; Schissler 1978, 59–71.

13. On the history of these experiments in selecting representatives to serve in the provincial administrative bodies, see Levinger 1992, 115–19; Zeeden 1940, 52–61; Obenaus 1969, 153–58, 165–76.

14. Koselleck 1981, 318–32.

15. Obenaus 1969, 166.

16. On regional variations in aristocratic political views, see Levinger 1992, 145–59; Obenaus 1988; Kehr 1977, 131; Treue 1951, 113–16; Hintze 1975, 46–48.

17. Eickenboom 1976, 63–66.

18. Obenaus 1969, 166. As Kondylis notes, the traditional role of the diets was to defend the "freedoms and rights" (Freiheiten und Gerechtigkeiten) of the corporate bodies of the realm. According to the traditional concept of representation, "the estates are the land, they don't represent it" (1986, 115, 118).

19. Rousseau [1762] 1966, 67.

20. Kant, "Über den Gemeinspruch: Das mag in Theorie richtig sein, taugt aber nicht für die Praxis," in Kant 1968, 11:151, 143–44, 153; Kant, Perpetual Peace, in Reiss 1991, 100–101.

21. Koselleck 1981, 188–89, 192–95.

22. "Vorstellung der Deputierten der Kurmärkischen Stände an den Staatskanzler vom 22. Januar 1811," in Meusel 1908–13, 2/1:229–35. Also, GStA PK, I. HA Rep. 92, Hardenberg, H 5, VII, Bl. 7–8 (M). The petition was written by Quast and Bredow-Schwanebeck (Meusel 1908–13, 2/1:229). The authors enclosed along with the petition passages from four royal proclamations: the Landtags-Rezeß of 26 July 1653, two documents of 1717 that acknowledged the Brandenburg nobles' legal rights, and the Assekurationsakte of 1798, in which Frederick William III reconfirmed the "privileges and freedoms" of the nobility upon his accession to the throne.

23. Regarding the formation of military alliances, the estates had been granted the right of "consent" (Bewilligung) (Meusel 1908–13, 2/1: 231).

24. Meusel 1908–13, 2/1:230.

25. Simon [1955] 1971, 76–78; Meusel 1908–13, 2/1:277–88, 308–13.

26. "Letzte Vorstellung der Stände des Lebusischen Kreises an den König, dem sich der Beeskow- und Storkowsche anschloß," in Meusel 1908–13, 2/2:3–23, excerpted in Simon 1955 [1971], 78–79. Marwitz completed this document on 22 Mar. 1811; it was accepted at the Kreistag in Frankfurt/Oder on 9 May, and delivered to Albrecht, the king's secretary, in Potsdam on 10 June (Meusel 1908–13, 2/1:3, n. 1).

27. Meusel 1908–13, 2/2:10.

28. On the ethos of paternalism, see Berdahl 1988, 131.

29. Meusel 1908–13, 2/2:12, 15, 17, 19–21.

30. Hardenberg, Immediatbericht to Frederick William III, 23 June 1811, in Meusel 1908–13, 2/2:25.

31. Meusel 1908–13, 2/2:24–30; Simon [1955] 1971, 74–76, 79–81; Berdahl 1988, 135–36; Steffens 1907, 83–84; Schissler 1978, 124–25.

32. Berdahl 1988, 125–26. These and other East Prussian petitions from this period are printed in Bujack 1889, 1–9, 11–17, 31–32, 35–36, 38–39, 45, 61–62.

33. Steffens 1907, 11–13, 28–29; also in Bujack 1888, 7ff. According to Steffens, the strongest protests of 1810–1811 against Hardenberg's reforms came from the eastern provinces: East Prussia, West Prussia, Lithuania, and Silesia (1907, 11–12).

34. Steffens 1907, 28–29.

35. Rohrscheidt 1894–95, 213, 222–23, 236–52.

36. Rohrscheidt 1894–95, 230, 237; Koselleck 1981, 201–2. For an additional discussion of the guilds' reactions to the *Gewerbesteueredikt*, see Vogel 1983a, 188–223.

37. On Hardenberg's economic philosophy and his responses to protests against his program, see, for example, Brose 1993, 33–41; Vogel 1983a, 135–97.

38. Steffens 1907, 18; also Simon [1955] 1971, 63.

39. Koselleck 1981, 193; see also Berdahl 1988, 126–27; Zeeden 1940, 161–62; Simon [1955] 1971, 62–63.

40. "Fernerweite Edikt über die Finanzen des Staats," quoted in Stern 1885, 172–73.

41. In addition to the eighteen noble *Rittergutsbesitzer*, there were nine representatives from the peasantry, each of whom was required to own at least one hide (*Hufe*) of land, and fifteen representatives from the municipalities. Of the representatives from the municipalities, nine were elected by the provinces at large and six by the individual cities of Berlin, Breslau (which was given two delegates), Königsberg, Elbing, and Stettin (Stern 1885, 173–74; see also Koselleck 1981, 194).

42. "Instruktion an die Regierungspräsidien vom 11 Februar 1812," in Stern 1885, 173–74; Zeeden 1940, 127–28.

43. Stern 1885, 178–79; Zeeden 1940, 128; Dieterici 1875, 48ff.

44. GStA PK, I. HA Rep. 77, Titel 321, Nr. 1, Vol. I, Bl. 124–25 (M). See also Stern 1885, 179–80.

45. Provisional National Representation to Hardenberg, 4 June 1812. GStA PK, I. HA Rep. 77, Titel 321, Nr. 1, Vol. I, Bl. 129–30 (M). See also Stern 1885, 180–81.

46. Hardenberg to Count Dohna-Wundlacken, draft of 6 June 1812, quoted in Stern 1885, 181.

47. GStA PK, I. HA Rep. 77, Titel 321, Nr. 1, Vol. I, Bl. 205 (M). Also in Stern 1885, 181–82.

48. Provisional National Representation to Hardenberg, 24 June 1812, quoted in Stern 1885, 182.

49. Hardenberg to the delegates of the Provisional National Representation, 15 July 1812 (draft), in Stern 1885, 182.

50. Frederick William III, cabinet order of 1 Aug. 1812, quoted in Stern 1885, 183. See also Zeeden 1940, 130.

51. Frederick William III, instruction to the Provisional National Representation, 9 July 1812, quoted in Koselleck 1981, 195.

52. Berdahl 1988, 141–42; Koselleck 1981, 195–97, 204–7; Stern 1885, 183–84.

53. Gerlach, essay on the Gendarmerie Edict, 1 Sept. 1812, GStA PK, I. HA Rep. 77, Titel 321, Nr. 1, Vol. II, Bl. 112 (M).

54. Sanden, comments in debate of 19 Aug. 1812, ibid., Bl. 60.

55. Lange, memorandum of 17 Aug. 1812, quoted in Klein 1965, 183.

56. "Bemerkungen der National-Versammlung über das Edict vom 30. Juli 1812 wegen Errichtung einer Gensdarmerie," 26 Sept. 1812, in Röpell 1848, 349–58.

57. Provisional National Representation to Frederick William III, GStA PK, I. HA

Rep. 77, Titel 321, Nr. 1, Vol. II, Bl. 363–64 (M). Concerning this petition, see also Stern 1885, 186–92.

58. The Gendarmerie Edict contained a provision that abolished the patrimonial justice powers of the landholding nobility (a proposal that had been floated unsuccessfully by Stein in 1808). In Sept. 1812, the Provisional National Representation voted to petition the king to demand the retention of estate owners' judicial powers in civil cases. Seven delegates from the bourgeoisie and peasantry, however, abstained from this resolution. Elsner, the representative of the Upper Silesian towns, argued that these powers were inimical to the principle of "equality before the law" and that "the majority of the nation certainly desires the abolition of patrimonial justice because it is an injustice to the greatest number of the citizens" (Bezzenberger 1898, 18). Ultimately, the nobles prevailed on this point, preserving their judicial authority over their estates until 1848 and their police powers until 1872 (Röpell 1848, 349; Ritter [1958] 1983, 230–31).

59. The seven non-noble dissenters were Schmidt, Rosemann, Jacob, Müller, Leist, Rump, and Ring. Of these, all except Ring (the delegate from the municipalities of the Neumark) were representatives of the *Bauernstand* (GStA PK, I. HA Rep. 77, Titel 321, Nr. 1, Vol. II, Bl. 315 [M].

60. Stern 1885, 219–20; see also 189, 206–7.

61. "Protocol of the Interimistische Landesrepräsentation," 7 Ap. 1815, in Stern 1885, 216–21. Though the initial vote to send this petition to the king was 22–13, a subsequent motion to address the petition to Hardenberg was approved 32–3. Koselleck offers a somewhat misleading description of this debate (1981, 211).

62. Quast, "Auszüge aus meinem Aufsatze über National-Repräsentation," BLHA, Pr. Br. Rep. 37, v. Quast/Garz, Nr. 86, Bl. 41.

63. Marwitz, "Entwurf einer Vorstellung der Kurmärkischen Stände an den König," July or August 1806, in Meusel 1908–13, 2/1:132–34.

64. Marwitz to Hardenberg, 14 Sept. 1814, in Meinecke 1899, 100–101.

65. Compare Berdahl 1988, 130–31:
For the nobles, the constitution was contained in provincial law. . . . Because of this understanding of the constitution, the nobility was itself, in a fundamental way, a provincial institution. The conflict between Hardenberg and the aristocracy was, at one level, a conflict between Prussian nationalism and Prussian provincialism.

66. Poselger, comments in debate of 13 Nov. 1812, GStA PK, I. HA Rep. 77, Titel 321, Nr. 1, Vol. II, Bl. 310–11 (M); also Stern 1885, 189.

67. Bock, comments in debate of 13 Nov. 1812, quoted in Stern 1885, 187–88.

68. Bock, "Über die Grundzüge der Constitution der National Repräsentation anzuzeigen," 12 Nov. 1812, GStA PK, I. HA Rep. 77, Titel 321, Nr. 1, Vol. II, Bl. 327 (M). On the constitutional views of Bock, Poselger, and Elsner, see also Zeeden 1940, 129–30.

69. Elsner, speech to the Provisional National Representation, 21 Jan. 1813, GStA PK, I. HA Rep. 77, Titel 321, Nr. 1, Vol. III, Bl. 48 (M).

70. Quast, speech of 21 Jan. 1813, ibid., Bl. 49.

71. Stern 1885, 197–200.

72. Provisional National Representation, "Aufruf an unsern Mitbürger," 13 Feb. 1813, GStA PK, I. HA Rep. 77, Titel 321, Nr. 1, Vol. III, Bl. 259 (M); see also Stern 1885, 201–2.

73. Stern 1885, 203; also 197–202; Sheehan 1989, 314–15.

74. Quoted in Sheehan 1989, 315.

75. Sheehan 1989, 315–23.

76. Zeeden 1940, 134–35; Stern 1885, 203–4.

77. Stern 1885, 207; also 215–16.

78. ["Heil und Segen unserer braven und rechtlichen Nation! Heil und Segen unserem guten, braven und gerechten Könige!"]. *Immediatkommission* (composed of Schrötter, Kircheisen, Schuckmann, and Stägemann) to Frederick William III, 21 Feb. 1814, GStA PK, I. HA Rep. 77, Titel 524, Nr. 8, Bl. 11 (M).

79. Frederick William III to the *Immediatkommission*, 9 Mar. 1814, GStA PK, I. HA Rep. 77, Titel 524, Nr. 8, Bl. 16 (M). Also ibid., Bl. 17–18; Stern 1885, 204–5; Klein 1965, 186–87.

80. "Eingabe der National-Repräsentanten vom 16. Februar 1814. Betreffend das Gens'darmerie-Edikt vom 30. Juli 1812," in Röpell 1848, 359–60. Seven bourgeois delegates (Brummer, Hübner, Ring, Leist, Müller, Schmidt, and Bock) partially dissented from this petition in an accompanying letter to Hardenberg of 16 Feb. (Bezzenberger 1898, 23).

81. Koselleck 1981, 205–6; Bezzenberger 1898, 20, 23–25, 33, 40.

82. Stern 1885, 205–11, 221–22.

83. Dönhoff to Hardenberg, Mar. 1815, quoted in Koselleck 1981, 210.

84. Petition of the Committee of East Prussian and Lithuanian Estates, 5 Apr. 1815, quoted in Müsebeck 1918, 162.

85. *Kurmärkische Ritterschaft* to Frederick William III, 13 Aug. 1814, GStA PK, I. HA Rep. 92, G. v. Rochow, A III, Nr. 1, Bl. 21, 24 (M); see also Müsebeck 1918, 159–61.

86. "Verordnung über die zu bildende Repräsentation des Volks," in Huber 1978, 1:61–62.

87. Hardenberg to the *Interimistische Landesrepräsentation*, 10 July 1815, in Stern 1885, 213.

88. This interpretation is developed most elegantly in Koselleck 1981.

89. As Hanna Schissler points out, Hardenberg's generous concessions to the aristocracy were hardly necessary, given that the landowning nobility had been both weakened economically and discredited politically by the military defeats of 1806–1807 (1978, 143).

90. Cf. Koselleck 1981, 209, 298.

Chapter 5

1. Fichte 1846, 274; Fichte [1808] 1968, 7, 13, 117.

2. Sheehan 1989, 342–46, 376–78; Schuurmans 1995, 304–55.

3. Sheehan 1989, 332. In the words of Hugh Honour, the romantics were "united only at their point of departure" (1979, 19). See also Sheehan 1989, 326–42; Lovejoy 1941, 257–78.

4. See, for example, Pinson 1934.

5. Brunschwig 1974, 247; also Kohn 1960, 50–51.

6. Kohn 1960, 49–68.

7. Sheehan 1989, 344.

8. Langewiesche 1996, 46–64.

9. Hroch 1996, 66; Deutsch 1953.

10. Anderson 1983, 47.

11. For example, Kohn 1960; Brubaker 1992; Greenfeld 1992; Jeismann 1992; François, Siegrist, and Vogel 1995; Hettling and Nolte 1996; Pickett 1996; Echternkamp 1998; Giesen 1998.

12. Anderson 1983, 40.

13. See, for example, Clark 1995, 22–66, 83–102; Pinson 1934; Sheehan 1989, 174–76, 561–62; Ergang 1931, 40.

14. Greenfeld 1992, 277; see also Giesen 1998, 80–102; Vierhaus 1987, 216–34.

15. Craig 1982, 197.

16. Bruford 1965, 290; Toews 1980, 24–25; Brunschwig 1974, 119–63.

17. According to Liah Greenfeld, there were 3,000 people in the German states with the profession of writer in 1771 and 10,650 in 1800 (1992, 298–99). See also Woodmansee 1984.

18. Darnton 1982, 1–41.

19. Hunt 1984, 180–212.

20. Raab 1978, 19–20, 25–26, 30–47; Sheehan 1989, 374–75.

21. Görres, "Die künftige teutsche Verfassung," in Raab 1978, 139–41.

22. Raab 1978, 48; Haake 1916, 29:327; Czygan 1911, 1:335–50.

23. "Verordnung über die zu bildende Repräsentation des Volks," in Huber 1978, 1:61–62.

24. Raab 1978, 52.

25. Koblenz Address, in Görres 1929, 13:xxviii-xxix.

26. Jahn, Über die Beförderung des Patriotismus im preußischen Reich, quoted in Kohn 1949, 419.

27. Kohn 1960, 91.

28. Quoted in Kluckhohn 1934, 158, 159.

29. Kohn 1960, 84–86; Schnabel [1932–37] 1987, 1:433–36. See also Düding 1984, 15–139.

30. Jahn [1810] 1991, 222.

31. "Thus will we preserve a free Empire, / By rank and estate everyone is equal! / Free Empire! Everyone equal! hurrah hurrah!" Quoted in Kohn 1949, 425.

32. Mosse 1975, 74–85; see also Jahn [1810] 1991, 230–38.

33. Schnabel [1932–37] 1987, 1:435–36; see also Pickett 1996, 78–94.

34. Jahn [1810] 1991, 193.

35. The party of the "olds" was known as the Altteutschen. Schulze-Wesen 1929, 56–62; Haupt 1907, 111–22.

36. Schnabel [1932–37] 1987, 2:253–55; Spevack 1997, 46–85; Sheehan 1989, 407; Wehler 1987, 2:337; Haupt 1907, 119–20.

37. Arndt, "Über Preußens rheinische Mark und über Bundesfestungen," in Haake 1915, 28:211.

38. Müsebeck 1913–14, 147; see also Haake 1915, 28:210–11.

39. Arndt 1934, 248–49.

40. Jahn [1810] 1991, 96, 79, 133, 187.

41. Mosse 1975, 79; Sheehan 1989, 406; Steiger 1966, 183–84.

42. Reimann's speech is quoted in Spevack 1997, 33. Fries Kluckhohn 1934, 133. See also Sterling 1950, 118; is quoted in Mosse 1975, 77.

43. Quoted in Brose 1997, 78–79. The full text of the speech is found in Kieser 1818, 104–10.

44. Rödiger, speech at the Wartburg Festival, in Spevack 1997, 34; and Brose 1997, 87. See also Kieser 1818, 114–27.

45. Spevack 1997, 35; Brose 1997, 87.

46. [Hoffmeister] 1818, 53–55. A slightly different account is found in Schulze-Wesen 1929, 85–86.

47. Arndt, *Geist der Zeit*, in Kluckhohn 1934, 141.

48. Quoted in Kohn 1960, 78–79, 76.

49. Arndt agreed with Jahn that race was an important factor in determining nationality, but he considered Germany racially pure. In In 1812, Arndt wrote, "The Germans have not been bastardized by foreign peoples, they have not become mongrels [*Mischlinge*]"; instead, "the fortunate Germans are an original *Volk*." Kluckhohn 1934, 136; see also Kohn 1960, 76–77.

50. Jahn [1810] 1991, 33–35.

51. Goldhagen 1996, 33, 77.

52. Wehler 1987, 1:377, 407–09; Stern 1885, 251–62.

53. Quoted in Stern 1885, 240. On the Emancipation Edict of 1812, see also Brammer 1987, 34–70.

54. Stern 1885, 228–29.

55. Sorkin 1987, 20; Rürup 1975, 74–94. See also Brunschwig 1974, 249–92; Katz 1980, 1–33; Goldhagen 1996, 49–54.

56. Quoted in Goldhagen 1996, 56–57.

57. Hunt 1996, 99–101.

58. Rühs, *Die Ansprüche der Juden an das deutsche Bürgerrecht*, quoted in Kohn 1960, 93–94; see also Sorkin 1987, 37.

59. Fries 1816, 248, 254, 258, 251, 241. (Fries's review was reissued the same year in pamphlet form, under the title *Über die Gefährdung des Wohlstands und Charakters der Teutschen durch die Juden*.)

60. ["daß diese Kaste mit Stumpf und Stiel ausgerottet werde, indem sie offenbar unter allen geheimen und öffentlichen politischen Gesellschaften und Staaten im Staat die gefährlichste ist"]. Fries 1816, 250, 244, 254, 256.

61. Fries 1816, 260–61.

62. Sterling 1950, 116. On Fries, see also Kohn 1960, 94.

63. *Westfälische Anzeiger*, 19 Oct. 1816, quoted in Steinschulte 1933, 214.

64. Menzel 1818, 52, 54–55. See also Kohn 1960, 95–96.

65. From a resolution adopted by the Heidelberg *Burschenschaft* in 1818, quoted in Haupt 1907, 105.

66. Carové 1818, 67, 70, 140, 196–97; Toews 1980, 85, 134–36. On the romantic nationalists' response to Carové's arguments, see Avineri 1963, 148–51.

67. Ascher 1991, 213, 215, 214. On Ascher's biography, see Hacks 1991.

68. Sorkin 1987, 20; Rürup 1975.

69. Quoted in Schulze-Wesen 1929, 59–60.

70. [Oken] 1817, GStA PK, XII. HA IV Flugblätter, Nr. 318, cols. 1557–58. See also Stacke 1881, 2: 684; Sterling 1950, 118.

71. [Oken] 1817, GStA PK, XII. HA IV Flugblätter, Nr. 318, cols. 1555–56.

72. See, for example, Hagen 1980.

73. Botzenhart and Hubatsch 1957–74, 2/1, 396–97; Hagen 1980, 76–77.

74. Wirth, speech at the Hambach Festival, 27 May 1832, in Müller and Schönemann 1991, 37.

75. Speech to the Frankfurt National Assembly, 26 July 1848, in Müller and Schönemann 1991, 30–31.

76. Müller and Schönemann 1991, 9, 11–15; Nipperdey 1983, 626–28.

77. Sterling 1950, 107–13.

78. See, for example, Stern 1961.

Chapter 6

1. Branig 1972, 246–48; GStA BPH, Rep. 192, Wittgenstein, VII, K 6(e), Bl. 5, 7–9, 16–19, 33–37.

2. Branig 1972, 248 (n. 5), 249; GStA BPH, Rep. 192, Wittgenstein, VII, B, Nr. 6, Bl. 21–27; VII, K 6(e), Bl. 34–35. See also Müsebeck 1911, 151–94; Schoeps 1963, 217–66.

3. Plehwe to Frederick William III, undated (May 1819?), (handwritten copy), GStA BPH, Rep. 192, Wittgenstein, VII, B, Nr. 6, Bl. 26. According to Plehwe's friend Ludwig von Gerlach, Plehwe had written an earlier letter to the king addressing him as *Du* in Dec. 1817 (Schoeps 1963, 261–62).

4. Hardenberg to Wittgenstein, 3 June 1819, in Branig 1972, 249.

5. See pp. 63–65 and 74–83.

6. Schissler 1978, 130–44; Rosenberg [1958] 1966, 220–26.

7. Wehler 1987, 1:363–66.

8. The king of Württemberg proposed a constitution in 1815, but an elected representative assembly rejected the document. A revised version was adopted by royal decree in 1819. Bavaria and Baden both implemented constitutions in 1818. Other German states that adopted constitutions during the decade after the Vienna Congress were Schwarzburg-Rudolstadt (1816), Schaumburg-Lippe (1816), Waldeck (1816), Sachsen-Weimar (1816), Sachsen-Hildburghausen (1818), Liechtenstein (1818), Hanover (1819), Brunswick (1820), Hesse-Darmstadt (1820), and Sachsen-Meiningen (1824, united with Hildburghausen in 1829). By 1848, only four German states remained without constitutions: Austria, Prussia, Oldenburg, and Hesse-Homburg (Sheehan 1989, 411–16, 393–99; also Haake 1921, 53).

9. Mager 1974, 343. On Hardenberg's plans for the reorganization of Germany, see also Sheehan 1989, 398–401; Botzenhart 1968, 26–32, 35–37.

10. Sheehan 1989, 400–403, 411, 417–19; Nipperdey 1983, 90–91; Aretin 1954, 718–27.

11. Haake 1915, 28:211; Müsebeck 1913–14, 147.

12. In Schmidt 1890, 100–121. See also Sheehan 1989, 398; Nipperdey 1983, 93–94.

13. Schmidt 1890, 104–05. Humboldt argued that since the "old constitution" of the Reich had been irretrievably lost, the "unification of Germany" would best be achieved through an "association of states" (*Staatenverein*) through which states would pool their resources for common defense and coordinate domestic policies. Such an arrangement, he noted, would depend on the "firm, consistent, and unwavering agreement and friendship of Austria and Prussia" (Ibid., 105, 107–8).

14. In July 1814, Stein and Hardenberg met at Frankfurt, concurring that "in every German state a *ständische Verfassung* should be established." That October, during the Vienna Treaty negotiations, Hardenberg supported an accord among Austria, Prussia, and Hanover, proposing *Landstände* with the right to assess taxes, participate in government spending decisions, and vote on legislation (Haake 1921, 52–53; Sheehan 1989, 398–400).

15. In Mar. 1815, Hardenberg received a letter from Justus Gruner, the governor of the Rhine district of Berg, requesting his support for a "secret association for

Germany." Declaring that Germany must be "united as *one* people under *one* ruler," Gruner called for the creation of a "constitutional bond" through the "unification of the German nation" under the Hohenzollern dynasty. Gruner informed Hardenberg of a secret organization led by *Justizrat* Carl Hoffmann, which sought to gather support for this plan in the smaller German states. Hardenberg approved Gruner's request on 5 June, without having informed the king or anyone else; and the chancellor secretly paid the costs of the organization out of Police Ministry funds. (Gruner to Hardenberg, 25 Mar. 1815, in Gruner 1906, 491–92, 497, 507; Haake 1915, 28: 215–17).

16. For example, Sheehan 1989, 421; Klein 1965, 192. Only Paul Haake has given a serious treatment of the ideas of Ancillon, who was by far the most intellectually interesting figure associated with the Prussian Reaction (See Haake 1920; also Haake 1915, esp. 28:182–209).

17. Ancillon to Crown Prince Frederick William, 28 Oct. 1813, quoted in Haake 1920, 61.

18. Ancillon, "Denkschrift über Verfassung in Preußen," undated (Apr. or May 1815), GStA PK, I. HA Rep. 92, Albrecht, Nr. 61, Bl. 2; also Haake 1913, 26:221. The date is implied by Haake 1915, 28:180–82.

19. GStA PK, I. HA Rep. 92, Albrecht, Nr. 61, Bl. 2–11; Haake 1915, 28:187–89.

20. Haake 1921, 53–57; also Haake 1913, 26:561–62.

21. Huber 1978, 1:61–62; Haake 1921, 55, 63–65.

22. On this question, Hardenberg's revisions to the original draft of the edict (which was written by his assistant Friedrich August von Stägemann) provide a partial answer. In several instances, Hardenberg replaced traditional political terms that appeared in Stägemann's draft with more modern and neutral ones. For example, he substituted the newer word "provincial estates" (*Provinzialstände*) for the more traditional "estates of the countryside" (*landschaftlichen Stände*). On the king's insistence, he used the word *Landes-Repräsentanten* in place of *Reichsstände*, because Frederick William wanted to avoid implying a connection to the former *Reichsstände* of the Holy Roman Empire (Koselleck 1981, 214–15).

23. On the fluidity of political alignments in Prussia during this era, see Levinger 1990a; Brose 1993.

24. Brose 1997, 84–85.

25. Quoted in Brose 1997, 88; see also Simon [1955] 1971, 134–35.

26. Hofmeister-Hunger 1994, esp. 201–3, 233–45.

27. Quoted in Haake 1917, 30:329–30.

28. GStA PK, I. HA Rep. 92, Hardenberg, H 15 ½, Bl. 1 (M).

29. Ibid., Bl. 42 (M).

30. Hardenberg, draft of a royal response to the Koblenzer Address, 19 Feb. 1818, ibid., Bl. 45 (M).

31. Kaufmann 1928, 33. Kaufmann does not identify the source of this remark.

32. Frederick William III to Hardenberg, 23 Feb. 1818, GStA PK, I. HA Rep. 92, Hardenberg, H 15 ½, Bl. 47 (M).

33. Hardenberg to Frederick William III, 10 Mar. 1818, GStA PK, I. HA Rep. 92, Hardenberg, H 15 1/2, Bl. 70 (M).

34. In a letter to Görres of 31 Jan. 1818, Hardenberg called the pamphlet's description of Görres's discussion with Hardenberg "richtig und sehr schön," with the exception of a minor inaccuracy regarding the abolition of *Leibeigenschaft* in Prussia. GStA PK, I. HA Rep. 92, Hardenberg, H 15 1/2, Bl. 39 (M).

35. Ibid., Bl. 63, 64 (M).

36. Ibid., Bl. 65.

37. Frederick William III, "An die Einwohner der Stadt Coblenz und der Städte und Gemeinde des Coblenzer Regierungs Departements," 21 Mar. 1818 (draft), ibid., Bl. 91 (M); see also Haake 1916, 29:366–67.

38. Frederick William III to Hardenberg, 21 Mar. 1818, GStA PK, I. HA Rep. 92, Hardenberg, H 15 1/2, Bl. 90 (M).

39. Haake 1917, 30:319–20.

40. Schnabel [1929–37] 1987, 2:253–55; Sheehan 1989, 407; Wehler 1987, 2:337. On Sand, see Heydemann 1986, 7–77.

41. De Wette to Sand's mother, 31 Mar. 1819, GStA BPH, Rep. 192, Wittgenstein, V, 5, Nr. 19, Bl. 3.

42. Ibid. On de Wette, see also Schnabel [1929–37] 1987, 2:255; Nipperdey 1983, 281–82.

43. Eylert, opinion on de Wette's letter (undated), GStA BPH, Rep. 192, Wittgenstein, V, 5, Nr. 19, Bl. 14.

44. Ibid., Bl. 15–16.

45. Ibid., Bl. 35. See also Schnabel [1929–37] 1987, 2:262; Wehler 1987, 2:341.

46. Pauli 1819, 306.

47. Carové, *Ueber die Ermordung Kotzebue's*, quoted in Pauli 1819, 314; see also 309–13.

48. Pauli 1819, 309.

49. Carové, *Ueber die Ermordung*, quoted in Pauli 1819, 314.

50. Hoffmeister 1969–77, 2:242–44, 455–68.

51. For example, Büssem 1974.

52. Hardenberg to Wittgenstein, 4 Apr. 1819, in Branig 1972, 248.

53. Wittgenstein, "Promemoria über Untersuchung der Umtriebe und Manahmen gegen sie," 24 June 1819, GStA BPH, Rep. 192, Wittgenstein, VII, B, Nr. 5, Bl. 2.

54. Quoted in Sheehan 1989, 407.

55. Simon [1955] 1971, 208.

56. Schoeps 1968, 169–210.

57. Cabinet order to the *Staatsministerium*, 11 Jan. 1819 (handwritten copy), GStA BPH, Rep. 192, Wittgenstein, V, 5, Nr. 22, Bl. 1–10; see also Levinger 1990a, 270.

58. Wehler 1987, 2:340.

59. Teplitzer Punkatation, 1 Aug. 1819, in Treitschke 1894–99, 2:634.

60. As early as Nov. 1818, Metternich had warned Prussian police minister Wittgenstein: "Central representation through deputies of the people means the dissolution of the Prussian state." He had urged that the Prussian king "never go further than the establishment of provincial estates," which he considered less dangerous than a central representative body (Metternich to Wittgenstein, 14 Nov. 1818, in Metternich-Winneburg 1881, 3: 171). By the time of the Teplitz Conference, Metternich had become convinced that "the most important positions in the Prussian state administration . . . are occupied by pure revolutionaries" and that the impending adoption of a "democratic constitution in Prussia" would seal the demise of that state (Metternich to Kaiser Franz, 1 Aug. 1819, ibid., 3:362).

61. Treitschke 1894–99, 3:756–61.

62. Levinger 1992, 282–84.

63. Hardenberg to Frederick William III, 3 May 1819, in Haake 1917, 30:344.

64. Haake 1917, 30:345–46; Stern 1894, 1:649–53; GStA BPH, Rep. 192, Wittgenstein, V, 6, Nr. 1, Bl. 6–12.

65. Haake 1917, 30:347; Stern 1894, 1:571–72.

66. Bernstorff, "Gutachten über den Verfassungsentwurf," undated (May 1819?), GStA BPH, Rep. 192, Wittgenstein, V, 6, Nr. 2, Bl. 22–26. This is an unsigned copy of the original, but it corresponds in its content to a memorandum attributed to Bernstorff by Ancillon (Ancillon to Wittgenstein, 20 May 1819, ibid., Bl. 37).

67. Ancillon to Wittgenstein, 20 May 1819, GStA BPH, Rep. 192, Wittgenstein, V, 6, Nr. 2, Bl. 35.

68. Albrecht, opinion on the constitutional question, undated (May or June 1819), quoted in Haake 1917, 30:351–52, note.

69. Schuckmann to Wittgenstein, 13 May 1819, GStA BPH, Rep. 192, Wittgenstein, V, 6, Nr. 2, Bl. 27. See also Büssem 1974, 232. For a more detailed discussion of these memoranda, see Levinger 1992, 288–94.

70. Haake 1919, 142–43.

71. *Gesetz-Sammlung* 1820, 10.

72. Meisner 1913, 35–46, 120–29. For a comparative perspective on theories of monarchical authority elsewhere in nineteenth-century Europe, see Kirsch 1999.

73. Quoted in Treitschke 1894–99, 3:21; see also Sheehan 1989, 408–9. Metternich offered a slightly clearer definition in Nov. 1820; he described the monarchical principle as "der Grundsatz, nach welchem die oberste Staats-Gewalt ungetheilt in den Händen des Monarchen bleibt und anderen Behörden nur eine regelmäige Mitwirkung bey bestimmten Zweigen der Gesetzgebung oder Verwaltung zugestanden wird" (Bailleu 1883, 190). Concerning the date of this document, see Treitschke 1894–99, 3:759–60.

74. The Bavarian charter stated: "The King is the head of state; he unifies in his person all the legitimate powers of the state and exercises them under the conditions established by the present constitution" (Barclay 1995, 8; Boldt 1975, 19).

75. Gentz completed a revised version of this essay on 5 Aug. 1819; the Karlsbad Conference began the following day (Meisner 1913, 184–85).

76. Gentz, "Ueber den Unterschied zwischen den landständischen und Repräsentativ-Verfassungen," in Klüber and Welcker 1844, 221–22, 225, 227.

77. Metternich to Wittgenstein, 14 Nov. 1818, in Metternich-Winneburg 1881, 3: 171.

78. Hardenberg, "Ideen zu einer landständischen Verfassung in Preußen," 11 Aug. 1819, GStA BPH, Rep. 192, Wittgenstein, V, 6, Nr. 4, Bl. 85.

79. Humboldt, "Denkschrift über ständische Verfassung," Oct. 1819, in Humboldt 1903–20, 12:389, 391.

80. Meisner 1913, 198.

81. Treitschke 1894–99, 3:131–41, 151–60; Stern 1894–1924, 2:1–61, 103–17.

82. The various powers entered the congress with widely differing agendas. Tsar Alexander favored a joint military campaign by all five Great Powers to quell the uprisings both in Italy and on the Iberian Peninsula. France and England, in contrast, expressed reluctance about any direct intervention and sent only subaltern officials to attend the Congress of Troppau. Austria and Prussia supported a middle course that would avoid any involvement in Spain or Portugal, seeking only to suppress the Italian revolts. Neither German power favored a joint European military alliance: Austria, whose Italian client states were among those involved in the uprisings, wanted to act alone, and Prussia, still saddled by crushing war debts from the Napoleonic era, was happy to remain on the sidelines (Treitschke 1894–99, 3:151–60; Stern 1894–1924, 2:118–27).

83. Treitschke 1894–99, 3:164.

84. Ibid., 3:160–83; Stern 1894–1924, 2:128–81.

85. For example, Büssem 1974; Obenaus 1984, 149. Stamm-Kuhlmann depicts Frederick William III as extremely reluctant to establish a constitution from the time of the Vienna Congress onward, though he acknowledges that the king made no final decision on this matter until 1820 or 1821 (1992, 416–44, 458–64). Brose, while emphasizing Frederick William's opposition to parliamentary rule, portrays the king as a moderate on social and economic issues (1993, 32–34, 38–50, 56–69). Two works that explore in detail the political events of 1819–1820 are Haake 1919, 32:109–80; and Treitschke 1894–99, 2:588–607, 3:68–130.

86. Frederick William III to Hardenberg, 2 Oct. 1820, quoted in Haake 1919, 32:164.

87. Stern 1886, 330, 328, 329. See also Haake 1919, 32:177–80; GStA BPH, Rep. 192, Wittgenstein, V, 6, Nr. 4, Bl. 81–82, 87–89.

88. *ADB*, 40:358–61.

89. Below is the complete text of *Oberhofmeister* von Schilden's note to Voß, under the heading "Äußerungen Sr. Majestät des Königs über die Einführung einer ständischen Verfassung" (handwritten copy), undated (written before 10 Oct. 1820), GStA PK, I. HA Rep. 92, Otto von Voß-Buch, B 19, Bl. 1 (M).

"I. Das Versprechen hiezu sey zwar gegeben, da aber über die Art und Weise seiner Erfüllung nichts bestimt sey, so ließen es sich durch eine, die Monarchie am wenigsten beschränkende Form der Verfaßung lösen.

"II. Die alten Stände wären ihrer früheren großen Rechte wegen, und durch gründete Verhältnisse nicht ganz wiederherzustellen. Sr. Majestät könnte sich aber ebensowenig entschließen, eine auf den neuen staatsrechtlichen Theorien gegründete Constitution zu bewilligen.

"III. Der König hält berathende Provinzialstände, die sich in wenig zahlreichen Ausschüssen versammeln, dem Zustande und der Lage des Staates am angemeßensten. Diese Provinzialstände würden sich nur mit den Gegenständen beschäftigen, die ihnen vom Könige zur Berathung vorgelegt würden. Bey ihrer Einführung wären die Verhältnisse der verschiedenen Provinzen sehr zu berücksichtigen.

"IV. Sr. Majestät urtheilten sehr besorglich über eine Versammlung von Reichsständen. Sie hielten solche für einen gefährlichen Centralpunct in welchem revolutionaire Absichten leise sich entwickeln könnten.

"V. Der König äußerte: sich nie entschlieen zu können, eine ständische Verfassung, die von ihm allein, aus gnädiger Absicht verliehen würde, beschwören(?) zu können. Jede neue Bekräftigung landesväterlicher Pflichten, die ihn während seiner während seiner ganzen Regierung geleitet hätten, wäre ihm ganz unmöglich.

"Es fanden hierbey noch sehr richtige und lebhafte Bemerkungen gegen die Bairischen und Würtembergschen neuen Verfassungen statt.

"Sr. Majestät berührten die gute Stimmung des größten Theils der Königl. Unterthanen, aber auch daß Vieles geschehen sey um von Seiten der Administration diese Stimmung zu verderben.

"Diese nachtheilige Würkung sey nicht ganz leicht zu heben.

"Die Gesetze der letzten Jahre wären zum Theil im neueren Geiste abgefaßt; ein förmlicher Rückschritt sey nicht möglich, wohl aber eine zweckmäßige Leitung und Anwendung dieser Gesetze, um größeren Nachtheil zu verhindern.

"VI. Es war dem König angenehm zu vernehmen, daß das Resultat meiner Unterredung mit dem Herrn Minister von Voß, mit dem Ansichten Sr. Majestät übereinstimmen.

"Besonders erfreulich war Sr. Majestät, was ich über des Herrn Ministers Meinung: wegen Vermeidung des ganz Alten und ganz neuen in ständischen Angelegenheiten sagen konnte, da der König bisher nur das Eine oder Andere Extreme in dieser Materie gefunden hätte, wenn er den Fürsten Metternich und einige wenige ausnähme.

"Der König wünscht also, in gerechter Anerkennung der bewährten Einsichten und der genauen Landeskenntniß des Herrn Minister von Voß, daß derselbe seine Ansichten über die zweckmäßige Einführung einer ständischen Verfassung, in einem kurzen Aufsatze, so schnell, als es die Wichtigkeit des Gegenstandes nur irgend zulasse, Sr. Majestät vorlegen wolle.

"Der König äußerte sich sehr gnädig und vertrauensvoll über den Herrn Minister von Voß und dessen bekannte Ergebenheit für Seine Person."

90. Voß-Buch, "Ueber Constitution und Central Repraesentation" (handwritten copy), 10 Oct. 1820, GStA BPH, Rep. 50, Frederick William IV, E 2, Nr. 1, Bl. 61 (M). (Another copy of this document is contained in GStA PK, I. HA Rep. 92, Otto von Voß-Buch, B 19, Bl. 2–3 (M).)

91. Below is the complete text of Schilden's letter to Voß, 9 Nov. 1820 (handwritten copy), GStA PK, I. HA Rep. 92, Otto von Voß-Buch, B 19, Bl. 4 (M).

"Euer Excellenz den Dank des Königs Majestät für den letzthin überreichten Aufsatz zu erneuern, ist die erste und sehr erfreuliche Veranlassung dieses Schreibens.

"Sr. Majestät haben in jenem Aufsatze Euer Excellenz vieljährige treue Anhänglichkeit an Ihre Höchste Person und an den Staat mit wahrem Wohlgefallen und gerechter Anerkennung wiedergefunden. Sie äußerten: der Minister von Voß hat Recht, aber man ist schon zu weit gegangen.

"Der König stimmt also für consultative Stände und deutet zuweilen auch auf einen wenig zahlreichen Central-Ausschuß hin, dessen Berufung ihm Allein verbliebe.

"Die zweite Veranlassung dieses Schreibens ist: die Mittheilung der dem Könige eingereichten Communal-Ordnungen. Euer Excellenz Gutachten darüber zu erhalten, ist der Wünsch des Königs.

"Mit ebenso merkbarem als wohlgegrundetem Vertrauen zu Euer Excellenz, hat der König mir befohlen, diesen Wünsch auszudrücken. Zugleich darf Euer Excellenz ich bemerken: wie(?) bei den nächsten Umgebungen des Königs die Ansicht befahl(?), daß eine Commission zur Revision der eingereichten Communal-Ordnungen, auch Untersuchung dessen, was hierin zur Ausführung kommen solle, und zur Einleitung ständischer Verfassungen gebildet werde, Euer Excellenz aber an der Spitze dieser Commission Sich befinden möchten.

"Ob Euer Excellenz dem Könige anheim stellen wollten: eine solche Commission zu ernennen, und Sich zu deren Leitung entschließen könnten, davon hängt nicht allein deren Gründung, sondern ganz besonders ihr Erfolg ab.

"Von den fünf Mitgliedern der bisherigen Communal-Commission, deren Arbeiten Euer Excellenz vorliegen, würde keines sich in der neuen Commission befinden, wohl aber Euer Excellenz Vorschläge von großem Einfluß auf ihre Zusammensetzung sein können.

"Euer Excellenz kennen die Lage der Sachen und die Stellung der Personen so genau, um Selbst einzusehen: wie entscheidend Ihr Entschluß und wie höchst wünschenswerth Ihre Einwürkung in diese so wichtige Angelegenheit sein wird. Genehmigen Euer Excellenz den erneuerten Ausdruck meiner höchsten Verehrung, mit welcher ich die Ehre habe zu sein."

92. Hardenberg noted in his diary on 11 Nov. 1820: "Plan du roi d'abdiquer que W[ittgenstein] m'a communiqué. C'est de peur de la constitution et de ses suites, de ses difficultés" (quoted in Haake 1919, 32:165; see also Treitschke 1894–99, 3:171–73).

93. Voß, opinion on the proposals for a communal ordinance, 16 Nov. 1820, GStA PK, I. HA Rep. 92, Otto von Voß-Buch, B 19, Bl. 5 (M).

94. Below is the complete text of Schilden's letter to Voß, 3 Dec. 1820 (handwritten copy), GStA PK, I. HA Rep. 92, Otto von Voß-Buch, B 19, Bl. 10 (M).

"Euer Excellenz Gutachten über die Communal-Ordnungen habe ich gleich nach der Rückkehr des Königs, Höchstdemselben zu überreichen die Ehre gehabt. Es hat solches im höchsten Grade den Beyfall des Königs erhalten.

"Sr. Majestät fanden es, zu Ihrem sichtbaren Wohlgefallen, mit Ihren eigenen Ansichten übereinstimmend. Äußerten aber, daß nicht Alle solche theilten.

"Dringender und wünschenswerther als je, scheint es mir daher, daß diesem entgegengewirkt werde. Von diesem, für das Wohl des Königs und des Ganzen, so wichtigen Gesichtspuncte auch früher schon geleitet, bin ich vielleicht in meinen Wünschen gegen Euer Excellenz in jener Beziehung zu weit gegangen und habe ich mich in den Mitteln zum guten Zwecke täuschen können. Eurer Excellenz besserer Einsicht unterwerfe ich mich gerne.

"Ich darf aber Ihnen nicht verhehlen, daß die Gefahr fortwährend sehr groß ist, und daß unter den bestehenden Persönlichkeiten und Umständen Vieles gewonnen seyn würde, weitere Nachtheile zu verhindern. Diese Ansicht allein vermochte mich(?) einer Commission zu erwähnen. Sie sollte nicht eigentlich der Verwaltung gegenüber, sondern mit ihr verschmolzen, zusammenberufen werden. Vielleicht gelänge es den Wunsch des Prinzen wegen einer Staatshaushaltungs-Commission mit der zur Einführung ständischer Verfassungen zu vereinigen. Das erste Geschäft würde dann das zweite wenigstens verschieben, und Zeit gewonnen werden.

"Euer Excellenz hoffe ich bald persönlich hier in Berlin aufwarten zu dürfen. Herzog Carl, Fürst Wittgenstein, Ancillon rechnen auch auf Ihre Ankunft.

"Euer Excellenz soll ich noch ganz besonders den Dank des Königs für die jüngsten Beweise Ihrer Anhänglichkeit, für das Gutachten, auszudrücken die Ehre haben. Zugleich gereicht es mir zur größten Freude Euer Excellenz noch die Gesinnungen von Wohlwollen und höchst gerechtem Vertrauen mitzutheilen, welche der König bei dieser Veranlassung mir auch das Neue für Sie äußerte.

"Genehmigen Sie den erneuerten Ausdruck der höchsten Verehrung, mit welcher ich zu verharren die Ehre habe."

95. Treitschke 1894–99, 3:173–74, 226; Haake 1919, 32:170.

96. On this point, see, for example, Brose 1993, 68–71; Stamm-Kuhlmann 1992, 555.

97. Wehler writes:

The late absolutist German state [of the eighteenth century] embodied anything but an unrestricted absolutist regime in which . . . all impulses originated with the monarch. In the Old Reich, absolutism remained always a tendency rather than a full reality. Everywhere a dualism persisted between the monarchical state [*Fürstenstaat*] and a nobility that was accustomed to the exercise of power. (1987, 1:339)

See also Blänkner 1993.

98. This discursive triumph of "Germany" over "Prussia" was not yet complete: for example, during the Revolution of 1848, the representative assembly convening

in Berlin was called the Prussian National Assembly. Such occurrences of the word, however, were rare after 1820.

Chapter 7

1. "Opinion concerning the *Kreis-* and *Kommunalordnung*," GStA BPH, Rep. 192, Wittgenstein, V, 6, Nr. 8, Bl. 15. This document is an undated and unsigned copy; "Minister v. Voß Januar 1821" is written in pencil at the top of the first page.

2. Branig 1965, 184, 191–92; Obenaus 1971, 1:415.

3. Developments in the Prussian Rhineland varied somewhat from the pattern analyzed here, both because the government faced challenges in integrating these new territories into the Prussian state after 1815 and because the Rhenish provinces had generally preserved a more vigorous system of local and regional self-government during the eighteenth century than was the case in the older Prussian provinces. Moreover, the political experience of the Rhineland during the Napoleonic era was strikingly different from that of the core Prussian provinces. As part of the Confederation of the Rhine, this region adopted the Napoleonic Code and reforms of the French Revolution, such as the abolition of feudalism and the introduction of a new system of municipal government. Much of this new legislation remained in force in the Rhineland after 1815. On developments in the Rhineland, see Sperber 1991, 12–136; Weitz 1970. On the neighboring province of Westphalia, which was politically similar to the Rhineland, see Reif 1979.

4. While there was significant overlap between the conservatism of the aristocracy and that of the civil service, important differences also existed, both in terms of these groups' motives and in terms of the theories they expressed. On the evolution of conservatism within the Prussian civil service, see the excellent works by Dittmer (1992) and Vogel (1983b), along with Rosenberg's classic *Bureaucracy, Aristocracy, and Autocracy* ([1958] 1966a).

5. Mannheim 1953, 95, 98–99, 117, 102, 115

6. Some insightful work has begun to move away from this view, arguing that conservatism must be understood as a fundamentally innovative and modern phenomenon. See, for example, Berdahl 1988; Neugebauer 1992; Dittmer 1992; Beck 1995; Ullmann and Zimmermann 1996. Berdahl, for example, writes that
the Prussian nobility traditionally justified, or "euphemized," its domination of the peasantry by means of an ideology of paternalism, that this paternalistic model of social relations began to dissolve under the capitalist transformation of agriculture at the end of the eighteenth century, and that the conservative politics of the nobility during the first half of the nineteenth century were determined by an effort to reestablish the lineaments of patrimonial rule and a paternalist ideology. (1988, 5)

7. For example, Ribhegge 1989.

8. For example, Valjavec 1951; Epstein 1966a, 12–20; Greiffenhagen 1967; Schoeps 1958, 22.

9. Especially Kondylis 1986, 63–206; Neugebauer 1992; Schoeps 1964, 28–45; Wehler 1987, 2:440–57; Christopher Clark 1993, 31–60.

10. Berdahl 1988, 6–7.

11. On this point, compare the interpretation of Kondylis, who argues that the first half of the nineteenth century marked the "downfall" of conservatism, coinciding with the demise of traditional hierarchical notions of the *societas civilis* (1986, 387–507). This is an insightful but also an idiosyncratic claim, because it

suggests that authentic conservatism disappeared forever at the very historical moment (the 1830s and 1840s) that the words "conservative" and "conservatism" were coined in Germany. (On the etymology of these words, see Vierhaus 1982, 3: 537–41.)

12. Brose 1993, 222–28, 239; Barclay 1995, 47–48, 84–98, 115–16, 120–26.

13. Sheehan 1989, 403–4.

14. On the malleability of tradition, see Hobsbawm and Ranger 1983.

15. See pp. 149–57.

16. The initial members of the Crown Prince's Commission, which was established on 19 Dec. 1820, were Crown Prince Frederick William, Wilhelm Ludwig Georg von Sayn-Wittgenstein-Hohenstein, Johann Peter Friedrich Ancillon, Kaspar Friedrich von Schuckmann, Daniel Ludwig Albrecht, and Friedrich von Bülow (Treitschke 1894–99, 3:173). The members of the second commission, which was established on 30 Oct. 1821, were the crown prince, Otto von Voß-Buch, Wittgenstein, Schuckmann, Friedrich Ludwig von Vincke, Albrecht, Ancillon, *Regierungspräsident* Schönberg, and Dunker (GStA BPH, Rep. 192, Wittgenstein, V, 6, Nr. 9, Bl. 1–21; Obenaus 1971, 411–12; Haake 1919, 32:170).

17. Letter of the Crown Prince's Commission to Frederick William III, Jan. 1822, GStA BPH, Rep. 192, Wittgenstein, V, 6, Nr. 9, Bl. 1–2, 21.

18. For example, *Kurmärkische Ritterschaft* to Frederick William III, 13 Aug. 1814, GStA PK, I. HA Rep. 92, G. v. Rochow, A III, Nr. 1, Bl. 21 (M); *Deputies of the Großen Ausschußes der Kur- und Neumärkischen Ritterschaft* to Frederick William III, 17 Mar. 1818, GStA PK, I. HA Rep. 74, H IX, Nr. 20, Bl. 23–24 (M).

19. Petition of the *Ritterschaftlichen Stände des Westhavelländischen und der Zauchischen Kreises* to Frederick William III, 15 Nov. 1819 (handwritten copy), GStA PK, I. HA Rep. 92, Hardenberg, H 28, Bl. 4–5 (M). See also Müsebeck 1918, 344–46; Treitschke 1872, 431–32.

20. Frederick William III to the nobles of Zauche and Westhavelland, 28 Dec. 1819, in Müsebeck 1918, 366.

21. See, for example, the petition by the *Kurmärkische Ritterschaft* to the king dated 29 Mar. 1820, protesting the abolition of the Brandenburg provincial credit association (*Landschaft*). The nobles of the Kurmark were deeply upset by this law, because the *Landschaft* was one of the only important provincial institutions that remained under the direct control of the estates, and they complained that the monarchy had "seized property of the estates without promising any compensation." But in this petition, composed at the height of the Spanish Revolution of 1820, the Kurmark nobles qualified their theoretical claims. Having repeated all of their arguments about the contractual basis of monarchical rule, they concluded their plea as follows: "Should Your Royal Majesty, for reasons unknown to us, reject the deed [*Verhandlung*] and contract with your faithful estates, then we ask, for now, only the protection of our property. We also request, in the near future, a hearing in Your Majesty's district court [*Landes Gerichte*]." The Kurmark nobles, in other words, equivocated about the status of the contract between the king and the estates. They now conceded that this contract might legitimately be overriden by a "law of the land," provided that this law were properly reviewed by the State Council and the Ministry of State. Deputies of the *Ritterschaft der Kurmärkischen Kreise* to Frederick William III, 29 Mar. 1820, GStA PK, I. HA Rep. 92, G. v. Rochow, A III, Nr. 5, Bl. 36, 39 (M).

22. For example, Frederick William III to Hardenberg, 16 Sept. 1822, GStA BPH, Rep. 192, Wittgenstein, V, 6, Nr. 12, Bl. 1; also Brose 1993, 63–64.

23. Koselleck 1981, 515–17; Rosenberg [1958] 1966, 221; Berdahl 1988, 374–80; Görlitz 1981, 218–20.

24. Brose 1993, 64. Other works that argue that the Prussian nobility was in decline by the early nineteenth century include Hagen 1989, 302–35; Botzenhart 1983, 450.

25. Brose 1993, 62–65; Koselleck 1981, 80–83, 515; Berdahl 1988, 77–90, 273–80.

26. Brose gives the following figures for the percentages of bourgeois appointees to various branches of the Prussian government: officer corps: 46 percent bourgeois in 1818; foreign service: 50 percent in 1830; top provincial administration: 76 percent in 1820; business department: 100 percent in 1824; leading Seehandlung staff: 88 percent in 1824; artillery officer corps: 58 percent in 1830 (1993, 58). See also Koselleck 1981, 680–90.

27. Koselleck 1981, 689.

28. Sitzungsprotokolle der Kommission des Kronprinzen, Dec. 1821, GStA BPH, Rep. 192, Wittgenstein, V, 6, Nr. 9, Bl. 15. In practice, there was some variation from this principle. In Brandenburg's Kurmark, this principle was observed: the nobility was granted twenty-two delegates, the towns fourteen delegates, and the peasantry eight. In West Prussia, however, the nobility received fifteen delegates, the towns thirteen delegates, and the peasantry seven delegates. In Saxony, the nobility received thirty-five delegates and the towns and peasantry a combined total of thirty-seven. In the Rhine provinces, the towns and peasantry received a greater representation than elsewhere: the nobility was awarded twenty-nine delegates, the towns twenty-five delegates, and the peasantry twenty-five delegates (Gesetz-Sammlung 1823, 131; 1824, 71, 102).

29. GStA BPH, Rep. 192, Wittgenstein, V, 6, Nr. 9, Bl. 18, 20. On the hybrid of traditional and modern logic in the Provincial Estates Law, see also Obenaus 1984, 202–9.

30. Stahl, quoted in Obenaus 1984, 203–4; see also Berdahl 1988, 221–22.

31. Quoted in Berdahl 1988, 222.

32. Rochow, "Was kann geschehen um dem Adel aufzuhelfen?" 1 Oct. 1823, GStA PK, I. HA Rep. 92, G. v. Rochow, A III, Nr. 10, Bl. 5 (M); see also Berdahl 1988, 225.

33. Petition of the Deputies of the Großen Ausschußes der Kur- und Neumärkischen Ritterschaft to Frederick William III, 17 Mar. 1818, GStA PK, I. HA Rep. 92, G. v. Rochow, A III, Nr. 1, Bl. 35 (M).

34. Brose 1993, 59–60, 65–66; Obenaus 1984, 486–91; Koselleck 1981, 589–99; Mieck 1965. The quote is from a letter by Frederick William III of 30 Nov. 1824, GStA PK, I. HA Rep. 92, Müffling, A 9, Bl. 2 (M), quoted in Brose 1993, 59.

35. The term Verbürgerlichung des Adels appears in Fehrenbach 1994; see also Vierhaus 1987, 235–48. Obenaus concurs that a "partial modernization" of Prussian society was achieved during the early nineteenth century (1984, 450). For similar arguments about the transformation of the social identity of the nobility, see Schissler 1978; Reif 1979; Koselleck 1981; Vetter 1978. On the "feudalization thesis," see Kocka, "The European Pattern and the German Case," in Kocka and Mitchell 1993, 25–27, as well as the various works in chapter 1, n. 10, of this study.

36. Rosenberg 1966b, 295.

37. See, for example, Eickenboom 1976, 68–76.

38. Marwitz to Hardenberg, 14 Sept. 1814, in Meusel 1908–13, 2/2:223, quoted in Kondylis 1986, 294.

39. Quast, "Auszüge aus meinem Aufsazze über National-Repräsentation," 28

June 1812 (?), BLHA, Pr. Br. Rep. 37, v. Quast/Garz, Nr. 86, Bl. 41. The document, which is in Quast's handwriting, is unsigned and undated, but it appears to be a copy of a memorandum to which Marwitz later refers in a letter to Quast of 25 Dec. 1812 (Meusel 1908–13, 2/2:168–71).

40. Voß to Quast, 2 Mar. 1812, BLHA, Pr. Br. Rep. 37, v. Quast/Garz, Nr. 134, Bl. 15. This letter appears to be the response to a letter from Quast, dated 24 Feb. 1812 (unsigned handwritten copy), ibid., Bl. 18.

41. See also Marwitz's memorandum of 1812, which declared that the landowning nobility was the "first member of the nation" and that it should "return to its original vocation" by becoming a "caste of warriors" that would lead the realm to victory in a patriotic war (Marwitz, "Über eine Reform des Adels," Jan. 1812, in Meusel 1908–13, 2/2:156–57).

42. "Marwitz über den ersten Brandenburgischen Provinziallandtag," 1824, in Meusel 1908–13, 2/2:343.

43. Quast, letter to the *Ritterschaft* of the *Ruppinschen Kreis*, 18 May 1820, BLHA, Pr. Br. Rep. 37, v. Quast/Garz, Nr. 91, Bl. 114–16.

44. Quast, memorandum of 30 Jan. 1822, in "Protokolle der Kommission zur Zusammensetzung der Provinzialstände," 1822, BLHA, Pr. Br. Rep. 37, v. Quast/Garz, Nr. 95, Bl. 7, 8, 9. On patterns of landownership, see Schissler 1978, 72–73, 159–85.

45. Obenaus identifies the provincial diets of Brandenburg, Pomerania, and Saxony as the most rigidly conservative ones during this period and those of the provinces of the Rhineland and Prussia (formerly East Prussia and West Prussia) as the most liberal (1988, 304).

46. See, for example, Schoeps 1968, 173–77, 183–86, 189–92, 195–97.

47. Klüber and Welcker 1844, 225, 221; see also chapter 6 above.

48. Haller [1820] 1964, 1:172, 1:359, quoted in Berdahl 1988, 234, 236. See also Sheehan 1989, 591–93; Nipperdey 1983, 317–18; Barclay 1995, 36; Wehler 1987, 2: 445–46.

49. Berdahl 1988, 236–45. The quotes are from Haller [1820] 1964, in Berdahl 1988, 238–39.

50. *Berliner Politisches Wochenblatt*, 6 Apr. 1833, 83, quoted in Beck 1995, 47.

51. Barclay 1995, 33–34, 40–41; Berdahl 1988, 246–55; Beck 1995, 43–45, 79–81; Schoeps 1964, 11–21; Kondylis 1986, 276–86, 305–6.

52. Tocqueville [1856] 1955.

53. Schoeps 1964, 31–32; see also Berdahl 1988, 255.

54. Stahl [1845] 1927, 6, 5, 8. On Stahl more generally, see Berdahl 1988, 348–73; Sheehan 1989, 593–96; Nipperdey 1983, 379–80; Wehler 1987, 2:452–54; Toews 1980, 248, 254; Füßl 1988.

55. Berdahl 1988, 367, 371–72.

56. Stahl [1845] 1927, 25–26, 31.

57. Stahl [1845] 1927, 8, 37–40, 44–47, 55–57; also Sheehan 1989, 595; Berdahl 1988, 369–70.

58. Schoeps 1964, 31.

59. Berdahl 1988, 256–63.

60. GStA BPH, Rep. 192, Wittgenstein, V, 6, Nr. 9, Bl. 2.

61. Ibid., Bl. 8, 10, 16–17, 19–20. See also "Allgemeines Gesetz wegen Anordnung der Provinzialstände," 5 June 1823, *Gesetz-Sammlung*, 1823, 129–45; Obenaus 1971, 412.

62. Neugebauer 1992, 326–27, 336–41.

63. Obenaus 1971, 412; see also 428–29, 437; Obenaus 1984, 419–47; Arndt 1902.

64. Rosenberg [1958] 1966, 203.

65. Schissler 1978, 130–44; Rosenberg [1958] 1966, 220–26.

66. Schissler 1978, 144.

67. Brose notes that King Frederick William III, "never convinced of his own infallibility," did not oppose a single recommendation of the Council of State from its formation in 1817 until his death in 1840 (1993, 63).

68. Obenaus 1971; Obenaus 1984, 516–51; Stamm-Kuhlmann 1992, 416–581; Barclay 1995, 49–126; Blasius 1992, 57–112.

69. See, for example, Dittmer 1992, 238.

70. Obenaus 1984, 205–6.

71. Neugebauer 1992, 390–98, 414–15; Obenaus 1984, 407–10, 583–94.

72. Dohna, letter of 24 Oct. 1824, quoted in Neugebauer 1992, 389–90.

73. Neugebauer 1992, 391–92.

74. The main historiographical approaches to this question are reviewed in Obenaus 1988, 305–8.

75. Obenaus 1988, 322–28.

76. Quoted in Obenaus 1984, 412.

77. Treitschke 1894–99, 5:141; quoted in Neugebauer 1992, 415.

78. Neugebauer 1992, 414–15, 435–37; Dittmer 1992, 194–95 (the quote is from Dittmer).

79. Quoted in Neugebauer 1992, 461–62.

80. The *Rittergutsbesitzer* Waner of Lissnau, petition of 9 Mar. 1843, quoted in Neugebauer 1992, 436–37.

81. Dittmer 1992, 239.

82. Quoted in Dittmer 1992, 177.

83. Dittmer 1992, 181–82.

84. "Allgemeines Gesetz wegen Anordnung der Provinzialstände," 5 June 1823, *Gesetz-Sammlung* 1823, 130.

85. See pp. 135–36 and 146–49, as well as Levinger 1990a.

86. Ancillon, "Gutachten über den Bericht der Kommission des Kronprinzen über den Entwurf Hardenbergs," 12 Jan. 1821, GStA BPH, Rep. 192, Wittgenstein, V, 6, Nr. 8, Bl. 22–23.

87. Wittgenstein, "Bemerkungen zu dem Entwurfe des Gesetzes für die Brandenburgischen Provinzial Stände," unsigned and undated (but contained in the same folder with the draft version of the law and the commission report of 14 Sept. 1822), GStA BPH, Rep. 192, Wittgenstein, V, 6, Nr. 15, Bl. 11.

88. Compare also the views of Voß, who declared on 5 Apr. 1818 that the adoption of a constitution was both "desirable" and "nearly inevitable": "Eine *Konstitution* [ist] für den Staat nach dem sich entwickelnden Geiste der Zeit, und für die Möglichkeit, daß doch in später Zukunft einmal irgend ein Regent demselben nicht entsprechen könne, allerdings wünschenswerth, und fast unvermeidlich." GStA PK, I. HA Rep. 77, Titel 514, Nr. 28, Bl. 256 (M).

89. Quoted in Sheehan 1989, 727.

90. Stahl [1845] 1927, 8; Barclay 1995, 96, 129, 187, 248–50; Füßl 1988.

91. Radowitz, quoted in Beck 1995, 66; see also Barclay 1995, 185–213; Sheehan 1989, 711–15.

92. Frederick William IV to Ernst Senfft von Pilsach, 9 July 1854, GStA PK, I. HA Rep. 92, Ernst Freiherr Senfft von Pilsach, B, Nr. 8, Bl 12 (M), quoted in Barclay 1993, 152.

93. Grünthal 1987, 46; see also Schwentker 1988; Retallack 1991.

94. On this point, see, for example, Barclay 1995, 49–55.

95. In this connection, it is noteworthy that nobles from East and West Prussia, many of whom strongly advocated a constitution during this era, were also generally more willing than aristocrats from other provinces to accept modifications to their traditional privileges, such as the abolition of patrimonial justice powers. (Obenaus 1988, 304–20). See also Neugebauer 1992, 415.

96. Dittmer 1992, 244.

Chapter 8

1. Henry E. Dwight, *Travels in the North of Germany* (New York: G. & C. & H. Carvill, 1829), 166, quoted in Knudsen 1990, 113.

2. Knudsen 1990 130, 114, 131.

3. Toews 1980, 211, 213, 216; Sheehan 1978, 20–21.

4. See chapter 3 above.

5. Langewiesche 1988, 28. On Hegel's theory of civil society, see also Sheehan 1978, 33–34; Manfred Riedel's essays "Hegels Begriff der 'bürgerlichen Gesellschaft' " and "Natur und Freiheit in Hegels Rechtsphilosophie," in Riedel 1975.

6. Hegel 1821, §182, §183, §185.

7. Ibid., §185, addendum to §185; §205.

8. Sietze, *Grundbegriff preussischer Staats- und Rechtsgeschichte als Einleitung in die Wissenschaft des preussischen Rechts* (Berlin: F. Laue, 1829), quoted in Toews 1980, 120.

9. On the traditions of Right, Center, and Left Hegelianism, the standard work is Toews 1980.

10. Whitman 1990, 233, 95.

11. Toews 1980, 357–59. (This quote dates from the autumn of 1841.)

12. Ruge, "Der preußische Absolutismus und seine Entwickelung" (1841), in Ruge 1988, 4:1–59.

13. Ruge 1988, 4:18, 58–59.

14. See chapter 2, n. 52.

15. Toews 1980, 357–58, 361.

16. Ruge, "Der preußische Absolutismus," in Ruge 1988, 4:58.

17. Brandt 1968, 5–7, 280–81.

18. Langewiesche 1988, 21.

19. Schneider 1952; Haake 1916, 29:305–10; Haake 1914, 247, 265; Brose 1993, 63.

20. Quoted in Langewiesche 1988, 26.

21. Quoted in Sheehan 1978, 39.

22. Schleunes 1979, 315–16; Baumgart 1990, 103; Nipperdey 1983, 451–82; Wehler 1987, 1:472–85; Schnabel [1929–37] 1987, 1:408–57; König 1972.

23. Schleunes 1979, 322, 323, 340. The most thorough recent account of nineteenth-century Prussian elementary schooling is Kuhlemann 1992.

24. Quoted in Langewiesche 1988, 18.

25. See chapter 3, n. 1, and chapter 4, n. 3.

26. "Proklamation an sämtliche Bewohner des preußischen Staates," 21 Oct. 1808, quoted in Baumgart 1990, 35.

27. In Winter 1931, 371.

28. "Promemoria" to Süvern's draft of an educational reform bill, 1819, quoted in Schleunes 1979, 332.

29. Draft of the school reform bill, 1819, quoted in Baumgart 1990, 79.

30. Schleunes 1979, 326–32. See also chapter 4, n. 6.

31. Barkin 1983, 33. The reference here is to a remark by David Landes (1969).

32. Quoted in Barkin 1983, 41. The second quote is from the Pennsylvania educator Enoch Wines, ibid., 48.

33. Report of the *Erziehungskommission* to Frederick William III, 5 Feb. 1821 (signed by Bishop Eylert, *Regierungsrath* Shulz, *Regierungsrath* Beckedorff, and *Consistorialrath* and Director Snethlage), GStA BPH, Rep. 192, Wittgenstein, V, 5, Nr. 26, Bl. 37, 38, 39, 50.

34. Beckedorff's opinion on Süvern's education reform bill, quoted in Schleunes 1979, 333.

35. Schleunes 1979, 333–34. The quote is from Beckedorff 1825, 32.

36. Beckedorff 1825, 32.

37. H. Brunnengräber, *Ludolf von Beckedorff: Ein Volksschulpädagoge des 19. Jahrhunderts* (Düsseldorf, 1929), 28, quoted in Schleunes 1979, 333.

38. Schleunes 1979, 332–35; Baumgart 1990, 88–102.

39. In Botzenhart and Hubatsch 1957–74, 2/1:394. See also chapter 3, n. 38.

40. On the several proposals for a Prussian *Kreisordnung*, see Unruh 1968.

41. Treitschke, "Der erste Verfassungskampf," 438–41; *Deutsche Geschichte*, 3:98–113.

42. Report of the third constituent committee (Friese, Köhler, Eichhorn, von Bernuth, Streckfuds, Daniels, Vincke), 7 Aug. 1820, GStA BPH, Rep. 192, Wittgenstein, V, 6, Nr. 4, Bl. 188, 159, 160. Part of this document is reprinted in Unruh 1968, 31–41.

43. Kant, "Beantwortung der Frage: Was ist Aufklärung?" in Kant 1968, 11:53.

44. GStA BPH, Rep. 192, Wittgenstein, V, 6, Nr. 4, Bl. 159.

45. Hagen 1980, 82–117. (The quote from Altenstein is on 82.)

46. See, for example, chapter 6, n. 21 and n. 22.

47. Humboldt, "Denkschrift über Preußens ständische Verfassung," 4 Feb. 1819, in Humboldt 1903–20, 12:232–35, 12:279–81; Treitschke 1894–99, 2:498–500.

48. Humboldt 1903–20, 12:293–94; Treitschke 1894–99, 2:499–500.

49. Hardenberg, "Ideen zu einer landständischen Verfassung in Preußen," 11 Aug. 1819, GStA BPH, Rep. 192, Wittgenstein, V, 6, Nr. 4, Bl. 84–85; reprinted in Treitschke 1894–99, 2:637.

50. Humboldt, "Denkschrift über ständische Verfassung," Oct. 1819, in Humboldt 1903–20, 12:389, 391.

51. *Gesetz-Sammlung* 1820, 10.

52. Heymann 1925, 157.

53. Quoted in Barclay 1995, 49.

54. Botzenhart and Hubatsch 1957–74, 2:208; see also chapter 2.

55. Barclay 1995, 51.

56. For a further discussion of these themes, see pp. 184–87 above and Barclay 1995.

57. Barclay 1995, 49, 51.

58. Quoted in Barclay 1995, 50.

59. I thank Dr. Eva Bliembach for calling this engraving to my attention and for explaining its iconography. Concerning radical political activism in Cologne during the early 1840s, see Sperber 1991, esp. 87–99, 105–20.

60. Obenaus 1984, 563–648.

61. Ibid., 521–51, 594–617.

62. Ibid., 649–50; Barclay 1995, 122.

63. Barclay 1995, 127–29.

64. "Thronrede Sr. Maj. des Königs von Preußen, bei Eröffnung des Vereinigten Landtages am 11. April 1847" (Leipzig: E. Pöhnecke & Sohn, 1847), 4, 11, 14, in GStA PK, XII. HA IV, Nr. 12. Concerning Stein and Hardenberg's views on representation, see, for example, chapter 3, n. 29.

65. GStA PK, XII. HA IV, Nr. 12, p. 5.

66. Trauttmansdorff to Metternich, 16 Apr. 1847, quoted in Barclay 1995, 128–29.

67. "Adresse des Vereinigten Landtages an Se. Majestät den König," in Bleich [1847] 1977, 1:26–27.

68. Bleich [1847] 1977, 1:28; see also Barclay 1995, 130.

69. Bleich [1847] 1977, 2:271; see also Balster 1848, 33–36.

70. Quoted in Sheehan 1989, 628.

71. Sheehan 1989, 628; Barclay 1996, 131–41; Obenaus 1984, 649–716.

72. Nor did any of the hundreds of petitions received by the United Diet directly challenge the principle of monarchical sovereignty. For a list of the titles of 474 such petitions, see Bleich [1847] 1977, 1:585–606.

73. Siemann 1985, 70.

74. On women's participation in the Revolution of 1848 through democratic women's associations, see Hachtmann 1997, 514–22.

75. Frederick William's own words were more prosaic and less fervently nationalistic: "Ich habe heute die alten deutschen Farben angenommen, und Mich und Mein Volk unter das ehrwürdige Banner des deutschen Reiches gestellet" (Siemann 1985, 70).

76. "Der deutsche Michel kann sich nur schwer zwischen Schlaf- und Jakobinermütze entscheiden." This title is found on the photograph of this print in the Bildarchiv Preußischer Kulturbesitz. The caption at the bottom of the picture reads: "Der deutsche Michel ist uneinig mit sich auseinander gegangen, wird sich aber bald wieder zusammenfügen." Anonymous lithograph, Leipzig, 1848.

77. Jahn, speeches to the Frankfurt Assembly, 15 Jan. and 17 Feb. 1849, in Jahn 1887, 2:1031–32, 1034. The vote regarding the abolition of hereditary nobility took place on 2 Aug. 1848.

78. Jahn 1887, 2:1021–22.

79. Though Jahn's position on the establishment of a hereditary Kaiser placed him in the conservative minority in the Frankfurt Assembly, on other issues he ranked as a moderate. A study of voting patterns in the Frankfurt Assembly of 1848 placed Jahn squarely in the middle of the political spectrum. Using a scale of 0 to 9, where 0 represented the most conservative delegates and 9 the most radical, Jahn's overall score was 5 (Matthiesen 1979, 130, note).

80. The vote count of 27 Mar. 1849 was 267–263 in favor of establishing a hereditary title of Kaiser (Siemann 1985, 197).

81. Speech to the Frankfurt Assembly, in Jahn 1887, 2:1035, 1038.

82. Sperber 1991, 124–25.

83. Boldt 1971, 75–76. Similarly, concerning the 1848 revolutionaries, Rudolf Stadelmann declares:

> But even these people who had their minds made up only wanted a cooperation, a division of power between the people and the government, between the legislation and the administration, between the chamber and the king. An aspiration to establish, over and above this liberal dualism, an absolute responsibility of the governed, an actual popular sovereignty, was only out-

lined by a very small circle of radicals, and even they had no clear conception of which organs must develop first to support a true self-government. (1975, 44).

84. Sperber 1991, 266. On the democratic monarchists, see also Seypel 1988, 153–57.

85. Sperber 1991, 226–27.

86. See chapters 5 and 6 above.

87. Carové 1848, 52, x.

88. Ibid., 77, 83, 55.

89. Proskauer 1974, 10:11–12. The most comprehensive study of Nees is Höpfner 1994, 9–102. I thank Dr. Höpfner for calling Nees's writings to my attention.

90. Nees von Esenbeck 1848, 8.

91. Proskauer 1974, 10:12.

92. Nees von Esenbeck 1848, 12–13, 5–6.

93. Langewiesche 1993b, 43–44.

94. Hachtmann 1997, 273–74.

95. Ibid., 274–78, 514.

96. Ibid., 581; see also 555–82.

97. Ibid., 624–27, 866–67, 884–85. (The quote is from 626.)

98. Oettrich 1848, 3–4.

99. Kletke 1848, 4. Langewiesche describes "democratic monarchy" as an unsuccessful "compromise formula" in 1848 (1988, 57).

100. Mattheisen 1979, 141–42.

101. Langewiesche 1988, 46.

102. Letter of 26 Mar. 1848, quoted in Langewiesche 1988, 47. The new Prussian government, headed by Ludolf Camphausen, was formed on 29 Mar. 1848.

103. Boldt 1973, 621. See also Boldt 1971; Mattheisen 1979, 124–26.

104. Gailus 1990, 129–32, 431–57; Schwentker 1988, 72–117, 144–81.

105. Hachtmann 1997, 514–22.

106. A revised version of this Prussian constitution was promulgated in Jan. 1850. On the question of whether the Prussian Revolution of 1848 should be regarded as a "failure," see esp. Grebing 1986, 93–95; Wehler 1987, 2:778–89; Hachtmann 1997, 887–92.

Chapter 9

1. See the review of recent historical scholarship on this issue on pp. 4–9.

2. Anderson uses the term "high center" to refer to the nature of political and religious authority in the premodern world, before the era of nation-states (1983, 40). My analysis suggests that this term may also be applied to the era of modern nationalism, at least in the case of Prussia.

3. Nipperdey 1983, 451–52.

4. Quoted in Jeismann 1996, 1:294; see also 1:291.

5. Sheehan 1978, 282. Sheehan asserts that for German liberals prior to the Revolution of 1848, "party is not an institution or even an entirely political category; it describes a shared inner, moral condition and a way of viewing the world. . . . The uncertainty that hangs over liberal views of the distribution of power between Volk and Staat was generated by the deep ambivalence many of them felt about the role of the state in German life" (1974, 163, 169). In a similar vein, Faber has argued

that the nineteenth-century liberals attempted a "dubious symbiosis between civil society and authoritarian state" (1975, 227).

6. Wolfgang Hardtwig makes this point in a study of public monuments erected in Germany between 1871 and 1914. These monuments, he argues, reveal that the German bourgeoisie continued to associate itself closely with the monarchy throughout the imperial era. He interprets this iconography as evidence of a general "bourgeois deficit" (*Defizit an Bürgerlichkeit*) in Germany (1990: 285–90).

7. For example, Sarcinelli 1990 (esp. the articles by Sarcinelli, Leggewie, Prätorius, and Oberreuter).

8. Botzenhart and Hubatsch 1957–74, 3:380. See also pp. 71–72.

9. Cabinet order to the *Staatsministerium*, 11 Jan. 1819 (drafted by Altenstein and revised by Hardenberg), GStA BPH, Rep. 192, Wittgenstein, V, 5, Nr. 22, Bl. 1; also Hardenberg to Wittgenstein, 28 Oct. 1818, in Branig 1972, 243. See also chapter 6 above.

10. Wehler 1985, 95–96.

11. For example, in a 1922 treatise, the prominent conservative legal theorist Carl Schmitt expressed his scorn for the chaotic nature of parliamentary rule:

> The essence of liberalism is negotiation, a cautious half-measure, in the hope that the definitive dispute, the decisive bloody battle, can be transformed into a parliamentary debate and permit the decision to be suspended forever in an everlasting discussion. Dictatorship is the opposite of discussion.
> ([1922] 1985, 63)

Concerning the unhappiness of many members of the German political elite with pluralistic parliamentary rule during the Weimar era, see also Dahrendorf 1967, 3–16, 188–203, 314–27, 348–80; Fritzsche 1990, 6–13, 230–36; Kershaw 1987, 254–55; Jarausch and Jones 1990, 303–6, 319–21.

12. Madison, *Federalist* 10, in Hamilton, Jay, and Madison [1787] 1901, 45–47.

13. This interpretive tendency is most pronounced among exponents of modernization theory, who present a normative model under which a premodern order, characterized by a feudal society and a monarchical political system, is ideally succeeded by a modern order defined by a capitalist economy and a government based on representative democracy. These analyses often depict societies that do not conform to this model as following a deviant or pathological course of historical development. The literature of modernization theory is discussed in Huntington 1976; Wehler 1975; Brose 1993, 3–8.

14. One excellent such comparative study already exists: Nolte 1990.

15. See, for example, Levinger 1990b.

16. On this point, compare Baker's definition of a revolution as a moment "in which signification itself seems to be at issue in social life, in which there is a consciousness of contested representations of the world in play" and "in which social action takes the form of more or less explicit efforts to order or reorder the world through the articulation and deployment of competing systems of meaning" (1990, 17).

17. On the concept of the *societas civilis*, see esp., Kondylis 1986.

18. See, for example, Sheehan 1989, 14–24.

WORKS CITED

ARCHIVAL SOURCES

Geheimes Staatsarchiv Preußischer Kulturbesitz, Berlin-Dahlem

Note: Repositories in the Geheimes Staatsarchiv that were formerly housed in the Zentrales Staatsarchiv, Dienststelle Merseburg, are denoted here by the mark "(M)."

Hauptabteilung I: Die alten preußischen Reposituren

Rep. 74 H, Staatskanzleramt, Generalia und Staatskanzleramt (M)
    II (Organisation der Behörden in den Provinzen)
    IX (Stände)
    X (Höhere Polizei)
Rep. 74 J, Staatskanzleramt, Departement für allgemeine Polizei (M)
    IV (Landschaftliche und ständische Verfassung)
Rep. 74 K, Staatskanzleramt, Departement für Handel und Gewerbe (M)
    II (Landwirtschafts Polizei)
Rep. 77, Ministerium des Innern (M)
    Titel 149, 320, 321, 322, 323, 489, 514, 523, 524
Rep. 89, Geheimes Zivilkabinett (formerly 2.2.1.) (M)
    Nr. 13906, 13913, 13919, 13920
Rep. 92, Nachlässe
    Albrecht
    Altenstein (M)
    Hardenberg (M)
    Müffling (M)
    Gustav von Rochow (M)
    Stägemann (M)
    Otto von Voß-Buch (M)
    Karl von Voß-Buch (M)

Hauptabteilung XX: Staatsarchiv Königsberg

Rep. 2, I, Oberpräsidium
    Rep. 2, II, Oberpräsidium
    Rep. 300, Graf von Brünneck I (Nachlaß Theodor von Schön)

Brandenburg-Preußisches Hausarchiv (contained in the Geheimes Staatsarchiv, Berlin)
Rep. 50, Friedrich Wilhelm IV (M)
   Rep. 192, Nachlaß Wittgenstein

Brandenburgisches Landeshauptarchiv (formerly the Staatsarchiv Potsdam)
Pr. Br. Rep. 2A, Regierung Potsdam
   I (Präsidialabteilung)
Pr. Br. Rep. 3B, Regierung Frankfurt (Oder)
   I (Präsidialabteilung)
Pr. Br. Rep. 37, von Marwitz/Friedersdorf
Pr. Br. Rep. 37, Neu-Hardenberg
Pr. Br. Rep. 37, von Quast/Garz

PUBLISHED PRIMARY SOURCES

Arndt, Ernst Moritz. 1807–1818. *Geist der Zeit.* 4 vols. Berlin: Realschulbuchhandlung.
———. 1934. *Volk und Staat: Seine Schriften in Auswahl.* Edited by Paul Requardt. Leipzig: Alfred Kröner.
Ascher, Saul. 1991. *4 Flugschriften.* Berlin: Aufbau Verlag.
Bailleu, Paul. 1883. "Metternich's Teplitzer Denkschrift." *HZ* 50:190–92.
Beckedorff, L[udolf von]. 1825. "Ueber den Begriff der Volksschule." In *Jahrbücher des Preussischen Volks-Schul-Wesens* 1.
Bezzenberger, Adalbert, ed. 1898. *Aktenstücke des Provinzial-Archivs in Königsberg aus den Jahren 1786–1820 betreffend die Verwaltung und Verfassung Ostpreußens.* Königsberg: Gräfe & Unzer.
Bleich, Eduard, ed. [1847] 1977. *Der Erste Vereinigte Landtag in Berlin 1847.* 4 vols. Berlin: Karl Reimarus; reprint, Vaduz: Topos Verlag.
Botzenhart, Erich, and Walther Hubatsch, eds. 1957–74. *Heinrich Friedrich Karl, Freiherr vom und zum Stein. Briefe und amtliche Schriften.* Rev. ed. 10 vols. Stuttgart: W. Kohlhammer.
Botzenhart, Manfred, ed. 1968. *Die Deutsche Verfassungsfrage 1812–1815.* Göttingen: Vandenhoeck & Ruprecht.
Branig, Hans, ed. 1972. *Briefwechsel des Fürsten Karl August v. Hardenberg mit dem Fürsten Wilhelm Ludwig v. Sayn-Wittgenstein, 1806–1822.* Veröffentlichungen aus den Archiven Preußischer Kulturbesitz, vol. 9. Cologne: Grote.
Bujack, [Georg]. 1887. *Das erste Triennium des Comités der Ostpreußischen und Littauischen Stände.* Königsberg: Emil Rautenberg.
———. 1888. *Nachtrag zum ersten Triennium des Komitees der ostpreußischen und littauischen Stände.* Königsberg: Emil Rautenberg.
———. 1889. *Das Commissorium der Landesdeputirten der Provinz Preußen und Littauen in Berlin im Jahre 1811.* Königsberg: Emil Rautenberg.
Carové, Friedrich W. 1818. *Entwurf einer Burschenschafts-Ordnung und Versuch einer Begründung derselben.* Eisenach: Bärecke.
———. 1848. *Souverainität der Deutschen Nation und Competenz ihrer constituirenden Versammlung.* Berlin: Verlag der Deckerschen Geheimen Ober-Hofbuchdruckerei.
Fichte, Johann Gottlieb. [1808] 1968. *Addresses to the German Nation.* Edited by George A. Kelly. New York: Harper Torchbooks.

————. 1846. *Johann Gottlieb Fichte's Sämmtliche Werke.* Edited by J. H. Fichte. Vol. 7. Berlin: Veit.

Fries, J[akob Friedrich]. 1816. Review of *Ueber die Ansprüche der Juden an das deutsche Bürgerrecht*, by Friedrich Rühs, 2d ed. In *Heidelbergische Jahrbücher der Litteratur* 9:241–64.

Gesetz-Sammlung für die Königlichen Preußischen Staaten. 1810–25. Berlin: Georg Decker.

Gneisenau, August Wilhelm Anton Neithardt von. 1911. *Gneisenau: Eine Auswahl aus seinen Briefen und Denkschriften.* Edited by Wilhelm Capelle. Leipzig: B. G. Teubner.

Görres, Joseph. 1929. *Gesammelte Schriften.* Edited by Günther Wohlers. Vol. 13, *Politische Schriften (1817–1822).* Cologne: Gilde-Verlag.

Haller, Carl Ludwig von. [1820] 1964. *Restauration der Staatswissenschaft.* 2d ed. 6 vols. Wintertur; reprint, Aalen: Scientia Verlag.

Hamilton, Alexander, John Jay, and James Madison. [1787] 1901. *The Federalist: A Collection of Essays by Alexander Hamilton, John Jay, and James Madison.* New York: Colonial Press.

Hegel, G. W. F. 1821. *Grundlinien der Philosophie des Rechts.* Berlin: In der Nicolaischen Buchhandlung.

Heydemann, Günther. 1986. "Der Attentäter Karl Ludwig Sand: 20 Briefe und Dokumente aus den Erlanger und Jenaer Studienjahren." In *Darstellungen und Quellen zur Geschichte der deutschen Einheitsbewegung im neunzehnten und zwanzigsten Jahrhundert* 12:7–77. Heidelberg: Carl Winter.

Hoffmeister, Johannes, ed. 1969–77. *Briefe von und an Hegel.* 3d ed. 4 vols. Hamburg: Felix Meiner.

[Hoffmeister, Karl]. 1818. *Beschreibung des Festes auf der Wartburg: Ein Sendschreiben an die Gutgesinnten.* [Essen]: Gedruckt in Deutschland und für die Deutsche.

Huber, Ernst Rudolf, ed. 1978. *Dokumente zur deutschen Verfassungsgeschichte.* Vol. 1. 3d ed. Stuttgart: W. Kohlhammer.

Humboldt, Wilhelm von. [1791] 1969. *The Limits of State Action.* Edited by J. W. Burrow. London: Cambridge University Press.

————. 1903–20. *Wilhelm von Humboldts Gesammelte Schriften.* Edited by Bruno Gebhardt. 15 vols. Berlin: B. Behr.

Hunt, Lynn, ed. and trans. 1996. *The French Revolution and Human Rights: A Brief Documentary History.* Boston: Bedford.

Jahn, Friedrich Ludwig. [1810] 1991. *Deutsches Volkstum.* Lübeck: Niemann; reprint, Aufbau-Verlag.

————. 1887. *Friedrich Ludwig Jahns Werke.* Edited by Carl Euler. Vol. 2. Hof: Rud. Lion.

Justi, Johann. 1758. *Staatswirthschaft, oder Systematische Abhandlung aller Oekonomischen und Cameral-Wissenschaften, die zur Regierung eines Landes erfodert werden.* 2d ed. Leipzig: Bernhard Christoph Breitkopf.

————. 1760. *Die Grundfeste zu der Macht und Glückseeligkeit der Staaten, oder ausführliche Vorstellung der gesamten Polizeiwissenschaft.* Vol. 1. Königsberg: Johann Heinrich Hartungs Erben.

Kant, Immanuel. 1968. *Werke in zwölf Bänden.* Edited by Wilhelm Weischedel. Vol. 11, *Schriften zur Anthropologie, Geschichtsphilosophie, Politik und Pädagogik 1.* Frankfurt: Suhrkamp.

Kieser, Dietrich Georg. 1818. *Das Wartburgfest am 18. Oktober 1817: Seiner Entsteh-

ung, Ausführung, und Folgen nach Aktenstücken und Augenzeugnissen. Jena: F. Frommann.

Kletke, G. M. 1848. *Entwurf zu einem Verfassungsgesetz auf den breitesten Grundlagen für den Preußischen Staat*. Berlin: Albert Gury.

Klüber, Johann Ludwig, and Karl Welcker, eds. 1844. *Wichtige Urkunden für den Rechtszustand der deutschen Nation*. Mannheim: Friedrich Bassermann.

Kluckhohn, Paul, ed. 1934. *Die Idee des Volkes im Schrifttum der deutschen Bewegung*. Berlin: Junker & Dünnhaupt.

Lehmann, Max. 1889. "Ein Regierungsprogramm Friedrich Wilhelm's III." *HZ* 61: 441–60.

Menzel, Karl Adolf. 1818. *Über die Undeutschheit des neuen Deutschtums*. Breslau: Graß, Barth.

Metternich-Winneburg, Richard, ed. 1881. *Aus Metternich's nachgelassenen Papieren*. Vol. 3. Vienna: Wilhelm Braumüller.

Meusel, Friedrich. 1908–13. *Friedrich August Ludwig von der Marwitz, ein märkischer Edelmann im Zeitalter der Befreiungskriege*. 2 vols. Berlin: E. S. Mittler.

Müller, Michael G., and Bernd Schönemann, eds. 1991. *Die "Polen-Debatte" in der Frankfurter Paulskirche: Darstellung, Lernziele, Materialien*. Schriften zur Internationalen Schulbuchforschung Schriftenreihe des Georg-Eckert-Instituts, vol. 68. Frankfurt: Moritz Diesterweg.

Nees von Esenbeck, Christian Gottfried. 1848. *Die demokratische Monarchie: Ein Gesetz Vorschlag*. Berlin: Julius Springer.

Oettrich, Eduard. 1848. *Mittel zur schleunigsten Abhülfe unserer jetzigen Noth*. Berlin: Leopold Lassar.

[Oken, Lorenz]. 1817. "Der Studentenfrieden auf der Wartburg." *Isis, oder Encyclopädische Zeitung*. No. 195.

Pauli, C. M. 1819. Review of F. W. Carové, *Ueber die Ermordung Kotzebue's*. In *Freimüthige, Literarische Blätter für Deutsche in Beziehung auf Krieg, Politik, und Staatswirtschaft* 1:305–41.

Raab, Heribert. 1978. *Joseph Görres, ein Leben für Freiheit und Recht: Auswahl aus seinem Werk, Urteile von Zeitgenossen, Einführung und Bibliographie*. Paderborn: Ferdinand Schöningh.

Rehberg, August Wilhelm. 1807. *Ueber die Staatsverwaltung deutscher Länder und die Dienerschaft des Regenten*. Hannover: bey den Gebrüdern Hahn.

Reiss, Hans, ed. 1991. *Kant: Political Writings*. Translated by H. B. Nisbet. 2d ed. Cambridge: Cambridge University Press.

Röpell, [Richard]. 1848. "Zur inneren Geschichte Preußens in den Jahren 1811–12." In *Uebersicht der Arbeiten und Veränderungen der schlesischen Gesellschaft für vaterländische Kultur im Jahre 1847*, 339–60. Breslau: Graß, Barth.

Rousseau, Jean-Jacques. [1762] 1966. *Du contrat social*. Paris: G. F. Flammarion.

Ruge, Arnold. 1988. *Arnold Ruge: Werke und Briefe*. Edited by Hans-Martin Sass. 5 vols. Aalen: Scientia Verlag.

Scheel, Heinrich, and Doris Schmidt, eds. 1966–68. *Das Reformministerium Stein. Akten zur Verfassungs- und Verwaltungsgeschichte aus den Jahren 1807/08*. 3 vols. Deutsche Akademie der Wissenschaften zu Berlin, Schriften des Instituts für Geschichte. Berlin: Akademie-Verlag.

———. 1986. *Von Stein zu Hardenberg: Dokumente aus dem Interimsministerium Altenstein/Dohna*. Schriften des Zentralinstituts für Geschichte der DDR, vol. 54. Berlin: Akademie-Verlag.

Schissler, Hanna, and Hans-Ulrich Wehler, eds. 1984. *Preußische Finanzpolitik, 1806–*

1810: Quellen zur Verwaltung der Ministerien Stein und Altenstein. Göttingen: Van-denhoeck & Ruprecht.

Schoeps, Hans-Joachim, ed. 1963. *Aus den Jahren Preussischer Not und Erneuerung: Tagebücher der Gebrüder Gerlach und ihres Kreises 1805–1820.* Berlin: Haude und Spenersche Verlagsbuchhandlung.

———. 1968. "Metternichs Kampf gegen die Revolution: Weltanschauung in Brie-fen." In *Neue Quellen zur Geschichte Preußens im 19. Jahrhundert.* Berlin: Haude und Spenersche Verlagsbuchhandlung.

Stahl, Friedrich Julius. [1845] 1927. *Das Monarchische Prinzip: Eine Staatsrechtlich-Politische Abhandlung.* Berlin: Weltgeist-Bücher.

Svarez, Carl Gottlieb. [1791–92] 1960. *Vorträge über Recht und Staat.* Edited by Her-mann Conrad and Gerd Kleinheyer. Wissenschaftliche Abhandlungen der Arbeitsgemeinschaft für Forschung des Landes Nordrhein-Westfalen, vol. 10. Co-logne: Westdeutscher Verlag.

Turgot, Anne-Robert-Jacques. 1844. *Oeuvres de Turgot.* 2 vols. Paris: Guillamin.

Vincke, Ludwig von. [1808] 1848. *Darstellungen der inneren Verwaltung Groß-britanniens.* Edited by B. G. Niebuhr. 2d ed. Berlin: G. Reimer.

Winter, Georg, ed. 1931. *Die Reorganisation des Preußischen Staates unter Stein und Hardenberg. Erster Teil: Allgemeine Verwaltungs- und Behördenreform. Band I: Vom Beginn des Kampfes gegen die Kabinettsregierung bis zum Wiedereintritt des Min-isters vom Stein.* Publikationen aus den Preußischen Staatsarchiven, vol. 93. Leip-zig: S. Hirzel, 1931.

SECONDARY SOURCES

Allgemeine deutsche Biographie. 1875–1912. 56 vols. Leipzig: Duncker & Humblot.

Althusser, Louis. 1969. "Contradiction and Overdetermination." In *The New Left Reader.* Edited by Carl Oglesby. New York: Grove.

Anderson, Benedict. 1983. *Imagined Communities: Reflections on the Origin and Spread of Nationalism.* London: Verso.

Ankersmit, Frank A. 1989. "Historiography and Post-modernism." *History and The-ory* 28:137–53.

Aretin, Karl Otmar Freiherr von. 1954. "Metternichs Verfassungspläne 1817/1818." *Historisches Jahrbuch im Auftrage der Görres-Gesellschaft* 74:718–27.

Aris, Reinhold. 1936. *History of Political Thought in Germany.* London: Allen & Un-win.

Arndt, Adolf. 1902. "Der Anteil der Stände an der Gesetzgebung in Preußen von 1823–1848." *Archiv des öffentlichen Rechts* 17:570–88.

Asselain, J.-C. 1984. *Histoire économique de la France du XVIIIe siècle à nos jours.* Vol. 1, *De l'Ancien Régime à la Première Guerre mondiale.* Paris: Seuil.

Augustine, Dolores. 1994. *Patricians and Parvenues: Wealth and High Society in Wil-helmine Germany.* Oxford: Berg.

Avineri, Shlomo. 1963. "A Note on Hegel's View on Jewish Emancipation." *Jewish Social Studies* 25: 145–51.

Baker, Keith Michael. 1990. *Inventing the French Revolution: Essays on French Political Culture in the Eighteenth Century.* New York: Cambridge University Press.

Balster, Friedrich. 1848. *Der Erste Vereinigte Landtag in Preußen: Ein Beitrag zur Geschichte.* Berlin: August von Schröter.

Barclay, David E. 1993. "The Court Camarilla and the Politics of Monarchical Res-toration in Prussia, 1848–1858." In *Between Reform, Reaction, and Resistance:*

Studies in the History of German Conservatism from 1789 to 1945, 123–56. Edited by Larry Eugene Jones and James Retallack, 123–56. Providence: Berg.

———. 1995. *Frederick William IV and the Prussian Monarchy, 1840–1861*. Oxford: Clarendon.

Barkin, Kenneth. 1983. "Social Control and the Volksschule in Vormärz Prussia." *CEH* 16:31–52.

Baumgart, Franzjörg. 1990. *Zwischen Reform und Reaktion: Preußische Schulpolitik 1806–1859*. Darmstadt: Wissenschaftliche Buchgesellschaft.

Beck, Hermann. 1995. *The Origins of the Authoritarian Welfare State in Prussia: Conservatives, Bureaucracy, and the Social Question 1815–70*. Ann Arbor: University of Michigan Press.

Behrens, C. B. A. 1985. *Society, Government and the Enlightenment: The Experiences of Eighteenth-century France and Prussia*. New York: Harper & Row.

Beiner, Ronald, and William James Booth, eds. 1983. *Kant and Political Philosophy: The Contemporary Legacy*. New Haven: Yale University Press.

Beiser, Frederick C. 1992. *Enlightenment, Revolution, and Romanticism: The Genesis of Modern German Political Thought, 1790–1800*. Cambridge: Harvard University Press.

Berdahl, Robert. 1988. *The Politics of the Prussian Nobility: The Development of a Conservative Ideology, 1770–1848*. Princeton: Princeton University Press.

Berding, Helmut. 1973. *Napoleonische Herrschafts- und Gesellschaftspolitik im Königreich Westfalen 1807–1813*. Kritische Studien zur Geschichtswissenschaft, vol. 7. Göttingen: Vandenhoeck & Ruprecht.

Bergeron, Louis. 1991. "The Revolution: Catastrophe or New Dawn for the French Economy?" In *Rewriting the French Revolution*. Edited by Colin Lucas. Oxford: Clarendon.

Bhabha, Homi K., ed. 1990. *Nation and Narration*. London: Routledge.

Blackbourn, David. 1998. *The Long Nineteenth Century: A History of Germany, 1780–1918*. New York: Oxford University Press.

Blackbourn, David, and Geoff Eley. 1984. *The Peculiarities of German History: Bourgeois Society and Politics in Nineteenth-century Germany*. Oxford: Oxford University Press.

Blänkner, Reinhard. 1993. " 'Der Absolutismus war ein Glück, der doch nicht zu den Absolutisten gehört': Eduard Gans und die hegelianischen Ursprünge der Absolutismusforschung in Deutschland." *HZ* 256:31–66.

Blanning, T. C. W. 1983. *The French Revolution in Germany: Occupation and Resistance in the Rhineland, 1792–1802*. New York: Oxford University Press.

———. 1986. "The Death and Transfiguration of Prussia." *Historical Journal* 29: 433–59.

———. 1989. "The French Revolution and the Modernization of Germany." *CEH* 22:109–29.

Blasius, Dirk. 1992. *Friedrich Wilhelm IV. 1795–1861: Psychopathologie und Geschichte*. Göttingen: Vandenhoeck & Ruprecht.

Bödeker, Hans Erich, and Ulrich Herrmann, eds. 1987. *Aufklärung als Politisierung, Politisierung der Aufklärung*. Studien zum achtzehnten Jahrhundert, vol. 8. Hamburg: F. Meiner.

Boldt, Hans. 1975. *Deutsche Staatslehre im Vormärz*. Düsseldorf: Droste.

Boldt, Werner. 1971. *Die Anfänge des deutschen Parteiwesens: Fraktionen, politische Vereine und Parteien in der Revolution 1848*. Paderborn: Ferdinand Schöningh.

———. 1973. "Konstitutionelle Monarchie oder parlamentarische Demokratie: Die

Auseinandersetzung um die deutsche Nationalversammlung in der Revolution von 1848." *HZ* 216:553–622.

Bornhak, Conrad. 1890. "Die preußische Finanzplan von 1810." *FBPG* 3:555–608.

Botzenhart, Erich. 1928. "Adelsideal und Adelsreform beim Freiherrn vom Stein." *Westfälisches Adelsblatt* 5:210–41.

Botzenhart, Manfred. 1983. "Verfassungsproblematik und Ständepolitik in der preußischen Reformzeit." In *Ständetum und Staatsbildung in Brandenburg-Preußen: Ergebnisse einer internationalen Fachtagung.* Edited by Peter Baumgart. Berlin: Walter de Gruyter.

Brammer, Annegret H. 1987. *Judenpolitik und Judengesetzgebung in Preußen 1812 bis 1847, mit einem Ausblick auf das Gleichberechtigungsgesetz des Norddeutschen Bundes von 1869.* Berlin: Schelzy & Jeep.

Brandt, Hartwig. 1968. *Landständische Repräsentation im deutschen Vormärz: Politisches Denken im Einflußfeld des monarchischen Prinzips.* Abhandlungen und Texte zur politischen Wissenschaft, vol. 31. Neuwied: Hermann Luchterhand.

Branig, Hans. 1965. "Die oberste Staatsverwaltung in Preußen zur Zeit des Todes von Hardenberg." *Jahrbuch für die Geschichte Mittel- und Ostdeutschland* 13/14: 182–99.

Brophy, James M. 1997. "Carnival and Citizenship: The Politics of Carnival Culture in the Prussian Rhineland, 1823–1848." *Journal of Social History* 30:873–904.

———. 1998. *Capitalism, Politics, and Railroads in Prussia, 1830–1870.* Columbus: Ohio State University Press.

Brose, Eric Dorn. 1993. *The Politics of Technological Change in Prussia: Out of the Shadow of Antiquity, 1809–1848.* Princeton: Princeton University Press.

———. 1997. *German History 1789–1871: From the Holy Roman Empire to the Bismarckian Reich.* Providence: Berghahn.

Brubaker, Rogers. 1992. *Citizenship and Nationhood in France and Germany.* Cambridge: Harvard University Press.

———. 1996. *Nationalism Reframed: Nationhood and the National Question in the New Europe.* Cambridge: Cambridge University Press.

Bruford, W. H. 1965. *Germany in the Eighteenth Century: The Social Background of the Literary Revival.* Cambridge: Cambridge University Press.

Brunner, Otto. 1968. "Vom Gottesgnadentum zum Monarchischen Prinzip." In *Neue Wege der Verfassungs- und Sozialgeschichte.* 2d ed. Göttingen: Vandenhoeck & Ruprecht.

Brunner, Otto, Werner Conze, and Reinhart Koselleck, eds. 1972–97. *Geschichtliche Grundbegriffe: Historisches Lexikon zur politisch-sozialen Sprache in Deutschland.* 8 vols. Stuttgart: Ernst Klett.

Brunschwig, Henri. 1974. *Enlightenment and Romanticism in Eighteenth-century Prussia.* Translated by Frank Jellinek. Chicago: University of Chicago Press.

Burger, Rudolf, Hans-Dieter Klein, and Wolfgang H. Schrader, eds. 1996. *Gesellschaft, Staat, Nation.* Veröffentlichungen der Kommission für Philosophie und Pädagogik, vol. 26. Vienna: Verlag der Österreichischen Akademie der Wissenschaften.

Büsch, Otto. 1997. *Military System and Social Life in Old Regime Prussia, 1713–1807.* Atlantic Highlands: Humanities Press.

Büsch, Otto, and Monika Neugebauer-Wölk, eds. 1991. *Preussen und die Revolutionäre Herausforderung seit 1789.* Veröffentlichungen der Historischen Kommission zu Berlin, vol. 78. Berlin: Walter de Gruyter.

Büssem, Eberhard. 1974. *Die Karlsbader Beschlüsse von 1819: Die endgültige Stabili-*

sierung der restaurativen Politik im Deutschen Bund nach dem Wiener Kongreß von 1814/15. Hildesheim: H. A. Gerstenberg.

Bußmann, Walter. 1990. *Zwischen Preußen und Deutschland: Friedrich Wilhelm IV: Eine Biographie*. Berlin: Siedler.

Calhoun, Craig J. 1998. *Nationalism*. Buckingham: Open University Press.

Canning, Kathleen. 1996. *Languages of Labor and Gender: Female Factory Work in Germany, 1850–1914*. Ithaca: Cornell University Press.

Childers, Thomas. 1989. "Political Sociology and the 'Linguistic Turn.' " *CEH* 22: 381–93.

Clark, Christopher. 1993. "The Politics of Revival: Pietists, Aristocrats, and the State Church in Early Nineteenth-century Prussia." In *Between Reform, Reaction, and Resistance: Studies in the History of German Conservatism from 1789 to 1945*, 31–60. Edited by Larry Eugene Jones and James N. Retallack. Providence: Berg.

————. 1995. *The Politics of Conversion: Missionary Protestantism and the Jews in Prussia, 1728–1941*. New York: Oxford University Press.

Craig, Gordon. 1982. *The Germans*. New York: G. P. Putnam's Sons.

Czygan, Paul. 1911. *Zur Geschichte der Tagesliteratur während der Freiheitskriege*. 2 vols. Leipzig: Duncker & Humblot.

Dahrendorf, Ralf. 1967. *Society and Democracy in Germany*. New York: W. W. Norton.

Dann, Otto. 1996. *Nation und Nationalismus in Deutschland 1770–1990*. 3d ed. Beck'sche Reihe, vol. 494. Munich: C. H. Beck.

Darnton, Robert. 1982. "The High Enlightenment and the Low Life of Literature." In *The Literary Underground of the Old Regime*. Cambridge: Harvard University Press.

Deutsch, Karl. 1953. *Nationalism and Social Communication*. Cambridge: MIT Press.

Dickey, Laurence. 1987. *Hegel: Religion, Economics, and the Politics of the Spirit*. Cambridge: Cambridge University Press.

Dieterici, Karl Friedrich Wilhelm. 1875. *Zur Geschichte der Steuer-Reform in Preußen von 1810 bis 1820*. Berlin: G. Reimer.

Dittmer, Lothar. 1992. *Beamtenkonservatismus und Modernisierung: Untersuchungen zur Vorgeschichte der Konservativen Partei in Preußen 1810–1848/49*. Stuttgart: Franz Steiner Verlag.

Doyle, William. 1982. *Origins of the French Revolution*. Oxford: Oxford University Press.

Droz, Jacques. 1949. *L'Allemagne et la Révolution française*. Paris: Presses Universitaires de France.

Dubois, Claude-Gilbert, ed. 1991. *L'imaginaire de la nation, 1792–1992*. Bordeaux: Presses Universitaires de Bordeaux.

Düding, Dieter. 1984. *Organisierter gesellschaftlicher Nationalismus in Deutschland (1808–1847): Bedeutung und Funktion der Turner und Sängervereine für die deutsche Nationalbewegung*. Studien zur Geschichte des neunzehnten Jahrhunderts, vol. 13. Munich: R. Oldenbourg.

Dülman, Richard van. 1977. "Die Aufklärungsgesellschaften in Deutschland als Forschungsproblem." *Francia* 5:251–75.

Dunlavy, Colleen. 1994. *Politics and Industrialization: Early Railroads in the United States and Prussia*. Princeton: Princeton University Press.

Echternkamp, Jörg. 1998. *Der Aufstieg der deutschen Nationalismus (1770–1840)*. Frankfurt am Main: Campus.

Eickenboom, Peter. 1976. "Der preussische erste Vereinigte Landtag von 1847." Ph.D. diss., Universität Bonn.

Eley, Geoff. 1986. *From Unification to Nazism: Reinterpreting the German Past.* London: Routledge.

Eley, Geoff, and Ronald Grigor Suny, eds. 1996. *Becoming National: A Reader.* New York: Oxford University Press.

Epstein, Klaus. 1966a. *The Genesis of German Conservatism.* Princeton: Princeton University Press.

———. 1966b. "Stein in German Historiography." *History and Theory: Studies in the Philosophy of History* 5:241–74.

Ergang, Robert Reinhold. 1931. *Herder and the Foundations of German Nationalism.* New York: Columbia University Press.

Evans, Richard. 1985. "The Myth of Germany's Missing Revolution." *New Left Review* 149–54:67–94.

Faber, Karl-Georg. 1975. "Strukturprobleme des deutschen Liberalismus im 19. Jahrhundert." *Der Staat* 14:201–27.

Faulenbach, Bernd. 1980. *Ideologie des deutschen Weges: Die deutsche Geschichte in der Historiographie zwischen Kaiserreich und Nationalozialismus.* Munich: Beck.

Fehrenbach, Elisabeth. 1974. *Traditionale Gesellschaft und revolutionäres Recht: die Einführung des Code Napoléon in den Rheinbundstaaten.* Kritische Studien zur Geschichtswissenschaft, vol. 13. Göttingen: Vandenhoeck & Ruprecht.

———. 1979. "Verfassungs- und Sozialpolitische Reformen und Reformprojekte in Deutschland unter dem Einfluss des Napoleonischen Frankreich." *HZ* 228:288–316.

———. 1994. "Adel und Bürgertum im deutschen Vormärz." *HZ* 258:1–28.

Foucault, Michel. 1972. *The Archaeology of Knowledge.* Translated by A. M. Sheridan Smith. New York: Pantheon.

Frader, Laura L., and Sonya O. Rose, eds. 1996. *Gender and Class in Modern Europe.* Ithaca: Cornell University Press.

François, Etienne, Hannes Siegrist, and Jakob Vogel, eds. 1995. *Nation und Emotion: Deutschland und Frankreich im Vergleich; 19. und 20. Jahrhundert.* Kritische Studien zur Geschichtswissenschaft, vol. 110. Göttingen: Vandenhoeck & Ruprecht.

Freud, Sigmund. 1989. *The Freud Reader.* Edited by Peter Gay. New York: W. W. Norton.

Fritzsche, Peter. 1990. *Rehearsals for Fascism: Populism and Political Mobilization in Weimar Germany.* New York: Oxford University Press.

Furet, François. 1981. *Interpreting the French Revolution.* Translated by Elborg Forster. Cambridge: Cambridge University Press.

Füßl, Wilhelm. 1988. *Professor in der Politik: Friedrich Julius Stahl (1802–1861). Das monarchische Prinzip und seine Umsetzung in die politische Praxis.* Göttingen: Vandenhoeck & Ruprecht.

Gailus, Manfred. 1990. *Straße und Brot: Sozialer Protest in den deutschen Staaten unter besonderer Berücksichtigung Preußens, 1847–1849.* Veröffentlichungen des Max-Planck-Instituts für Geschichte, vol. 96. Göttingen: Vandenhoeck & Ruprecht.

Gall, Lothar. 1985. "Liberalismus und 'bürgerliche Gesellschaft.' Zu Charakter und Entwicklung der liberalen Bewegung in Deutschland." In *Liberalismus,* 162–86. Edited by Lothar Gall. 3d ed. Königstein: Athenäum.

Gayot, G., and J.-P. Hirsch, eds. 1989. *La Révolution française et le développement du capitalisme.* Lille: Revue du Nord.

Geertz, Clifford. 1973a. "The Cerebral Savage: On the Work of Claude Lévi-Strauss." In *The Interpretation of Cultures.* New York: Basic.

Geertz, Clifford. 1973b. "Ideology as a Cultural System." In *The Interpretation of Cultures*. New York: Basic.

Geyer, Michael, and Konrad H. Jarausch. 1989. "The Future of the German Past: Transatlantic Reflections for the 1990s." *CEH* 22:229–59.

Giesen, Bernhard. 1998. *Intellectuals and the Nation: Collective Identity in a German Axial Age*. Translated by Nicholas Levis and Amos Weisz. Cambridge: Cambridge University Press.

Göbel, Karin, Theodor Kohlmann, Heidi Müller, and Konrad Vanja. 1989. *Auf's Ohr geschaut: Ohrringe aus Stadt und Land vom Klassizismus bis zur neuen Jugendkultur*. Schriften des Museums für Deutsche Volkskunde Berlin, vol. 16. Berlin: Reiter-Druck.

Goldhagen, Daniel Jonah. 1996. *Hitler's Willing Executioners: Ordinary Germans and the Holocaust*. New York: Alfred A. Knopf.

Görlitz, Walter. 1981. *Die Junker: Adel und Bauer im deutschen Osten. Geschichtliche Bilanz von 8 Jahrhunderten*. 4th ed. Limburg: C. A. Starke.

Gray, Marion W. 1977. "Der ostpreussische Landtag des Jahres 1808 und das Reformministerium Stein: Eine Fallstudie politischer Modernisation." *Jahrbuch für die Geschichte Mittel- und Ostdeutschlands* 26:129–45.

———. 1986. "Prussia in Transition: Society and Politics under the Stein Reform Ministry of 1808." *Transactions of the American Philosophical Society* 76.

Grebing, Helga. 1986. *Der deutsche Sonderweg in Europa 1806–1954: Eine Kritik*. Stuttgart: W. Kohlhammer.

Greenfeld, Liah. 1992. *Nationalism: Five Roads to Modernity*. Cambridge: Harvard University Press.

Greiffenhagen, Martin. 1967. *Das Dilemma des Konservatismus in Deutschland*. Munich: R. Piper.

Grimm, Dieter. 1988. *Deutsche Verfassungsgeschichte 1776–1866: Vom Beginn des modernen Verfassungsstaats bis zur Auflösung des Deutschen Bundes*. Edition Suhrkamp, vol. 1271. Frankfurt am Main: Suhrkamp.

Groh, Dieter. 1983. "Le *Sonderweg* de l'Histoire Allemande: Mythe ou Réalité." *Annales: Economies, Sociétés, Civilisations* 38:1166–87.

Gruner, Justus von. 1906. "Justus Gruner und der Hoffmannsche Bund." *FBPG* 19: 167–89.

Grünthal, Günther. 1987. "Bemerkungen zur Kamarilla Friedrich Wilhelms IV. im nachmärzlichen Preußen." In *Friedrich Wilhelm IV. in seiner Zeit: Beiträge eines Colloquiums*. Edited by Otto Büsch. Berlin: Colloquium Verlag.

Gschnitzer, Fritz, Reinhart Koselleck, Bernd Schönemann, and Karl Ferdinand Werner. 1992. "Volk, Nation, Nationalismus, Masse." In *Geschichtliche Grundbegriffe: Historisches Lexikon zur politisch-sozialen Sprache in Deutschland*, 7:141–431. Edited by Otto Brunner, Werner Conze, and Reinhart Koselleck. Stuttgart: Ernst Klett.

Guha, Ranajit. 1997. *Dominance without Hegemony: History and Power in Colonial India*. Cambridge: Harvard University Press.

Gumbrecht, Hans-Ulrich. 1978. "Für eine phänomenologische Fundierung der sozialhistorischen Begriffsgeschichte." In *Historische Semantik und Begriffsgeschichte*, 75–102. Edited by Reinhart Koselleck. Stuttgart: Klett-Cotta.

Haake, Paul. 1913, 1915, 1916, 1917, 1919. "König Friedrich Wilhelm III, Hardenberg und die Preußische Verfassungsfrage." *FBPG* 26:523–73; 28:175–220; 29:305–69; 30:317–65; 32:109–80.

————. 1914. "Die Errichtung des preußischen Staatsrats im März 1817." *FBPG* 27: 247–65.

————. 1920. *Johann Peter Friedrich Ancillon und Kronprinz Friedrich Wilhelm IV von Preußen.* Munich: R. Oldenbourg.

————. 1921. *Der preußische Verfassungskampf vor hundert Jahren.* Munich: R. Oldenbourg.

Habermas, Jürgen. [1962] 1989. *The Structural Transformation of the Public Sphere: An Inquiry into a Category of Bourgeois Society.* Translated by Thomas Burger and Frederick Lawrence. Cambridge: MIT Press.

————. 1970. "Technology and Science as 'Ideology.' " In *Toward a Rational Society: Student Protest, Science, and Politics.* Translated by Jeremy J. Shapiro. Boston: Beacon Press.

————. 1979. "Legitimation Problems in the Modern State." In *Communication and the Evolution of Society.* Translated by Thomas McCarthy. Boston: Beacon Press.

Hachtmann, Rüdiger. 1997. *Berlin 1848: Eine Politik- und Gesellschaftsgeschichte der Revolution.* Bonn: J. H. W. Dietz Nachfolger.

Hacks, Peter. 1991. *Ascher gegen Jahn: Ein Freiheitskrieg.* Berlin: Aufbau-Verlag.

Hagemann, Karen. 1996. "Nation, Krieg und Geschlechterordnung. Zum kulturellen und politischen Diskurs in der Zeit der antinapoleonischen Erhebung Preußens 1806–1815." *GG* 22:562–91.

Hagen, William W. 1980. *Germans, Poles, and Jews: The Nationality Conflict in the Prussian East, 1772–1914.* Chicago: University of Chicago Press.

————. 1989. "Seventeenth-century Crisis in Brandenburg: The Thirty Years' War, the Destabilization of Serfdom, and the Rise of Absolutism." *American Historical Review* 94:302–35.

————. 1991. "Descent of the *Sonderweg*: Hans Rosenberg's History of Old-Regime Prussia." *CEH* 24:24–50.

Hall, John A., ed. 1998. *The State of the Nation: Ernest Gellner and the Theory of Nationalism.* New York: Cambridge University Press.

Hardtwig, Wolfgang. 1990. "Bürgertum, Staatssymbolik und Staatsbewußtsein im Deutschen Kaiserreich 1871–1914." *GG* 16:269–95.

————. 1993. *Der monarchische Staat und das Bürgertum.* 3d ed. Munich: Deutscher Taschenbuch Verlag.

Harootunian, H. D. 1988. *Things Seen and Unseen: Discourse and Ideology in Tokugawa Nativism.* Chicago: University of Chicago Press.

Hartung, Fritz. 1954. *Deutsche Verfassungsgeschichte vom 15. Jahrhundert bis zur Gegenwart.* 6th ed. Stuttgart: K. F. Koehler Verlag.

Haupt, Hermann. 1907. *Karl Follen und die Gießener Schwarzen: Beiträge zur Geschichte der politischen Geheimbünde und der Verfassungs-Entwicklung der alten Burschenschaft in den Jahren 1815–1819.* Mitteilungen des Oberhessischen Geschichtsvereins, Neue Folge, vol. 15. Giessen: Alfred Töpelmann.

Heffter, Heinrich. 1950. *Die deutsche Selbstverwaltung im 19. Jahrhundert: Geschichte der Ideen und Institutionen.* Stuttgart: K. F. Koehler.

Hellmuth, Eckhart. 1982. "Aufklärung und Pressefreiheit: Zur Debatte der Berliner Mittwochgesellschaft während der Jahre 1783 und 1784." *Zeitschrift für Historische Forschung* 9:315–45.

————, ed. 1990. *The Transformation of Political Culture: England and Germany in the Late Eighteenth Century.* Studies of the German Historical Institute, London. London: Oxford University Press.

Herzog, Dagmar. 1996. *Intimacy and Exclusion: Religious Politics in Pre-Revolutionary Baden.* Princeton: Princeton University Press.

Hettling, Manfred, and Paul Nolte, eds. 1996. *Nation und Gesellschaft in Deutschland: Historische Essays.* Munich: C. H. Beck.

Heymann, Ernst. 1925. "Das Testament König Friedrich Wilhelms III." *Sitzungsberichte der Preußischen Akademie der Wissenschaften, Philosophisch-Historische Klasse, 1925,* 127–66. Berlin: Akademie der Wissenschaften.

Hintze, Otto. 1896. "Preußische Reformbestrebungen vor 1806." *HZ* 76:413–43.

———. 1962. "Das monarchische Prinzip und die konstitutionelle Verfassung." In *Gesammelte Abhandlungen zur allgemeinen Verfassungsgeschichte.* 2d ed. Vol. 2, *Staat und Verfassung.* Edited by Gerhard Oestreich. Göttingen: Vandenhoeck & Ruprecht.

———. 1975. "The Hohenzollern and the Nobility." In *The Historical Essays of Otto Hintze.* Edited by Felix Gilbert. New York: Oxford University Press.

Hobsbawm, E. J., and Terence O. Ranger, eds. 1983. *The Invention of Tradition.* Cambridge: Cambridge University Press.

Hofmeister-Hunger, Andrea. 1994. *Pressepolitik und Staatsreform: Die Institutionalisierung staatlicher Öffentlichkeitsarbeit bei Karl August von Hardenberg (1792–1822).* Veröffentlichungen des Max-Planck-Instituts für Geschichte, vol. 107. Göttingen: Vandenhoeck & Ruprecht.

Honour, Hugh. 1979. *Romanticism.* New York: Harper & Row.

Höpfner, Günther. 1994. "Nees von Esenbeck (1776–1858)—ein deutscher Gelehrter an der Seite der Arbeiter." In *Beiträge zur Nachmärz-Forschung,* 9–102. Schriften aus dem Karl-Marx-Haus, vol. 47. Trier: Karl-Marx-Haus.

Hroch, Miroslav. 1996. "From National Movement to the Fully Formed Nation: The Nation-building Process in Europe." In *Becoming National: A Reader.* Edited by Geoff Eley and Ronald Grigor Suny. New York: Oxford University Press.

Hubatsch, Walter. 1975. "Stein und Kant." In *Stein-Studien: Die preußischen Reformen des Reichsfreiherrn Karl vom Stein zwischen Revolution und Restauration.* Studien zur Geschichte Preußens, vol. 25. Cologne: Grote.

Hull, Isabel. 1996. *Sexuality, State, and Civil Society in Germany, 1770–1815.* Ithaca: Cornell University Press.

Hunt, Lynn. 1984. *Politics, Culture, and Class in the French Revolution.* Berkeley: University of California Press.

Huntington, Samuel P. 1976. "The Change to Change: Modernization, Development, and Politics." In *Comparative Modernization: A Reader,* 25–61. Edited by Cyril E. Black. New York: Free Press.

Ibbeken, Rudolf. 1970. *Preußen 1807–1813: Staat und Volk als Idee und in Wirklichkeit.* Veröffentlichungen aus der Archiven Preußischer Kulturbesitz, vol. 5. Cologne: Grote.

Iggers, Georg. 1983. *The German Conception of History: The National Tradition of Historical Thought from Herder to the Present.* Middletown: Wesleyan University Press.

———. 1995. "Zur 'Linguistischen Wende' im Geschichtsdenken und in der Geschichtsschreibung." *GG* 21:557–70.

James, Harold. 1990. *A German Identity, 1770–1990.* London: Weidenfeld and Nicolson.

Janson, Helmuth. 1963. *45 Lesegesellschaften um 1800 bis heute.* Harmonie-Almanach, Mannheim. Bonn: Stein-Verlag.

Jarausch, Konrad H., and Larry Eugene Jones, eds. 1990. *In Search of a Liberal*

Germany: Studies in the History of German Liberalism from 1789 to the Present.
New York: Berg.

Jeismann, Karl-Ernst. 1996. *Das preußische Gymnasium in Staat und Gesellschaft.* 2 vols. Stuttgart: Klett-Cotta.

Jeismann, Michael. 1992. *Das Vaterland der Feinde: Studien zum nationalen Feindbegriff und Selbstverständnis in Deutschland und Frankreich, 1792–1918.* Stuttgart: Klett-Cotta.

Jelavich, Peter. 1995. "Poststrukturalismus und Sozialgeschichte—aus amerikanischer Perspektive." *GG* 21:259–89.

Jones, Colin. 1991. "The Bourgeois Revolution Revivified." In *Rewriting the French Revolution,* 69–118. Edited by Colin Lucas. Oxford: Clarendon.

———. 1996. "The Great Chain of Buying: Medical Advertisement, the Bourgeois Public Sphere, and the Origins of the French Revolution." *American Historical Review* 101:13–40.

Jones, Larry Eugene, and James N. Retallack, eds. 1993. *Between Reform, Reaction, and Resistance: Studies in the History of German Conservatism from 1789 to 1945.* Providence: Berg.

Jones, P. M. 1995. *Reform and Revolution in France: The Politics of Transition, 1774–1791.* Cambridge: Cambridge University Press.

Katz, Jacob. 1980. *From Prejudice to Destruction: Anti-Semitism, 1700–1933.* Cambridge: Harvard University Press.

Kaufmann, Paul. 1928. "Görres im Kampfe gegen die preußische Reaktion." *Historische Jahrbuch im Auftrage der Görres-Gesellschaft* 48:31–41.

Kedourie, Elie. 1993. *Nationalism.* 4th ed. Oxford: Blackwell.

Kehr, Eckart. 1965. "Zur Genesis der preußischen Bürokratie." In *Der Primat der Innenpolitik. Gesammelte Aufsätze zur preußisch-deutschen Sozialgeschichte im 19. und 20. Jahrhundert,* 31–52. Edited by Hans-Ulrich Wehler. Veröffentlichungen der historischen Kommission beim Friedrich-Meinecke-Institut der Freien Universität Berlin, vol. 19. Berlin: de Gruyter.

———. 1977. "The Social System of Reaction in Prussia under the Puttkamer Ministry." In *Economic Interest, Militarism, and Foreign Policy.* Edited by Gordon Craig; translated by Grete Heinz. Berkeley: University of California Press.

Kershaw, Ian. 1987. *The Hitler Myth: Image and Reality in the Third Reich.* Oxford: Oxford University Press.

Kirsch, Martin. 1999. *Monarch und Parlament im 19. Jahrhundert: Der monarchische Konstitutionalismus als europäischer Verfassungstyp—Frankreich im Vergleich.* Veröffentlichungen des Max-Planck-Instituts für Geschichte, vol. 150. Göttingen: Vandenhoeck & Ruprecht.

Klassen, Peter. 1929. *Die Grundlagen des aufgeklärten Absolutismus.* List Studien: Untersuchungen zur Geschichte der Staatswissenschaft, vol. 4. Jena: Gustav Fischer.

Klein, Ernst. 1965. *Von der Reform zur Restauration: Finanzpolitik und Reformgesetzgebung des preußischen Staatskanzlers Karl August von Hardenberg.* Berlin: W. de Gruyter.

Knudsen, Jonathan B. 1986. *Justus Möser and the German Enlightenment.* Cambridge: Cambridge University Press.

———. 1990. "The Limits of Liberal Politics in Berlin, 1815–48." In *In Search of a Liberal Germany: Studies in the History of German Liberalism from 1789 to the Present,* 111–31. Edited by Konrad H. Jarausch and Larry Eugene Jones. New York: Berg.

Kocka, Jürgen. 1986. *Arbeiter und Bürger im 19. Jahrhundert: Varianten ihres Ver-hältnisses im europäischen Vergleich*. Munich: R. Oldenbourg.

———. 1988. "German History before Hitler: The Debate about the German *Son-derweg*." *Journal of Contemporary History* 23:3–16.

Kocka, Jürgen, and Allan Mitchell, eds. 1993. *Bourgeois Society in Nineteenth-century Europe*. Oxford: Berg.

Kohn, Hans. 1949. "Father Jahn's Nationalism." *Review of Politics* 11:419–32.

———. 1960. *The Mind of Germany: The Education of a Nation*. New York: Charles Scribner's Sons.

Kondylis, Panajotis. 1986. *Konservativismus: Geschichtlicher Gehalt und Untergang*. Stuttgart: Klett-Cotta.

König, Helmut. 1972. *Zur Geschichte der bürgerlichen Nationalerziehung in Deutschland zwischen 1807 und 1815*. Berlin: Volk und Wissen Volkseigener Verlag.

Koselleck, Reinhart. 1972. Introduction to *Geschichtliche Grundbegriffe: Historisches Lexikon zur politisch-sozialen Sprache in Deutschland*, 1:xiii–xxvii. Edited by Otto Brunner, Werner Conze, and Reinhart Koselleck. Stuttgart: Ernst Klett.

———. 1973. *Kritik und Krise: Eine Studie zur Pathogenese der bürgerlichen Welt*. Frankfurt am Main: Suhrkamp.

———. 1981. *Preußen zwischen Reform und Revolution: Allgemeines Landrecht, Ver-waltung und soziale Bewegung von 1791 bis 1848*. 3d ed. Stuttgart: Ernst Klett.

———. 1985. "*Begriffsgeschichte* and Social History." In *Futures Past: On the Se-mantics of Historical Time*, 73–91. Translated by Keith Tribe. Cambridge: MIT Press.

Koselleck, Reinhart, Hans Boldt, Werner Conze, Görg Haverkate, and Diethelm Klip-pel. 1990. "Staat und Souveränität." In *Geschichtliche Grundbegriffe: Historisches Lexikon zur politisch-sozialen Sprache in Deutschland*, 6:1–154. Edited by Otto Brunner, Werner Conze, and Reinhart Koselleck. Stuttgart: Ernst Klett.

Koshar, Rudy. 1989. "Playing the Cerebral Savage: Notes on Writing German History before the Linguistic Turn." *CEH* 22:343–59.

Krieger, Leonard. 1957. *The German Idea of Freedom: History of a Political Tradition*. Boston: Beacon Press.

Krüger, Gerhard. 1978. *. . . grundeten auch unsere Freiheit: Säptaufklärung, Freimaure-rei, preußisch-deutsche Reform, der Kampf Theodor v. Schöns gegen die Reaktion*. Hamburg: Bauhütten.

Kuhlemann, Frank-Michael. 1992. *Modernisierung und Disziplinierung: Sozialgeschichte des preußischen Volksschulwesens 1794–1872*. Göttingen: Vandenhoeck & Ru-precht.

Kühn, Erich. 1902, 1903. "Der Staatswirtschaftslehrer Christian Jakob Kraus und seine Beziehungen zu Adam Smith." *Altpreußische Monatsschrift* 39:325–70; 40: 1–61.

Lacan, Jacques. 1977. *Écrits: A Selection*. Translated by Alan Sheridan. New York: W. W. Norton.

Landes, David. 1969. *The Unbound Prometheus: Technological Change and Industrial Development in Western Europe from 1750 to the Present*. London: Cambridge Uni-versity Press.

Landes, Joan. 1988. *Women and the Public Sphere in the Age of the French Revolution*. Ithaca: Cornell University Press.

Langewiesche, Dieter. 1988. *Liberalismus in Deutschland*. Neue Historische Bibliothek. Frankfurt am Main: Suhrkamp.

———. 1993a. "Liberalism and the Middle Classes in Europe." In *Bourgeois Society in Nineteenth-century Europe*, 40–69. Edited by Jürgen Kocka and Allen Mitchell. Oxford: Berg.

———. 1993b. *Republik und Republikaner: Von der historischen Entwertung eines politischen Begriffs*. Stuttgarter Vorträge zur Zeitgeschichte. Essen: Klartext.

———. 1996. "Kulturelle Nationsbildung im Deutschland des 19. Jahrhunderts." In *Nation und Gesellschaft in Deutschland: Historische Essays*, 46–64. Edited by Manfred Hettling and Paul Nolte. Munich: C. H. Beck.

———. 2000. *Liberalism in Germany*. Princeton: Princeton University Press.

La Vopa, Anthony J. 1992. "Conceiving a Public: Ideas and Society in Eighteenth-century Europe." *JMH* 64:79–116.

Lee, Loyd E. 1980. *The Politics of Harmony: Civil Service, Liberalism, and Social Reform in Baden, 1800–1850*. Newark: University of Delaware Press.

Lehmann, Max. 1902–5. *Freiherr vom Stein*. 3 vols. Leipzig: S. Hirzel.

Lestition, Steven. 1993. "Kant and the End of Enlightenment in Prussia." *JMH* 65: 57–112.

Levinger, Matthew. 1990a. "Hardenberg, Wittgenstein, and the Constitutional Question in Prussia, 1815–22." *German History* 8:257–77.

———. 1990b. "La rhétorique protestataire du Parlement de Rouen 1753–1763." *Annales: Economies, Sociétés, Civilisations* 45:589–613.

———. 1992. "Imagining a Nation: The Constitutional Question in Prussia, 1806–1825." Ph.D. diss., University of Chicago.

———. 1998. "Kant and the Origins of Prussian Constitutionalism." *History of Political Thought* 19:241–63.

Levinger, Matthew, and Paula Franklin Lytle. Forthcoming 2000. "Myth and Mobilization: The Triadic Structure of Nationalist Rhetoric." *Nations and Nationalism: Journal of the Association for the Study of Ethnicity and Nationalism* 6.

Lévi-Strauss, Claude. 1962. *The Savage Mind*. Chicago: University of Chicago Press.

Lindenfeld, David F. 1997. *The Practical Imagination: The German Sciences of State in the Nineteenth Century*. Chicago: University of Chicago Press.

Link, Jürgen, and Wulf Wülfing, eds. 1991. *Nationale Mythen und Symbole in der zweiten Hälfte des 19. Jahrhunderts: Strukturen und Funktionen von Konzepten nationaler Identität*. Stuttgart: Klett-Cotta.

Lovejoy, Arthur O. 1950. *The Great Chain of Being: A Study of the History of an Idea*. Cambridge: Harvard University Press.

Mager, Wolfgang. 1974. "Das Problem der landständischen Verfassung auf dem Wiener Kongreß 1814/15." *HZ* 217:296–346.

Makowski, Ilse. 1988. *Emanzipation oder "Harmonie"—zur Geschichte der gleichnamigen Mannheimer Lesegesellschaft in der ersten Hälfte des 19. Jahrhunderts*. München: K. G. Saur.

Mannheim, Karl. 1953. "Conservative Thought." In *Essays on Sociology and Social Psychology*. Edited by Paul Kecskemeti. New York: Oxford University Press.

Marchand, Suzanne L. 1996. *Down from Olympus: Archaeology and Philhellenism in Germany, 1750–1970*. Princeton: Princeton University Press.

Mattheisen, Donald J. 1979. "Liberal Constitutionalism in the Frankfurt Parliament of 1848: An Inquiry Based on Roll-Call Analysis." *CEH* 12:124–42.

McGovern, William Montgomery. 1941. *From Luther to Hitler: The History of Fascist-Nazi Political Philosophy*. Boston: Houghton Mifflin.

Meinecke, Friedrich. 1899. "Zur Geschichte des Gedankens der preußischen Hegemonie in Deutschland." *HZ* 82. 1:98–104.

Meinecke, Friedrich. [1906] 1977. *The Age of German Liberation, 1795–1815.* Edited by Peter Paret. Berkeley: University of California Press.

──────. 1911. *Weltbürgertum und Nationalstaat: Studien zur Genesis des deutschen Nationalstaates.* 2d ed. Munich: R. Oldenbourg.

Meisner, Heinrich Otto. 1913. *Die Lehre vom monarchischen Prinzip im Zeitalter der Restauration und des Deutschen Bundes. Untersuchungen zur deutschen Staats- und Rechtsgeschichte.* Vol. 122. Breslau: M. & H. Marcus.

Mieck, Ilja. 1965. *Preussische Gewerbepolitik in Berlin, 1806–1844: Staatshilfe und Privatinitiative zwischen Merkantilismus und Liberalismus.* Veröffentlichungen der Historischen Kommission zu Berlin, vol. 20. Berlin: de Gruyter.

Mitchell, B. R. 1992. *International Historical Statistics: Europe, 1750–1988.* New York: Stockton.

Mommsen, Wolfgang J. 1981. "Gegenwärtige Tendenzen in der Geschichtsschreibung der Bundesrepublik." *GG* 7:149–88.

Mosse, George L. 1975. *The Nationalization of the Masses: Political Symbolism and Mass Movements in Germany from the Napoleonic Wars through the Third Reich.* New York: Howard Fertig.

Münchow-Pohl, Bernd von. 1987. *Zwischen Reform und Krieg: Untersuchungen zur Bewußtseinslage in Preußen 1809–1812.* Veröffentlichungen des Max-Planck-Instituts für Geschichte, vol. 87. Göttingen: Vandenhoeck & Ruprecht.

Müsebeck, Ernst. 1911. "Siegmund Peter Martin und Hans Rudolph von Plehwe, zwei Vertreter des deutschen Einheitsgedankens von 1806–1820." In *Quellen und Darstellungen zur Geschichte der deutschen Burschenschaft und der deutschen Einheitsbewegung,* 2:75–194. Heidelberg: Carl Winter.

──────. 1913–14. "E. M. Arndts Verfassungspläne für das zukünftige Deutschland aus den Jahren 1807–15." *Der Greif: Cotta'sche Monatsschrift* 1:134–47.

──────. 1917. "Zur Geschichte der Reformbestrebungen vor dem Zusammenbruche des alten Preußens 1806." *FBPG* 30:115–46.

──────. 1918. "Die märkische Ritterschaft und die preußische Verfassungsfrage von 1814 bis 1820." *Deutsche Rundschau* 174:158–82, 354–76.

Neugebauer, Wolfgang. 1992. *Politischer Wandel im Osten: Ost- und Westpreußen von den alten Ständen zum Konstituttionalismus.* Stuttgart: Franz Steiner Verlag.

Neuhouser, Frederick. 1990. *Fichte's Theory of Subjectivity.* Cambridge: Cambridge University Press.

Nietzsche, Friedrich. [1887] 1989. *On the Genealogy of Morals.* Translated and edited by Walter Kaufmann. New York: Vintage.

Nipperdey, Thomas. 1983. *Deutsche Geschichte 1800–1866: Bürgerwelt und starker Staat.* Munich: C. H. Beck.

Nolte, Paul. 1990. *Staatsbildung als Gesellschaftsreform: Politische Reformen in Preußen und den süddeutschen Staaten 1800–1820.* Historische Studien, vol. 2. Frankfurt: Campus.

Obenaus, Herbert. 1969. "Verwaltung und ständische Repräsentation in den Reformen des Freiherrn vom Stein." *Jahrbuch für die Geschichte Mittel- und Ostdeutschlands* 18:130–79.

──────. 1971. "Die Immediatkommission für die ständischen Angelegenheiten als Instrument der preussischen Reaktion im Vormärz." In *Festschrift für Hermann Heimpel zum 70. Geburtstag am 19. September 1971,* 1:410–46. Veröffentlichungen des Max-Planck-Instituts für Geschichte, vol. 36/1. Göttingen: Vandenhoeck & Ruprecht.

————. 1980. "Finanzkrise und Verfassungsgebung." In *Preußische Reformen 1807–1820*, 244–65. Edited by Barbara Vogel. Königstein: Anton Hain Meisenheim.

————. 1984. *Anfänge des Parlamentarismus in Preußen bis 1848*. Düsseldorf: Droste.

————. 1988. "Gutsbesitzerliberalismus: Zur regionalen Sonderentwicklung der liberalen Partei in Ost- und Westpreußen während des Vormärz." *GG* 14:304–28.

Parker, Geoffrey. 1996. *The Military Revolution: Military Innovation and the Rise of the West, 1500–1800*. 2d ed. Cambridge: Cambridge University Press.

Pickett, Terry H. 1996. *Inventing Nations: Justifications of Authority in the Modern World*. Westport: Greenwood.

Pinson, Koppel. 1934. *Pietism as a Factor in the Rise of German Nationalism*. New York: Columbia University Press.

Pocock, J. G. A. 1985. *Virtue, Commerce, and History: Essays on Political Thought and History, Chiefly in the Eighteenth Century*. Cambridge: Cambridge University Press.

Proskauer, Johannes. 1974. "Christian Gottfried (Daniel) Nees von Esenbeck." In *Dictionary of Scientific Biography*, 10:11–14. New York: Charles Scribner's Sons.

Raeff, Marc. 1983. *The Well-ordered Police State: Social and Institutional Change through Law in the Germanies and Russia, 1600–1800*. New Haven: Yale University Press.

Reder, Dirk Alexander. 1998. *Frauenbewegung und Nation: Patriotische Frauenvereine in Deutschland im frühen 19. Jahrhundert (1813–1830)*. Kölner Beiträge zur Nationsforschung, vol. 4. Cologne: SH-Verlag.

Reichardt, Rolf, and Eberhard Schmitt, eds. 1985. *Handbuch politisch-sozialer Grundbegriffe in Frankreich*. Vol. 1. Munich: R. Oldenbourg.

Reif, Heinz. 1979. *Westfälischer Adel 1770–1860: Vom Herrschaftsstand zur regionalen Elite*. Göttingen: Vandenhoeck & Ruprecht.

Reinalter, Helmut, ed. 1986. *Freimaurer und Geheimbünde im 18. Jahrhundert in Mitteleuropa*. 2d ed. Frankfurt am Main: Suhrkamp.

Retallack, James. 1991. "Ideology without Vision? Recent Literature on Nineteenth-century Conservatism." German Historical Institute, London. *Bulletin* 13, no. 2 (May):3–22.

Ribhegge, Wilhelm. 1989. *Konservative Politik in Deutschland: Von der Französischen Revolution bis zur Gegenwart*. Darmstadt: Wissenschaftliche Buchgesellschaft.

Riedel, Manfred, ed. 1975. *Materialien zu Hegels Rechtsphilosophie*. 2 vols. Frankfurt am Main: Suhrkamp.

Riley, Patrick. 1983. *Kant's Political Philosophy*. Totowa: Rowman & Littlefield.

Ritter, Gerhard. 1927, 1928. "Der Freiherr vom Stein und die politischen Reformprogramme des ancien régime in Frankreich." *HZ* 137:442–97; 138:24–46.

————. [1958] 1983. *Freiherr vom Stein: Eine politische Biographie*. 2d ed. Stuttgart: Deutsche Verlags-Anstalt; reprint, Frankfurt am Main: Fischer Taschenbuch.

Rohrscheidt, K. v. 1894–95. "Die Aufnahme der Gewerbefreiheit in Preussen in den Jahren 1810 und 1811." *Zeitschrift für Social- und Wirthschaftsgeschichte* 3:93–108, 204–57.

Rosenberg, Hans. [1958] 1966a. *Bureaucracy, Aristocracy, and Autocracy: The Prussian Experience, 1660–1815*. Harvard Historical Monographs, vol. 34. Cambridge: Harvard University Press; reprint, Boston: Beacon Press.

————. 1966b. "Die Pseudodemokratisierung der Rittergutsbesitzerklasse." In *Moderne deutsche Sozialgeschichte*, 287–308. Edited by Hans-Ulrich Wehler. Neue wissenschaftliche Bibliothek, vol. 10. Cologne: Kiepenheuer & Witsch.

Rürup, Reinhard. 1975. "Die 'Judenfrage' der bürgerlichen Gesellschaft und die Entstehung des modernen Antisemitismus." In *Emanzipation und Antisemitismus: Studien zur "Judenfrage" der bürgerlichen Gesellschaft*. Kritische Studien zur Geschichtswissenschaft, vol. 15. Göttingen: Vandenhoeck & Ruprecht.

———. 1992. *Deutschland im 19. Jahrhundert 1815–1871*. 2d ed. Deutsche Geschichte, vol. 8. Göttingen: Vandenhoeck & Ruprecht.

———, ed. 2000. *The Problem of Revolution in Germany, 1789–1990*. Oxford: Berg.

Sahlins, Marshall. 1985. *Islands of History*. Chicago: University of Chicago Press.

Sarcinelli, Ulrich, ed. 1990. *Demokratische Streitkultur: Theoretische Grundpositionen und Handlungsalternativen in Politikfeldern*. Opladen: Westdeutscher Verlag.

Schama, Simon. 1989. *Citizens: A Chronicle of the French Revolution*. New York: Alfred A. Knopf.

Scheel, Heinrich, ed. 1982. *Preußische Reformen—Wirkungen und Grenzen*. Sitzungsberichte der Akademie der Wissenschaften der DDR, Nr. 1/G. Berlin: Akademie-Verlag.

Schieder, Theodor. 1992. *Nationalismus und Nationalstaat: Studien zum nationalen Problem in modernen Europa*. Edited by Otto Dann and Hans-Ulrich Wehler. 2d ed. Göttingen: Vandenhoeck & Ruprecht.

Schissler, Hanna. 1978. *Preußische Agrargesellschaft im Wandel: Wirtschaftliche, gesellschaftliche und politische Transformationsprozesse von 1763 bis 1847*. Kritische Studien zur Geschichtswissenschaft, vol. 33. Göttingen: Vandenhoeck & Ruprecht.

Schleunes, Karl A. 1979. "Enlightenment, Reform, Reaction: The Schooling Revolution in Prussia." *CEH* 12:315–42.

Schmidt, Wilhelm Adolf. 1890. *Geschichte der Deutschen Verfassungsfrage während der Befreiungskriege und des Wiener Kongresses 1812 bis 1815*. Edited by Alfred Stern. Leipzig: G. H. Meyer.

Schmitt, Carl. [1922] 1985. *Political Theology: Four Chapters on the Concept of Sovereignty*. Translated by George Schwab. Cambridge: MIT Press.

Schnabel, Franz. [1929–37] 1987. *Deutsche Geschichte im neunzehnten Jahrhundert*. 4 vols. Freiburg: Herder; reprint, Munich: Deutscher Taschenbuch Verlag.

Schneider, Hans. 1952. *Der preußische Staatsrat 1817–1918: Ein Beitrag zur Verfassungs- und Rechtsgeschichte Preußens*. Munich: C. H. Beck.

Schoeps, Hans-Joachim. 1958. *Konservative Erneuerung: Ideen zur deutschen Politik*. Stuttgart: Ernst Klett.

———. 1964. *Das andere Preußen: Konservative Gestalten und Probleme im Zeitalter Friedrich Wilhelms IV.* 3d ed. Berlin: Haude und Spenersche Verlagsbuchhandlung.

Schönbeck, Otto. 1907. "Der kurmärkische Landtag vom Frühjahr 1809." *FBPG* 20: 1–103.

———. 1912–13. "Die Einkommensteuer unter den Nachfolgern Steins: Ein Beitrag zur Geschichte des Ministeriums Altenstein-Dohna." *FBPG* 25:117–77.

Schröttler, Peter. 1997. "Wer hat Angst vor dem 'linguistic turn'?" *GG* 23:134–51.

Schulze, Hagen. 1985. *Der Weg zum Nationalstaat: Die deutsche Nationalbewegung vom 18. Jahrhundert bis zur Reichsgründung*. Deutsche Geschichte der neuesten Zeit. Munich: Deutscher Taschenbuch Verlag.

———. 1996. *States, Nations and Nationalism: From the Middle Ages to the Present*. Translated by William E. Yuhill. Oxford: Blackwell.

Schulze-Wesen, Karl. 1929. *Das Vermächtnis der Urburschenschaft: Zeitgenössische Urkunden und Berichte ausgewählt und durch eine Darstellung verbunden*. Berlin: Verlag der Deutschen Burschenschaft.

Schuurmans, Frank T. W. C. 1995. "State, Society, and the Market: Karl Sigmund Altenstein and the Languages of Reform, 1770–1807." Ph.D. diss., University of Wisconsin.

Schwentker, Wolfgang. 1988. *Konservative Vereine und Revolution in Preussen 1848/49: Die Konstituierung des Konservatismus als Partei*. Beiträge zur Geschichte des Parlamentarismus und der politischen Parteien, vol. 85. Düsseldorf: Droste.

Scott, Joan Wallach. 1996. *Only Paradoxes to Offer: French Feminists and the Rights of Man*. Cambridge: Harvard University Press.

Sellin, Volker. 1978. "Politik." In *Geschichtliche Grundbegriffe: Historisches Lexikon zur politisch-sozialen Sprache in Deutschland*, 4:789–874. Edited by Otto Brunner, Werner Conze, and Reinhart Koselleck. Stuttgart: Ernst Klett.

Sewell, William. 1980. *Work and Revolution in France: The Language of Labor from the Old Regime to 1848*. Cambridge: Cambridge University Press.

———. 1994. *A Rhetoric of Bourgeois Revolution: The Abbé Sieyès and What Is the Third Estate?* Durham: Duke University Press.

Seypel, Marcel. 1988. "Die Demokratische Gesellschaft in Köln während der Revolution von 1848/49." Ph.D. diss., Cologne.

Sheehan, James J. 1974. "Partei, Volk, and Staat: Some Reflections on the Relationship between Liberal Thought and Action in Vormärz." In *Sozialgeschichte Heute: Festschrift für Hans Rosenberg zum 70. Geburtstag*, 162–74. Edited by Hans-Ulrich Wehler. Kritische Studien zur Geschichtswissenschaft, vol. 11. Göttingen: Vandenhoeck & Ruprecht.

———. 1978. *German Liberalism in the Nineteenth Century*. Chicago: University of Chicago Press.

———. 1989. *German History 1770–1866*. Oxford: Clarendon.

Siemann, Wolfram. 1985. *Die deutsche Revolution von 1848/49*. Neue Historische Bibliothek. Frankfurt am Main: Suhrkamp.

———. 1995. *Vom Staatenbund zum Nationalstaat: Deutschland 1806–1871*. Neue Deutsche Geschichte, vol. 7. Munich: C. H. Beck.

Simms, Brendan. 1997. *The Impact of Napoleon: Prussian High Politics, Foreign Policy, and the Crisis of the Executive, 1797–1806*. Cambridge: Cambridge University Press.

Simon, Walter M. [1955] 1971. *The Failure of the Prussian Reform Movement, 1807–1819*. Ithaca: Cornell University Press; reprint, New York: Howard Fertig.

Smith, Anthony. 1986. *The Ethnic Origins of Nations*. Oxford: Basil Blackwell.

———. 1991. *National Identity*. London: Penguin.

Smith, Helmut Walser. 1995. *German Nationalism and Religious Conflict: Culture, Ideology, Politics, 1870–1914*. Princeton: Princeton University Press.

———. 1996. "Geschichte zwischen den Fronten: Meisterwerke der neuesten Geschichtsschreibung und postmoderne Kritik." *GG* 22:592–608.

Sorkin, David. 1987. *The Transformation of German Jewry, 1780–1840*. New York: Oxford University Press.

Sösemann, Bernd, ed. 1993. *Gemeingeist und Bürgersinn: Die preußischen Reformen*. FBPG, n.s., Beiheft 2. Berlin: Düncker & Humblot.

Sperber, Jonathan. 1985. "State and Civil Society in Prussia: Thoughts on a New Edition of Reinhart Koselleck's *Preussen zwischen Reform und Revolution*." *JMH* 57:278–96.

Sperber, Jonathan. 1991. *Rhineland Radicals: The Democratic Movement and the Revolution of 1848.* Princeton: Princeton University Press.

Spevack, Edmund. 1997. *Charles Follen's Search for Nationality and Freedom: Germany and America, 1796–1840.* Cambridge: Harvard University Press.

Stacke, L[udwig]. 1881. *Deutsche Geschichte.* Vol. 2. Bielefeld: Velhagen & Klasing.

Stadelmann, Rudolph. 1975. *Social and Political History of the German 1848 Revolution.* Translated by James G. Chastain. Athens: Ohio University Press.

Stamm-Kuhlmann, Thomas. 1992. *König in Preußens großer Zeit: Friedrich Wilhelm III. der Melancholiker auf dem Thron.* Berlin: Siedler.

Stedman Jones, Gareth. 1983. *Languages of Class: Studies in English Working Class History, 1832–1982.* Cambridge: Cambridge University Press.

———. 1994. "Kant, the French Revolution, and the Definition of the Republic." In *The Invention of the Modern Republic.* Edited by Biancamaria Fontana. Cambridge: Cambridge University Press.

Steffens, Wilhelm. 1907. *Hardenberg und die ständische Opposition 1810/1811.* Veröffentlichungen des Vereins für Geschichte der Mark Brandenburg. Leipzig: Duncker & Humblot.

Steiger, Günter. 1966. "Das 'Phantom der Wartburgverschwörung' 1817 im Spiegel neuer Quellen aus den Akten der preußischen politischen Polizei." *Wissenschaftliche Zeitschrift der Friedrich-Schiller-Universität Jena, Gesellschafts- und Sprachwissenschaftliche Reihe* 15:183–212.

Stein, Robert. 1918–34. *Die Umwandlung der Agrarverfassung Ostpreußens durch die Reform des neunzehnten Jahrhunderts.* 3 vols. Königsberg: Bon's Buchhandlung.

Steinschulte, Walter. 1933. "Die Verfassungsbewegung in Westfalen und am Niederrhein in den Anfängen der preußischen Herrschaft (1814–1816)." *Jahrbuch des Vereins für Orts- und Heimatkunde in der Grafschaft Mark* 46/47, part 2.

Sterling, Eleonore O. 1950. "Anti-Jewish Riots in Germany in 1819: A Displacement of Social Protest." *Historia Judaica* 12:105–42.

Stern, Alfred. 1885. *Abhandlungen und Aktenstücke zur Geschichte der preußischen Reformzeit 1807–1815.* Leipzig: Duncker & Humblot.

———. 1894–1924. *Geschichte Europas seit den Verträgen von 1815 bis zum Frankfurter Frieden von 1871.* 10 vols. Berlin: Wilhelm Hertz.

Stürmer, Michael. 1983. *Das ruhelose Reich: Deutschland 1866–1918.* Berlin: Severin und Siedler.

Sweet, Paul R. 1978. *Wilhelm von Humboldt: A Biography.* Columbus: Ohio State University Press.

Taylor, A. J. P. 1946. *The Course of German History: A Survey of the Development of Germany since 1815.* New York: Coward-McCann.

Tocqueville, Alexis de. [1856] 1955. *The Old Regime and the French Revolution.* Translated by Stuart Gilbert. Garden City: Doubleday.

Toews, John Edward. 1980. *Hegelianism: The Path toward Dialectical Humanism, 1805–1841.* Cambridge: Cambridge University Press.

———. 1987. "Intellectual History after the Linguistic Turn: The Autonomy of Meaning and the Irreducibility of Experience." *American Historical Review* 92: 879–907.

Treitschke, Heinrich von. 1872. "Der erste Verfassungskampf in Preußen (1815–1823)." *Preußische Jahrbücher* 29:313–60, 409–73.

———. 1894–99. *Deutsche Geschichte im neunzehnten Jahrhundert.* 5 vols. 4th ed. Leipzig: S. Hirzel.

Treue, Wilhelm. 1951. "Adam Smith in Deutschland: Zum Problem des 'Politischen

Professors' zwischen 1776 und 1810." In *Deutschland und Europa: Historische Studien zur Völker- und Staatenordnung des Abendlandes*. Festschrift für Hans Rothfels, 101–33. Edited by Werner Conze. Düsseldorf: Droste.

Tribe, Keith. 1984. "Cameralism and the Science of Government." *JMH* 56:263–84.

————. 1988. *Governing Economy: The Reformation of German Economic Discourse 1750–1840*. Cambridge: Cambridge University Press.

Ullmann, Hans-Peter, and Clemens Zimmermann, eds. 1996. *Restaurationssystem und Reformpolitik: Süddeutschland und Preußen im Vergleich*. Munich: R. Oldenbourg.

Unruh, Georg-Christoph von. 1968. "Die Kreisordnungsentwürfe des Freiherrn vom Stein und seiner Mitarbeiter 1808–1810–1820." *Westfälische Forschungen: Mitteilungen des Provinzialinstituts für westfälische Landes- und Volkskunde* 21:5–41.

Valjavec, Fritz. 1951. *Die Entstehung der politischen Strömungen in Deutschland 1770–1815*. Munich: R. Oldenbourg.

Vernon, James. 1994. "Who's Afraid of the 'Linguistic Turn'? The Politics of Social History and Its Discontents." *Social History* 19:81–97.

Vetter, Klaus. 1978. *Kurmärkischer Adel und Preussische Reformen*. Veröffentlichungen des Staatsarchiv Potsdam, vol. 15. Weimar: Hermann Böhlaus Nachfolger.

Vierhaus, Rudolf. 1982. "Konservativ, Konservatismus." In *Geschichtliche Grundbegriffe: Historisches Lexikon zur politisch-sozialen Sprache in Deutschland*, 3:531–65. Edited by Otto Brunner, Werner Conze, and Reinhart Koselleck. Stuttgart: Ernst Klett.

————. 1984. *Deutschland im Zeitalter des Absolutismus (1648–1763)*. 2d ed. Deutsche Geschichte, vol. 6. Göttingen: Vandenhoeck & Ruprecht.

————. 1987. *Deutschland im 18. Jahrhundert: Politische Verfassung, soziales Gefüge, geistige Bewegungen*. Göttingen: Vandenhoeck & Ruprecht, 1987.

Vogel, Barbara, ed. 1980. *Preußische Reformen 1807–1820*. Königstein: Anton Hain Meisenheim.

————. 1983a. *Allgemeine Gewerbefreiheit: Die Reformpolitik des preußischen Staatskanzlers Hardenberg (1810–1820)*. Kritische Studien zur Geschichtswissenschaft, vol. 57. Göttingen: Vandenhoeck & Ruprecht.

————. 1983b. "Beamtenkonservatismus. Sozial- und verfassungsgeschichtliche Voraussetzungen der Parteien in Preußen im frühen 19. Jahrhundert." In *Deutscher Konservatismus im 19. und 20. Jahrhundert. Festschrift für Fritz Fischer zum 75. Geburtstag und zum 50. Doktorjubiläum*, 1–31. Edited by Dirk Stegmann, Bernd-Jürgen Wendt, and Peter-Christian Witt. Bonn: Verlag Neue Gesellschaft.

Wagner, Wilhelm. [1922] 1956. *Die preußischen Reformen und die zeitgenössische Philosophie*. Cologne: Kölner Universitäts-Verlag.

Wahl, Adalbert. 1908. "Die französische Revolution und das neunzehnte Jahrhundert." *Zeitschrift für Politik*, o.s., 1:157–92.

Wahrman, Dror. 1995. *Imagining the Middle Class: The Political Representation of Class in Britain, c. 1780–1840*. Cambridge: Cambridge University Press.

Walker, Mack. 1971. *German Home Towns: Community, State, and General Estate, 1648–1871*. Ithaca: Cornell University Press.

Wehler, Hans-Ulrich. 1975. *Modernisierungstheorie und Gesellschaft*. Göttingen: Vandenhoeck & Ruprecht.

————. 1985. *The German Empire, 1871–1918*. Translated by Kim Traynor. Leamington Spa: Berg.

————. 1987. *Deutsche Gesellschaftsgeschichte*. Vol. 1, *Vom Feudalismus des Alten Reiches bis zur defensiven Modernisierung der Reformära, 1700–1815*, and vol. 2,

Von der Reformära bis zur industriellen und politischen "Deutschen Doppelrevolu-tion" 1815–1845/49. Munich: C. H. Beck.

————. 1995. *Deutsche Gesellschaftsgeschichte.* Vol. 3, *Von der "Deutschen Doppelre-volution" bis zum Beginn des Ersten Weltkrieges 1849–1914.* Munich: C. H. Beck.

Weis, Eberhard, ed. 1984. *Reformen in rheinbündischen Deutschland.* Munich: R. Old-enbourg.

Weitz, Reinhold K. 1970. "Der niederrheinische und westfälische Adel im ersten preussischen Verfassungskampf 1815–1823/24. Die verfassungs- und gesellschafts-politischen Vorstellungen des Adelskreises um den Freiherrn vom Stein." Ph.D. diss., Universität Bonn.

Whitman, James Q. 1990. *The Legacy of Roman Law in the German Romantic Era: Historical Vision and Legal Change.* Princeton: Princeton University Press.

Woodmansee, Martha. 1984. "The Genius and the Copyright: Economic and Legal Conditions of the Emergence of the 'Author.' " *Eighteenth-century Studies* 17:425–48.

Zeeden, Ernst Walter. 1940. *Hardenberg und der Gedanke einer Volksvertretung in Preußen 1807–1812.* Historische Studien, vol. 365. Berlin: Emil Ebering.

Ziekursch, Johannes. 1908. *Das Ergebnis der friderizianischen Städteverwaltung und die Städteordnung Steins, am Beispiel der schlesischen Städte dargestellt.* Jena: H. Costenoble.

INDEX

Page numbers followed by t. indicate tables